The Fight for Home

The Fight for Home

How (Parts of) New Orleans Came Back

DANIEL WOLFF

BLOOMSBURY

New York   Berlin   London   Sydney

Published by Bloomsbury USA, New York

All papers used by Bloomsbury USA are natural, recyclable products made from wood grown in well-managed forests. The manufacturing processes conform to the environmental regulations of the country of origin.

LIBRARY OF CONGRESS CATALOGING-IN-PUBLICATION DATA

Wolff, Daniel J.
The fight for home : how (parts of) New Orleans came back / Daniel Wolff.—1st U.S. ed.
p. cm.
Includes bibliographical references.
ISBN 978-1-60819-479-7
1. Urban renewal—Louisiana—New Orleans—History—21st century. 2. City planning—Louisiana—New Orleans—History—21st century. 3. Hurricane Katrina, 2005—Social aspects—Louisiana—New Orleans. 4. Hurricane Katrina, 2005—Economic aspects—Louisiana—New Orleans. 5. New Orleans (La.)—Population—History—21st century. 6. New Orleans (La.)—Social conditions—21st century.
7. New Orleans (La.)—Economic conditions—21st century.
8. New Orleans (La.)—Biography. I. Title.
HT177.N49W65 2012
307.34160976335—dc23
2011050140

First U.S. Edition 2012

1 3 5 7 9 10 8 6 4 2

Typeset by Westchester Book Group
Printed in the U.S.A. by Quad/Graphics, Fairfield, Pennsylvania

Contents

Conclusions

Introductions

Like a Tree Planted by the Rivers

(January 2006)

It's seven-thirty on a January morning, and it feels as if this ground-floor meeting room is underwater. The light coming in through the west window looks damp; there's a smell of mold; the whitewashed cinder-block walls sweat. And the eleven men sitting behind school desks could be half drowned.

They're ex-addicts. Or they're hoping to be ex-addicts. Most of the men here are in the middle of their initiation period: trying to stay straight for ninety days. It's like trying to hold their breath that long.

"These are the men of Bethel Colony South," says their leader, Pastor Mel. He's a dark-skinned man with a shaved head, a hooked nose, and a black moustache. The glint in his dark eyes makes him look a little like a pirate or a riverboat gambler. Broad-shouldered, over six feet tall, wearing a blue work shirt and blue jeans, he carries himself like an old high school athlete, now in his fifties. He's an ex-addict, too.

Mel calls what he runs "a transformational ministry." The men have tough, dulled faces, lots of broken noses and scars, tattoos on hands and arms. Some might be called white, some black, some Latino or Native American. Most look to be in their thirties or forties. Most are homeless. On the desk in front of each of them, there's an open notebook, a pen, and a Bible.

"You notice how, when you start drawing near to God," Pastor Mel says from the front of the room, "people start drawing near to you? . . . The

more you grow in God's righteousness, the stronger you will become."
He reads from the first psalm, first three verses: "Blessed *is* the man that
walketh not in the counsel of the ungodly . . . But his delight *is* in the law
of the LORD . . . And he shall be like a tree planted by the rivers of water,
that bringeth forth his fruit in his season . . . and whatsoever he doeth
shall prosper."

Mel, wearing reading glasses, jabs his finger in the air as he interprets
the text. The "ungodly," he says, include crackheads—like many of these
men were, like he once was. Don't return to "those old things," Mel declares; "move when they start talking negative!" He addresses each man
by name, calls on them to delight in the Lord. They answer when spoken
to, but only a few seem eager. The rest, under the fluorescent light, look
logy, submerged.

"I thought that was a good devotional for this morning," Mel concludes. "Amen?"

Some of the men offer a quiet "Amen."

Mel doesn't think that's good enough. He lifts his voice: "Most people
are searching for the meaning and purpose of life. You *know* what the
meaning and purpose of life is. And that's to serve God!"

If they serve, the text says, they shall prosper. Like a tree planted by
the rivers. In this room, as the damp light streams in against the damp
wall, the metaphor can't help but carry associations.

Five months ago today—almost to the hour of the morning—
Louisiana governor Kathleen Blanco asked President George W. Bush to
declare a state-wide emergency. A hurricane named Katrina was about
400 miles from the mouth of the Mississippi. Here at Bethel South, in
the Gentilly neighborhood of New Orleans, the men were boarding up
the building and deciding whether to leave.

Sunday at ten a.m., New Orleans mayor Ray Nagin ordered a mandatory evacuation of the city. It was, in some ways, a success. In less than
forty hours, more than a million people fled the metropolitan area, twice
as many as had ever evacuated a U.S. city before. But some 50,000 remained, the majority of them poor and elderly.

"I want Brother Dwight to stand up," Mel says, "and talk about his
experience with the hurricane." Dwight is a puffy-eyed black man in a
green sweater, a black knit UNC cap pulled over his hair. He starts slowly,
a little shy, looking down at the yellow and green linoleum, not sure what
to say.

"About ten of us chose to stay with Pastor. We didn't know what the situation was going to bring and, being that this is a low-lying building, we figured we'd go over to the seminary." The New Orleans Baptist Theological Seminary is just across the street. "'Cause we felt more stable at the seminary; they had generators and food and bottled water and things like that.

"Hurricane came," Dwight goes on. "It was three when it hit. Wasn't that bad. Matter of fact, myself, other members of Bethel South, and some staff that was at the seminary were outside smoking, two or three o'clock in the morning. We had to kinda push the door open. But you know the wind—it was Category 3—wasn't that bad."

The National Hurricane Center says that by the time Katrina reached New Orleans, wind velocities had actually gone down. Most of the city was hit with a Category 1 or 2 storm. But the tidal surge, when it reached the Louisiana coast, was eighteen to twenty-five feet high.

"The next morning when we woke up . . . about six o'clock in the morning, I could still see grass on the ground. By eight o'clock, I couldn't. By ten o'clock, water was a couple feet deep. We could see one of the manhole covers behind the seminary just pop off the ground. Just popped up like, uh, Old Faithful. The geyser." At six-thirty Monday morning, three levees near the seminary started to fail; at nine-thirty, they were failing "catastrophically."

"We still didn't know the extent of the devastation that was being caused by the levee being broke," Dwight continues. "Finally, the news showed a bird's-eye view—from a helicopter, I guess—of the Ninth Ward. How the water was coming in. It was devastating, but still, we didn't see it firsthand."

Then a friend of Mel's decided he needed to go back to his house "to get his insurance papers out the attic . . . The Pastor asked me to go with him. I hadn't been no farther than the seminary, so I didn't know what to expect. He had a canoe. Not a canoe!" Dwight smiles at himself, at getting it wrong. "He had a flat-bottomed boat. We were paddling. And I'm seeing dead dogs and cats and dogs stranded on top of cars and people stranded on top of houses . . . It was—it was frightening, you know? You had people standing on top of houses waving for helicopters, and the helicopters just passing them by."

By early Monday morning, Gentilly was thigh-deep in water. Then came a second wave of flooding. Soon 80 percent of the city was submerged. Everything was swept aside: people, buildings, trees standing by the river.

Pastor Mel and his remaining men discovered that Bethel South was relatively dry and started using it as a staging area. "We had found a couple boats . . . We had maybe four boats," Dwight says. "And we was going off in different directions. People were calling. Pastor had put the word out that if anybody needed a little refuge to come to Bethel South. And told them where we were.

"Then there were some guys—some volunteers, I mean; no one was getting paid because this wasn't part of FEMA—there was some guys coming to the corner there"—Dwight gestures toward the front of the room—"in a motorboat. We were dry here! It was four feet deep over there." He points to his right. "And about four feet deep over there." He points to his left. One of the men laughs. "And we were dry here. But those guys were coming in motorboats and taking people to the interstate, where a helicopter was picking them up and taking them to the Superdome. I don't know if they were going to the Convention Center at that particular time. But anyway, they would come up four or five times a day . . . They'd say, 'You got any people there?' And they'd pick everybody up."

The rescue operation wasn't supposed to be run by a bunch of ex-addicts and volunteers. FEMA, the Federal Emergency Management Agency, had been designed to come into situations like this and provide food, water, transportation. But since the attacks on the World Trade Center four years earlier, the agency had been downsized and put under the jurisdiction of Homeland Security. Its leadership not only was inexperienced but had taken to calling disaster relief an "oversized entitlement program" and recommending victims should look to "faith-based organizations" instead of government.

It wasn't till Tuesday night that FEMA declared the flood "an incident of national significance." By then it was becoming clear, as a House and Senate committee would later put it, that the response in New Orleans was "a national failure, an abdication of the most solemn obligation to provide for the common welfare."

Twenty-five thousand survivors took shelter in the Superdome, with about as many over at the Convention Center. In Gentilly, "most of the people were coming to the shopping center up there," Dwight gestures north, "because it was a dry spot. And they could sit down and rest their feet. But behind that—and most of the place—was flooded.

"I know one particular time, I went up there—Pastor sent me up there—and there was ten people up there. And one of the people who was waiting to get rescued, he had about four big bags. And he say, 'Help me with my property.' But I noticed that some of the stuff had price tags on it. And I say, 'Well, brother, that's a little loot there.'" Dwight smiles. "'You can't bring that with you, now.' And he say, 'Well why? It's mine.' And I say, 'But it's stolen property.'"

He shakes his head. So do some of the other men, who seem amused at their role in the disaster. "They were looting everything up there, while *we're* rescuing people . . . We would bring them here and feed them and shelter them and give them dry clothes to put on, and then the guys would come in the boat . . . Anyway," Dwight suddenly trails off, "that's about it. Thank you for letting me get up here and talk."

Pastor Mel thanks Dwight, walks around to the front of his desk, and sits on its edge, facing the men. He has more he wants to say about this; there are lessons to be learned.

"See, growing up here all my life," Mel begins, "hurricanes don't bother me. We've gone through Betsy, all the hurricanes that have come through. So that really didn't bother me. But I called Mom, and I said, 'Mom, you'all really need to get out of here.' I called Miss Clara, my fiancée at the time, I said, 'Clara, I want you to pack up.' Me and Leroy and a couple of other guys went over to her house and put things up on buckets and up on tables . . .

"Like Brother Dwight said," Mel laughs, "the manhole covers started popping off. The water was coming out of the drains, it was coming out of the manholes, and it was coming from different directions; we didn't know where it was coming from! We didn't have any idea the levee had broken . . ."

He motions outside.

"It was time to come back to the community. We knew that the people in the community were going to need some help. We got a lot of old people back here." Eighty-five percent of those who eventually died in the flood were fifty-one or older.

"We brought people in, brothers! We brought people in, and we fed them. We had a couple old ladies who were the first people we brought in, a couple old white—" He catches himself. "Ladies who were white, we got them clothed, fed them. And then we just started fanning out in the community and bringing people in. We rescued about seventy people . . ."

Mel's voice has started to climb toward a preacher's cadence. He's re-working Dwight's story into a parable: the ex-addicts and the flood.

"We had a little boat with a little motor on it. We went out the back

gate of the seminary . . . Lee remembers this!" Lee, some mix of Hispanic and black, smiles in the back row. "Lee was pulling people on his
back! He would load them up in a boat, put the rope on his back"—
Pastor Mel mimes this, hauling an invisible rope, stomping a few steps
like some barge man—"and he was pulling people through the water."

"Praise God!" one of the men answers.

"Lee was a soldier!" Mel continues, his voice now a shout. "And he
hung with Pastor the *whole* time!" Then he shakes his head. "Brother
Dwight got mad with me sometimes. 'Cause we pushed ourselves to the
point of exhaustion . . ." Mel's voice quiets for a moment; he laughs.

"We were going to my mom and dad's house in Pontchartrain Park to
check. Well, before we could get there, we met a guy who had a boat. And
he was gonna rescue his dad . . . So we went to his house. At his house,
his dad and his brother—his dad was eighty years old, had had a stroke,"
Mel's voice is rising again. "Standing on a five-gallon bucket, his head
was just above the water." Mel holds his hand below his chin and strains
as if to stay above the surface. "The man had been standing in the water
all day, shivering like a wet puppy . . . So somehow we got to him, and let
me tell you, brothers, by this time I was exhausted. I said, 'God, God,
you gotta help me. You gotta help me' . . . Finally we were able to get the
guy up on my shoulders . . . and just pulled him into the boat . . . And
then we just continued to go back and continue to go back and continue
to get people . . ."

Mel begins to list the names of the men of Bethel South who stayed
and helped. "Those brothers hung in! And you know, coming from the
community that we from: we are people that the world *discounts* . . . people
who others would say was a drain on the system . . . people who society
would say *are* nothing, will *be* nothing, you know?" The pastor's voice is
up now, brassy, sounding the charge. "I'll challenge them anytime! And
I'll put *my* men against *anybody's* men when it comes down! When the
going gets tough, you brothers *know* how to hang in there!"

Murmurs from the men, amens.

"Because you already *been* in tough situations! You've already *had* a
tough life! I don't want some Harvard PhD with me when I got to go and
rescue and help somebody." A chuckle from someone. "You brothers
hung with me! We did it *together*! We rescued those people! And we still
here, helping the community." His voice falls with the last line.

There's the parable. It's about faith and service, that obligation for the
common welfare. The flood was a test of these, and the government

failed. But the men here—and citizens throughout the city—passed gloriously.

After a moment of quiet, all stand and sing a ragged, thumping version of "Can't Nobody Do Me Like Jesus." Mel calls out the variations— "Can't nobody love me like Jesus . . . Can't nobody bless me like Jesus"—and the men sing them back, clapping, one fellow banging counterrhythms on a desktop. It's as if the singing could somehow lift this damp cinderblock room, lift it and dry it out.

The meeting is about to end. Mel shouts, "Attitude check?" and all the men respond in unison, "Praise the Lord!" Then the pastor goes over their duties for the day. Some are janitors at the seminary, some will be gutting houses, some will be driven downtown to get medical care. The assignments given, one of the men comes forward to give a closing prayer.

But Mel isn't done.

"We had a lot of mud here," he says slowly, looking out the ground-floor window. "Those poor people back there didn't have a chance. They didn't have a chance . . . just awful." There's still no firm death toll from the storm; estimates vary from 1,200 to more than 1,800. Mel takes a deep breath.

"They say that this was a natural—a *natural* disaster. This wasn't a natural disaster. This was a *man-made* disaster in that it wouldn't have *been* flooded if the levees were built properly."

The man waiting to say the closing prayer shifts his weight from foot to foot.

"It would *not* have flooded. We *would* have survived . . . Now the government is holding up money because they say Louisiana is this and Louisiana is that. *Give* the people the money! *Let* 'em rebuild. Deal with the politicians who steal, and let the people not suffer anymore."

Some of the men are nodding; others seem anxious to get the day started.

"In Mississippi, because there's a Republican administration—" Mel interrupts himself. "And I gotta tell you I voted for George Bush. I voted for George both times." But Mississippi, he goes on, is a Republican state, so it's getting more money than Louisiana, even though it has only half the number of damaged homes.

This isn't a parable anymore—this is politics—but his voice starts climbing back to its preacher tone.

"Now, you know, America's built on my forty acres. And a mule.

Many of us have bought and paid for our property here in New Orleans. And now they telling us we have to go? I don't think so. I don't *think* so! I know the property we have, we're not going anywhere."

"Amen."

"The property we have in New Orleans East, the property my mom and dad has in Pontchartrain Park. We not going *anywhere*! And we'll do whatever it takes to stand! To hold on to land that we paid for, that's been in my family—" Again he interrupts himself. "The *first* time our family has owned a home! *Owned* a home! So you think we're going to let that home go? No, we're *not* gonna let that home go. We're gonna re-build! And we're not going to let anybody stop us."

There's an amen, but the men look a little fidgety. Real estate isn't their first concern.

"*Government* should step forward . . . It's *their* fault the levees caved in, and now they don't want to help the people to come back! They want to make New Orleans what they call a 'smaller footprint.' What that says is: 'I don't want poor people and people who don't look like me here anymore!' If you're not wealthy, and you're not from a certain class or culture . . ." Mel leaves the thought dangling.

Earlier this month, Mayor Nagin's Bring New Orleans Back Commission came out with its master plan for the city's recovery. It's proposing that certain heavily damaged areas be considered "non-viable," with no rebuilding allowed. If in the next few months, a "critical mass" hasn't returned, these areas will either be bought by the city or seized through eminent domain. Then the houses will be razed, and the empty land turned into green space. Or "consolidated" for large-scale development. Almost all the areas designated non-viable are majority black and poor.

"But New Orleans has *always* been a place where we *all* got along." Mel's voice is high and excited. "Even during the civil rights, even in segregation, whites and blacks lived side by side. You can go across the street, the next block, and you have a white family in a black neighbor-hood, or a black family in a white block, coexisting right alongside. That's *always* been here in New Orleans! This has always been a gumbo. And that's never gonna change. God loves color! God loves diversity! You know, if everybody looked like me and Zach, it would be a pretty poor world, wouldn't it?"

"Yes, it would," someone answers. "Amen!" There are soft laughs in the room.

"So we going to do what's necessary, brothers. To stand with people.

Who the city or the state or the federal government wants to take their properties."

With that, Mel finally seems satisfied. The question isn't Katrina; that test is over. The question is the recovery: how—or if—the city comes back.

There's a short closing prayer addressed to "Father God," then Mel once again shouts: "Attitude check?"

"Praise the Lord!"

As the men start filing out, some stop to speak. One says he came to New Orleans from East L.A. Some 20,000 Latinos have migrated here looking for recovery work. But he didn't have the right identification papers, and he found himself without a job or a place to stay. "So I ended up at the seminary. Now I found peace."

"You found," Mel smiles, "what ninety percent of the world is looking for."

When the men have dispersed, Mel walks through the two-story building. He calls it "a refuge . . . away from the world." It was once a bar, a Moose lodge, an optical lab. Then, for a decade, it was a crack house. "We came in and started to clean up." Off the kitchen is his small, plain room with a tightly made bed, a single bookshelf. Nearby, the men's quarters look like an improvised barracks, bunk beds neatly separated by hanging plastic.

Mel pauses, looks around.

"I grew up here in New Orleans. First in the Lafitte Projects, and then Dad moved down to the first black subdivision in the South: Pontchartrain Park. Which is now destroyed through the hurricane. Grew up out there, went to John F. Kennedy High School . . . in the era of integration . . . After that, I went into business for myself—college for a couple years, then business for myself . . . Did very well. Ran political campaigns, owned nightclubs, flooring company, flower shops, anything I could do to make money. My dream was to become a millionaire.

"Wound up in the nightclub business. Started drinking a lot, using drugs, started snorting cocaine, then smoking crack. Lost my family, lost everything that I owned, but I gained everything. During that time—I was living on the street for three years—during that time I got to know God. Through Jesus Christ His Son."

At the height of his addictions, Mel heard a preacher on the car radio, talking about God being "a father to the fatherless and a husband to the widow." He pulled to the side of the road. "God, you gotta help me," he prayed. "You gotta help me. I want to be a man. God, if you are a father to the fatherless, be *my* father . . ." Mel describes his own dad as a hard worker and a devout Catholic, "[but he] wasn't around much . . .

"Then God took me off of the street and put me in the New Orleans Baptist Theological Seminary. Had no money, had no nothing." He smiles. "Took me out of a homeless shelter, put me right into the seminary because I desired to sincerely know God. And I have an undergraduate pastoral ministry degree in psychology. And I'm into my master's in psychology and Christian counseling."

After seminary, he worked with addicts at the original Bethel Colony in North Carolina. Then "God said it was time to open up the ministry [here] . . . With no money! No money. Borrowed ten thousand from Mom and Dad. Was working for Mom and Dad, so saved another ten thousand . . ."

At that point, Mel says, God "started sending men into my life . . . God was re-fathering me . . . [giving] me the chance to pour my life into the lives of others. Power and authority is given to serve. To serve! Not for selfish gain. To serve." He's nodding for emphasis. "Jesus said . . . 'The greatest among you will be the one who serves others' . . . That's the answer! . . . And it's not that hard. It's not that hard . . ."

The ministry has been open a year and a half. "The work is for men," Mel explains. ". . . Because we believe that men are the key to the families . . . We've found when a man is redeemed and returned to a position of respect and authority in his home, that affects his whole family. One of the threads that runs through *all* of the men here is the absence of a father."

He looks to the ceiling for a moment.

"New Orleans is a sin city . . . You can go down Bourbon Street and get whatever you want. You can get drugs, you can get prostitutes, you go to strip bars . . . And I used to do those things before I was a pastor; I came from that kind of life . . . The destruction is there. You've got voodoo in this city. You've got all manners of ungodly. . . . I can't propose to speak for God. But I can say to you that God is not pleased with New Orleans. Neither with America. Take it however you want."

He smiles.

Mel's work is about individual recovery, but in the flooded ruins of his city, he sees the possibility of a larger redemption. And he's not alone. As the *Washington Post* puts it: "The worst natural disaster in American history . . . has begun to unleash some inventive ideas." Across the Gulf, planners are proposing to "turn the main coastal road into a beachfront boulevard; pull major retail back into the historical city centers; build high speed regional rail connected to local streetcar systems." Low-income housing projects will make way for "mixed-income and pedestrian-scale redevelopment." In the words of one of the authors of the mayor's master plan, "We have this incredible, once-in-a-lifetime opportunity to re-engage and re-calibrate . . ."

Mel's hopeful, but he's also cautious about who exactly is going to re-calibrate whom. "The other word I've heard used is they want to make this a *boutique* city." His dark eyes sharpen. "You know: you come in and you've got entertainment, good food, you've got gambling and all of this, and then you go back to your home. But what about the people who live here? What about us?"

He's seen the maps that "green-dot" non-viable areas. "I just got to be brutally honest . . . My feeling is that the reason they don't want New Orleans East and the Ninth Ward to come back is it's a large African American population. I've heard through some pretty reliable sources that what the federal government wants to do is build high-rise condo-miniums along the river down to Holy Cross. Wait it out so that the people in those areas don't come back—and then shore up the levees to what they need to be, and *then* bring in condominiums, golf courses . . .

"I got to tell you: we're gonna fight." Shaking his head with convic-tion. "There's just no way. Even if we are a house with no houses around us for a block or two. You know, that's not bad! People live like that in the country." He smiles. "So that jack-o'-lantern effect they say is going to happen if people don't come back?" Empty lots like the gaps in a jack-o'-lantern's grin. "That's okay. That'll just give the people who live here a little more room! . . .

"But the answer is *not* government taking the land and then selling it to developers with sweetheart deals to make megabucks. No, that's not the answer. And we're not going to go for it! We're gonna stand. Lot of people coming back. Some are not; they found other opportunities else-where. God bless 'em and we're glad for them. But those God has called to stay in New Orleans, we're gonna stay. And we're gonna fight."

The fight for home has special meaning in New Orleans. The flood dam-aged an estimated 220,000 buildings, more than 70,000 of them beyond repair. But as Mel steps outside his ministry, the scene could be almost any street in any inner city in the country. Without any levees breaching, scores of American towns have the same boarded-up businesses, the

same falling-down apartment buildings, the same emptiness. In the nineties, neighborhoods in Cleveland lost almost 20 percent of their population, parts of Philadelphia lost over 20 percent, sections of Detroit over
30 percent. More than 800,000 manufacturing jobs disappeared in what's
now known as the Rust Belt. In the half century since the "golden age" of
the 1950s and '60s, the real growth rate of the U.S. economy has declined
every decade.

On this street, it's hard to tell flood damage from what was already
destroyed by this ongoing national emergency. The most obvious sign of
Katrina is the large X that's spray-painted on the front of Mel's building.
It's about the size of a man's chest, and there's one on every structure
down the block. Unintelligible at first, they look like *veves*: the geometric, stylized Haitian voodoo drawings used to call up gods and spirits.
But these *veves* are government-made. Four days after the flood, the
National Guard finally arrived in the city in force. These insignia mark
their house-to-house searches. Between each of the X's arms are initials
and numbers. The top of this X has a date, 9/9, which means that was the
first check of this building: a week after the flood. The left of the X shows
which unit of the National Guard inspected. The right quadrant is to
draw attention to hazards on the property: gas leaks, trapped animals,
unstable structures. And the bottom of the X is for the dead: in this
case a 0.

Mel decides to drive over to his parents' house and, on the way, take a
look at how the recovery is going in different neighborhoods. His first
stop is across the street at the Theological Seminary. It sits up on a slight
ridge, and its glassy classrooms and two-story residential halls look like
there never was a flood.

New Orleans is often described as a sunken bowl, but that's not quite
right: half of the city is at or above sea level. Ironically, its high ground
is mostly thanks to flooding. For centuries, the Mississippi River regularly overflowed, depositing thick layers of silt along its banks, and it
was on this natural levee that the French established a trading post. Goods
from the interior could be shipped down the Mississippi, off-loaded here,
and transported through the bayous to Lake Pontchartrain and then
out to the Gulf of Mexico. Imports from the Old World took the reverse
route. Never a manufacturing city, New Orleans was instead a kind of
router: a "nexus," as it's been called, between North America, South
America, and the Caribbean.

It's in and around this old city—the *vieux carré* or French Quarter—that the different races lived close together in what Mel calls a gumbo. Others refer to it as a "back-alley" pattern: masters occupying the higher, drier ground, slaves and other workers in nearby low-lying alleys.

But this district, Gentilly, was part of the swamp that lay between the Mississippi and Lake Pontchartrain. Besides the ridge where the seminary sits, it was mostly cypress trees, palmetto grass, snaky creeks. It wasn't until the early twentieth century that these back swamps were drained and subdivided. Around the same time, the passage from river to lake was modernized by digging what's now known as the Industrial Canal. It was the beginning of what was supposed to be a prosperous, safe, engineered future.

Mel drives down from the seminary, around the corner, and into a subdivision called Gentilly Woods. Given the opportunity to build new neighborhoods on reclaimed ground, the city created a future closely modeled on the laws of Jim Crow. "Indeed," says one history, "new highly-efficient pumps installed in 1917 have been identified as *the* agents for racial segregation in New Orleans." Gentilly Woods was built to be all white, its segregation written into its deeds. On these once tree-lined streets, David Duke grew up to be a grand wizard of the Ku Klux Klan.

Now, as Mel drives slowly past, many of the trees are down. Only a few vehicles use the cracked, broken roads. There are no street signs; the stoplights aren't working. The rows of ranch houses sit silently with gaping windows and roofs covered by blue tarps. Each boarded-up front door is spray-painted with its own *veve*, while piles of crumbled sheetrock wait on the curb.

Mel pauses to point out a rare sign of life: a work crew hooking up a trailer. It's one of 300,000 FEMA ordered as emergency housing. "This was in the papers the other day," Mel says, "that these FEMA trailers are costing sixty thousand dollars apiece to outfit them and get them in place. If they were to give every homeowner sixty thousand dollars to rebuild their place," Mel says, "you wouldn't have a problem . . . *Give* the people the money!"

He leaves Gentilly Woods, the only indication being a slight bump as he crosses a drainage ditch. But once he's on the other side, Mel announces: "This is where I grew up." Pontchartrain Park looks almost identical; the same company constructed both subdivisions. But David Duke's childhood landscape was all white, Pastor Mel's all black.

The Park, as it's known, is a ring of suburban-looking streets and cul-de-sacs that fan out from a former golf course, now weeds and dust. Before the flood, about 1,000 families lived here. Mel drives through blocks of 1950s ranch houses, all empty, some with their front doors barricaded, some wide open. A *veve* on one reads 9/22, three weeks after the levees breached.

At a house with a ruined bathtub out front, Mel stops. There's a little garden, brown from salt water, and a statue of the Virgin Mary. The small dead trees by the entryway still lean in the direction the flood pushed. Mel unlocks the front door and steps inside.

At first the darkness blinds. Somewhere ahead, water is running: a leaking pipe? As light trickles in, the black slowly turns into shadow. There are no walls, only their skeletons: two-by-four framing, stained with mold, wires dangling.

"This was the living room," Mel says. He steps over some rubble. "The dining room. There was a bedroom in back." Exposed pipes and aluminum vents hang from the ceiling. "This was the bathroom. Mom and Dad's room was back here. This was a den; they were real comfortable in here. Had a wide-screen TV." Mel looks like a child in the wet shadows, his face younger, more anxious, his hands crossed in front of him. "We were a big family. You can see where we added on . . . This is a carport we enclosed."

Now he unlocks the back door and steps out into a small fenced yard. A pine has toppled over and crushed a storage shed. Battered fences go off in every direction, separating now-empty houses.

"And there wasn't anything you could salvage. Absolutely nothing. The water was so toxic, everything had to be thrown away." Except Mel's parents couldn't bear to get rid of their family photos or the account books. They're neatly stacked on the brown lawn as if they could be dried and recovered. The account books are an off-yellow and fat from the water, their pages stuck together in a single mass. The old Kodachrome slides are crazed beyond recognition, smears of red and blue.

"This is our home. This is where we grew up at. This is the *family*'s home. Christmas, New Year's, Thanksgiving: five sisters and a brother . . . This is where we meet, this home. All we've ever known. So yeah, it's special. And we're not giving it up . . ."

In the silence, a faraway truck passes. There are a few faint bird calls: crows. A low wind rustles the fallen trees. It's like touring some historical site, some battlefield. The dirty brown line, eight feet up the side of the house, marks where the flood waters settled after they won.

"I'm so glad that I spent three years living on the street. Material things . . ." Mel shrugs. "It just doesn't mean that much to me anymore. God worked it that I can find contentment in whatever situation I'm in . . . That connection to family, those who have their family intact: *that's* a joy—"

His cell phone interrupts: a man in trouble, wanting to join the program. Mel gives instructions, then clicks off. When he starts speaking again, it's about the state of his city before the flood.

"I call New Orleans the happy plantation. And the reason I call it that is because people were just so content, so satisfied, so okay with a service job that paid five or six dollars an hour. If you lived in New Orleans before the flood, you could live cheap. You could find an inexpensive place to live, and you could live cheap."

The city's population had been declining for nearly a half century. From its peak of around 600,000 in 1960, it had shrunk to 450,000. Fifteen percent of its housing units were vacant, as were nearly a third of the apartments owned by the city housing authority. That helped drive median rent down to around $650 a month. But almost half the city's residents were making less than $25,000 a year. And nearly a quarter were living at or below the poverty line.

That's why some have described Katrina as less a break in history than an acceleration: "All of a sudden, time sped up." The city was already getting emptier, the economy already struggling. From this perspective, the flood sent it plummeting in the direction it had long been leaning.

Mel sees the happy plantation as a deliberate, profit-making arrangement. "I felt like the business community didn't input into the community in New Orleans 'cause they wanted to keep a service-oriented economy for the tourist business . . . Mr. Nagin, when he came into office, he had a great opportunity to help people . . . [He] had the equity because he was the CEO here of Cox Cable. He had the opportunity because he sat on boards with Fortune 500 companies." Mel believes New Orleans could have followed Atlanta's path: become a Sunbelt city with a revitalized school system, prosperous business sector, rising population. Instead, its median annual income before the flood was $8,000 lower than Atlanta's.

"What we did in New Orleans," Mel says, "we kept everything substandard . . . Those who lived in New Orleans and owned businesses, they moved into surrounding areas. Now, everything around New Orleans—Metairie, Mandeville, Covington, Slidell—those places are doing wonderful." Mel squints as he rattles off the names of suburban towns. Between 1960 and 2000, the city's racial demographics flipped: from two-thirds white to two-thirds black. It amounted to another kind of evacuation: decades-long, everyday, slow-motion.

"The businesspeople, they make their money here and bring it there. They support the Little League, the Boy Scouts, all of those things—Boys and Girls Clubs—the things that make a difference. But what was going on in New Orleans, they did not support." He gestures past the ruins of Pontchartrain Park. "What they didn't understand, that was draining *everybody*. Crime started getting worse. The educational system continued to get worse . . .

"[Mayor Nagin] had the ear of those who are in power to say, 'Look, we need to all move forward together!'" Mel forms a circle with both hands and jumps it from place to place, bundling. "Not the white population only—and the business community only. We need to move *everybody* forward! And he could have partnered. He could have pushed and partnered: 'All right, if we don't do this, none of us will move.' We know people in business want to make money. So, if people in business want to make money"—Mel's shoulders hunch, pushing an invisible rock uphill—"they'll do what's necessary to provide the environment to make money. And if they would have provided the environment, everybody would have moved forward together."

He drops his shoulders.

"But that didn't happen . . . Only three percent of the businesses here in New Orleans were owned by African Americans. And if you don't own anything, you don't have anything. Given the opportunity, you *can* move ahead. But you got to have opportunity. And all the time you can't create that opportunity for yourself.

"When I went into business for myself, age eighteen, a lot of people thought I was crazy: 'You can't do that!' . . . You *can* do it—but you gotta have somebody to push and to believe in. You gotta come from some kind of stock that says that you can." Mel points at the now-empty houses of Pontchartrain Park. A teacher lived over there, a post office worker here; that man was in the military. The Park was all about taking the opportunity and getting ahead.

"Now, we know we're always gonna have poor people. [But] the Bible says, as a Christian, the man who don't work don't eat. If you give a man an opportunity and he doesn't take care of it, shame on him." Shaking his head. "I'm a great believer in someone working hard and helping himself. Even if he gotta start at the bottom. Because if you're faithful with a little, you'll get more! If you work hard, you'll get more."

The bright sun bounces off his brown skin, brings out the gray in his moustache.

"[Mayor Nagin] had the opportunity to change the city," Mel repeats. As he speaks, Nagin is facing a mayoral primary against dozens of white challengers. An African American, he was elected in 2002 as a so-called de-racialized candidate, drawing not only black voters but 80 percent of the white, including widespread support from the business community. But today, for the first time in decades, the depleted city may have as many white voters as black. With that white vote splintered and as the sole viable African American running, Nagin has done a 180. He's become racialized, denouncing his own commission, declaring that all neighborhoods should be viable. He's now promoting what he calls a free market approach: if you have the means, you should be able to return to your home. Two weeks ago, on Martin Luther King Jr. Day, Mayor Nagin declared it was time to rebuild "a chocolate New Orleans! . . . The city will be a majority African-American city. It's the way God wants it to be. You can't have New Orleans no other way."

Mel shields his eyes from the sunlight.

"This will always be a chocolate city? No. This will always be a city of people. *People*," Mel says. "This will be a city of people. Of all colors. Human." His voice is soft but emphatic. "There's only one race I know, the human race. Ain't no black race, no white race. There's a human race. Ain't no other race but that. We're different, but together we can move forward."

He stands in his parents' backyard. Around him are block after block of empty homes. Even with a bright sun beating down, it smells of decay, of mold, as if the city was still struggling to surface.

Solidarity Not Charity

(February 2006)

It was a church; now it's a dormitory. And a volunteer center. And a distribution point for tools and clean water, legal services and health care.

Before the flood, it was the Greater Mount Carmel Baptist Church, a modern yellow-brick structure, one story, with a concrete courtyard surrounded by a wrought-iron fence. It sits not far from Claiborne Avenue, one of the main thoroughfares through the Ninth Ward. The waters that Pastor Mel saw as a test of faith ruined this sanctuary, soaking the hymnals, destroying the pews.

Standing outside the former church is a round-faced, pink-cheeked woman in her late twenties. "When we came in," she explains, "we had to gut out all the sheetrock and plaster. And then do mold remediation, which involved scrubbing with bleach, cleaning it up, vacuuming, removing all the dead mold particles . . . We actually went through that entire process, and then had volunteers stay here, who then got sick from the mold—and we had to do it all over again."

Around her, a crowd of fifty or so mills through the courtyard. They're mostly sleepy-looking, white, college-age. In the early morning light, some scoop yogurt, some drink from plastic water bottles. Short-haired girls wear blue bandannas; boys are in baseball caps; both genders have work boots, flannel shirts, blue jeans. An older hippie with a gray beard tries hard to wake up. Cell phones, sweatshirts, backpacks: it looks like a college field trip.

"We had to replace all the metal conduits, all the electrical wiring in the entire building up to where the floodwater was, so all the sheetrock is down, and we haven't been able to put it back up until we can get an electrician to pull all the wire, bend and hang new conduit, get that all in place; we did have blankets up on the walls to kind of create temporary walls, until we identified that it was actually a very serious fire hazard."

The run-on narrative pauses briefly as she steps inside the church. Here's an office area outlined by new two-by-fours but without walls. The church has become see-through: a temporary structure for a transient population.

A slightly older, rougher-looking crew occupies the office. They have the matted blond dreadlocks of gutter punks, used to sleeping in public parks, panhandling. Piled in the corners are more backpacks, dyed scarves, water bottles. An acoustic guitar is being passed around.

The next designated area looks like the sleeping quarters over at Pastor Mel's ministry. There's even a small handwritten sign above one of the double-decker bunks: LOVE WITH ALL YOUR HEART. But there're no Bible passages here. Instead, tacked onto the exposed two-by-fours are posters for upcoming demonstrations, instructions on how to deal with the New Orleans police, maps of the city, job schedules, notices about a women's group, a note card asking if anyone's driving to New York next week.

"We're pretty fortunate," the woman continues. "In the neighborhood for blocks in any direction, nobody else has electricity, much less plumbing." The neighborhood is St. Claude, part of the Ninth Ward, south of Gentilly. It used to be home to about 12,000 people, 90 percent of them African American, 40 percent living at or below the poverty line. Now the streets are all but deserted.

The woman is joined by one of the few black people in the compound: a short, round man she introduces as Suncere. He's got dreadlocks tipped with small blue beads and a quick, mischievous smile. An organizational chart posted near the office includes a photograph of him with the title "Relief Coordinator." The two of them make their way through the dormitory-like room and out the back of the church to a parking lot that's now a staging area. Here, long tables are stacked with face masks, rubber gloves, Tyvek coveralls, goggles. Blue plastic barrels store water. Piles of bicycles wait to be repaired.

Off to the side is a small structure made of blue tarp. Taped to it, a sign: SHOWERS EMPOWER. "We've got a direct line running from the hot water heater . . . We're looking to improve these, so they drain a little bit better."

Every morning, groups of volunteers leave here and fan out into the surrounding blocks. "When we go into the houses to do the mold remediation and the gutting, we wear the Tyvek suits, gloves, the respirators; that's to keep the mold spores off our clothes and skin—so showering and having laundry facilities is actually critical to our health—otherwise we'd bring all of those mold spores into the living environment with us." Her sentences stream together, picking up speed. "At times we've had up to three hundred volunteers staying between these two buildings and the tent city and had only two showers operating—it's been a real crunch and a real compromise for a lot of people—even just to shower in something like this is a big shift for a lot of the folks who stay with us."

If this former church looks like Pastor Mel's ministry, the two populations have gathered for what seem like opposite reasons. Where the ex-addicts are trying to get off the streets, these white kids are volunteering to get on them. They've left their homes or their college campuses—given up the comforts of reliable heat, electricity, and water—to live in and help rebuild one of the poorest neighborhoods in the country.

Out near the improvised showers, a guy with wire-rimmed glasses is showing a trio of college-age women how to screw air filters onto the sides of their face masks, then fit the masks snugly over bandannas and loose hair. "That way, if you get hit by a two-by-four, they'll stay on."

"Hit by a two-by-four?!" one woman asks, laughing.

Handmade signs designate the different staging areas: BLEACH. BUCKETS. GLOVES. "The boots we take and dunk in a mild bleach solution, inside and out . . . The respirators we wipe down . . . The Tyvek suits and paper suits . . . we just throw away."

Back in the church's main sanctuary, out past the pulpit and the baptismal font, the pews have been cleared away. In their place are lines of cots with exhausted volunteers fallen across them, their hoodies pulled up over their heads. It's shadowy and quiet, the windows taped over with brown paper. Suncere listens, smiling, to a rundown of the work the volunteers do: remove garbage, clean out homes, spray down mold, nail on roof tarps.

All of this is being organized by a group called the Common Ground Collective. It sprang up right after the floods, when a local resident and ex–Black Panther named Malik held an emergency meeting with a few friends. Since the government couldn't—or wouldn't—provide the relief people needed, they decided regular citizens would have to step up. With a total of fifty dollars, they started the collective, designing a logo of a clenched fist—the Black Power fist—holding a hammer on one side and a medical cross on the other.

They then issued a call for help, which was quickly answered by community organizers from across the country. Many were veterans of two and three decades of grassroots political work and protest. One described his activism as beginning with "anti-apartheid and animal rights issues in the mid-1980s." Another dated her involvement to the mid-1970s, organizing around "a broad range of issues from environmental justice and worker rights to peace and global justice." A third said she'd worked as a Peace Corps volunteer, then taught political science, focusing "mostly on corporate globalization and war." Many were self-defined anarchists, veterans of the 1999 protest against the World Trade Organization, the "Battle in Seattle."

For these organizers, post-Katrina New Orleans was the next logical place both to continue that battle and to start a different kind of struggle. Protests had been largely muted since the attacks of 9/11, but here was a chance for direct action. According to Common Ground's handbook, the floodwaters "exposed long-standing injustices faced by residents of the lower-income communities of color." As the mainstream media put it, Katrina was a "pulling back of the veil that hides poverty in America." The week the levees breached, the U.S. Census Bureau reported that the national poverty rate had risen for the fourth straight year. And New Orleans was among the nation's poorest cities.

Commentators hoped the floods would become a "watershed in the debate over poverty." When President Bush first addressed the nation from the ruined city, he, too, recognized its "deep, persistent poverty . . . [with] roots in a history of racial discrimination." The president later suggested that what would "break the cycle" and "lead the economic revival of the Gulf Coast" was basic American "entrepreneurship."

Common Ground took a more radical approach. The free market system was not the solution but part of the problem. Statistics showed that over the nation's last quarter century, "most of the [economic] gains have been concentrated in a small percentage of the work force." In a nation with a widening gap between rich and poor, the disparity in New Orleans was the second largest among major American cities. "As activists working for social change," the Common Ground handbook declares, ". . . [we] tend to be reactive and spend the bulk of our energy pushing against state power." Now New Orleans offered a chance for something new. The floods had leveled the state: everything from local government to the medical system to schools and law enforcement had essentially been washed away. That put organizers "in a position to be proactive in filling the void."

The response has been enormous. In the past five months, Common Ground has gone from a handful of people gathered around a kitchen table to a network of more than 1,000 volunteers and sixty full-time organizers. Almost all are from out of town, and almost all are white. According to the handbook, they've already served close to 50,000 residents. As Common Ground sees the political landscape, its volunteers are "a new generation of Freedom Riders," vowing to "use the privilege we have to support as many communities as we can to come back home." The collective's slogan, emblazoned on signs around this former church, is SOLIDARITY NOT CHARITY.

"At this point," the woman explains, "what we're looking to do is not to be leading so much as *join* with community members—join with the pastors and the reverends of the churches—and have *them* lead and have us support them—have community members that they choose, that they pick for the right positions . . . Of course, that will depend on how it plays out with the politics, with the real estate, and the funding."

Common Ground's long-term goal isn't simply to open a debate or even to provide aid, but to help create "a revolutionary transformation of society." This early February morning, these college students, punks, and organic farmers will be gutting houses so the residents of St. Claude can come back: part of the fight for home. But eventually, Common Ground hopes to set up "workers' cooperatives to develop economic engines to provide good paying jobs." The cooperatives and these shared living quarters are a deliberate alternative to the concept of private property. They're trying to operate via shared decision making, without a hierarchy of leadership. The idea is that the model Common Ground creates here will then spread nationwide.

Out in the church courtyard, a woman with a clipboard is asking people to sign up for work assignments. As the jobs slowly fill, the volunteers peel away. Suncere says he's driving across the bridge to drop off workers at various Common Ground sites. His first stop will be the Lower Ninth.

The Industrial Canal divides the Ninth Ward. The upriver side, closer to the French Quarter, is known as the Upper Ninth. Suncere heads onto the Claiborne Avenue Bridge and midway across looks down into the Lower Ninth.

If Gentilly and St. Claude were ruined by the floods, this neighborhood was all but erased. From the bridge, the view is diced and blurred by iron superstructure, so it's hard to get any perspective. Are those life-sized cars stuck on rooftops or toys? Is that a barge wedged on a street, a wide-screen TV tangled in the power lines? And can that really be acres of rubble with only a handful of houses left standing?

As Suncere comes down off the bridge, the landscape starts to pull into focus. This must have been ten or twelve blocks once. It all seems to have been lifted up, turned over, and mashed together. The contents of a hundred homes are heaped in giant piles that include the homes themselves. Suncere drives past slowly, as if to pay respect. Among mountains of pink insulation, a purple tricycle. The broken trunk of a tree jutting through a picture window. A single unbroken jelly glass on the arm of a blue sweater next to multicolored tangles of telephone wire. Close up like this, the wreckage exerts a strange pull. This is what remains of people's lives—the stuff they worked for—all shredded and impossibly jumbled together. Years of accumulation exposed on the street. The world turned inside out.

Before the flood, the Lower Ninth was home to 19,500 people, almost all African American. Thirty-six percent were living in poverty, about three times the national average. In a city known for its high crime and homicide rates, the Lower Ninth was called "the murder capital of the murder capital." But it might also have been called the capital of home ownership. New Orleans was full of people who had spent their whole lives here: the highest percentage of native-born residents of any major American city. When the flood tore the Lower Ninth apart, three-quarters of its residents had been living in the same houses for five years or longer. And 60 percent owned their homes, an even higher rate than the city as a whole.

This corner of the Lower Ninth—almost under the Claiborne Avenue Bridge and pressed up against the Industrial Canal—is often called Backatown. It's a generic term for former swampland set back from what's considered the front of town, the high ground along the Mississippi. Five months ago, at around seven-thirty in the morning, 900 feet of Backatown's levee collapsed. It went with a boom, a giant wave of water smashing houses and spinning them down the streets. Along with Pastor Mel's Gentilly neighborhood, Backatown had the largest number of deaths by drowning. As Suncere drives carefully between the mounds of rubble, residents are still missing, bodies are still being found.

This morning, workers with jackhammers are repairing the levee. Suncere stops nearby. In the middle of the ruin, a single blue house has somehow survived, and it's become Common Ground's headquarters in the Lower Ninth. Suncere leaves the car in the rutted dirt road—there's no traffic to block—and starts greeting volunteers with bear hugs. One soft-spoken man with a blond ponytail explains why Backatown is so empty, why there aren't even FEMA trailers here.

"FEMA built their trailers so they had to have sewage hookups. It's not like an RV where you can just have a septic kind of deal. Therefore, they can't move into this neighborhood, because there's no way for the sewage to be dealt with. They also have to have power." He squints into the light wind; it smells of dust and oil and mold. "Whereas Chalmette, hit just as hard by the storm, on the other side—in the white neighborhood over there"—he points east—"there's FEMA trailers everywhere. There's power back on; there're businesses open . . . There's not very many people back [there], but they're providing services . . . not bulldozing the whole neighborhood. Here, they're talking about bulldozing it. Redeveloping it. Buying out city blocks."

Mayor Nagin's original master plan put a green dot on Backatown and labeled it "Area for Future Parkland." It was described as "heavily damaged," with "insufficient" population and a low likelihood of even half its residents returning. After inspecting the area, an official from the Department of Homeland Security concluded: "There's nothing out there that can be saved." Common Ground volunteers say that when they first arrived, there weren't even any insects left.

Out of the little blue house steps one of the original members of the collective. Brandon is almost movie-star good-looking: a buff white man in his late twenties, short beard, close-cropped dark hair, gray eyes, a deep cleft in his chin. In an organization that is trying not to have leaders, he certainly looks like one. He squats in the ragged front yard and tries to explain how he—and Common Ground—ended up in Backatown.

Brandon didn't know Malik before the flood, but they'd both worked on the national campaign to free the Angola Three. "Former Black Panther party members that were incarcerated . . . that were in solitary confinement," Brandon explains, ". . . after being framed." As a fellow Panther, Malik was friends with all three. As a twentysomething radical activist, Brandon was drawn to the cause and got to know Robert "King" Wilkerson, the one member who was released in 2001.

When the flood struck, King was stranded in his New Orleans home. Brandon and a friend drove the 500 miles from their home in Austin, Texas, to make sure he was all right. When they reached the city's border, they were stopped at the security barricades. Though FEMA was clearly struggling to respond, and the National Guard was hampered by having key brigades deployed in the Iraq War, Brandon watched as officials repeatedly turned away volunteer rescuers and other help. From where he stood, it looked like they were letting the city drown. "We saw what they were doing, and it was like, 'What the fuck is this, man? What the fuck is this?' And we felt a moral obligation to do something about it." His voice is slow, angry, insistent. After their attempted rescue, they drove back to Austin "completely demoralized."

A few days later, they got a call from Malik: "'Man, I need help. There are these white dudes in Algiers, and they're armed, and they're *policing* the community. And they're like beating the shit out of us. They're putting guns in our faces; several young men have been shot.'" Brandon's voice rises to sound like Malik. "'They're working with ICE agents and with federal agents and with the New Orleans police department. And they're zip-tying the hands of all the young black men and bringing them to this Greyhound station.'"

Brandon's gray eyes go flat, unblinking.

"And so what we did was, we armed ourselves. Intensely. And we came. It wasn't an armed confrontation—we didn't shoot at each other—but it *was* an armed confrontation."

It was after this face-off—vigilantes versus radicals—that the small group gathered around Malik's kitchen table and founded Common Ground. But Brandon was still intent on rescuing the stranded member of the Angola Three. He crossed the bridge from Algiers into New Orleans alone. "I was able to get through the National Guard checkpoint . . . I went as far as I could on the highway, until there was water." Then he left a note with his name and contact info and started swimming. He was eventually stopped by the authorities and had what he calls "a big confrontation with the power structure and with law enforcement and the military. All this crazy shit occurred." He says he finally convinced a rescue boat to help him and was able to bring the ex-Panther back to Malik's. The confrontations, the show of weapons, the rescue helped turn Brandon into a hero in what he calls "the radical communities."

Pumped by his success and frustrated by the government's response, he admits that he got "kind of crazy . . . I was guerrilla-warfare-oriented at the time." Where the collective was trying to provide food and medicine to stranded residents, "I was, like, 'No! What we need to do is get guns and go in the fucking swamps! And we'll see how long that war in Iraq lasts if they've got a guerrilla movement in the swamps!'"

Brandon smiles at himself.

"My friend finally calmed me down. And I realized, okay, this isn't going to be the best thing to do against the U.S. government." Instead, he says, "we came back to this wonderful thing that had occurred. Called Common Ground. Where there was a health clinic, sixty to a hundred activists living at Malik's house . . . It was just unbelievable!

"The radical communities organized and started sending in aid . . ." Brandon's hands whirl in small circles. "That's when we decided to start the Ninth Ward Project." The reverend at Mount Carmel Baptist offered his church. "And so we said, 'Well, what needs to happen for residents to be here?' We asked the residents, they told us, and we started gutting homes. And taking mold out of homes. At the time, most people didn't support it. 'Cause they said it was dangerous. And toxic. But there was no other choice if the people were going to keep their homes." Brandon turns both his palms upward, as if this was obvious.

Common Ground was soon running one of the few relief efforts in the Upper Ninth. "And then we realized they weren't letting residents return to the *Lower* Ninth . . ." Though much of the city had been reopened by then, the Lower Ninth stayed barricaded. The city had declared the area too damaged and too dangerous for reentry: non-viable. Brandon wanted to move into Backatown and, symbolically anyway, establish the people's right to return. Otherwise, the city was liable to seize the whole area.

Malik had begun crisscrossing the country, speaking where he could, raising funds. He was often gone, and a core committee of between four and twenty organizers handled the logistics of the relief work, trying to practice and model what they called direct democracy. But for the more important decisions, the mostly white and out-of-town anarchists tended to defer to Malik. He was their senior, a local, and a member of the black community. In this case, Brandon went to Malik, and Malik okayed the idea. When the owner of the blue house agreed to loan it to the collective, Brandon and the soft-spoken, ponytailed man snuck past the barricades and started living here.

"It's so shocking to me," Brandon says in his Texas twang. "Because we *been* here. We been here the whole time almost." He stands and starts walking toward the levee with a quick cowboy stride. He's wearing a tight shirt, jeans, a dark baseball cap.

"FEMA basically gave money to the city, and the city has given aid and fixed places up in a very selective manner. Where they want the homeowners to be, they've turned water back on, power back on, gas back on, done debris removal. And in areas that developers have wanted—or where the people are predominantly black and they want to move people out and change the complexion of the city—they've restricted services."

Brandon talks in that same run-on style, organizer's speed. Meanwhile, he keeps tugging at the bill of his cap, readjusting it, as if there was a right way for it to sit, but he can't quite find it.

"I remember an entire nation watching these images on TV, right? Of these impoverished, neglected people, you know? Wading through water. Standing on rooftops for a week. Sometimes ten days. Knocking holes in their attics. And then I remember them being left at the Superdome and the Convention Center." He tugs at his cap. "And they were begging God to help them. And we watched elderly people die on camera because the government couldn't get a bottle of water to them. And it was hot. And they were left to die. And we all collectively said, 'Never again. How could this happen in the United States?' You know? And a few months later, we're still doing it to them! The government's still doing it to them."

He points to the jackhammers pounding at the levee.

"They've been trying since 1968 to widen this canal by taking property from these homeowners. So now that the storm's come, they've shipped [residents] across the country—when they could have shipped them across the river. But they didn't. And [the evacuees] have to battle FEMA constantly, 'cause FEMA's threatening to kick them out of the hotels they're staying in; they never have the energy to try to fight and get back here. And they [the city] are using this as an opportunity to take the land. To use eminent domain." He gulps air between sentences.

"That makes it easy to organize, though. 'Cause on the left hand of the spectrum, we're all concerned about it being an historically neglected community that's having their land taken . . . And on the right hand of the spectrum, it's easy to reach out to the right on this issue because of the private property rights implications and our constitutional freedoms. So," he grins, "we do a lot of AM talk shows. And we try to encourage people to stand on common ground."

Brandon steps over water pooling from a broken main and arrives at a giant, iron-red barge. During the flood, it punched through the breach in the levee and landed here. He peers under the barge, jabs at a pile of debris, kicks a scrap of linoleum flooring—all with a barely controlled fury.

"If this was in Florida?" He tugs his cap. "If this happened in Florida, an area that was predominantly second homes? And there was even one body thought to be out in this mess?" He gestures across the rubble. "They would have people in white suits going through looking for bones, looking for remains. Because it would be respectful." Tugs cap. "But because they're historically neglected, and they're black, and they have no voice, it's okay to come in and just scoop all this stuff out." He nods toward a backhoe in the distance. "They say, 'We looked for bodies.' But there's four hundred still missing! 'We can't find them.' What do you mean, 'we can't find them'? You find them! You know? You find them."

He spins and heads back to the blue house, walking fast in his black work boots. Finally he slows and exhales.

"When you take a day off and realize there's so much need still, it's kinda harsh. So a lot of us get sick . . . I cough a lot. I smoke a lot, too . . . And many of us drink a lot." He smiles at himself. "So, many people who come down here to volunteer? They stay . . . You come here, and it's like you can't leave." A bigger smile now. He looks around at the ruined landscape that's become his home. "You can't possibly leave when you realize what your presence does."

Suncere is running late. He pulls away from the blue house and heads farther out Claiborne Avenue. Big oil tanks rise on the horizon. Without street signs or stoplights, drivers are working on the honor system: contractors in pickups stopping at intersections to wave each other into traffic. Suncere watches out his window, slumped back but attentive. As the car bumps along the broken streets, it jiggles the blue beads that tip his dreads.

Like Brandon, Suncere is one of Common Ground's senior citizens. In his mid-thirties, he has a black goatee, a slight moustache, big belly, and broad chest. Under his left eye is a tattoo: the outline of the continent of Africa.

He was, he says, a street-corner drug dealer back in Washington, D.C. Then he became a community organizer. Recently he took what he calls "an activist sabbatical. 'Cause I had gotten really disappointed. Totally fried." He retreated from D.C. to Asheville, North Carolina, to recover.

"A friend of mine—who normally don't get out of bed till twelve o'clock—calls me up at seven o'clock in the morning, crying. And I thought something had happened with him and his girlfriend." He shakes his head a little, the dreadlocks barely moving. "He was like, 'You got to stop ignoring what's happening in the world and get active again.' He said, 'Man, they're killing our people down there.'" Suncere's face goes stony. "I went next door, and I just caught it: . . . Bush was giving his cowboy speech about how he was going to pull in troops from Iraq and come down here to 'speak the language of violence, which is the only language that these people seem to understand down here.' And I was like: 'Huh?'"

Three days after the flood, President Bush gave a television interview. "There ought to be zero tolerance," he said, "of people breaking laws during an emergency such as this. Whether it be looting, price gouging at the gasoline pump, or taking advantage of charitable giving, insurance fraud." The president announced there were 22,000 National Guard troops on site or on the way to Louisiana and Mississippi. "If they need more guard, there will be more guard." At the same time, Louisiana governor Blanco was declaring that the Guards "have M-16s and are locked and loaded. These troops know how to shoot and kill and I expect they will."

The way Suncere heard it, they were "basically saying, 'We're going to go down there and murder some black people.' That hurt a lot. I mean, prison-industrial complex, poor education, poor housing is a covert way of putting us back in slavery. But for him just to be so open with it? . . . To basically bitch-slap us in front of the whole world? . . . [That] was an embarrassment. That couldn't go down." He's shaking his head hard. "To boot, over in the corner [of the TV screen], there was a Dow Jones indicator. And number one on the stock market was Louisiana Real Estate! . . ." He gives his sly grin. "So I said, 'If I don't take my black self down here to help my folks out, I might as well get a potato peeler and start peeling off my skin.'"

He owned a pickup truck and began trying to gather money and supplies. "And surprisingly, I got a little bit of help from the left, but all the Republicans in my neighborhood helped organize the relief. And raised like seven hundred bucks! And I'm like, 'If Republicans can see this is fucked up, then everybody else should. And act on it.'

"My original plan," he goes on, "was to come down here, drop off the relief, grab as many black people as I could, throw them in my truck, and hope to God the state trooper didn't stop me having so many people going back to North Carolina. We had three safe houses set up for them."

He smiles again. "I didn't have a driver's license at the time . . ." He twirls one finger at his temple. "Sometimes it takes crazy people to do things like this. I be the first one to tell you, I'm crazy as hell. But I did it in the spirit of my people. I figured if I was standing on the corner selling crack with five different police agencies and stick-up boys floating around me, then fuck it, I could go down here and do this."

Suncere managed to make it through the roadblocks around New Orleans and found his way to Malik's. "I landed the day Common Ground started. Completely by accident or all on purpose, depending on how you look at it. My intention, like I say, was to go back home with as many people as I could. But I saw the situation that Malik was in. And Malik was a former Panther, so he's my elder . . . I was like, 'It would be a great honor to die for this man if I have to.'" His voice is soft.

"For about three and a half weeks, I had to sleep with a nine-millimeter carbine rifle. To protect us against whatever element was going to come through that door . . .'Cause we had a big problem with the white militias. Malik told me they dropped eighteen black men within a period of a week and a half. I was like, 'Either I stand now or forever hold my peace.' All those books I done read, all those long-ass political educations I done sat through, mean absolutely nothing if I didn't stay. So I wound up staying a little longer than I was supposed to."

Like Brandon and many of the other volunteers, Suncere has given up his former life to work with Common Ground. "I made a two-year commitment . . . I'm going to stay until I see some type of flower bloom from all this, from the work we're doing. Malik gave me two assignments here on the east bank. And we're all helping a lot of people. Not everybody. But we are making a dent in all this tragedy."

Suncere was first sent to Houma, Louisiana. "Down in the bayou . . . We got down there the night of Rita." Hurricane Rita came ashore twenty-five days after Katrina. It brought winds of between forty and fifty knots and a nine-foot storm surge. Houma, seventy miles southwest of New Orleans, was heavily damaged. "And we were the first people there. When I say the first people there, there was no FEMA, no Red Cross, none of that . . . That night was very traumatic for me. 'Cause I seen a lot of poverty before, but I never seen anything like that. For instance, when we pulled over to the Exxon gas station—we couldn't go no further—the parking lot at the Exxon was full of people who had just lost everything that they had . . . I was trying to give them boxes off the distro truck, but they really didn't need that at the time. Not at that moment. So I spent a lot of time having people cry on my shoulder and everything. For a couple of weeks, I used to have nightmares about that night."

Suncere pauses.

"Yea, so we developed a relationship with the folks in Houma through that experience. We been there, like, ever since . . . It was very beautiful being a part of that community . . . I have family down there for the rest of my life. The racial dynamics? . . . You got Native American people, you have the Cajuns . . . Of course you have African American down there, but you also had Vietnamese as well . . ." With a rueful grin, he declares: "My intent was to come down here and help black people out. Anybody else along the way, but my intent was to help black people out. But Malik has put me in a very unique position where I can help four different races of people at the same time, including my own."

Suncere thought he'd stay in Houma awhile. But as soon as he had a distribution center up and running, "Malik was like, 'Yo! . . . You gotta open up two distros simultaneously. *And* they're forty miles apart. *And* the good news is they're two of the most racist parishes we have down here! . . . Here's five hundred dollars. Good luck.'" Suncere gives a big grin.

One distro was in Phoenix, a small community of about 300, south of New Orleans in the bayous of Plaquemines parish. Suncere describes the town as "majority black . . . politically strong" in a predominantly white area. He set up a distribution center and helped clear land for FEMA trailers. "Another service that we did: we used to go around and pick up caskets and put them in the back of my truck and take them back to the gravesites. Along with, like, house gutting and everything."

The other distro, Suncere says, nodding out the window, "we're on our way to: St. Bernard."

Claiborne Avenue has now turned into Judge Perez Drive, less a main street, more a highway complete with strip malls. The drive was named for Judge Leander Perez, an all-powerful political boss of St. Bernard starting in the 1920s and an arch-segregationist. Judge Perez Drive is the borderline where Pastor Mel's gumbo ends and the rest of Louisiana begins.

The parish isn't in the city of New Orleans. In fact, it used to be so rural that in the great flood of 1927, influential city residents convinced the Army Corps of Engineers to deliberately blow its levees. That way, the surge supposedly aimed at the city population would only displace a few trappers and fishermen. St. Bernard remained mostly swamp and bayou until the forties, when big industry moved in: American Sugar, Kaiser Aluminum, and what is now known as ExxonMobil.

Then in 1960, six years after the *Brown v. Board of Education* decision, a federal judge enforced an order to desegregate the New Orleans schools.

At first Louisiana considered closing its public education system rather than integrate. After much resistance, the city school board decided that if integration had to come, it would be in a working-class neighborhood far from downtown. They picked the Ninth Ward, where a quarter of the city's African Americans then lived, but which had remained predominantly white. On November 14, 1960, U.S. marshals escorted three black first-grade girls into one school and one into another. All of them passed through screaming crowds of white "cheerleaders," spitting and waving Confederate flags. At a rally the next evening, Judge Perez addressed his fellow segregationists. "Don't wait for your daughter to be raped by these Congolese. Don't wait until the burr-heads are forced into your schools. Do something about it now!" One of the things they could do was leave. Within weeks, Perez had opened St. Bernard's schools to "dispossessed" students. Out of the 1,000 white children who been registered in the now-integrated schools, 600 shifted over to St. Bernard.

By 2005, the parish had grown to 67,000 residents and was more than 90 percent white. Largely working- and middle-class, they found jobs in the huge sugar refineries, the oil treatment and storage facilities, as shrimpers and oystermen, and in the fast-food and chain stores that lined Judge Perez.

Now, as Suncere looks out, the destruction is different from back in the Ninth. Instead of piles of brick and splintered wood, there's the plastic and aluminum of lightweight strip mall facades. A big yellow Midas Muffler sign lies slantways across an empty parking lot, a fiberglass canopy has collapsed onto shut-down gas pumps, the all-glass front of a Wendy's is now all-plywood.

On the morning when Pastor Mel's men were stepping outside to have a smoke in relative calm, three of St. Bernard's four surrounding levees had already breached. The parish was still mostly marsh; what was habitable land had been created by levees, drainage canals, and holding ponds. To the north ran the shipping canal known as MR-GO: the Mississippi River Gulf Outlet. Seventy-six miles long, it was designed as a shortcut between the city and the Gulf. But during the hurricane, it served as a funnel, directing the storm surge toward the Ninth Ward. And when MR-GO overflowed, a giant lake formed over low-lying St. Bernard.

The official designation was "complete destruction." The waters shifted a storage tank at the Murphy Oil refinery, releasing an estimated 1 million gallons. All told, some 7 million gallons of oil mingled with the flood-waters in southeast Louisiana, a leak two-thirds as big as Alaska's *Exxon Valdez* spill. Weeks later, when the toxic lake had finally dried out, inspectors surveyed St. Bernard's nearly 27,000 homes. The number they found habitable: six.

As Suncere stares at the wreckage, less than a third of the population has returned. And that count is by day, when property owners come back to make repairs. At night, most of St. Bernard's residents go elsewhere, leaving the parish almost as empty as Backatown. The Walmart over there is closed, a temporary health clinic set up in its parking lot. Suncere points out that many of its patients are being treated for depression. "Now, when we're here gutting homes and giving them food, sometimes we see it as a goody-goody thing to do or whatever." But, he says, the suicide rate in the area has almost tripled in the past year. "So, in my orientation with the volunteers who come down here, I try to let them know you're doing more than just a good deed. You very possibly may be saving someone's life."

The strip malls are empty because not enough people have returned. Many national chains have a minimum customer base required to open a store. Meanwhile, residents stay away because—among other things—no stores are open. At a building supply place that is up and running, long lines of people wait for high-priced sheetrock. But mostly it's blown-out drugstores and clothing outlets and Popeyes.

"My job," Suncere says, "is to go out and scout areas that have had no help—none whatsoever—and put my ear to the ground. Talk to the community and find out what they need. Then go back to the central committee and let them know that I need supplies and everything and support." As well as gutting and distribution, Suncere has helped set up other programs in St. Bernard. "We've got a tree removal service down here." It's an example of how Common Ground would like to change the economy. "The local people own the business and learn the skills of tree care and tree health." There's also a propane exchange and a grocery program. "Our grocery program: they give us a shopping list, the money, we go shopping for them. That's only for people who don't have cars." There are no supermarkets reopened in St. Bernard.

The distribution center is in another loaned church. As he pulls up, Suncere nods at a handmade sign. "We've changed the name of Common Ground out here. It's called Project Hope. It's sponsored by Common Ground." The reason for the name change? "The politics out here is really crazy." That's all Suncere will say. St. Bernard's overwhelmingly white population may not want charity from—or solidarity with—a program founded by an ex–Black Panther. And supervised by a guy with the continent of Africa tattooed under one eye.

This distro center looks a lot like the one in the Upper Ninth: full of out-of-towners, almost all white kids in blue jeans and bandannas. "The big story is definitely not me," says Suncere. "The big story is the volunteers and how they come down here. And how they're motivated. And how young they are. These college students come down here on their spring break and their Christmas break . . . That gives me a lot of hope for the future."

His business done, on the way back to New Orleans, Suncere decides to visit a local homeowner he worked with early on. He takes a right off Judge Perez into Daniel Park, a small subdivision built between drainage canals in the town of Violet. Six or seven blocks wide and a couple of long blocks deep, the development once consisted of blueprint-straight streets and houses that were all variations on the same design: one-family, one-story, brick, with overhanging eaves to shade a little patch of yard, a car-port to the side.

"The southern hospitality is like crazy," Suncere is saying. "People cook for us. I mean, they don't have anything, and they're cooking for us. They're helping us build things like site projects. They're offering their homes to us."

Today, the yards in Daniel Park are high yellow grass, the trees broken, windows bashed in, fences all aslant. The *veves* spray-painted on these houses say the Kentucky National Guard came through 9/16, two weeks after the flood. More than four months have passed since.

Down a long straight block, humps of dead appliances sit by the curb: stoves, iceboxes. The nearly identical houses wait under the bright sun, most of their car-ports empty, sometimes an abandoned vehicle left to rust on flat tires. The smell is of garbage and drying marshland. There's almost no sound: no hammering, little traffic. Way down the street, a crew is chain-sawing the big trunk of a limbless tree. It's Project Hope. "We did a lot of houses in this," says Suncere.

The small town of Violet was an exception in St. Bernard parish: about 40 percent of its 8,500 residents were African American. Within Violet, this subdivision of Daniel Park had been designated one of the parish's two "blighted" areas. It now just looks like an empty suburb. Almost at the end of the block, near the levee that cuts off the far horizon, some signs of life flutter against the Louisiana sky: an orange U.S. Marine Corps flag and, above it, the blue-on-red flag of the Confederacy.

Grinning, Suncere recalls why he first stopped at this house. "Actually, it was a dare." He and a co-worker were driving around, "and when I look up in the air, I see this huge-ass Confederate flag. So I knocked on his door, and, my God! What I met was this little short-built man. And he was just in tears! That we had come to help him." Suncere pauses. "He had told me about things that he had participated in prior . . . but he was pretty much a changed man."

On closer inspection, the Confederate flag has a slogan printed across it: HERITAGE NOT HATE. Suncere steps out of the car.

"What's up, Mike? I didn't think you were here."

The short-built man is out working next to his carport.

"Yea, I'm always here. How y'all makin' out today?"

Mike is big-bellied, maybe in his fifties, with close-cropped gray hair and a carefully kept white goatee. He's as short and wide as Suncere, but his skin is sun-raw pink. He's shoveling some dirt to set steps in front of his FEMA trailer.

"Gotta open up dis garage a little bit," he explains, wheezing as he speaks. He's packed into a white T-shirt, white shorts, white socks and sneakers, with big blue tattoos on both forearms. "One board at a time, baby. One board at a time."

Suncere laughs and encourages him: "All right!"

Mike levels the mud at the foot of the steps. "Nobody work together, nuthin' gets done." He's got a Cajun accent and grunts between sentences, sweating.

An American Red Cross van pulls up. Mike's pug-tailed dog starts barking and spinning on his chain. Almost before the volunteer can lean out and ask, Mike's waving her off. "I'm fine, dear. Thank you."

Now he rests on his shovel for a moment, looks at the steps. "I ain't goin' nowhere. Been here since I'm eight years old. I'm not goin' *anywhere*." He scrapes dirt out from under the trailer, his breath coming short. "My mom lost her house next door. 'Cause da water hit da back and messed up da structure. So we got to bulldoze dat one. But dey ain't gettin' mine." He shakes his head for emphasis, his eyes focused on the work in front of him. "Whatever it takes for me to rebuild it, dat's what's gonna happen." The Red Cross van is now down the street and out of sight.

"[The government's] being okay," Mike says carefully. "Dey got a big task ahead of dem." He pats down the dirt with the flat side of the shovel. "Dey need to do more. Instead of spending all dis money on dese trailers, dey need to help rebuild our homes. Dat would be da *wise* thing to do wit da money."

He walks around the back of his empty house, grabs a cinder block, hauls it to the trailer. Mike moves as if he's had military training: precise, a little on tiptoes. It turns out his father was the Marine.

"Do what you gotta do. But by da time you get da insurance money— what little bit you got left of it after livin' on generators and tryin' to survive—you don't have da money to do what you *need* to do. All you can do is scrounge what you can and save what you can. And go from dere." He drops the cinder block in the mud. "I mean, dey're doin' da best dey can, I would imagine."

He nods toward Suncere's dark, dreadlocked silhouette.

"Now, Common Ground and Suncere and dem: dey help *clean* da houses." Mike shakes his head in admiration. He points past where the Confederate flag flies and down toward the end of the street. "I got a guy all da way in da back dat wasn't comin' back, was gonna demolish his house . . . [Project Hope is] gonna clean out his house. He's an old fellow, can't do it by hisself. Now he's comin' back. It makes a difference."

He sets his shovel against the trailer, pauses for a breath, his big belly under his T-shirt, his blue eyes intense. "And den dere was a Vietnam vet right up da street. He was in dere by hisself; da man can hardly move. Dey went in dere and busted ass and cleared dat one out wit him. And he sat down and wanted to cry, man! It was *wonderful*. You get more help from da groups, da nonprofits, den I think you do from da federal government."

Again, he shakes his head. "Without dem, I wouldn't be as far along as I am. My wife and I gutted ours before we even knew dey was down here. But . . . dey gutted dat one. Dat house, dat house." He's pointing up his street past piles of rubbish. "Dey gonna gut dat house, dat house. Four or five down da street dey're still workin' on. I told 'em to take my mom's roof . . . if dey need the timbers." He shrugs. "Why bulldoze if people can use da lumber? Dey're helpin' people, and it helps dem. So it helps da community." He shrugs again.

Nodding at the empty lot next door, he adds: "I actually tore dat down by myself. I said if anyone's gonna tear down my family house, it's gonna be me . . ." He starts back shoveling. "My mom's doing okay. She's sixty-seven years old. She found a place up in Mississippi. She says dat's where she's stayin', so . . ." Another shrug. "Gotta do what you gotta do. But everybody's just petrified of dese levees now."

Mike and his family evacuated about 300 miles north, came back a month later, and had been staying with a cousin on the other side of the Mississippi River. "Got my trailer about a mont' ago." Mike nods at the white rectangle. "Then it took forever to get da lights on. Had to fix da sewage myself 'cause dey didn't have da trailer jacked up high enough . . . I mean, dere's five of us stayin' dere, and you get waste goin' trew! . . . I fixed dat myself. I played in waste back dere for a day! Straightenin' it out . . . Dey showed up day before yesterday, and I done had it fixed." Mike's blue eyes are focused now, his back has stiffened.

"You can't wait. You *can't*. It's not dere fault. Dey have to wait for da paperwork. Den dey give dem specs on how high da trailer needs to be and where da pipe should be, and dere specs are *wrong*. Dere specs are way wrong!"

As he hears himself say this—that his government is way wrong—he gives a surprised smile. "I mean, I'm not a plumber, but anybody dat does plumbin' will tell ya: you gotta have a drop on dat pipe. I think it's like tree inches in ten feet, or someting like dat."

It sounds like a joke: the government doesn't know that shit runs down-hill. But instead of laughing, Mike folds his thick arms across his chest and looks past the flagpole.

"I'm just lost for time. I don't even look at da calendar anymore, don't even look at da clock. When I get up, I start doin' what I can do. When I get tired, I go take a shower and eat a little bit of somethin' and go to bed." He considers. "I had to medically retire. I haven't worked in four years be-cause of my back. And my heart condition. I got two stents in my right coronary artery. And my wife's a cancer patient. But we're not goin' no-where."

Up the street, a black woman steps out of her FEMA trailer, shakes a red rug in the air, returns inside.

"What's nice about [Common Ground] is dey like to work with da fam-ily." Now Mike unfolds his thick arms, embracing air. "I mean, you had a lady two houses down dere, across da street. It was her, her two children, and her husband was cleaning out da house . . . And dey done had dat house half gutted out. And [Project Hope] and dem was going to go start on another house dat no one was dere . . . So I said, 'Wouldn't it be more feasible to help da family dat's dere?' And he said yeah."

Mike pauses a moment in wonder.

"He agreed. He said it was a good idea."

The government can't get the slant on the sewage line right, while the Common Ground volunteers—the long-haired kids and black radicals like Suncere—are not only here and helping, but they listen to him. They heard Mike's ideas and changed their plans. Maybe that doesn't equal a revolution. Maybe New Orleans and St. Bernard Parish aren't headed for a new society. But they listened.

"It made a big impact on dat family, you know?" Mike gives a small smile of pride. He's stopped work for now and is concentrating on what he's saying, making sure it comes out the way he wants. "It's just somethin', that it takes a disaster to bring people togetta like dey should be." He points down at the muddy ground. "Dis neighborhood's gonna come back as a family. Not as neighbors but as a *family*." Now he points up in the air, as if testifying. "It done started."

A Walk Around the Block

(June 2006)

Five months have passed. It's June 2006.

On what appears to be an abandoned street, a beat-up white trailer sits in front of a two-story pale green house. The house seems deserted, but in the branches of a small tree by its driveway, someone's wedged a truck tire at about eye level. Propped inside it is a circle of ragged, stuffed animals. They look like they're standing watch.

The front of the house has been spray-painted with CATS OKAY 10/13 and LEAVE CATS HERE. The sidewalk is blocked by big plastic storage tubs, some full of pet food, some planted with flowers. A closer look reveals that the flowers are plastic.

It's been ten months now since Katrina, and this short street—four or five houses long—is completely still. A breeze comes up, and from the second story of the pale green house comes the mysterious, slightly spooky sound of wind chimes.

A small hand-lettered sign hangs on the front fence:

ARE YOU FEELING UNLUCKY LATELY?
REMEMBER
He Who Lives By the Sword Shall Die by the Sword.
So—Please Put Your Swords Away!
P.S. What goes around comes around if given enough time.
You'll Get Yours.

A rubber snake has been stretched like a warning along the top of the fence.

It's not clear what street this is—all the street signs are gone—but the neighborhood is called Holy Cross. It's on the Mississippi River end of the Lower Ninth, a mile from Backatown. Six to eight feet above sea level, Holy Cross is this area's front of town. Before the hurricane, it had about 5,500 residents in 1,900 households. It was 90 percent African American, with 30 percent of the population living at or below the poverty level.

In the distance, a white man steps out of a driveway. He walks briskly down the middle of the deserted street till he gets to the house with the stuffed animals. Yes, he explains, the house is unoccupied. But the owner, Patsy, comes by nearly every day. "She's a social worker who recently retired. Very conscientious person."

The man has a hard-vowel, midwestern accent. He's white-haired, middle-aged, in a dark purple shirt with a black bag over one shoulder. His name is Mark.

"She takes care of the animals, feeds the animals. I feed a few animals myself." He smiles. "I'm surprised how many cats are still around. So we're feeding them pretty regularly."

Mark surveys the empty street. On one end, the early afternoon sun pours over the edge of a grassy levee. The first house is a hollow shell, its front entrance crisscrossed with yellow emergency tape. In its mailbox, someone's stuck a toy green frog with one arm raised, beneath it the words VOO DOO ON YOU! Then comes Patsy's, then a smaller house with a fallen pine almost completely covering its porch and driveway. A three-story brick building occupies the corner of the block; the sign over its main entrance reads: TH S J. S MES 19 0. Its windows are mostly broken, its roof missing shingles, a playground out front overgrown with weeds.

That, Mark explains, was the Thomas J. Semmes Elementary School. Built in 1900. Named after a Confederate senator. "The school was closed down about fifteen years ago, when they consolidated." It was then bought by a not-for-profit associated with a local politician. "New Orleans being New Orleans, stuff like that happens all the time."

In the last half of the twentieth century, as the city's population fell, schools and other services were consolidated. Here in Holy Cross, the emptiness was accelerated by Hurricane Betsy. It hit in the fall of 1965 with 150-mile-per-hour winds that helped flood Backatown and St. Bernard Parish. Though natural high ground like the French Quarter and

Holy Cross stayed dry, the hurricane provided yet another reason for people to leave.

During the subsequent decades, this short street, the block it's on, and the area in general fared a little better than Backatown, partly because of the Holy Cross School. "Holy Cross," as Mark puts it, "was the anchor of this neighborhood."

The school is three blocks away. Its main structure—a three-story brick Italianate building—is on the former site of a sugar plantation. The Brothers of the Holy Cross bought it in 1859. When Katrina struck, Holy Cross was serving some 500 middle school and high school boys on a seventeen-acre campus.

"Long as I been here," Mark says, "which is since 1980, I've watched the buses going constantly back and forth: five, ten, fifteen buses a day. The reason for that, of course, was that . . . tuition was so high that nobody from the Ninth Ward could really afford to go there . . . So [the students] came from places like Metairie and Kenner and midcity." It was reverse migration: white families who had fled to the suburbs sending their children back to the old Catholic school, even though it was in this low-income, predominantly black part of town.

Katrina provided a chance to change that. Within two months of the levee breach, the managing board announced Holy Cross School would be moving across the canal, closer to downtown. Since then, there's been no word about what will happen to the campus. If the school was an anchor, the neighborhood is now adrift.

Mark tries to explain what made this neighborhood, this block, so unique. "I think a large piece of the action here is the [St. Claude Avenue] bridge. We were cut off from the city in lots of ways. But one of the nice ways was crime . . . There wasn't all that burglary, the drive-by shooting and so forth. That all happened on the other side of the canal." He gestures with his chin down toward the levee. "So, though you had to be patient with that bridge going up and down and losing time, it protected you. In a real way. It protected you.

"And today," he goes on, "you can look at the concrete of that bridge protecting you from the water. Because if it wasn't for that concrete, we would look like Claiborne looks." The wave that washed whole blocks away in Backatown was diverted by the reinforced foundation of the St. Claude Bridge. Holy Cross got more than eight feet of water, but its houses weren't torn up and mashed together. It looks more like Gentilly and St. Bernard: buildings drained of life but still standing.

"You know what must have been neat?" Mark continues, then answers himself. "Before they built anything." Standing in the middle of the deserted street, he launches into an impromptu history lesson.

The Ninth Ward was laid out in the mid-nineteenth century, when New Orleans was the third-largest city in the nation and growing. Ninety-nine percent of all of the goods being transported from west of the Appalachians came down the Mississippi and were off-loaded here. There was trade in cotton, sugar, indigo, corn, lumber, and human beings.

Downtown New Orleans had the busiest slave market in the South: twenty-five auction blocks complete with holding pens, 300 dealers, and thousands of men, women, and children up for sale. Slaves were more than just laborers; they were a kind of currency, often used as collateral on mortgages. In those prewar years, New Orleans was considered a city "poised on the brink of commercial success." That success was based on trade, entrepreneurship, and a definition of private property that included dark-skinned people.

Then came the Civil War. For white New Orleans, it was a disaster as real as any flood. The city was occupied by Union troops. Emancipated slaves poured in, looking for work and more than doubling the black population. Many ended up living in the swampy lowlands of the newly created Ninth Ward. By the time peace was declared, the city's racially based social system was in ruins.

The recovery that followed was called Reconstruction. For a dozen years, reformers tried to create a new New Orleans. In 1869, the schools were integrated; in 1872, Louisiana elected its first black governor. But by the 1880s, the old guard was back in place, and Reconstruction was over. The state once again banned interracial marriage and resegregated its educational system. Thomas Semmes, for whom the school at the end of the block was named, chaired a committee that put white supremacist laws back into the state constitution.

New Orleans would continue to grow, but with the advent of a national railway system, it would never again dominate trade. Here in Holy Cross, plantations were cut up and streets run through them. Mark gestures toward the levee and says there used to be a convent for Ursuline nuns there. "In 1923, when they built that canal, they had to totally demolish it . . . But that's why they call this street right along the canal Sister Street. There was a little railroad that ran down where St. Claude is now, and this area was all truck farms. And they would bring all the produce to the French Market to sell. All truck farms here!"

While Backatown was filling with freed slaves and their descendants, Holy Cross was largely settled by German immigrant farmers. "When you first bought this property around here," Mark goes on, "you had to buy a whole block at a time. This is like 1910, 1915 . . . And the guy who built this house here"—he points to his own place, an elegant old white house opposite the abandoned school—"he bought this whole block here. And his family lived off of that block, by selling pieces over twenty and thirty years."

A piercing horn interrupts him. Mark barely blinks. It's a regular occurrence—a tanker coming down the Industrial Canal. It signals the St. Claude Bridge; the bridge beeps as it rises; traffic halts. Then the ship passes, and the bridge beeps back down into silence.

Grinning, Mark says that this is actually North Rampart Street. Rampart is legendary in the city's history, "the Broadway of New Orleans negroes." It's where slaves were allowed to gather and dance, where Louis Armstrong helped invent jazz, where the city's music stars—from Fats Domino to Dr. John—cut their hits. But all that's part of the distant skyline.

"They keep the same names," Mark explains, "even though the canal blocks everything off. You got North Rampart. You got Burgundy." He turns to point to the next street, pronouncing it Ber-GUN-dee. "You got Dauphine; you got Royal." Meanwhile, Holy Cross's avenues are named for former plantation owners: Deslonde, Forstall. The street that forms the end of the block, just past the Semmes School, is Jourdan Avenue, commemorating one of the city's largest slaveholders.

This semirural, hidden neighborhood has been Mark's home for thirty-five years. He has no doubt that he'll stay and rebuild. As he puts it, laughing a little, "I never really left." Instead of evacuating right away, Mark had waited to see how bad Katrina would really be. Soon it was too late. "It took exactly eight minutes for the water to go from my floor to my ceiling. Eight minutes! Saved the pets and some water, a little bit of food, some clothes. But eight minutes doesn't give you much time."

After two or three days, the water fell to about chest high, "and you could wade." The only other person still on the block was Patsy. "She was here for like ten days; I was here for twelve."

Mark did go away for a couple of weeks, then returned for good in early October. By then, Mayor Nagin had declared a look-and-leave policy for the Lower Ninth: residents could come during daylight hours to look at their homes, but they had to leave by dusk. Like Brandon, Mark broke the curfew, but it wasn't to foment political change. He's a land-lord. As well as the big white house he's standing near, he owns a one-story brick apartment building next to it and a couple of rentals around the corner. "I dug in my heels . . . and I just started working on my houses . . . I had to hide from [the National Guard] at nighttime."

He looks down the block. The only other sign of life is a big dog, some German shepherd mix, sleeping in the middle of the street. Mark nods at it and says, "[Mine] got eaten by wild dogs . . . There were three months here where there were no people and no garbage. So whatever dogs were around were famished. My dog was twenty-eight pounds, probably made a good snack. Never found him; never found him."

He shakes his head.

"You can always get another dog . . . but you gotta get over the last one."

The shepherd mix, Mark says, is a stray. "Patsy calls him Buddy. 'Cause he roams the neighborhood, and people seem to give him food. Patsy feeds him. Definitely a stray dog, but very quiet, nonchalant."

Then very quietly, nonchalantly, Mark heads back down the empty street, starts his car, and carefully drives around the sleeping dog. Once again, the block is still.

North Rampart stops at the levee. There're only a few homes on Sister Street: an A-frame with blue roof tarp, a little bungalow knocked off its foundation, and a redbrick house on a larger lot. The front porch of the brick house has been stacked with rusted bicycles, broken lawn chairs, hunks of cardboard. 905 SISTER STREET is painted on a piece of plywood by the front gate and BEWARE OF PIT BULLS next to it. Out by the beat-up mailbox, a Ken doll and a Barbie doll have been carefully arranged: both naked, riding bareback on a plastic palomino. There's another hand-lettered sign on a piece of poster board:

LOOTERS *You're Too Late. I've Already Been Looted!*
There's nothing left worth having.
NO DRUGS. NO JEWELRY. MOVE ON.

The next left is Burgundy. Its silence is broken by another man emerging from a driveway. This time it's a black man, maybe in his early forties, with a receding hairline. His name is Lathan: small head on a big body, slightly pop-eyed, a dark goatee.

"These are mine," he says, pointing to two houses side by side. "This one," a small bungalow, "and this fourplex." The fourplex is divided down the middle by a green cinder-block staircase that gives access to second-story apartments. Both buildings need major repairs.

Lathan says he's owned the bungalow since the early nineties. A few years ago, he added the fourplex. "The only reason I bought that one was 'cause—" He pauses. "They selling dope out the house . . . and my kid's playing out in the street! So when it finally went into foreclosure, I say I gotta get it just to protect this one," nodding at his bungalow. "I saw the neighborhood going down fast. And like I told my neighbors, 'You ain't ever gotta worry about that no more.' No, no, no."

As he speaks, he keeps moving—now stepping toward his house, now coming back—as if he has places to go, things to do, can barely afford the time to talk. He paces off, jingling his key chain, then takes a brief instant to stand and stare at his fourplex, hand on chin. "I'm waiting for them to tell me the moisture level is low enough so I can start rocking it." There's power in the neighborhood—he points toward some streetlights—but not in his buildings. "I'm in the process of working with Entergy . . . They got to come and give me a meter for these, but they're just overwhelmed . . . We on the comeback," he adds. "I see my neighbors pretty regular now . . . At least we *can* come back." After six months, the look-and-leave curfew finally ended a few weeks ago. But Lathan's still commuting daily from Baton Rouge.

His bungalow, he explains, is generations old. "Oh yes! We can't do anything unless we go through the historical society. They tell you what color to paint it, to put shutters on it or not, what type of windows to put in it. I like that! That's why I bought here." He laughs with pleasure.

Most of the buildings in Holy Cross date from 1880 to 1936. Just across the Industrial Canal, the neighborhood became an industrial port with transfer stations and shipyards, but Holy Cross stayed isolated. And the residents fought to keep it that way. In the eighties, when the Army Corps of Engineers proposed widening the canal, Holy Cross organized a neighborhood association and got placed on the National Historic Register. Unlike the uptown mansions of the Garden District, this is a working-class historic area of mostly small, black-owned homes.

Lathan studies his bungalow. "I made the mistake of covering it up with vinyl siding. That was before I really got into it. But if I have any money left over, I'm gonna take the siding off and have it painted." He spins, hands on hips, and points deeper into Holy Cross. "As a matter of fact, I'm in the process of buying another one. I close Thursday on it."

On this block, the fight for home may not have the religious overtones of Pastor Mel or the political convictions of Common Ground—but buying property in Holy Cross is still an act of faith. Right after Katrina, the Speaker of the U.S. House of Representatives declared that rebuilding the city didn't make sense. "It's a question that certainly we should be asking. It looks like a lot of that place could be bulldozed." As some urban planners and scientists put it: "New Orleans naturally wants to be a lake." For residents like Lathan, buying real estate is betting against those odds.

It helps that, nationwide, the average house value has gone up an astonishing 129 percent over the past decade. And the recent introduction of subprime mortgages has opened the dream of home ownership to more and more low-income families. As Lathan looks down his empty street, 70 percent of Americans either own or are buying their homes, the highest rate in the nation's history. To feed that demand, 2 million new houses are being built each year. In fact, as the country's manufacturing sector continues to fade, home construction accounts for a third of all economic growth. It's a big part of what the United States makes today: houses.

Poverty-stricken, losing population, New Orleans had been one of the metropolitan areas that wasn't benefiting from the real estate boom. And immediately after the floods, already low house prices dropped by almost 45 percent. But soon the pendulum started to swing back. "There was a sort of urgency," as one realtor put it, "to buy anything that was standing and livable." Many thought that real estate would help drive the city's recovery, the same way it had been driving the national economy. First a huge influx of federal money; then blocks of low-priced, often historic houses would be refurbished as part of the master plan for a smaller, more affluent metropolis.

Congress did approve $30 billion in immediate relief. And Representative Richard Baker, a Republican from Baton Rouge, proposed an additional $80 billion to restore infrastructure, help homeowners, and allow business to come back. The Baker bill had some of the scope of Franklin Roosevelt's New Deal legislation or the post–World War II Marshall Plan, and at first it had bipartisan support. But by the end of January, President Bush's White House had turned on it, saying the bill threatened to "put government in the real estate business." According to free market beliefs, lasting recovery would come not with federal help but through entrepreneurship and private enterprise.

On this block in Holy Cross, that leaves the rebuilding largely up to people like Mark and Lathan.

"The one I'm closing on Thursday," Lathan continues, "they got something up here with stained glass." He swivels to point out an architectural detail on a house across the street. "And I don't know what it is, but apparently it's worth money. And," he adds, "it's missing . . . Every day I come down here, it's a surprise."

It's hard to believe in recovery when, ten months after the floods, houses in Holy Cross continue to be stripped of everything from copper pipes to stained glass windows.

"There's a lady around the corner, she comes down here pretty regular by herself. I tell her, 'Look, you don't want to hang out here, baby.' I want her to have a whistle, so if I hear a whistle, I can run around there." Lathan's speaking fast now, eyes wide. "Like, I was talking to a guy with the feds. And he said the police force is still as big as it was, but the population is smaller. I mean, we have more police per." He puts one hand over the other, illustrating how police ought to be able to cover his neighborhood. "So, I should see cops all the time. But I don't." He shakes his head, then smiles. "Like they said, the crooks made it back first!"

He stops to laugh.

"But it's all right, it's all right. We can't wait to get back home."

With that, Lathan starts to walk away, then stops.

"My personal opinion?" He raises his arms like he's sighting down a rifle. "When they had those people in the Superdome? The mayor should have announced: 'This is *my* house! Anybody here is a guest in *my* house! If you're caught with a weapon, you'll be shot on sight.'" He pulls the trigger on his invisible gun. "'If you're caught doing wrong, we got a new law: martial law.'" He's shifted from laughing to a hard anger.

He drops his arms and checks his cell phone. "I gotta go."

Again he starts to leave, then stops.

"Oh, it's a ghost town. And now I see more people than I ever did. 'Cause at one time I come down here and—" He ends the sentence by spreading both arms and shrugging. "It was eerie . . . And the smell? My insurance adjustor—I had a garage back there—my insurance adjustor refused to go in. 'Cause the smell . . ."

He looks away.

"I still don't know what; I just had them bulldoze it."

Lathan walks around to the driver's side of his truck. "Oh, this is better," he adds. "When we were getting dark at five o'clock, man, I had to roll out. I don't know who around here!"

He laughs.

"I can't wait till it's over."

It's getting to be late afternoon. From the end of Burgundy, a left on Jourdan Avenue completes the block, returning to where Buddy the dog was sleeping. He's moved on, but a small cluster of people now stand in front of the Semmes school.

A white guy with a red goatee introduces himself as "Father Joe Campion, St. David Church." He's in a ball cap, shorts, and a PURPLE KNIGHTS T-shirt. "I was up in New York visiting my parents when Katrina came. Just drove in today."

As Father Joe sees it, the fight for home has just begun here in Holy Cross. "Property rights, that's gonna be a big issue. I'm flat against using eminent domain." He's soft-spoken, chews gum. "I think we should have each person decide what they're going to do. A lot of them are gonna be in such a financial pinch that they're not going to have much choice at all but to sell what they have. But that should be *their* option. Shouldn't be taken away. The biggest thing we were worried about were the developers. Wanting to come in beforehand and just take up the property." He smiles. "I don't think that's gonna happen. People are resolute about that."

He gestures behind him toward Backatown. "I don't know if you saw that group Common Ground over there? They're gonna stay put." He laughs a little. "So you got some battle going on here. And the frustration of the federal government not getting things going, city government, state." Shakes his head. "I find most helpful has been the college kids and the faith-based groups coming down. I got six groups coming down this summer, working just here in the Lower Ninth Ward. That's gonna be very impressive."

Father Joe points to a house across the street. It's a double shotgun: twin cement stairs lead to twin front doors with a semicircular glass fanlight above each. The house is a bright yellow-green, almost the color of the spring grass coming up in its small yard.

"Carolyn . . ." Father Joe says, nodding at the double doors. "Carolyn [is] a trip. She moved in a few months ago, long before anyone else did. And she's got the utility post up there. And since his FEMA trailer"— pointing two houses down—"came in today, I imagine hers will come in. And there're a few down there," pointing the other way.

The light's starting to orange toward sunset. It strikes the panes of the twin fanlights. Out one door comes a broad woman with a yellow kerchief covering her hair. "I'm Carolyn . . . That's Father Joe Champion, our parish priest."

Carolyn's wide, short frame nearly fills the door. She's brown-skinned with a broad nose, almond-shaped eyes, and a welcoming smile. There's a touch of the troublemaker in the way she turns the priest's name into Champion. She's wearing blue jeans and a white T-shirt with SAVE THE TIGER printed on the front. When she walks, it's with an awkward roll, as if something hurts. But the smile is overwhelming. She invites the little crowd on the street to come in.

It's dark in her house, and there are few walls. The rooms are separated by blue tarp. "This is my brother Raymond. Who's enjoying himself." A gray-haired black man is sitting on the edge of a cot, watching TV and eating. Later, Carolyn will explain how she hadn't seen her brother for ten years when she found him in the crowds at the Superdome. "He's eating my famous fried fish. And that's my daughter, Kyrah."

Kyrah is sitting on a bed in the other half of the double shotgun. She's watching her own TV. Kyrah looks to be in her late teens with pulled-back short hair, her mother's almond eyes, and a bright smile. Father Joe gives her a hug and asks when she got in. "Last week," she says. Her freshman year at New York's Syracuse University has just ended.

A neighbor appears from down the block. It's becoming a small, noisy party.

"I just took my laundry in," Carolyn announces. "From the front yard! . . . I have to use the knuckles," she shouts over the racket. "Now look what I got." She points to a modern washing machine sitting in the middle of what must have once been the living room. "When the trailer comes, I'm gonna stick it in the shade and plug it in somewhere. But I'll still hang 'em on the line, 'cause I like that smell." Another big smile.

"Come see," she says, inviting her guests to tour her home.

A shotgun is typically one room wide and two or three deep: a long, narrow rectangle you could supposedly fire a shotgun straight through. Carolyn's double is two of these under one peaked roof, with a wall down the middle. She thinks it was built in the mid-nineteenth century; it's on an 1875 map as part of a truck farm.

The shotgun design seems to have arrived in New Orleans with refugees from the Haitian revolution of 1804. The immigrants included *gens de couleur libres*—free people of color—and their influx changed the racial makeup of the city. By 1840, New Orleans was 60 percent white, about a quarter black slaves, and almost 20 percent free people of color: as racially fluid and complex as any American city. One writer describes the shotgun as having a "distinct mulatto identity." It combined elements of the houses built by Haiti's original inhabitants, the Arawak, with the rectangular Yoruba homes that slaves remembered from West Africa. By the time the shotgun came to New Orleans, it featured a shaded porch facing the street, high interior ceilings, and large rooms that stretched back to kitchens and courtyards. The design worked as a kind of air conditioner, letting hot air rise while pulling a cooler breeze from front to back. It's more African, more tropical, than it is European. Almost 10 percent of the on-street houses in New Orleans used to be shotguns, and Holy Cross was dotted with them: brightly colored masks, their private lives hidden behind. One expert calls the style "an architecture of defiance."

"I'm gonna pretend I'm turning on a light," Carolyn says, reaching toward a nonexistent wall switch and adding a "click!" As she walks her slow, side-to-side walk back into the dark, she pushes aside a blue plastic tarp that divides the occupied part of the house—the big front rooms— from the rest. She points to a bed frame standing on its side: "Now, that's my closet." She moves past a nonfunctioning bathroom. She enters the double kitchen with its ruined cabinets. Finally she points out the humped floor on the back porch. That, she says, "[is] the only damage I really, really have." But the house is a gutted shell. The high ceilings have been torn out, exposing the roof joists. All the wiring and plumbing had to go, which is why Carolyn doesn't have lights and has been scrubbing the family laundry on a washboard.

When she returns to the little party, Father Joe has moved onto the porch. Carolyn goes out there, too. Kyrah stands just inside the torn front-door screen in a pink Betty Boop T-shirt and purple shorts. She giggles as her mother puts her arm around Father Joe's waist. "Well, we friends," Carolyn grins. "Let's pretend."

"Friends!?" he grunts. "Who helped gut this house out? Huh?"

"Okay," with an immense smile, "we more than friends. They gonna bring the trailer," she adds seriously.

"Tomorrow," Kyrah puts in, "or Thursday."

"Been waiting long enough," Father Joe answers. Mike, in St. Bernard Parish, got his FEMA trailer six months ago.

"I'm gonna have a special-needs," Carolyn explains, meaning a trailer equipped for someone with disabilities: her bad knees. Carolyn plans to rebuild the double shotgun while living in the trailer.

"One stubborn woman" is what Father Joe calls her, and Carolyn—in a stage whisper, her eyes full of glee—explains.

"I was gonna ride it out . . . My niece came and jerked me by the arm! And they literally put me in the car. And I was still screaming to my neighbors, 'Get out! Get out!' And the man that was right next door"— she turns to look at the empty gray house beside hers—"I kept telling him to leave . . . That's the lady they found dead in the driveway right here." She half points between the two houses, then folds her arms across her chest. "And they thought it was me! They said, 'Carolyn Parker was dead.'" She makes a big-eyed look of horror. "Can you imagine? . . ."

"You and Fats Domino," says Father Joe, and they both laugh. The rock-&-roll star had been rumored drowned but eventually was rescued from his home, a dozen blocks from here.

Before the flood, on a spring night like this—when there were street-lights working and people in the houses—Carolyn's family might sit out in the dusk and talk sideways, from porch to porch, or visit with folks walking by. But this evening the block is empty.

Carolyn points out the black and red *veves* on the front of her home. It was first checked on 9/22, about three weeks after the flood. She was still up in mid-Louisiana then, staying with relatives. The ASPCA checked on 9/29 and 9/30: "This is how many times they were trying to catch my dog . . . They couldn't find him." She's unsmiling now. "Some people say they seen him the last time, that he was alive and running from the animal control." The dog, she explains, "[was] a puppy I found on top of the bridge, the St. Claude Bridge. It was a little-bitty thing, newborn, like a little sno-ball, and I nursed him from that. And"—she brings both hands down each side of her face as if brushing away a thought—"and it's like a kid . . . I miss him."

After evacuating, she tried to call Kyrah, "but I couldn't! We had no electricity, no phone, no communication . . . We was in the country."

Kyrah, at college in Syracuse, was getting frantic messages from her two brothers that their mother was reported dead. When mother and daughter finally connected, "I actually cried," Kyra says. "It was a mix of crying and screaming and yelling at her."

Carolyn tried to come back home immediately, but the Lower Ninth was cordoned off. "The policeman stopped me at the foot of the bridge. I told him, 'Officer, all I want to do is . . . see if my house is still standing.'"

She wasn't allowed. A month later, in October, she tried again, and this time a guard recognized her. And told her she was dead.

"Pinch me!" was Carolyn's response.

As she walked through the emptiness of Holy Cross, a neighbor told her the same thing, and somehow it fit. "When I came to see my house," she says now, "there was a deep breath I had to take. 'Cause everything down here was, like, dead." She looks around slowly. "It was like I was walking into death. . . . Everything was *gray*."

She saw her house was still in one piece and took pictures of the ruined interior. "In a swirl, like it had gone down a drain."

A couple of months later, on Kyra's Christmas break, the two of them returned to start the cleanup. Father Joe met them. It was clear to Carolyn that someone had been through the swirl of her possessions and helped themselves. Mother, daughter, priest, and another parishioner salvaged what they could, shoveling out the river mud that covered the hardwood floors, pulling down the rotted walls. Volunteers from the Alleluia Group—a self-described "charismatic, ecumenical, Christian community"—had come down from Georgia to volunteer. "The Alleluia Group came in and pretty much finished off everything that we couldn't do," Kyrah recalls. " 'Cause we weren't tall enough and didn't have ladders." The team also gutted another parishioner's house and started on St. David. Father Joe held a pre-Christmas service outside the battered church.

During that time, Mayor Nagin's Bring New Orleans Back Commission held its first public meeting at the Sheraton Hotel. Holy Cross had been designated an "Infill Development Area," subject to land seizure and developer's plans. Carolyn put on a brown print housedress and, with a black purse over her shoulder, made her way downtown through the ruins. Inside the Sheraton, she kept running into people she knew. And they kept telling her she was dead.

When the time came for public comment, she walked to the microphone and politely introduced herself. "I came to this meeting to find what your *vision* for the Lower Ninth Ward." Her voice was a little hesitant at first, in front of the cameras and the crowd. "I heard *nothing* really for the Lower Ninth Ward." As her confidence grew, she emphasized her points by tossing her head. "Those are my *family*, my *friend*, my *neighbor*. I been down there—yes, I'm telling my age—fifty-nine years! And I know who *been* here, I know who *came*, and I know who *went*."

Now, standing on her porch, describing the scene, she says, "It looked like they didn't understand me, right? So that's what made me pause."

After the pause, she leaned in to the mike. "I'm here for those persons who cannot get back to New Orleans," scanning the panel, which included Mayor Nagin, "and I don't think it's right if you try and take our property." A voice gave a faint thank-you; her two minutes were up. "Because like I said," Carolyn continued, *over my dead body!* I didn't die with Katrina! Bye." And she spun from the mike, the crowd applauding and shouting.

"I think they heard me," she says now, grinning. The moment was replayed on C-SPAN; NPR picked it up. Carolyn says someone asked President Bush about the woman at the Sheraton. Here on her porch, Carolyn reenacts the president's back-and-forth with reporters. "The man said, 'Well, President, the lady say you'll get it over her dead body.'" Carolyn's big smile reemerges. "'I have no comment.' 'But the lady say—' 'Well, I don't know how she really, really feel.'"

Now, with this small party going on in the midst of her still-dark neighborhood, she adds, "I'll tell you how I really, really feel. I love New Orleans. I love the Lower Ninth Ward. And I'm not going *anywhere*." She gives a proud smile, looking at her gutted house. "'Cause I'm home. I'm home. These are my friends. These are my neighbors. And I love that."

She's been staying here, illegally, since February. "It was supposed to be look-and-leave. I came in a U-Haul. And with flashlights and batteries. And candles!" She gives her troublemaking grin. Carolyn and her brother Raymond started camping in the bare bones of her gutted home. That first night, she remembers, "I lit up the whole house! . . . It was glowing on the corner, and it was total darkness all around . . . So the police came, and I let them in. And he said, 'Don't you know you're supposed to look and leave?' I said, 'The last time I noticed, I owned this house!'" She tosses her head and grins some more. "So, look-and-leave went to look-and-stay."

They've been camping ever since: bathing in water hauled from the corner fire hydrant, watching battery-run TVs, cooking off a propane barbeque grill that doubles as a heater. The Red Cross gave them hot food and blankets. "They thought it was so cute: two senior citizens breaking violations." Carolyn laughs.

Someone suggests throwing a block party to show they're back: putting tables out on Jourdan Avenue and having everyone cook.

"Next year," says Carolyn. "My knees will be ready." She's scheduled for a knee replacement operation. And by next year, she figures, the neighborhood should be back. Looking out on the block, she ticks off the status of each house. The one to her north, "the landlord has." And the one to the south, "I find out this couple's not coming back, so that's probably up for sale. The next house right behind it, I don't know if he's coming back. 'Cause that's a senior citizen."

The sun has now set, and the mosquitoes are starting to come out. It's time for the small party to break up. Carolyn says goodnight to everyone, then locks the front gate against stray dogs. She carefully pulls the front door closed and locks it, too—against looters. Soon the block is still again, the only light the blue flicker of her TV.

A Lot of Limbo

They've Not Done What They Needed

(June 2006)

It's a bright June morning. Pastor Mel is standing in Backatown, just down from the blue house. He's admiring the white concrete of the new levee, some fifteen feet high and almost finished.

"See, they're coming up with the wall! Amen. That's a whole lot better than what we've seen." Mel's bareheaded, in a freshly pressed pale blue shirt, the sun gleaming off his dark skin. "When I first came back here, a month after, there were trees in the street, houses in the street. Right over here . . . was where the barge came through. Under the barge was a school bus."

Visiting Backatown has become a pilgrimage for both locals and visitors; buses on "disaster tours" regularly roll through its blasted streets. It's one of the city's ground zeroes and a measuring rod for how the recovery is going. The greatest change since last winter—since Brandon strode through here, tugging at his ball cap—is that some of the houses and mashed debris have been hauled away. That's left empty lots, often with only a set of stairs rising to nothing. Even where houses remain, green palmetto grass and high weeds have taken over. Here and there, the skeleton of an old car lies like some big, sleeping animal. The emptiness touches Mel, sets him off.

"Ninety-nine percent of the people who lived back here were black . . . [Most] actually owned their homes . . . You had some drugs, just about like in every community. But these were all families along here, man. All families. This was all *people*." He gestures down the rutted streets, the empty blocks. "I would ride through here. For drugs . . . But the fact of the matter is, brother, just about any neighborhood in America you can find it. If it's not crack, it's Oxycontin. And if it's not Oxycontin, it's heroin. If it's not heroin, it's prescription drugs." Behind him, a dull red pickup truck has been left where the flood deposited it, nose buried in the dirt, rear sticking up in the air. "And if it's not that, it's alcohol; alcohol is a drug. So, you can find it anywhere in America . . . It's just everywhere now, man."

He looks at the weeds coming up in the streets.

"All [these] people are displaced. And they wanted to come home. But what do you come home to? The city is trying; the state is trying. A catastrophe of this magnitude, only the federal government has the resources to address it. And they've not done what they needed to . . . They should be pouring money in here, not worrying so much about who's gonna get what. Of course, putting in safeguards so that money is not wasted. But we're finding money is already being wasted on the federal level! You've got a group of guys who are getting the contracts, and those are all connected to the Republican Party. And well connected . . . They don't call that patronage; they just call it, 'Well, we're dealing with our friends.'"

So far, Congress has allocated a little under $16 billion in emergency funding to the Gulf Coast. Most of the first $1.5 billion was awarded either without any bidding or with limited competition. Two of the major contractors hired for the recovery are represented by a lobbyist who was a former head of FEMA—and also served as President Bush's campaign manager. And when the Army Corps of Engineers signed subcontracts worth over $6 million to put blue tarps over damaged roofs, they paid as much as ten times the going price. The result: the blue plastic that dots many neighborhoods was nailed up at an average rate of $1,200 an hour.

"We're exasperated here," Mel says, hands on hips, the wind blowing his shirt. As he looks across Backatown, it seems to call up what isn't working, who isn't being heard. "We just don't understand why we can set up voting in Iraq, but in this past election, displaced people had to come into town. Where they *could* have set up satellite centers in Houston and other areas . . ."

The Democratic mayoral primary took place in April. Sixty percent of the city's pre-storm population was still scattered across the country, most of them African American and seen as potential Nagin voters. There was a proposal to put voting machines in evacuee centers such as

Houston, Atlanta, and Birmingham, but Governor Blanco and a coalition of politicians opposed the idea: former residents living outside Louisiana would either have to mail in absentee ballots or make the trip home. The state assembly even defeated a proposal for satellite voting *within* the state—until protests forced them to back down.

Only about a third of the city's registered voters turned out for the primary. And of the 300,000 displaced residents, only about 21,000 managed to vote. The results showed blacks still representing a thin majority, but turnout in Gentilly, for example, was around 80 percent of what it had been in 2002's mayoral election. In the Lower Ninth, it was around 40 percent. Nagin pulled about a third of the total vote, while three white candidates split most of the rest. In the runoff, Nagin's "racialized" strategy paid off, but just barely. He ended up with 52 percent of the total: 80 percent of the black vote and 20 percent of the white. Lieutenant Governor Mitch Landrieu—son of the city's last white mayor and brother of the sitting U.S. senator, Mary Landrieu—got a total of 48 percent.

The elections drew national comment, not so much because Nagin won, but because the vote indicated that a major American city was heading back to being majority white. In the *New York Times*, the drop in low-income residents was heralded as a chance "to break up zones of concentrated poverty." President Clinton's former chief of staff for HUD predicted that New Orleans would end up smaller, "and I'm not sure if that's the worst thing in the world." Displaced families might get a chance to live "in other parts of the state or in other parts of the country, live in neighborhoods where they have access to good schools, safe streets and quality jobs." Meanwhile, Congressman Baker—the same whose Baker Bill had proposed billions for recalibrating the city—was overheard saying to lobbyists: "We finally cleaned up public housing in New Orleans. We couldn't do it, but God did."

To Pastor Mel, it's all part of the shift toward a boutique city. Before the floods, just over half of the city's population rented. "Lot of people who were renters—even had lease situations—landlords are kicking them out . . . saying they want to repair their property . . . They're going to court, and they're just being kicked out." His cell phone rings; he thumbs it mute. "Because [landlords] here in New Orleans see they can get more money . . . Properties that once rented for four, five hundred dollars a month are now at a thousand. And this is from people who can't afford it, who could barely afford it before the storm."

The floods are now estimated to have destroyed 140,000 of the city's housing units, the majority of them low-income. More than half its rental units were damaged. Even with fewer people in the city, rents have gone up an average 70 percent.

Again, the disaster seems to have sped up time, pushing the city in a direction it was already headed. In the decade before the flood, New Orleans had cut the number of its low-income units almost in half. When Katrina struck, a third of the apartments held by the Housing Authority of New Orleans (HANO) were already boarded up: some to be "modernized," many declared beyond repair. Forty-nine thousand people were living in the city's public housing, 20,000 of them in the "Big Four" developments: Lafitte, St. Bernard, C. J. Peete, and B. W. Cooper. HUD had already targeted the Big Four for closure, and since the floods, they've sat empty, fenced off in case residents try to return.

Mel surveys the desolation of Backatown, distant backhoes dumping wreckage into waiting trucks. "We got people who *want* to come home. Who we need to set up trailer parks for. FEMA's willing to do it. But we got some local politicians here who don't want people who don't *look* like them in their community!" He's animated now, emphasizing points by swinging from side to side, preaching in this newly made wilderness.

"They're afraid of—" He shrugs. "Whatever. 'You can't come to my park because me and my children and my dog have to go here every day!'" He smiles tightly. "You're afraid that something is going to happen in your community?" Mel asks the question of the far-off city skyline. "I just don't—" Then stops himself, starts over.

"We all got to make some kind of sacrifice. And if that means that somebody who don't look like me"—tapping his chest with both hands—"that's different—they may even be struggling in life—they come in the community? It's *my* responsibility, now, to try to befriend you and help you in any way that I can." His voice rises. "We want everybody in the United States to help us here in New Orleans." He pronounces it New Or-lee-ins. "But you got people here in New Or-lee-ins who don't *want* people who don't *look* like them to be *in* the park. So they can run their *dog*. That's shame on some of us in New Or-lee-ins."

The recovery has raised the possibility of doing away with decades of segregated housing patterns. But Mel doesn't see it happening. And one of the reasons, he believes, is the court system.

His ministry, Bethel Colony South, recently faced eviction proceedings. "And the judge didn't want to hear anything. And we *had* money. We were not avoiding the lease-purchase agreement." Mel acts out the dialogue: "'I don't want to hear it. The man didn't get his money each month.' 'But Your Honor, the man didn't want to *accept* the money. He wanted to change the lease agreement . . . We would have lost fifteen thousand dollars.' 'Well, . . . I'm sorry: we rule against you.'"

Pastor Mel, looking out at the new concrete levee, gives a broad, complicated smile.

"Now, a ministry that was established from *nothing*—God gave us everything we had, we started with no money—that before the storm was helping thirty-five men—we've helped a hundred and twenty men over that year's time—that a judge decided that, well, because a hurricane has come, and the landlord wants the property back—"

He doesn't end the thought but jumps to connect it with the larger situation.

"And a lot of the judges are doing that . . . You can come and sit in the court; you don't have to take my rendition of it. Go sit in court and watch the travesty that's going on. They're *poor* people!"

He stops abruptly and just stares, blinking in the morning light. The white concrete levee draws a line across the empty neighborhood.

Pastor Mel drives back over the Industrial Canal, travels the fifteen minutes it takes to reach Gentilly, and parks around the corner from his ministry's former location. In front of him is a modern-looking one-story gray building set on a fairly large lot. There's a smaller building out back and a trailer parked to the side.

"This is just another gift from God," Mel declares.

He steps into the concrete yard that surrounds the building.

"We went to court, and the judge threw us out. And in twenty-four hours—twenty-four hours!—wanted us to move our whole ministry." His face tightens. He'd promised his men a place to stay and a chance to go straight. And there he was, faced with having to put a dozen of them back on the street.

"I'm trying to figure out where we gonna go from here. God had me drive around the corner. And there was a FOR SALE sign out in front of this. This used to be what's called New Life Ministries. And the pastor of this church, I went to seminary with! So I called. And he said, 'Mel, you would not understand—but then again, I know you *will* understand. Me and my wife, we're not coming back to New Orleans. We've taken a church in Ohio. [But] we've put our names on [this building's] mortgage, and we've had to pay one thousand dollars a month since the hurricane to keep our credit intact . . . Me and my wife, we prayed *last night* that God would help us to do something so we could get out from under the burden. Here it is, this morning, you're calling asking to buy it!' He said, 'Whatever we need to work out, we're gonna work out!'"

Mel is so excited by retelling this story that he's jiggling on the balls of his feet.

"Now, the money we had for rent—that our landlord over here wouldn't take?—that was twenty thousand dollars. That's *exactly* what we needed to put on this building to secure the building! So God had already had this set up for us." He shakes his head in wonder. "He gave us *more* than we had! We have a much better facility. And we've got central air here; over there we were using fans. God is great! Amen, amen!"

He's chuckling at the glory of it when a well-dressed elderly woman steps into the compound. She looks out of place in this neighborhood: a middle-class woman in a pale blue jacket, turquoise blouse, gold earrings, red lipstick. It's Mel's mother, here to see the new property.

He starts showing her around, starting with a new set of showers in the back courtyard. "The men who are on the program," he explains, "they do the work." He lifts the flap of a white tent. "This is where we keep our food supplies." Boxes of canned goods, long tables, a refrigerator running off an extension cord. His mom murmurs her approval.

Inside the main building, there's a little kitchen, the plumbing still raw. "Now we got a commercial sink. It's small, but it gets the job done." Beyond that, double-decker bunks line the building's single room. "We got one, two, three, four, five, six, seven, eight, nine, ten bunk beds. That the New Orleans Baptist Theological Seminary was throwing out after the hurricane. And it's much nicer than what we already had! So God blessed us and gave us even better." There are no closets: the men's clothes hang off the end of the bunks. Toilet supplies in plastic bags sit on the headboards. As Mel tours the room with his mother, a man sleeps quietly in one of the lowers.

Up front, chairs are set facing a desk. "And this is where we hold class, where we eat . . . Everything we have is all stuff that we've salvaged, that people were throwing away after the hurricane. All the couches."

He stops to consider.

"I know Katrina hurt a lot of people, but it gave us a fresh start. And I think it's given a lot of people a fresh start. Because stuff that we thought that we used to have to have, we're finding out that we really don't have to live with it. You know, it's not the material things that we've had in life. People have learned dependence on God—because that's the only one that can carry any of us through this. But also their connection with family has been so important for them. Because those that lost family members"—he shakes his head—"they're really struggling. Those that didn't, they're just very thankful that their families are intact."

Mel's cell phone buzzes. It's his father.

"Yes, sir, we're on our way. All right, Dad, we'll see you in a minute."

Mel and his mom drive the same route he drove last winter: past the Theological Seminary, through Gentilly Woods, into Pontchartrain Park. FEMA trailers still sit in driveways; blue tarps still cover roofs.

As they pull up to the family house, Mel's mother says she and her husband evacuated and only returned to the city six months ago. "It hasn't changed much since. In the inner city, Lower Nine, even out here, it hasn't changed much. The only thing that's happened here is a house is gutted. And a tree has been cut down."

They get out of the car, and the first thing Mel's mother does is bend down and pick some stray sticks off the lawn. Then, she stops and looks at her pale yellow house. The Virgin Mary still stands out front. Black iron grilles cover the windows and doors. She opens the entrance grate— the wooden front door is broken—and steps inside.

There are no walls, no insulation, no sheetrock. All the wires and plumbing are exposed. A layer of dust covers the tiles in the entryway, and water still drips somewhere toward the back.

Mel's father—Melvin senior—joins them in the ruins. He's a gentle-looking man, light-skinned, with short gray hair. "See," he says in a soft voice, "some of this wood was under water for two weeks. *Salt* water."

"Three weeks," his wife puts in.

"That's what you get when you pay off your mortgage." If it's a joke, he's not smiling. He has a poker face, thin slits for eyes. "But it could have been worse."

The same way Mel looked young standing in this house, his parents look old. Or maybe it's just the contrast between their age and the work that needs to be done. They don't say much.

"Eventually," Mel's father announces slowly, breaking the silence, "we gotta try to get back some way. Repair it."

"I forgot we got that leak here." Pastor Mel points toward a pipe in what had been the kitchen. Spray bounces off the wrecked tile floor. "It won't cut off." He heads off to deal with it.

"We had flood insurance," his father says quietly, with his slight Louisiana lilt, "and we got very little. Very little. And those people who didn't have flood insurance are getting a hundred and fifty thousand dollars . . ."

A hundred and fifty thousand has become the magic number. In February, the state announced its plan for distributing federal relief money, dubbing the program Road Home. This month, $9 billion in federal community development block grants has been targeted to "help Louisiana residents get back into their homes or apartments as quickly as possible." The maximum payout per household is $150,000. So far, no money has been distributed.

Road Home is offering homeowners three options: they can stay and rebuild, sell their house to the state and relocate in Louisiana, or sell and move out of state. The maximum payment goes for rebuilding. Mel's parents still aren't sure what they'll do.

"The insurance adjustors?" Mel's mother gives a halfhearted smile. "First thing they told us: what they *can't* pay us for. Flood: they maxed it out. The policy. But we didn't have a lot of flood; we had more homeowner's insurance. And *that* we didn't get paid for." She's shaking both hands, bracelets jangling. The money they did receive, she says, was "just a drop in the bucket. It's very disheartening."

Across the Gulf, insurance companies are declaring damages are due to wind and mold, not water, so flood policies won't apply. And what payouts homeowners do receive will be subtracted from Road Home's hundred and fifty thousand. Mel's father says it's as if his family is being punished for having insurance, for doing the right thing.

"At our age," Mel's mother offers, "we don't want to take everything we have to go back into rebuilding a home. Melvin [senior] will be seventy-five. Right, Melvin? In November. And I'll be seventy-four in October. And there are thousands of people like that. Especially in our community. We've been out here since 1962."

She raises one hand. "They're just throwing the ball at us and telling us: do. But we can only do so much. They talk about loans? Loans sound great . . . but at our age? Our home was paid for. I don't want to take out a loan for thirty years. We won't be here . . ." She shakes her head in exasperation. "We didn't ask for any help to gut the home and everything. But if we can get monies in, and we can get contractors, we can move forward."

Her husband gestures out toward Pontchartrain Park. "All these people who lived here are over seventy years old, and they're just not coming back, you know? You have real estate people who are out there waiting. So they can take you for little or nothing." A slight smile. And what the realtors will do, he says, "is rebuild. And then sell. And then make a ton of money." He gives a resigned, gentle shrug.

"Well, we hope not," says his wife, more assertive, feistier. "With God willing, I want to come home."

The two of them stand there, the water splashing on their former kitchen floor.

"Just asking them to give us a break. Come down and look at ordinary people." She swirls her hand. "We're not wealth, you know. We came from good stock, but we were poor. We worked ourselves up. Melvin and I with our family? We never asked anybody for anything. We raised our seven children, educated them . . . We wanted the American Dream like everybody else. We struggled to get this home. And paid for it. And it's all gone. And that hurts."

Her husband wanders off into the dark to help with the plumbing. Mel's mother stands in the ruins and starts talking about what the realtors can't get: her memories.

"We didn't have very much when we moved here." She points out where the wringer washing machine once stood, the stools for her seven kids, the homemade cabinets to store toys. "My husband . . . he was a teacher . . . He had a job after school, and he would clean up office buildings downtown . . . This is how he made the extra money to bring home. 'Cause teachers only got paid once a month, and it wasn't enough. And he wanted me to be the homemaker, so I stayed home with my seven children. It was rough, but we were happy. We thought this was the White House when we moved in here!"

The short, lively woman looks around at the moldy wood as if for inspiration. She swerves back to her childhood and how she got from there to here.

"Before [my family] moved into public housing, we lived in a house where you could have chickens in the backyard . . . Many the mornings we'd go: 'Ma, can we have eggs?' We'd run out to the little henhouse and get eggs. Ma would fry them in a great big iron skillet." She remembers the corn they planted in their Depression-era yard and the tomatoes. "Take the tomatoes off the vine, run to the faucet and clean them off, get the salt shaker . . . Best tomatoes you ever ate! Those were happy times. But we were poor. We didn't have indoor plumbing or anything like that, no electricity . . ."

She gestures to where the wires once ran in this house, now left dangling. And as she looks around the empty shell, it takes her back to when she and her sister would walk to the drugstore, the game they'd play as they passed houses. "My sister would say, 'This is mine.' And I'd say, 'This is mine!'" She grins, looking girlish. They could dream of their future homes, but what they couldn't figure out was: "How did they get that? This is where we lived . . . but how did they get that? I knew there was something out there that was better . . ."

The answer—for her family, anyway—began when they started building public housing. "Which they call the projects now." Around 1940, New Orleans opened six public housing developments, four for blacks and two for whites. They were part of a national push that grew out of the Depression. During and after World War II, in a golden age of near full employment, the country set out to fulfill Franklin Roosevelt's goal of "adequate, safe, and sanitary housing [for the] working poor." More than 450 developments went up nationwide, most of them large-scale complexes like Chicago's Robert Taylor Homes and Detroit's Charles Terrace Complex. The Lafitte Development, where Mel's mother moved, consisted of blocks of low, redbrick homes facing grassy courtyards shaded by oaks. "And we moved in there when I was first year of high school. About 1946. It was beautiful! We had hardwood floors, hot and cold running water, a hot water heater. Everything!" She smiles.

Most American cities didn't have enough adequate housing, but the pressure was especially acute in New Orleans. It had emerged from the war as the country's second-busiest port. With veterans returning and the rural population migrating into the city to find work, its white population grew by almost 15 percent, "nonwhite" by more than 20. In the postwar reconstruction that followed, New Orleans was a national leader. Its large-scale housing developments were the first to be ratified by the Federal Housing Administration and have since been called "some of the best public housing built in the United States." Lafitte had not only tile roofs and iron trelliswork but federally funded nursery schools, on-site medical services, garden clubs.

In all, New Orleans built 9,000 new units. But there were 19,000 applicants for public housing in 1947—and double that the next year. Twenty percent of the new homes went to families on relief; the rest were reserved for the working poor: domestics, dock workers, taxi drivers. The developments were designed to be temporary—a little like Pastor

Mel's ministry—a stopping place for families coming out of poverty and heading for the middle class.

While living in Lafitte, Mel's mother met her future husband. "I was at Booker Washington High School . . . We were on a picnic . . . And I guess we clicked that day, but he was, you know, in the seminary." A small smile. "Anyway . . . by the time it was ready for my graduation from high school, he had left the seminary . . . We decided we'd made up our minds: we wanted to get married. We did. And Melvin went into the military. In the air force. He was working as a chaplain's assistant."

They had Mel junior, their first child, in Sacramento, California. Over the next decade, they added six more kids, including two sets of twins. Back in New Orleans, they were living in housing, Mel's mother recalls, "constructed for the returning veterans from the Korean crisis. It was run by the federal government." But then that, she says, was demolished.

"They wanted us to move back in the projects around the city? I didn't want that." She touches the center of her chest, just below her gold necklace. "I grew up in the Lafitte housing development, and it was just a beautiful place to live and everything was safe. But times change, and people change, and I didn't want to move there. I didn't want to take our children back there."

The change took little more than a decade. In the late forties, urban redevelopment in New Orleans was "stopped cold by political opposition." Then the Federal Housing Act of 1949 shifted the target population from the "deserving poor" to "families that had been poor for generations." By the time Mel's family was considering reentering public housing, white evacuation to the suburbs had begun. That not only lowered the city's tax base but drew business away. New Orleans went on to build 5,000 additional low-income units, but the construction was no longer first-rate. At the same time, maintenance of the old developments fell off. And the segregation that had always been part of the Big Four now began to feel permanent. Instead of temporary stops on the way to the American Dream, public housing complexes got the reputation for being "federal ghettoes" occupied by the "chronically unemployed." As Mel's mother puts it, they went from developments to projects.

So the family chose instead to test the free market. They felt sure they'd be able to find a place: Mel's father had steady work and was getting his B.A. from Xavier University; they were decent, religious folk. But a long search produced little. They'd been paying sixty dollars a month rent,

Mel's mother says, "and we knew we could afford a hundred dollars . . .
But nobody would touch us. Nobody." First they had to find a neighborhood that accepted blacks. Then, they needed a big enough place for two
adults and seven kids. Finally, it had to be within a teacher's budget.

The only house they found scared Mel's mother. "Rats came out at
night." By this time—1960—20 percent of the city's housing was considered "substandard." As the black population grew and the white
population evacuated, more and more families ended up in falling-down,
overcrowded homes. The lack of loans and mortgages for black home-
buyers created a similar situation across the country. As the National
Commission of Race and Housing concluded: "Housing is the one com-
modity on the American market that Negroes . . . cannot purchase freely."

The way Mel's mother remembers it, she ran into a young woman who
was about to move out of a house in Pontchartrain Park. "And I said, 'Oh
my God! We'd like to have it' . . . [Pontchartrain Park was] the first
black—well, it was colored in those days—subdivision in the country.
With the golf course around it."

Pontchartrain Park had been Mayor DeLesseps "Chep" Morrison's
solution to the "Negro problem." By the end of World War II, New Orleans
was 30 percent black, a growing voting bloc that the mayor couldn't afford
to ignore. At the same time, he had to appease white voters by maintain-
ing segregation. He fell back upon the separate-but-equal doctrine, legal-
ized a half century earlier in *Plessy v. Ferguson*. Then, a mixed-race New
Orleans shoemaker named Homer Plessy had been arrested for trying to
sit in a whites-only railroad car. The subsequent ruling had affirmed a
state's right to provide separate-but-equal accommodations for blacks
and white. Now, as New Orleans Negroes demanded adequate housing,
education, and recreational facilities, the mayor proposed an exclusively
black and exclusively middle-class subdivision on 366 acres of former
marshland.

The city built the golf course, the surrounding park, and a "Negro
bathing area," while private philanthropists developed the housing. Purchase prices were underwritten: a family could put $25 down and pick a
house model starting at around $11,000. With the help of the G.I. Bill,
the average thirty-year mortgage in Pontchartrain Park was between $50
and $100 a month.

Even so, the move almost wiped out Mel's family. "We only had twenty-
five dollars to our name when we moved in this house," his mother recalls. They were able to make it because Mel's father "didn't have to clean

offices anymore; he was able to sell automobiles." Mel's mother grimaces a little. "But they gave him such a hard time at the dealership, because they really didn't want, um, colored men to work there at that time."

Still and finally, they had a home. It was, as Mel said, the first in the history of the family: a sign of changing times.

Once they'd moved in, they discovered that only some things had changed. Their new home was within walking distance of an amusement park, Pontchartrain Beach, with a midway, a roller coaster, and a kiddieland. "We could see the Ferris wheel from the front lawn." The seven kids were beside themselves. "All of them were jumping up, all seven. 'We want to go there this week! And tell Daddy to come home early so we can go ride on the Ferris wheel . . . Ma, can we go? Can we go?'" Mel's mother, standing in the wreckage of her home, can still mimic the excitement in their voices from forty years ago.

The trouble was that the amusement park was on land leased from the Orleans Parish Levee Board. And the lease specifically stated the midway and rides were for whites only. "I had to tell them, very painfully, that because we were colored we were not allowed to go there." So the Ferris wheel twirled on the horizon, hopelessly out of reach. "They would sit on the weekends, just about every weekend . . . crying. You know? To be able to go to Pontchartrain Beach."

Two summers after they moved in, the Civil Rights Act of 1964 forced the amusement park to integrate. "It was a happy day. But it didn't last very long." Whites stopped coming; repairs and maintenance fell off; soon the rides were too rickety to be safe. The Ferris wheel was now open to them, but Mel's mother wouldn't let her children on it. "It just went down," she recalls, "and was gone."

Still, Pontchartrain Park remained an island of middle-class African American life. "We raised our children," Mel's mother declares, "in peace and tranquility. With the door open. They could come and go. Left our windows open at night! . . . [And] the children were able to go to some integrated schools." Mel attended John F. Kennedy High School. "He was one of the few colored to graduate there, with some of the other young men and women who lived out here in the Park."

Their first son went on to his father's alma mater, Xavier, to get a degree in pharmacy. And his five sisters all went to college. "Out of those seven children," Mel's mother says, "we have eighteen grandchildren. And we have nine great-grandchildren." She reels off the numbers with obvious pride, standing in the ruins of her home, immaculate in her blue jacket, the sound of her bracelets rattling and water dripping in the dark.

Then Mel dropped out of college. "He was always a businessman at heart. Like his dad." As she's about to go on, Mel comes back in the room and takes up the story from there.

How he opened up a florist shop and invested the profits in a nightclub. "It was called the New York Times." He looks embarrassed. "I went through New York one time and had a party, and I came back and called it the New York Times . . . We used to have the Neville Brothers, Luther Kent 'Trick Bag' . . . Willie T . . ." And then the nightclub led to drugs. "Gave her a lot of grief," Mel says, looking toward his mother. "A lot of grief."

She looks right back at him. "Maybe not as much as you think you did."

Mel describes her waiting up nights, "not knowing if she was gonna get a call, if I was dead or alive. She cried many a night. I heard her cry sometimes—times when I would stay clean for a while and then I'd call up and say, 'Ma, I fell. . . .'"

"But you also remember I told you I'd never give up."

"Yea," he answers.

"I don't think there are enough words, Melvin, to tell you how proud Dad and I are of you. And you know that."

"God!" is Mel's answer. "God. God."

"We know that . . . but you cooperated, too."

"I came kicking and screaming, Ma." He smiles.

"God is good, as you always say." Mother and son laugh together. ". . . Do you remember Paw-Paw saying that?"

And that takes Mrs. Jones one final layer deeper into family history. Her father, Pastor Mel's grandfather, was a small man, five foot three, who sold perfume door to door from "a little brown handbag . . . My dad was a foreigner," Mel's mother explains.

"He was from India," Mel puts in, ". . . but I'm *black*!" He's both mock serious and emphatic. "I'm *black*. Let's make no mistake about that."

Again, they're both laughing.

Early in the twentieth century, when Paw-Paw took his place in the gumbo of New Orleans culture, "he belonged," Mel's mother says, "to the white race. Because they weren't from Africa . . . He believed, I think, deep in his heart, that he was not of our race . . . I remember when he got ill one time, we brought him to Charity Hospital . . . They put him on—at that time—the white side . . . My mother was upset . . . because she was afraid they wouldn't let her in [to visit] . . . When we were growing up," she continues, "he tried to send us to school in the French Quarter, where children of different nationalities were. And my mother didn't approve . . . 'Cause she thought . . . it would harm us later on. Because we were really colored . . . So we went to the public school with the colored children." Her shoulders rise in a held shrug.

Again, she looks around at her gutted house. It's been a long road here.

"We're hoping to come home. And I pray every day that God will set everything in motion for us. That either we can tear this house down and rebuild on this spot . . ." Or what? She doesn't offer an alternative but jumps instead to the rest of her prayer. "And that other people are able to come back. And hopefully be just a bit of family in this community that we had at one time. Melvin [senior] and I may not be here when it's *all* done, but our children will be here. And hopefully one of them will live in this house." She smiles.

"All this is going to have to be torn down."

Mel's father has drifted into the backyard and is waving his hand at the back of their home.

"Just dry rot . . . We're going to do the best we can. We hope we can live ten years longer," he nods, "and do what we can to kinda help the children . . . As we started off raising them, we will continue to raise them. And they will continue to come back, like they did Sunday for Mother's Day . . ."

There's a quiet moment. Then Mel's father points out into Pontchartrain Park.

"Some people over here are starting to put their place back together. Other people . . . haven't done anything. Many, many people are not coming back."

He has an idea about that. Almost half of the Pontchartrain Park residents were fifty or older. Many came here, as he did, soon after the subdivision opened, and now they're too elderly to take on the rebuilding. "I made a suggestion to one of the banker friends of mine that what they do is build a home for the retired people. And let it be three stories high: first story would be shopping and all of that, swimming, and then you got two stories [residential]. And do it all the way across." He points off toward the horizon. "And then those people who are young can rebuild their houses. And we would call [the retirement home] Pontilly: Pont-chartrain Park and Gentilly Woods." He smiles slightly at the idea of the two neighborhoods, built to be separate-but-equal, now merging. "That would keep a lot of elderly people still in this area."

It's the kind of large-scale public building project that once helped families like his. But while the Baker Bill had some of that scope, it's been defeated. The mayor still doesn't have a master plan. The city council has announced it's formulating its own, but that hasn't happened yet. Meanwhile, today's newspaper has a story about HUD deciding not only to close but to demolish the Big Four. Instead of large public works, the recovery is moving house by house, family by family, chore by chore.

"All those trees," Mel's father says, pointing to the remaining scraggly pines, "are gonna have to come down."

His wife joins him and explains how they've managed to get even this far.

"We were blessed . . . —that's my wonderful son!—with the ministry and the men. They've just been so wonderful to us. They'll come at any time, if they have the time, and they'll do some things for us. They came and picked up the bulk of the things: the refrigerators, the stoves, the air-conditioning units. But other than that, we haven't had any assistance at all."

Her husband is quiet, looking out at the neighborhood.

"And every day," his wife says, "we see on the television how it's the greatest natural disaster to have happened in the United States since the Great Fire in San Francisco. In 1906, I believe. And Katrina has topped it. And I'm wondering—and I pray—" She stumbles over her words. "Well, what are they trying to do for us?"

It isn't 1906. Or 1946. It's June 2006. In this year's State of the Union address, President Bush made only a glancing reference to the city's recovery.

"We're not coming with our hands out!" Mel's mother frowns into the glare of the sun. "Give us the insurance money; don't take it *away* from the grant that they're going to give us. That would afford a lot of people," sweeping the neighborhood with a hand, "to say, 'All right. We can do something with this.' And come back home."

She pauses a moment. Sunlight falls on her blue jacket and gold hoop earrings. There's a streak of gray in the dark hair along each temple.

"Forty years we lived here. And just can't . . ." she pauses to find the word. "eliminate that. In nine months, ten months, or even a year. The memories will always be here." She looks around. "Many happy days were spent with the children in this yard."

Mel's mother starts to shrug and then holds it, shoulders up toward the sky. Finally she exhales.

She and her husband stand silently in the backyard. Then they walk slowly back through the shell of their house and out to the front. A few flowers have been replanted in the little garden. They stop by the Virgin Mary. Mel's mother calls it her "sign to come back." Mel's father places white rosary beads on the statue. As he prays, his wife bends down to pull a weed.

Got to Do What You Got to Do

(August 2006)

It's a year after the floods, and short-built Mike out in St. Bernard Parish is home.

It's astonishing.

Astonishing how normal his house looks: comfortable, suburban, with a large-screen TV hanging from a newly painted wall, a ceiling fan spinning slowly in the damp air. And that much more astonishing because the trip through the Ninth Ward out Judge Perez Drive still crosses a blasted landscape. The ruined strip malls remain vacant. The Kentucky Fried Chicken and the Popeyes are still boarded up. There's a McDonald's sign, but all the yellow plastic has been ripped out of its arch. Of the thousand or so businesses once located in St. Bernard, fewer than 10 percent have reopened.

The ExxonMobil plant did, just three months after the flood. So did Domino Sugar. Pickup trucks sit outside the latter, and there are caps of fire on the tips of some of the exhaust chimneys. But the vehicles parked in front of the multiplex theater are backhoes.

Between the vacant malls are undeveloped, low green fields. Some of these have been turned into trailer parks. Under a blue sky with white wispy clouds, FEMA trailers sit in T-square-straight rows: each row twenty trailers long and two trailers wide, with ten or fifteen rows per site, all set behind new mesh fence like a refugee camp. A guard is posted at each entrance gate. Across Louisiana, 73,000 families are now living in FEMA trailers. And in St. Bernard alone, 1,600 families are still waiting to get one.

Chalmette High School, "Home of the Fighting Owls," is open again. During Katrina, it filled with five feet of water: "a mixture of marsh bottom mud, oil and gasoline, fish and grass." In the weeks that followed, the superintendent lost patience with FEMA and hired a local construction company. Part of the building reopened a couple months after the flood, far ahead of schools in New Orleans. The parish is still so small—less than a third the size it was—that this one school now serves the student population that used to need three high schools and nineteen other public and private elementary and middle schools.

Past Chalmette, down Judge Perez Drive, most of the squat brick houses in the Daniel Park subdivision are still unoccupied. Thick green vines have climbed the fences, softened the dead trees, deformed windows and doors. Cars have been left for trash with hoods and trunks gaping open. Every once in a while, there's a white FEMA trailer.

Almost at the end of one of these long, ruined streets, there's Mike's house, his U.S. and Confederate flags flying out front.

Inside, Mike is sitting on a pale brown sofa, his shirt off, air-conditioning on. His round gut hangs over his shorts, blurry tattoos on both shoulders, chest, and back. Behind him, curtains frame new windows. In the kitchen, a new black coffee machine sits on an unfinished countertop below new blond cabinets. There's a new silver stand-up fridge and big greenish containers of bottled water. Ask him what he's been doing for the past six months—since Suncere found him leveling the steps up to his trailer—and he'll give a three-word answer: "Redoing the house."

Across the room, on a matching brown sofa, is his wife, Kim. She's very thin with straight brown hair to her shoulder, big glasses, and big teeth. Her skin is whiter than her husband's: less time outdoors. She's wearing a knee-length white T-shirt with bright red lettering: KATRINA THAT BITCH.

"Two of us?" Kim says, grinning. She's missing a lower tooth. "I never thought we could do it. But we were determined. We were going to *get in* our house."

When Suncere came by, they'd just gotten their trailer. "So dat's when we moved over here." Mike nods toward the back. They did the house gutting mostly by themselves and with their own money. They did get some early aid from FEMA, but Mike can't remember how much. He turns to his wife.

"Twenty-five hundred dollars, two thousand dollars?"

"From FEMA?"

"Yeah. When we was all the way in Monroe."

"Twenty-five hundred."

"Dat's it. Dat's what we got from FEMA."

They also received some private insurance money. "It took months," Kim says, "for them to even acknowledge they owed us anything." The couple received their check a few weeks ago, when the rebuilding was almost done.

"For six thousand dollars," Mike says. He puts his head down and stares a second. Six thousand dollars to rebuild his home.

Over in Mississippi, a federal judge has just heard a case in which some 3,000 policyholders are suing Nationwide Mutual for not selling flood insurance—and for not paying out on the policies it did sell. Similar suits are being filed against a half dozen other companies.

Mike and Kim made do with their savings and what disability pay they receive. Mike used to work for a nearby marine outfit that sold and repaired recreational fishing boats. He was a jack-of-all-trades, fixing outboards, repairing electrical systems, helping to put up storage buildings. The business reopened just a month after the flooding—one of the first to do so—and it's been doing well, selling replacements for all the boats lost in the hurricane. "I called my boss right after da storm . . . and I said, 'Man, I'd love to come help you rebuild.' Dat was my intent." But it didn't happen. "I just can't do what I want to do."

Five years ago, he had a heart attack. "I was already having the problems with my back and arthritis. So, I was seeing a doctor for dat. And I was taking dat medicine for arthritis. And then . . . just all of a sudden, I hit da floor. The day before, da whole week before: fine, nothing. I was working; I take the Vioxx. Hey, da medicine worked. But I ended up with a major heart attack."

He estimates that his medical bill is "six hundred something dollars a month. And my wife," he explains, "she's a lymphoma patient." Kim believes she got cancer by living next to the Murphy Oil Refinery. The stretch of the Mississippi River between here and Baton Rouge is often called "Cancer Alley." "I can't get any help for her. I can't get any insurance for her because of da little money I make. She's got to travel all da way to Houma just to get her port cleaned. She's got a port underneat' her skin, ya know, in case it should come back on her, again. I don't know, it's just . . . it's just . . ." He slows, fumbles. "A loss for words on dat situation . . ."

Their other potential source of recovery money is Road Home. "We've signed up for dat . . . We ain't heard nuttin' . . . Dey got all our information and everything. We've told 'em how much we collected from insurance . . . I just got a call da other day saying da first appointment I can get is December 1!" That's four months away.

The same way the federal government is privatizing—hiring Blackwater USA, for example, to provide security in Iraq—Louisiana has brought in a "global professional services firm," ICF International, to run Road Home. The argument is that private companies are more efficient and cost-effective than government. The state board of ethics raised the possibility of a conflict of interest, since ICF had drawn up the Road Home plan in the first place. But the contract's been signed.

Now Mike grins and acts out his phone conversation with an ICF/Road Home employee.

"'So should I bring my receipts?' She says, 'Well, what kind of receipts you have?' 'Well, for my roof, for my plumbing, for my electric, for my appliances: dis, dat, and de other.'" She didn't seem to know the answer. "'Well . . .' I said, 'I'm bringing dem all.' Dat was it! 'See you December 1.'" So far, more than 30,000 Louisiana homeowners have applied for Road Home. No checks have been issued.

Mike started rebuilding by borrowing some sections of fire hose. "I went and got dem off da side of da road and hooked dem to da fire hydrant. Pushed da mud out wit da fire hydrant." When the floors were washed clean, the moldy, waterlogged sheetrock had to be torn off.

Kim goes and gets a plastic box half full of snapshots. The first is of their street dank with mud, all the houses empty, no signs of life. It looks like a river bottom. "Dey had to come trew here," Mike says, "with a big humongous bulldozer. To push da mud and da muck and da cars and everything else out of da middle of da street."

Then comes a picture of a floor with pink insulation stuck to what looks like the bottom of a mattress. Mike has a hard time figuring out which way to hold the photo. "Dat's da bedroom. Dat's da ceiling on top of da bed. Everything flipped upside down. Dere's da window."

The other interior shots show more of the same: jumbled belongings, wet insulation, a layer of mold over everything. "That's what fell on our bed," Kim says cheerfully. "We had a king-size bed. Which was pushed into the closet! It was a bed that you couldn't move otherwise." Shakes her head. "I was amazed when I walked in here and I looked in there. How the heck the bed got into the closet?"

"Floated," Mike says. "Oh yeah, dat water came in and started swirlin'. . . ."

"I'd left my jewelry there. My husband got in that bed, and my jewelry was sitting right on the top of all of that mess!"

She smiles. Mike smiles.

He says they gutted without safety masks or any other protection. "I came in here with a pair of gloves, boots, jeans, and T-shirt. Put it on da curb!" There's a picture of Mike in knee-high rubber boots next to a gray pickup. "Yea, dat's my brother-in-law's truck. It was wedged between a tree and my house. He lived across da street over dere."

Next is a picture of the interior with the sheetrock off, nails showing, the wood black with mold. The ceiling opens to the sky. When they'd dumped the walls and insulation on the curb, the bare timbers were still moldy from weeks underwater. It all needed to be pressure-washed. "We did ours like three times," says Kim.

Mike explains that Project Hope, the volunteer group organized by Suncere and spun off from Common Ground, "sprayed it two, tree times. And dey had some kind of, uh, organic bacteria that eats bacteria and was supposed to kill it." He looks up at the ceiling. "Dere was actually green fungus growin' from under da attic floorboards. I ripped all of dat out"—he claws with one hand—"and then I had it soda-blasted." Soda blasting uses a mixture of sodium bicarbonate—baking soda—shot through compressed-air guns. "Dat wasn't cheap, either, but we had to do it . . . And I still let it sit—it still sat here another two, tree months before I did anything with it: to make sure after dat."

"To make sure nothing grew back," Kim says with a chuckle. She bunches one hand and pulls it downward to indicate mold slowly growing back.

"You can't do it. You cover it up and den, what happens den? You end up wit something like dat—what was dat? Legionnaire's disease or something like dat . . . Like dat black mold what dey call—I don't remember da name of it." *Stachybotrys* has been found growing in houses all across the Gulf Coast. Residents blame the black mold for eye irritation and their lingering "Katrina coughs."

Next, Mike and Kim show a picture of the front of their house with its *veves*: ILL 9-16 and KEN 10-19. "Yea, da people from Kentucky was smart enough to spray-paint on da glass. The people from Illinois spray-painted on da brick!" A cackle of laughter. "I'll get it off. I'll get some paint thinner or somethin' and scrub it. Or somethin'."

"The day we took these pictures?" Kim adds. "They found his friend's mother. Down the street. In her house . . . From what they say, she was determined to stay." Her body had lain there, undiscovered, from the end of August until sometime in January.

The next snapshot is of a wall of white containers set in rock. "Oh, that's the cemetery," Kim explains. "Where my dad is."

"My dad and her dad. We went and checked."

"Yea, we have family in there," Kim says brightly. "We went over there just to check." Because of the danger of flooding, most graves in the region are aboveground. "They had a boat in the cemetery and that, but it seemed like all the graves and that were fine. I mean, my mom's little name thing and all was gone, but I knew where she was."

Kim is cheerful enough, but the graveyard picture gets to Mike. He pauses. Takes a couple deep breaths. Collects himself.

"I been hangin' doors and doin' plumbin' and all of dat myself. But as far as da sheetrock and da floor, we had a crew come in and do dat, I mean, and air-condition', you know . . . My wife's ex-husband came in. It was seven somethin' thousand dollars for dem to do it. Dey had a crew of Mexicans come in and, whew! Dey knocked it out like nuttin', you know? I mean, dey really great at dat! Dey came in; dey didn't play."

In the middle of the gutting and rebuilding, Mike had to go to the hospital for a week. "Basically, a—" he begins to explain, when Kim cuts in.

"A nervous breakdown."

"A typical nervous breakdown type situation." Mike shrugs his tattooed, sunburnt shoulders. "I'd just had enough . . . Every day you walk outside and see your stuff sittin' out dere in front your house." Points to the street. "And it just . . . took its toll on me." His eyes begin to glisten.

During the weeks that their possessions sat out on the curb, the Army Corps of Engineers was fixing the levee at the end of the block. Their trucks, Mike explains, "kept flyin' trew here . . . tearin' things up."

"You could feel the house shaking," Kim says, jiggling in her chair to demonstrate.

The constant noise, the long hours of work, the cramped FEMA trailer, and all their goods on the street: one day Mike had enough. He stepped out in front of an Army Corps truck. "I had a .45 caliber. Stuck it to one of da fuel tanks . . . 'If you don't slow this son of a bitch down, I'll blow your truck up.'"

"Shut their work down for a day," says Kim, a little proud.

"And da cops come flyin' back here. One of dem's talkin' to me, da other one he's from Black—what d'ya call it? The private security."

St. Bernard Parish has been privatizing, too. Using federal relief money, it's been hiring Blackwater personnel to supplement its local police and sheriff departments. Across Louisiana in the first four months after the flood, Blackwater received some $42 million to provide various kinds of security.

"[The Blackwater guard], he's got my face down and sayin' I ain't no kind of man—dis, dat, and de other . . . Da older cop, he says, 'Let him up off da ground and take dem cuffs off him, and you'll find what kind of man he is' . . . [The Blackwater guard] come back dere like he's G.I. Joe . . . tacklin' and shovin' your face down in da dirt. Sayin' I endangered his life! He wasn't nowhere around here; how'd I endanger his life?"

They took Mike to the Tulane hospital for rest and evaluation. "My mom says I shouldn't feel it . . . but there's still a lot of depression. You look around, you know?"

Kim cuts in: "But he also grew up on this street. He's used to what this street was. Before."

"Dis is home," Mike says. "Been home all my life. I grew up down the road in Plaquemines till I was about five and came here then. And I been here ever since . . . We'll keep pushin'," he adds after a pause. "We'll keep pushin', Pop." He looks to the ceiling, red-eyed. "It's all I can do. Can't afford to do anything else."

Again he takes a deep breath.

"When we first came back, everyone was sayin' it was unsafe. But . . . what you gonna do? FEMA's puttin' trailers in for you to live; you can't stay in a hotel. Who's gonna come and rebuild it for you? I mean, it's depressing, but you got to keep on goin' . . . One board at a time!" he adds, and laughs a little.

"In between hospital stays." His wife grins. "First him, then me, then me again. Then we wind up doing it!"

They fall into a silence.

After a while, they start talking about the looting that's been going on since they returned.

"When we first came back, if your door was open—"

"They'd take your stuff!"

"Even with da mud up to your knees, they'd be comin' in your house and . . . takin' whatever dey could find." Mike says he never had to use a gun. "But I have a couple!" He laughs. ". . . I wouldn't want to do dat to anybody. But if it comes to my family, I *will* stand up and protect dem."

"We couldn't leave our house when we were first back working on it."

"Tools and—"

"One of us always had to be around."

"Not dat we didn't trust da neighbors. It was da other people."

"It was the other people."

"And I think it was mostly contractors dat were working for FEMA—"

"—that were doing it! Yeah."

"I actually watched dem," says Mike. "Boy a couple of houses down, his house was cleaned out. [This guy] was loadin' up his tools in a big front-end loader. He was takin' all da Snap-on tools . . . I went down dere and told him: 'Man, you can't take dat man's tools!' He says, 'Well, I seen dem dere.' I say, 'Yea, you seen dem dere, but dat don't mean dey're free for da takin'!'" Mike gives a big shrug.

The five of them—Mike, Kim, a daughter, and her two kids—moved into this house last month. "We didn't have everything done." There was no hot water, for example. "But we moved back in, anyway. Such close quarters in dere, you know." Mike nods toward where the trailer still sits.

"We ready for them to take it!" Kim puts in, waving her hand and grinning like a teenager. "I'm done with it! I'll take a cold bath till we get our hot water heater!"

From a back bedroom, a blond granddaughter, three or four, wanders in. As she takes the little girl up in her arms, Kim declares proudly that theirs is the one house on the street that's been fully renovated—that it's a kind of model, an inspiration.

"Dat's what my mom tells me," Mike responds. "I get all depressed and sad—"

Kim interrupts in a high-pitched voice, mimicking her mother-in-law: "Well, Mike, you don't realize how far you'all got." She grins. "I got a girlfriend says she *wished*—my next door neighbor across the street tells me all the time—'I *wish* I was as far as you are.'"

Mike stares ahead. "You got to. That's the way I was brought up."

"Got to do what you got to do," Kim says. Which seems to settle things for a moment.

Mike breaks the silence. "Don't make it any easier!" He lets loose with one of his cackling laughs. "I don't wait on da government for anything," he adds, and turns to look out on the street. "Dere's a few more comin' back. Dey tryin' to come back; it's just takin' 'em a little bit longer. Dey all just tryin' to hold on to da dollar. Instead of spendin' it, I guess." He chuckles.

"It ain't even half," Kim says.

"I doubt if it's a tird. But da ones who are willin' to come back," Mike shrugs, "dey doin' what dey have to do . . . Everyone helps da other one. If dey have a tool you need—hey!—dere's no problem with any'ting like dat. If dere's somethin' I know dat someone needs, I try to help 'em. Like I say, I can't do a lot of da manual labor anymore." Shrugs. "But I'll get someone over dere dat can help me and show 'em how. Or do what I can do."

The neighborhood's lack of progress bothers both of them. "'Cause you walk outside," Kim says, "and look at everybody else's mess."

"Just bein' empty," Mike adds, "it's a big difference. From hearin' da kids out in da street. I mean . . ." He shakes his head as if to clear it. "It wasn't all good, you know, but dere was life."

Their granddaughter has wandered off. A younger dark-haired boy in a little baseball uniform has now crawled up on Kim's lap.

"They're cleaning up better out here in Chalmette," says Kim. Chalmette, where the high school is, was St. Bernard's biggest city. It had a population of over 30,000, and as Mike and Kim see it, residents there are getting first priority on rebuilding. "Like they forgot from [Chalmette] down," says Kim. "They just forgot us."

"A lot of people up dat way," Mike says, "dere like we don't have any common sense. We don't have any education, we fishermen. We from *down the road*."

"Yeah," Kim echoes, "we're from down the road." The grandson on her lap cries a little, shifts around.

"It's not all of dem, but some of dem figure dere more educated so dere lives are worth—" Mike stops to rephrase. "Not dere lives; dere *better off* than you. Like you're white trash or black trash or whatever. 'I got more,' ya know? So what!? You die with a few more toys; you can't take 'em wit you." Mike shrugs, then laughs. "It all comes down to da workingman. I don't care how you look at it."

He sees the same attitude in New Orleans. "I mean, New Orleans is a big part of Louisiana. But without the surrounding parishes? . . . Where do ya think New Orleans gets all its seafood at? What dey gonna do, start buying it from Japan or Korea or something? Not everybody, but a good percentage of da people down here, dat's all dey know. Commercial fishing. You know, dey did dat all dere lives with dere dads and dem."

"All the surrounding parishes is what make New Orleans; not New Orleans," Kim declares. "And I'm from New Or-lee-ins!" She giggles. "I'm from the Ninth Ward, actually."

Their grandson is still crying. "He's teethin'," Mike explains. "Come here, Paw-Paw. Come here, *mon pé*." He takes the boy on his lap.

Now the granddaughter comes back in the room, and the four of them make a family portrait: the sun coming through the oval glass in the front door, Mike with the little boy lying on his tattooed, graying chest, his wife in her Katrina T-shirt, the blond grandchild standing nearby.

As Mike sees it, they had no choice but to rebuild. "We would have had to go find a house. And wit da amount of money I got from insurance? No way! Dey ain't no way . . . Da house properties everywhere went skyrocket. It would have been a thousand dollars or better for a house, or even to rent an apartment. And I can't afford dat. I can't. I can't hardly afford our medicines . . . I mean, we live on a fixed income. Her with her cancer, me with heart problems and back problems. We got our check on da tird; we totally broke!" Mike grins.

"But we in our house!" Kim laughs.

The little boy is playing with his own pink toes.

Clear-eyed, Mike looks into the middle distance. What's left to do on the house, he adds, is "basically just the trim and a hot water heater."

"Counter," says his wife.

"A countertop and da sink. I got my stove and oven outside, just waitin' . . . Plumber came dis morning and pressurized everything . . . It takes two hundred dollars just to get a damn permit to turn gas on!" He hands his grandson back to Kim and crosses his thick arms over his bare chest. "I mean, it was money dat we needed to hold on to—in case somethin' happened or whatever." He throws his hands into air. "But dat's the only way it's gonna roll."

Enough people have come back to St. Bernard for a Home Depot to open. "I go up dere," Mike says, "and basically get raped. Da prices are so high. Dey scabbin' off of everybody! . . . I know supply and demand, but dere's no way you can tell me a piece of sheetrock went from tree dollars to ten to tirteen dollars like it did. It cost dat much more to make it 'cause dere was a storm?" He raises his voice. "Dey were still buildin' houses! It didn't go up when the houses was boomin'!"

As to the businesses along Perez Drive: "Dey just cleanin' dem out and lettin' dem sit."

"They not gonna build them back like they was," Kim says. "They waitin' to see how many people come back."

"Yea, dey waitin' till—what did dey say: over tirty-five or forty percent of da people come back?" It's the same dilemma as months before: stores waiting for customers, customers waiting for stores. "You still got to go all the way cross da river to make any kind of groceries. To go to a Kmart, or a Walmart, or anyting like dat."

"How many people gonna stay down here," Kim asks, "when you can't even go to a grocery store?"

Mike decides to take a quick tour of the neighborhood.

He drives down the block past the ruins of his mother's house. Though it's been at least six months since he "pushed it over," no one will haul it off. "'Cause dey think a church group knocked it down. So dey not gonna get *paid* to clean it up . . . Now, everybody thinks it's a dump site." His mother has bought a trailer across Lake Pontchartrain in Slidell. "She says after a while, when she gets her trust back in da levees and dat, she might build on da slab. She'll have to build da slab higher then, because she won't be grandfathered in."

This spring, FEMA announced its new regulations for rebuilding. To qualify for flood insurance, homeowners in the worst-hit areas—including here in St. Bernard, the Lower Ninth, Gentilly—will have to lift their homes at least three feet above the estimated height of a "hundred-year storm." According to a federal recovery coordinator, these new regulations "will enable people to get on with their lives." But the eight-month delay in issuing the new rules was a long time to leave homeowners in limbo. Some have been forced to get on with their lives elsewhere.

Mike passes four or five empty houses till the street ends at a locked iron gate. Here, there's a drainage ditch covered with lilies. A white egret walks on its bright green surface. Past the ditch is the levee, a grassy mound. Behind it, the view stretches across brown flat bayou sheared of all its ground cover. Here and there are the gray, twisted trunks of old cypress trees. Off on the horizon is the man-made channel, MR-GO.

"All back dere," Mike says, turning to the brown stretch of bayou, "just before you get to MR-GO, dere used to be camps. Where people would go for a weekend? Dey just gone. Nothing left. History . . ."

The Army Corps of Engineers has raised this levee four feet. "Probably wouldn't hurt to be a little bit higher." Mike grins. "If another hurricane came today . . . then it would be another situation. Because I can't do it twice."

Instead of going back up his street, he takes the next one over. It's got bigger houses and shows more signs of recovery: lawns mowed, security gates up. "People's takin' care of business," Mike grunts. But when he gets around to the street behind his home, the neighborhood is ravaged. Heaps of trash ten feet high line both curbs.

There are volunteer work crews back here: mostly young, college-age, in sunglasses and sweatshirts. One says he's from Boise, Idaho, been down a week, hopes to gut a house a day. Passing a Habitat for Humanity group, Mike shouts out the car window, "We appreciate it! Just watch da rats and da snakes."

Soon it grows still. More shattered windows, collapsed porches, the electric lines slumped with vine. Bushes cover rooflines, and cars sit with weeds growing up through their engine compartments. Mike points out an empty area right behind his house. "Dat was just a place dat we kept clean for kids to play baseball. And families would go dere to have barbeques on birthdays for dere kids. Or just get-togethers . . . I used to keep all of dis cut right here, and now I can't even get in dere."

A block or two farther, Mike spots a low-eaved brick house with plywood over its windows and a fresh sign stapled near the front door. "Dat house with da orange tag is for demolishin' . . . First time I've seen dem. Although I don't really ride around da neighborhood dat much."

Both St. Bernard and New Orleans have set the first anniversary of Katrina, just a few weeks away, as their remediation deadline. Houses not showing signs of repair will be declared a public nuisance, the owners given ten days to respond before demolition. New Orleans calls it the Good Neighbor Plan. Out here, they've already torn down about a thousand homes.

Mike gets out and walks through knee-high grass till he reaches the sign. It's quiet. A dog barks somewhere. He stops, lights a cigarette, then reads the sign out loud.

ORDER OF INVOLUNTARY DEMOLITION. NO REPAIR,
REHABILITATION, RECONSTRUCTION, OR MAINTENANCE
ACTIVITY IS APPARENT AT THIS ADDRESS.
THIS PROPERTY APPEARS TO BE ABANDONED.

Mike stares at it, smoking his cigarette.

"Back in here was a lot of Section 8 homes. Doubles and dat. Dat were lived in by families and belonged to—" He pauses for the right word. "Slumlords." Section 8 dates back to FDR and the thirties: a program that subsidizes rent for low-income families. In majority-white St. Bernard, where three-quarters of the houses were owner occupied, renting was suspicious. Section 8 became code for black people. It was one of the main reasons Daniel Park was designated a blighted area.

Now the Section 8 housing is getting tagged with this new orange *veve*. In St. Bernard, remediation seems targeted to make the parish even whiter.

"You got a lot of people dat's gonna take and try to buy some of dese houses for two, tree, four, five thousand dollars and renovate dem. And den go and rent dem out for fifteen hundred dollars a month. You know? Dey're not looking to turn dem over and sell 'em or help anybody. Dey lookin' to capitalize."

Mike gets in the car and slowly circles the streets till he's back home. In the midst of the ruins, his house looks like an outpost, flags flying.

There's a man waiting in Mike's carport. A tall, skinny, white guy, he's bald on top with a scraggly reddish beard and a long, matted blond ponytail. Mike greets him like an old friend: he's one of the main organizers for Project Hope.

The organizer says he's from California and first came down this street when it was "a super ghost town. Mike was one of the only people here at all." Suncere had set up the Common Ground distribution center, but by then it had spun off and become Project Hope. "[Common Ground] just grew up so fast!" the organizer says. "They went from a backyard operation to having a thousand people living in a church. Within months! They got built up so fast that they didn't have the infrastructure to support satellite groups . . . We just felt we needed to have our own center and be able to make our own decisions. And it worked out better that way. It's better to decentralize things."

At that, Mike starts praising Project Hope's work. How they helped "wit da cleaning out and dat. And went on to other neighbors and helped dem clean out dere houses and do what dey could for dem."

"A bunch of kids camped out in a church" is how the organizer describes it. "College kids . . . We kinda just built a camp. And did a real shoestring budget, super shoestring. But effective. 'Cause we had people who were willing to work and actually enjoyed camping . . . It kinda shows that you get regular people to start doing work—that know how to work? And still have their hearts turned on? And aren't wrapped up in bureaucratic systems? You can get a lot done. You can get *more* done."

The two men stand in the shade of the carport. "I just don't tink da government's on da right stance," says Mike. "I still say dat."

Kim comes out the back door, says hello, and starts taking the laundry off the line.

"Check it out," says the organizer. He talks quickly with a slight sibilance: his words tend to whistle. "St. Bernard Parish Council passed an ordinance. That said if a house wasn't already a rental property, the only way it could become a rental property is if you rent to *blood relatives*. Which then got challenged by a group in New Orleans."

The challenge declared that the ordinance perpetuated the parish's history as "a segregated, predominantly white community." And the parish admitted as much. One councilman said it was meant "to maintain the demographics." Another was more direct: "[It's] to block the blacks from living in these areas."

"Dat's senseless!" Mike explodes. "If someone needs a home, and a home's dere, and someone's willing to rent it—damn it, let dem have someplace to live!" He's up on the balls of his feet, shifting his weight from side to side. "Dat's outrageous."

"It's in the courts," the organizer explains in his soft, patient voice. "Filed in federal courts."

"Dat'll never stand!"

The organizer raises his bony shoulders in a shrug. "The numbers are that ninety-three percent of homeowners are white." His eyebrows lift. "And so it's just right on the numbers. It just totally takes out a group of people."

"Dey, dey"—Mike's stuttering with anger—"dey trying to make it sound like dat anyone coming out of New Orleans is a drug dealer. And dat's not true. See, 'cause back here, we used to have a lot of problems wit it. And I tink dey're tryin' to avoid dat situation. But anybody, *anybody* can buy or sell or deal drugs. I don't care what color you are or who you are. You know? It could be your own blood relative you rent da house out to, destroyin' your property and doin' it. Now, come on!" He laughs, red in the face.

From behind them, folding laundry, Kim joins in. "I was just in court for a child custody case. Because I live on this street—"

Her husband interrupts: "Da judge doesn't want da child back here." He gestures toward the street.

"The law-yer"—Kim drawls the word—"said it's possible that *I* could be criminal. I don't even have a speeding ticket or anything! But I could possibly be a criminal. Because of where I live."

Mike cackles. "You can look around, see my neighbors." He gestures wide with one tattooed arm. Across the way, a black teenage girl sits on the front porch of a FEMA trailer with her mother. "We all live here. I mean . . ." Mike shrugs, smiles a little. "I mean, I had some neighbors back here who were white who were total . . . I can't say what I want to say. But asses! You know? And . . . we all get along great back here. If one of us has a barbeque, it don't take much for dis family, dat family . . ." He's gesturing down the street again.

"It sounds like they've been trying to do that kind of stuff for a long time," says the Project Hope organizer. He has a way of nodding when he speaks, as if to see that everyone is following his argument, that everyone agrees. "A lot of people are getting blocked in more than one way. There're so many resources that are coming in, but they're not supporting people *directly*." He presses his palms together, gently but forcefully.

"My daughter tried to make a loan," says Kim. "To buy a house that was damaged a couple streets back."

"Said dey can't make a loan," Mike speaks in tandem with her, " 'cause da house is damaged."

"And they said because the house is damaged, she has to come up with so much—"

"Ten percent."

"Yeah, ten or twenty percent down. In order to buy it. And, like, she said, 'Ma, if I had that, I could do it on my own.' "

"And then people who got their flood insurance money," the organizer continues softly, "their mortgage companies told them they had to pay off their whole note." He grins in some combination of disgust and amazement. According to the New Orleans newspaper, "Mortgage holders have first claim on insurance payouts. If the insurance pays off the mortgage, an owner could be left owning a destroyed home and a piece of land in a largely abandoned block."

"I paid off my mortgage!" Mike almost shouts. "I paid off my mortgage, and da rest of it went into dis house. Dat's why it's not finished."

The organizer nods. It's like he's conducting a backyard seminar, turning Mike's specifics into general political points. "It's the money game that doesn't make sense."

"Our government is screwy," Mike answers.

Another long nod of agreement. "Yea. Inept. Doesn't work. Then people come back," the organizer adds, that sibilance in his voice, "and the only job for them is Exxon or Murphy Oil."

"Yeah!"

"So they work these twelve-hour shifts, a lot of times at night; they have no energy left. Totally shot."

"Oh, they wore out." It's starting to sound like Pastor Mel's ministry: call and response.

"And they're living back in these trailers." The organizer points past Daniel Park. "It's funny how inept it is. But it's not funny. Because there're people living it. They're breaking all the time." As Project Hope sees it, the government is "dangling" the Road Home grants in front of a desperate public, promising relief payments and then saying, "No, it'll be a couple months." The organizer sags his bony knees to illustrate the toll that takes.

Kim has gone inside with the laundry. When she comes back out, she has her grandson in her arms.

"When you think just from a straight economics point of view," the Project Hope guy is saying, "then you screw the people. You may make your books make sense, but what is that? That doesn't make sense. In actuality . . . the priorities stay on making money."

Kim chimes in, the baby climbing up her T-shirt. "I've been living in this parish most of my life, and it's always been Chalmette and Arabi. Down this way," brushing a bug away, "they forget us." She laughs. The baby gives her a big smile in response.

"It'll work out," Mike says, a little wearily. "It's just gonna take a long time. But it'll work out."

"People complain about the parish," says Kim, shifting the baby on her hip. She's standing on the edge of the backyard now, near the unmowed lot where Mike talked about there being rats and snakes. She keeps the boy in her arms. "But this is home," she continues. "I mean, we didn't have to come back. We chose to come back. 'Cause this is home." She says it with soft determination, then looks down at the smiling baby. He's got two new bottom teeth.

We Sitting Here Waiting

(August 2006)

Back in New Orleans, the silhouettes of roofers against a clear blue sky are like large, unexpected birds. Their call: the thudding of nail guns. The green and pink Manchu Food Store is open. Cars swish by. Folks are out on the corner. Live oaks, green with leaves, cast intricate shadows on the still-broken sidewalks. A year after the floods, there are signs of change.

In the Upper Ninth, a lot of wreckage remains. But here a crew is rebuilding a front porch: the old lumber has been stripped off, the new treated beams are being cut and nailed into place. The crew head is from Brooklyn, speaks with a Jamaican accent. The guy on the table saw has long dreads down his back: a musician from Florida. It's a frontier town, attracting workers from all over.

In Backatown, the new white concrete levee stretches from the Claiborne Avenue Bridge to a former cypress swamp, Bayou Bienvenue. The wall is 4,000 linear feet of "structure concrete and flowable fill material," 500 tons of reinforcing steel, 2,250 steel H-pilings. It cost $33.5 million, part of the over $1 billion allocated to rebuild the city's levees. FEMA put the Army Corps of Engineers in charge; it, in turn, subcontracted this job to a firm based in Baton Rouge.

This morning, two of the workers are up on the far end of the wall. Both are white guys, the younger in a pickup truck, wearing an LSU cap, reflecting sunglasses, a gold wedding band. "November twentieth, I think, was the first day we were out on the site. And we been out here since. Workin' seven days a week." He fiddles with his wedding ring as he talks.

Sitting across from him is an older, gray-haired man with big arms and belly. "We been out here ten hours a day, seven days a week, since November *fourt'*," he corrects. He's got a Cajun accent, but lighter than Mike's.

"Is that when we got out here?" the younger guy asks.

"Yup. And it was nonstop . . . We were very lucky wit the weather. It was a dry winter; coulda been worse. We had about a hundred and fifty people. Wit the pile drivers and all . . ."

"It was pretty high-profile," says the guy in the truck. Four Army Corps inspectors were "on the job full-time . . ." The official completion deadline was the first anniversary of the floods, still about three weeks off, but by June 1, he says, "we had it built. President Bush came out to get his picture taken with the workers. Then everybody scattered."

On one side of the white wall is the Industrial Canal. On the other, Backatown: grassy with more empty lots. The older worker hacks a little, spits, then makes a broad sweep of the neighborhood with one hand. "They have until the end of the mont', da owners, to see if they're gonna want to rebuild. Or do whatever. Or put a claim on dere *in*-surance. And if they don't file, they gonna demo. They gonna demo whatever people don't cooperate."

"Yeah," says the younger guy, ". . . they have a list of addresses that they go to: the people who have already signed, filed, or whatever. And that's why they're jumping around from spot to spot."

In the distance, with almost no sound, yellow backhoes set their metal teeth, pull out a chunk of house, dump it on a big pile. Workers in lime-green vests hose down the wreckage. Where St. Bernard is posting demolition notices, and greater New Orleans hasn't gotten that far, Backatown is already being cleared away.

"There's nobody coming here to rebuild anythin'," says the older worker. "It's not worth it. There's rats and—" He shrugs to a stop.

"This was one of the worst areas," the young guy says, then checks himself. "Well, not the worst, but one of the poorest areas."

"Poorest neighborhood in New Orleans," his co-worker insists. He sits, arms resting on knees, hands crossed, tired. "It's bad enough that they're blaming the Corps of Engineers dat dey blew it up." That rumor has been going since Katrina: that the boom of the levee collapsing was the sound of it being dynamited. "Naw! Naw. This wall was forty years old. And it was put together *cheap*."

Post-flood studies have indicated that while some water overtopped Backatown's levee, the major breach occurred from underseepage: water digging beneath the wall till it collapsed. The pilings weren't sunk deep enough; the soil was too sandy and weak. This spring, in a 6,000-page report, the Army Corps of Engineers "formally admitted its mistakes were responsible for the levee fracture."

The older man hacks again and spits. Today's his last day on the job. "Tonight? . . . I bought a bottle of Cabo Wabo tequila." He holds his hand two feet off the ground to show the size of the bottle. "That come from Cabo San Lucas. It's mine tonight!"

On one of Backatown's abandoned streets, inside a lot marked off with yellow emergency tape, a backhoe gnaws away at somebody's former home. It takes its ponderous time carting the wreckage over to a waiting dump truck. The driver of the truck stands nearby: a stocky black man with a little gray in his sideburns and beard, dark sunglasses, a lime-green hard hat. He starts talking without an introduction and goes without a break.

"I'm so pissed off it's ridiculous; this happened a year ago; this ain't happened last week! It looks like it happened last week, but this happened a year ago." He speaks rapidly, with a Louisiana burr, his voice deep and insistent, like the bass singer in a gospel group.

"This is a crime scene here. The government should be put on trial for this here . . . Ain't *nuthin'* been done. Few contractors, Corps of Engineers: it's totally fudged up. They're holding these people hostage to where they can't come back to their house. They, they, they . . ." He slows, tries to make his point: "Eventually they done *took it*. This is ridiculous here. I've never seen nothing like this here. This didn't happen last week; this happened a year ago! Ain't *nothing been done*."

His back is to the house being torn down. He looks out across the emptying landscape.

"They don't have no choice: the government is going to take their house regardless. They're gonna say it's *contaminated*. And the longer they deviate and procrastinate to *keep* the people from coming back"— hand pushing forward, knuckles out—"the house becomes *more and more* contaminated. With mold . . . just eats the house, totally. So, people who may have gotten insurance money for their property, been willing to come in here and do it for themselves, if they got the insurance check Monday, well, Tuesday they was ready to come in? But now, but now, the government has *stopped* them. Because there's contractors. Who don't even *live* here and don't even *care* about this community. 'Cause they have nothing to lose. Nothing. Only to gain tremendously for the work that's being done—*supposedly* that's being done."

His eyebrows rise under his hard hat.

"It's *not* being done. These contractors," shrugs shoulders, "who don't even *live* here and don't even *care* about this community."

The debris removal in New Orleans is contracted to three out-of-state companies, each getting around $500 million. Environmental Chemical Corp. (ECC) from California is doing most of the work in the Ninth Ward. ECC's previous jobs include cleaning up Superfund sites domestically, removing land mines after the Persian Gulf War, and doing school repair in Iraq. Nonunion, privately owned, its backhoes are filling this man's truck as he speaks.

"I don't be in their meeting room with them, but what they say is, 'We need more money. Because whatever time we deadlined, we didn't realize it would cost whatever.' And now it done escalated! Our government is going to get desperate and just pay them." He throws both hands forward in disgust. "Where local contractors who can do the same thing—much better and much faster—because they will have to answer to this community . . . A local contractor would have to answer to *these people*." He nods toward the invisible homeowners out in the ruins of Backatown. "They would be accountable and responsible to the people of this community. And even of this city and this state. Many a contractor done came in here since the beginning of this disaster who done just took money from this city and from this state, and they ain't been heard from since. And haven't done *nothing* . . ."

A recent report from the U.S. Government Accountability Office put the overall figure for "improper and fraudulent payments" connected to Gulf Coast cleanup at almost $1.5 billion.

"Some people been sixty, seventy years living here. They know nothing else. And wherever they are, they are *not* happy. They're being stressed out. And eventually what's going to happen—" He pauses to catch a quick breath. "They are going to die."

Nods in affirmation.

"'Cause *everything* has been taken away from them. If you a eighty-year-old man or a eighty-year-old woman who's been living in whatever house," gestures out at the landscape in disgust, "for sixty or seventy years, and that's all they know? Well, now they in maybe Houston or Atlanta or whatnot. They are not comfortable there, they're not eating right, they're not taking their medication; they're gonna eventually *die*."

His truck is nearly loaded. He has to cut his speech short.

"This is a crime. I'm gonna always be angry about this. Gonna always be angry."

Across Backatown, at Common Ground's blue house, someone's hung a hand-lettered cardboard sign: AUGUST 29TH *DEADLINE* FOR HOMEOWNERS TO CLEAN, GUT, BOARD UP FLOODED HOUSES OR THE CITY WILL SEIZE AND DEMOLISH PROPERTY. Beneath it, a smaller sign says Backatown is exempted. On this block, there are hardly any houses left to seize. But the fight here, Brandon's and Common Ground's fight, was to stop the city from seizing the land itself, and that continues. Another sign reads: EMINENT DOMAIN FOR WHO?

A year after the floods, the collective says it's hosted and organized 10,000 volunteers. They continue to gut houses; there's now a three-to-five-month waiting list. The Mt. Carmel Baptist Church has been restored, and volunteer housing has shifted to another donated church building in the Upper Ninth. Here in Backatown, college-age kids bustle around the distro center, handing out tools and bottles of water.

Compared to when Brandon arrived in defiance of the curfew, the operation now seems established. Most volunteers only stay for a week or two. They've heard of Malik, Common Ground's founder, but never met him: he's mostly out fund-raising. They have no news of Suncere, either. One speaks vaguely of Brandon being away somewhere; maybe Lebanon? It's strange, as if the original organizers have simply vanished.

Common Ground has just passed through what's been called its "heyday . . . [of] anarchist influence." Leadership is more anonymous, more communal. That's occasionally resulted in the feeling of "a driverless bus careening down the road at top speed." Still, the blue house remains a symbol of resistance and a center of activity. The collective hopes to open a Lower Ninth Ward health clinic any day now. It's established a women's center, a community garden, a bike repair operation, and anti-racist workshops for its volunteers, still largely young, from out of town, and white.

On the edge of Backatown, heading toward Holy Cross, there's a large modern school with mustard yellow exterior walls and dark purple trim. A sign out front proclaims this is DR. MARTIN LUTHER KING JR.

ELEMENTARY FOR SCIENCE AND TECHNOLOGY. Its windows are streaked with dirt. Inside, the classrooms are deserted: desks scattered, ceilings fallen, blackboards marked with what look like graphs and turn out to be water lines. In the growing heat, there's a faint smell of fish and mold.

Before the floods, MLK was a source of pride in the Lower Ninth. Its 715 students were drawn from one of the poorest areas in the city: 96 percent qualified for free or reduced-price lunch. Yet it boasted such high test scores and strong attendance records that, eleven days before Katrina, officials spotlighted MLK by using its campus for the school year's opening day ceremonies.

Before the floods, New Orleans had as weak a school system as any in the nation. Three-quarters of its eighth graders weren't at the "basic skills" level in English; almost that many failed in math. Fewer than half the kids who entered kindergarten graduated from high school. The student population had gone from 58 percent African American in 1960 to 94 percent by 2005, and, like the Ferris wheel in Pastor Mel's childhood, the result was neglect. Not only were the schools failing their students, but the system was some $265 million in debt. The FBI was investigating "multiple instances of fraudulent behavior," including $20 million that remained unaccounted for.

By the start of the twenty-first century, 70 percent of America's black children went to predominantly black schools—and more than 80 percent of white kids were in predominantly white ones. New Orleans was an extreme example of this school resegregation and abandonment. Before the floods, the state had brought in a private accounting firm that specialized in downsizing failing businesses; it started closing city schools and firing personnel. Louisiana was on the verge of dismissing the city school board and taking over altogether, creating its own "Recovery School District." And then the hurricane hit. Nearly 90 percent of the city's schools were damaged, and the district shut down for the remainder of the year.

"This is a tragedy," declared economist Milton Friedman. "It is also an opportunity to radically reform the educational system." A state official echoed that position, calling the floods a "once-in-a-lifetime opportunity to reinvent public education." Within three months, the state legislature had seized control of 107 of New Orleans's 128 public schools. It then fired all 7,500 district employees, including every teacher in the system.

At the flooded, mud-encrusted MLK, Principal Doris Roché Hicks was determined to reopen, and quickly. Born and raised in the Ninth Ward, Dr. Hicks had been principal since the school opened. "People were talking about writing us off," she told a national magazine. "It was personal for me." She and her staff believed reopening would serve as "proof that this neighborhood is not doomed. People would come back, because the school was back." And the opposite held, too: if there were no schools in the Lower Ninth, families would stay away, these neighborhoods would remain empty.

Within two months of the flood, MLK staff began meeting regularly. "We decided if King was going to open," said a third-grade teacher, "we'd have to do it ourselves." The state-run Recovery District declared the school structurally unsound and announced that MLK wouldn't be ready for occupancy for another three years—or maybe five. Dr. Hicks thought there were other factors at work. "I was angry because there were people in the city where I was born who did not believe that children of color should be educated in an appropriate environment."

Citywide, FEMA had committed $354 million for school rehab, but the Recovery District was slow to draw it down. In mid-March, Dr. Hicks and her staff decided to go outside the system. First she and the Southern Christian Leadership Conference staged a protest, demanding at least a temporary home for MLK. Then she turned to Common Ground. Would its volunteers help with gutting and cleanup?

Not only was it a popular local cause and an opportunity to accomplish what the government apparently wouldn't, but the request came during spring break, when Common Ground had hundreds of college-age volunteers. Joined by members of the community, young people in white hazmat suits gathered at MLK. Many had OPEN THIS SCHOOL painted on their backs. They were met by police officers and the news media.

The subsequent publicity helped convince school officials to reopen MLK. Today, the first day of the 2006–7 school year, teachers and students are in a temporary building across the canal. But the MLK staff hopes to be back in the Lower Ninth by the second anniversary of the floods, a year from now.

Across St. Claude Avenue, the Holy Cross School has some temporary, gum-brown structures lined up next to its abandoned main building. Squads of football players in blue helmets run drills on the adjacent fields. Next semester, the school is scheduled to leave for good.

A nearby house has its porch stuffed with ruined furniture. In the shadows over its front door, a solar-powered Virgin Mary flashes blue and white. Down the street, a pink brick house has its pink wood shutters pulled closed and its pale green doors locked. Above, roofers talk and laugh, slapping down shingles and then hitting them with nail guns. A sign out front, half-hidden by a FEMA trailer, reads: TO GOD BE THE GLORY.

Around the corner is a white shotgun with floor-to-ceiling windows. All are boarded over with raw plywood, but spray-painted in red on the front is: NOT 4 SALE @ ANY $ I'M STAYING PUT! Stuck on a telephone pole is another sign penciled on a scrap of white paper: WELCOME & THANKS NATIONAL GUARD (AND BRAD PITT!!) YOU CAN COME BY ANYTIME!!

After the floods, for about six months, 15,000 National Guard troops patrolled the city. With the poorest, most dangerous neighborhoods all but empty, the crime rate plummeted. One expert called Katrina "one of the greatest crime-control tools ever deployed against a high-crime city." But in the first three months of 2006, as residents returned and the Guard pulled out, there were seventeen killings. Over the next three months, thirty people were killed. And over a weekend this past June, five teenagers were shot to death. A stabbing the next day brought the city's mid-year death toll to fifty-three. There was talk of a turf war among returning drug dealers. It didn't help that the New Orleans Police Department (NOPD) is known as "arguably one of the most brutal, corrupt, and incompetent police units in the United States."

"We've had enough," Mayor Nagin declared, and got 360 National Guard troops redeployed into the city. While many welcomed them, others had grown tired of what felt like a military occupation. The police chief reassured citizens: "You will have to look for them to find them. They will not be uptown, downtown, or in the French Quarter. Our people will be there." Instead, the Guard was assigned to the same areas that had once been designated non-viable: Gentilly, the Ninth Ward. Here in Holy Cross, behind the streets of empty houses, big camouflaged humvees watch from the tops of the levees.

As to Brad Pitt, the movie star visited Holy Cross a month ago. "It's a bit shocking," was his reaction. "It's a bit disturbing. There's a lot of limbo—a persuasive feeling that there's little action." But he also saw what he called "a real opportunity here to lead the nation in a direction it needs to be going, and that is building efficiently." Along with Global

Green USA, he's co-sponsoring a competition for new multifamily home designs with "net zero" energy consumption. The actor's put up an initial $200,000, and the president of the Holy Cross Neighborhood Association is calling it "the first real development project in the Ninth Ward . . . People don't like change," she adds, "but if there ever was a time for it, this is it."

The change on Burgundy Street is slight. There's now a FEMA trailer next to the fourplex apartment house. The pop-eyed, energetic Lathan arrives in his pickup and, with the help of his son, Ethan, unloads a pair of tired-looking, secondhand air conditioners and grunts them over to the porch.

Lathan waves at the FEMA trailer and snorts, "It's been there four months. The air conditioner's *been* broken: it has a short in the wiring or something. They're supposed to come out and replace it. We come downstairs to shower, brush our teeth. Other than that, we sleep up here." He points to a second-floor apartment in the fourplex, then back at the trailer. "It's an outhouse!" He laughs.

"You can see the neighborhood on the comeback." He turns to look at his gray and blue bungalow next door: the family home before the floods. "Right now our main project, we getting this house together. We got it rocked up, wired." Plus he's getting the rental apartments ready in the fourplex and has closed on his house over on Chartres Street (he pronounces it Charters). "We workin' on all three at the same time."

He starts up the path toward the bungalow. Lathan still talks in spurts, constantly moving away and coming back, as if there was a job to be done just around the corner. "My son and I are doing most of the work. We're not contractors, so don't laugh at us." He goes through a bunch of keys, unlocks the door, steps in.

"This was the living room. And it's still going to be the living room." It's big, with a temporary beam propped up where a wall has been taken out. Father and son have gotten the gray sheetrock nailed, but it hasn't been taped or painted. Power tools sit on benches; a stepladder is propped in the corner.

"Well, it's better than it looks!" Lathan says, laughing. "This is my bedroom. My office." The rooms are dark. As he paces through them, he seems suddenly stunned by how little they have to show for months of labor. "We workin' on it; we workin' on it. We timed it: [Ethan] starts school next week. So I'm gonna be by myself. Wow." He circles the unfinished rooms, smiling, a little uncertain. "And hopefully, by this time next week, his mother will be staying out here with us, too. So, we be like family again." His wife still hasn't moved back from Baton Rouge.

Lathan wanders toward the front door. "That's pretty much it," he begins, then remembers something. "If I find my plumber? I'm gonna put my foot in his ass! He got my money, and I ain't seen him since!" He flicks one hand. "I bought all the material: the copper. Yeah. I gave him pretty much. And he vanished . . . He got my money, and he's gone . . ." Pause. "Look like I gotta get a book on plumbing." He laughs and walks quickly out the door.

Lathan approves of the National Guard returning to Holy Cross. "You see them mainly, I guess, about nine o'clock at night . . . rollin' around. But they patrol the neighborhood pretty good." He nods. "I like that. I guess that's our security right now. As a matter of fact, you know what? I do see a difference." He nods again as if it's just come to him. "I do see a difference."

As Lathan heads upstairs to the apartment, his son keeps an eye on the air conditioners. A teenager with a thin moustache, yellow ball cap worn backward, hip-hop slouch, Ethan says he'll be a junior this year. His high school is back over the canal. It's called McDonogh #35. John McDonogh, a nineteenth-century slave owner, left part of his fortune to New Orleans to build schools, including separate buildings for freed blacks. Until 1917, Negro education in New Orleans was capped at fifth grade. That year, as a result of protests by parents and other community members, McDonogh #35 became the city's first black high school. By the time of the floods, it had become a magnet school for students labeled gifted and talented.

Its first floor, Ethan says, was heavily damaged. "But they got it back together by now. It look good." As with MLK, the school board has been slow about reopening it. But parents and other supporters packed a recent meeting, and this week McDonogh #35 will be one of only five city-run schools to offer classes.

The major change in the educational landscape is that thirty-four of the schools opening this week will be privately run charters. With all its teachers let go and their union effectively shut down, New Orleans has become an ideal place to test what's been called an entrepreneurial model of public education. This year, Philadelphia will have 13 percent of its students in charters, Detroit close to 20, and Washington, D.C., will have almost 30 percent. But the new New Orleans will lead the country: nearly

60 percent of the kids who've made it back will be enrolled in charter schools, most of them run by national education firms.

Ethan mentions how there was talk about turning McDonogh #35 into a charter. "But they did it the original way. The way it was." As a magnet school, McDonogh #35 had high enough test scores and strong enough community support to resist the trend. But even McDonogh #35 is finding out what it's like to stay public in a privatized landscape. "They got a lot of different teachers," Ethan says. "A lot of teachers didn't come back. 'Cause, I guess, they moved. Or they couldn't come back." He speaks softly, with sleepy but sharp eyes. "A lot of new teachers."

Lathan returns from upstairs and starts explaining how the only insurance money they got was for the bungalow. "So I'm on a budget." He raises his eyebrows and laughs. "Looks like I should be back at work in October. If nothing else comes in the way." He steps away, steps back. "I was a bartender. In the French Quarter. At a hotel." He says he started at seventeen and has been bartending for twenty-four years, then wipes his face. "My job took a big hit, too. In the particular area, in the bar, it had not only been hit but—what do you call that?" He pretends not to know. "Looted? They went in there and just *ransacked* the place." He makes a disgusted expression, then laughs a little. "So . . . I got nothing but time."

Around the corner, on North Rampart—where, months ago, Buddy the dog slept undisturbed in the middle of the street—there are now signs of activity. The big, fallen pine that covered the house next to Semmes school has been cut up and hauled off. Where it fell, the section of fence has been replaced with green corrugated plastic. From behind it comes the owner: a short white guy called Joe. He plops down on a drink cooler.

"You want to know what I think about New Orleans? My home?" He's in his sixties, sweaty from work, keeps wiping his forehead with his black-and-white horizontally striped shirt. His thick black hair, streaked with gray, sticks out to one side.

"He's in a bad mood," his wife, Linda, interrupts. She stands behind him, on the walkway into their home. She's bigger than he is, red-faced, with thick glasses and strong arms.

"I'll tell you the truth," Joe goes on. "The politicians are so bad here. *Everything's* corrupted. That's what I think about New Orleans."

His wife can't bear to listen. She ducks back into their small, dark house.

"That is why I'm *not* coming back," Joe says, pointing to the ground between his feet. He hitches up his camouflage pants and waves one hand. Twenty feet behind him, Linda has started pulling objects out of the house and throwing them into a metal wheelbarrow.

"All the money they're supposed to be saving for health care from Lotto? There's not a dime. The schools? The teachers? The police? The firemen? All of that's gone! Somebody got rich on it. That's what I think about my city. And I loved my city at one time." Hot and tired, his small black eyes squinting in concentration, he leans forward to explain.

"People around here are struggling." He gestures up the street, deeper into Holy Cross. "They can't come back. They don't even have insurance." His Louisiana drawl lengthens each word. "They don't have no kind of income. On disability. Retirement. They go to get the money from this [Road Home] grant; they can't do it . . . So how you gonna rebuild?" He spreads both arms like he's asking a question, but he isn't. "It's impossible to rebuild."

Behind him, Linda throws one thing too many into a red plastic grocery, which crashes to the ground.

"The only thing I can do is try to sell these lots. This house," he points across the street to a yellow bungalow, "that house," a peach one next to it and nearly identical, "and this house." He jacks a thumb over his shoulder to where Linda is gutting. "Try to sell them all. Go somewhere else."

Like Lathan, Joe worked as a bartender. And also like Lathan, he was an entrepreneur, investing his money in real estate, putting together a local, three-house empire. But Joe's empire has collapsed.

"This used to be a beautiful neighborhood." He waves his hand at the length of the block. "But you had killings in front of the house here," he says, pointing all the way to his left. "You had killings on the levee," pointing all the way right. "You had car thefts," back left. "They steal the cars; they burn the cars all around the corner," both hands to the right. "So what kinda life is around here?" Again, it's not a question. "You don't have a life."

"We only have from the end of August," Linda shouts from the door, "to clean out these three houses." She's talking about the demolition deadline. "The city," she shouts, "is gonna take it away from us." Joe continues to sit as she comes out of the house with a bunch of neatly folded shirts and pants. She dumps them into the wheelbarrow.

"All I can say," Joe continues, "is I'm very angry with my own city . . . Born and raised here. Born in 1941 . . . What year did we move here, Linda?"

"Thirty-five years," she shouts.

"Thirty-five years in this house," Joe repeats. "This neighborhood here coulda been a Garden District . . . The streets were beautiful . . . All this was—" he sweeps his hand up and down the street—"was flowers! This was beautiful!"

Joe dates the neighborhood's collapse not to the floods but to the late sixties, early seventies, "when things started to downfall." In 1962, three African American girls integrated the Semmes school next door. They were spat on and struck with baseball bats. Their teachers called them niggers. Whites started moving out, and real estate prices fell.

By the eighties, prices were low enough that Joe and Linda could buy the twin houses across the street. "This was going to be our retirement: fixing up the houses, renting them out." But they never got to it, and then the floods came. Now, a year later, they're stuck with three badly damaged buildings.

"This is the first chance we got to get in there and clear everything out," Joe says. "Nothing is salvageable. Nothin'."

Inside their dark home, Linda is walking gingerly, waving a small red flashlight. She shows where the water came to: twelve feet up the wall, almost to the ceiling. She points to a half dozen glass-fronted cabinets, each packed with cups, mugs, figurines. She calls it her "collection . . . about three thousand ceramics." Next, she turns the flashlight to the opposite wall, where floor-to-ceiling shelves are crammed with thousands of moldy video tapes and DVDs. That's Joe's collection. He also invested in turntables, eight-track players, monitors, big stereo speakers. Everything lay underwater for weeks and then sat, untouched, for a year. Now it all seems to be rotting into a single, unidentifiable mass.

"Everything's mumble-jumble," is how Linda puts it. She plows deeper in: gray-haired, puffing. When she moves anything, a cloud of bugs flies up. The air gets closer, hotter. "Oh, Lord. This is the kitchen."

She steps down past an overturned freezer, two refrigerators. Shelves of canned goods have collapsed on the floor. She picks up a souvenir license plate, raps it to get the grime off. It says: HOLY CROSS SCHOOL, GO TIGERS! "We were collectors of everything." She wipes her brow and chuckles. "FEMA gave us five thousand for our contents. No, no: they gave us six thousand for the contents, and they gave us five thousand to repair the house." She rolls her eyes to the ceiling. "You cannot buy the sheetrock with the five thousand. Believe me. [And] they're only letting me have thirty-six dollars in food stamps." She makes a funny curtsy with her big hips. "Go figure. The government," she begins, then sighs, then begins again. "The government is helping the war."

The statement seems to have slipped out, but once it has, she keeps going, looking at her ruined possessions, emphasizing each word.

"I understand they got to help the soldiers, but," in a rush, "*they need to bring them home.* I don't like Bush," she whispers. "I don't like no politician, really, but I don't like Bush. There's too many, too many people died . . . I know deep down, I know it had to be done because of 9/11." She hunches her shoulders. "But . . . to lose so many sons, you know?"

She gets quiet, takes a deep breath, steadies herself. Then she starts to make her way back toward the rectangle of light that is the front door.

Outside, the sun is bright, the heat starting to overwhelm. Joe's been shoveling, but he stops to point next door to Patsy's house.

"She'll tell you an entirely different story," he says. "That we got a beautiful city. Don't let her bullshit you on that . . . She's from the hippie generation: 'Everything was beautiful. Everything is *still* beautiful!'" He goes back to shoveling.

Patsy, owner of the mysterious house with the wind chimes and the rubber snake, turns out to be a big woman in a purple pants suit. She has a square, childlike face framed by hair that's going gray in front, is reddish in back, and has been pulled up in two small braids held by blue plastic clips. She looks to be about sixty.

"I'm a packrat to begin with," she says. She's sitting out on the curb in a plastic lawn chair. "I had so much stuff in my yard!" She smiles.

"My son and his fiancée lived in the blue house on the corner, and they had five cats and five dogs . . . I had three dogs and one cat . . . And then we had the box turtles and the parakeets." She blinks her eyes innocently. "And the frogs that we had been pulling out of the fish pond." When they got word of the approaching hurricane, "we brought them all in." She and her son and their pets decided to ride it out on her second floor: a little Noah's ark, as she says. She watched the water "coming like white rapids! Like waves." She makes a long rolling motion with both arms, then points down to the corner. "We were using that stop sign as a gauge? It would go down a little bit," lowers her pale white arm, "and then it would rise again," arm up.

She talks about the days after the flood: people trapped on the St. Claude Bridge, the party atmosphere after stores were raided, the slow drop in her bottled water supply, the sound of gunfire at night. "It was a mess. A big scary mess . . . Eventually we didn't even light a candle at night because we didn't want them to see us. I mean, I didn't want to be taken to the Superdome or to the Convention Center." Finally they left in her son's truck: three people, eight dogs, six cats. They evacuated "thirteen hundred miles to Greenville, Michigan. I didn't think anyplace was that far from home!"

It's gotten too hot on the sidewalk. Patsy rises and walks slowly toward her house. She's followed by a yellow-brown German shepherd wearing a purple handkerchief around its neck: Zee-zee. A FEMA trailer is parked just inside the fence. Next to it are two black mannequins draped with Mardi Gras beads. Potted plants sit on unhinged doors; pieces of furniture hunch under gray tarps.

"I used to have a pretty yard," she says, and sighs. She finds a seat on a rusting metal glider. "Anyway, we ended up getting back in November. And for the first three months that we were back, I would open up those garage doors," pointing to her house. "I'd open them up," unfolds both hands, stares at them, "and I'd just close them again." She snaps her hands together. "I didn't even know where to begin. I did not know *whe-ere* to begin . . . There're so many little sentimental things.

"Bobo!" she suddenly shouts. She's trying to quiet another dog that's barking in her trailer. Then she goes back to sitting ladylike, her big body in an almost formal posture.

"I just have been slow-ly, slow-ly, slow-ly going through stuff with my hands." She bends over to paw through imaginary belongings. "And the treasures that I'm finding! Little plastic dinosaurs from when my son was a baby. He's twenty-three now." She laughs. "All of his little plastic animals and his toys and his cars."

She's been sorting for half a year. When it got to be too much, "I would just shut those garage doors and start working in the yard. You know? I just wanted to do something." She squints her eyes and flaps her hands to both sides. "Totally mindless. Chopping wood and getting rid of the debris and stuff like that. Anyway, this is where I spend most of my time." She looks at the dirt beneath her feet. "Cleaning the yard."

Patsy moved to Holy Cross in 1978. By then, the neighborhood had made the transition to majority black, and she remembers her school-age son called their house "the white neighborhood." She laughs. She says she likes the "live-and-let-live" attitude on the block and "the country-in-the-city kind of feel."

"These were my favorite albums," she suddenly says, pointing to thirty or forty LPs stacked in a grocery cart. All of them are badly water damaged, most of them stuck together. "I don't know if I can save them, but there they are. My old Neil Young and my Carly Simon and my Joan Baez and my Dylan. I don't know what I'm gonna do with them. I guess I can clean them?" She looks away as if she doesn't want to think about it. Her wind chimes tinkle overhead.

"But I don't have anything to play them on!" This comes out as a shout, and her laughter suddenly swerves toward tears. "But I'm comin' back! This is my home. I've been here twenty-eight years. I could have moved." She smiles her big, slightly goofy smile.

Right after the storm, Patsy took what savings she had, got a loan from the Small Business Administration (SBA), and put a down payment on a house uptown. Her son and his girlfriend have been living there.

"So far, about three hundred families are back. Or are planning on coming back." That's three hundred out of the nineteen hundred families that used to live in Holy Cross. Patsy refolds her hands in her lap.

"The other night on the news, they were talking about a lot of people going into depression. It's like the loss of a loved one . . . There's a big hole or space," she spreads her arms in a circle, "that has to slow-ly be filled with new energy. It's like a black hole or something . . . Other people have said the same thing to me: it just seems like we're sleepwalking . . ." She looks quizzical, as if she's not sure she knows what she's saying. "It's like a bad dream that you think you're gonna wake up from," takes a breath, "but you don't . . .

"People are just constantly fighting with their insurance companies and FEMA and SBA. I ended up having to retire from my job. I worked for the Department of Social Services for thirty years. And I was eligible to retire in September?" She wipes her forehead. "Then Katrina happened in August. And I couldn't get back by the state's deadline . . ." She widens her eyes. "But I had my thirty years in, so I was able to retire." Takes a breath. "I managed a caseload of two hundred families . . ." Now, sorting through her stuff, dealing with insurance, is a "full-time job. I couldn't imagine myself going back to work."

She stands slowly and heads back out toward the street. Next to the pile of black mannequins are animal cages. "I've been scrubbing these. They're the kennels we evacuated with. And there're stacks and stacks of them. And I want to have them handy in case that we have to go again."

Next door, Joe and Linda are still throwing ruined electronics out on the curb. Patsy steps to the middle of the street and calls Zee-zee over.

"My wonder dog," she says. She picks up a hoop decorated with purple feathers and—whistling and clicking—persuades Zee-zee to jump through it. "Whee! See that's a Ninth Ward dog for you!"

Down at the end of the block, beyond the Semmes school, Carolyn's double shotgun looks unchanged. She and her daughter, Kyrah, now live behind it in a FEMA trailer. "We received this on June the sixth," Carolyn says with her big grin. "So we'd been staying in the house from February to June. It's a long time, huh?" Five months in a gutted house with no water or electricity. "When they brought the trailer, it was right on time . . . The temperature started really getting up there . . . So I was grateful."

The trailer is air-conditioned but small. Carolyn can walk from one end to the other with five or six steps, her big hips nearly banging its sides. There's one bed that mother and daughter have been sharing. Meanwhile, Carolyn's brother Raymond is still sleeping in the gutted shotgun along with her grown son, Rahsaan.

Carolyn crosses from the trailer to the house. A blue tarp still separates the front of the house from the back. The rooms are still raw space outlined by wall studs. Extension cords bring power (no more batteries), and the two white refrigerators—"given to us by the Salvation Army"— are plugged in and running. "We moving up!" Carolyn says, giggling.

She finds Rahsaan sitting on his bed, his attention on a video game. He's a black man in his early thirties, almost as wide as he is tall, with a precise, educated voice and a round face behind glasses. "I'm here for a little while . . . but you never know, you never know . . ." He punches at the game controller. "I just came back from San Diego, where I've been the last year or so, wrapping up my . . . master's in arts in international relations." Before that, he was in Japan teaching English to what he calls "corporates."

It's stifling inside, and Carolyn soon moves out to a chair on the shaded front porch. "We trying to get the neighbors to come back so we can clear this up." She nods at her street. "As far as complaining, we don't have that much complaining. We sitting here waiting."

"Thank you, Lord," her brother Raymond chimes in, "for helping us get as far as we got. Thanks for *surviving*."

He's seated on the other side of the porch, legs over its edge. Kyrah and Rahsaan wander out. Kyrah is wearing a white T-shirt with a cartoon of a rabbit across her chest; it says TRIX. She did some modeling in high school, and her fashion statement this afternoon includes bright red shorts and a brown cap she wears sideways on her close-cropped hair. She's scheduled to go back to Syracuse soon. "Class of '09," she says.

"People have to understand these houses are totally gone. And for some people to rebuild, we have to wait and see what others want to do." Kyrah's talking about the continuing worry that the government will condemn the neighborhood if more families don't come back. Joe and Linda's decision to leave means three fewer occupied houses; Lathan's two are still empty, and it's not clear yet if Patsy or her son will be able to stay. "It's just a really slow, slow process," the teenager says, "of everybody depending on somebody else."

Carolyn moved into the double shotgun in 1971, just after Rahsaan was born. She'd grown up in Backatown, and coming to Holy Cross was literally a move up: to a more prosperous neighborhood on higher ground. Hers was the first African American family on this block. When she first arrived, a man across the street went around telling homeowners: "You might as well go because the neighborhood's gone." He'd send his dog out, Carolyn believes, to crap on her lawn. She finally got mad enough where "I'd take a scoop, pick the dog stool up, and I'd throw it on his house!" She smiles grimly. "I could see if I'd done them something, but I didn't do nothing. I just moved into the neighborhood."

Eventually she built a life here, and when she got divorced, she fought for and kept the house. Rahsaan was one of the few local kids who went to the Holy Cross School; he then graduated from Louisiana State University. Kyrah was an honors student at MLK Elementary, got into an elite high school, and earned a full scholarship to Syracuse.

"This was her greatest moment!" Carolyn says of her daughter heading to college. But within a week of her getting there, the hurricane struck. "And it looked like all this joy just turned into a disaster . . . It was almost like you couldn't breathe. Everything you had accomplished all your life . . . everything was just gone. Like that. And something just said, 'Breathe . . . accept what has happened.'"

Carolyn looks out on the street with a slow gaze.

"We will never go forward," she says slowly, "if we don't let this pass . . . I'm tired of waiting," she adds with a laugh, "[but] you have to embrace it. You have to *work it out*." She emphasizes the last words with both hands. "Because when you're gutting your houses—I don't care if you're just cutting the grass . . . it lets out somethin' that need to be, really, withdrawn from your body. It's like . . . like a *spirit*. To enable you to go on."

Kyrah jumps in. Compared to her mom's deliberate way of speaking, she's all sophomore eagerness. "New Orleans was expecting Katrina to come sometime. I know when I was in eighth grade, seventh grade, our teacher always used to explain to us: the wetlands is what holds Louisiana together." She tents her fingers into a little universe. "We lost about ten years' worth of wetlands in one year." She pulls her fingers apart. "Without that wetlands sitting in front of the coast in Louisiana, New Orleans is always gonna be the first thing hit."

Before Katrina, the region was losing 16,000 acres of marsh a year. Man-made levees channeled the Mississippi so it couldn't feed the wetlands; oil companies dug transportation canals through the bayous; developers filled in swamps. The marshes around New Orleans have been called "the fastest-disappearing land mass on earth."

"This was something we always knew was coming," Kyrah repeats. But when it came, many didn't or couldn't evacuate. "So many people in the Ninth Ward died because we are a *poor* people. We broke as a joke down here." Carolyn nods in agreement. "We didn't even have transportation! Most of the Ninth Ward jumps on that St. Claude bus to get to work, to get to school . . . Lower Nine don't *have* money. A lot of us sitting here screamin' and hollerin' now 'cause we don't know where to *get* money. Most of us live from check to check."

That starts her brother Rahsaan. He's wearing black Nike shorts and has a black do-rag dangling to his broad shoulders. He speaks as if at a podium. "My message to Congress, to the government in general, to the governor of our great state of Louisiana: get it in gear! Stop fooling around and send the money down here! . . . We now have a neighborhood plan, and we're ready to go."

He means the city council's recently completed master plan. After surveying Holy Cross residents, it calls for a commercial strip along St. Claude Avenue, shops and apartments on the Holy Cross School site, and a riverfront park. Rahsaan is ready for the planning to stop and the rebuilding to start. "I'm telling you straight out: we're sick of sitting down here and waiting for even the basic amenities that everyone else is enjoying . . . And another thing, another thing: don't think that because we're staying in a FEMA trailer things have gotten a little bit more special!"

"Man," says Kyrah, giggling, "we were living in the Flintstones time before the trailer got here!"

She describes how her other brother evacuated to Texas and has decided to stay. Rahsaan says that makes sense; Kyrah agrees. About

250,000 Gulf Coast evacuees have remained in Texas. "Instead of coming back here. Trying to find a school. Trying to find a job. It's too hectic
right now." For the first time, Kyrah looks sad, the light out of her eyes.

"Especially for those of us who fall between the ages of twenty-two
and forty," says Rahsaan. "Myself included. We're finding great difficulty
in trying to fit in what's left of the economic infrastructure here. There
are jobs here, but they're only employing people from ten to twenty
hours a week." Rahsaan, with his newly earned master's degree, is working at a downtown restaurant. "Hopefully, [the hours] will get better as
the [tourist] season gets ready to start."

Tourism has long been one of the city's main economic drivers. From
its peak as the nation's third-largest city in 1840, New Orleans dropped
to seventeenth by World War I. Its port was still active, but the city had
been, as one observer puts it, "largely left out of the industrial revolution." Instead, its economy seemed to pass almost directly from slavery
to service. As early as the 1880s, writers such as Lafcadio Hearn and
George Washington Cable had begun to create its romantic image of
blowsy, slightly debauched decay. By the last half of the twentieth century, with manufacturing jobs and longshoreman work both dropping
by 80 percent, the city depended more and more on tourism. Its only
significant pre-flood growth was in low-wage service work: bartenders
in the French Quarter, chambermaids in the big hotels, cooks, taxicab
drivers.

New Orleans may have started a century earlier, but much of the rest
of the country now has a similar arrangement. In the mid-1960s, the
United States became the first nation in the world to have most of its jobs
in the service economy. Today, the service sector accounts for 80 percent
of the country's workforce. On this block, Lathan, Joe, Patsy's son
Adrian, and Carolyn all made their living in "leisure and hospitality."
And now both Kyrah and Rahsaan do, too.

"Most of these jobs are running eight-fifty an hour," says Rahsaan.

"Unless you're doing construction," Kyrah points out. "Actually, the
only thing is construction. Because if you try to work at a hospital,
they're not letting you do that; they're only allowing the people who have
seniority . . . The people at Popeyes," she continues, giving a look of disgust, "told me I was overqualified. They said, 'You're too smart to fry
chicken.'" She throws both hands in the air. "Thank you! But I need a
paycheck!" She's spent the summer working at a clothing store in a shopping mall downtown. Part-time.

Carolyn's brother, Raymond, interrupts: "There's Mark over there." Mark is the gray-haired man who stayed through the floods, whose dog was eaten.

"Hey, Mark!" Carolyn calls, and adds a piercing whistle. ". . . He was on his motorbike and fell." Mark's right arm is in a sling, his left in a cast. He's limping and walking very slowly.

"All right, man. How ya doin?" Raymond shouts.

Mark stops. "Not good. I'm in a lot of pain." Pause. "Everything okay?"

"Oh yeah," Raymond answers.

Mark slowly raises the arm in the cast, waves, and starts to limp back toward his house.

He gets to the middle of the block and stops. His moustache is neatly trimmed, but his hair is uncut and a slight white beard creeps up his jawbone.

"I guess I'm alive," he says. "I've got five broken ribs. Broken shoulder. Broken collarbone. Broken thumb . . . and, uh, there's something else but I forget what it is . . . Hit something in the road on Franklin Avenue. About nine-thirty at night . . . You know, you're tooling down the road, got no problems—of course, the road is totally unlit, no streetlights, totally deserted— . . . and all of a sudden, wham!" He woke up in an ambulance. "And they took me to the trauma center in—what's it again?—Elmwood."

Before the floods, Mark probably would have been taken to Charity Hospital, the city's largest inpatient facility, housing the area's only Level 1 trauma ward. But Charity has been closed since Katrina, as have half the hospitals in the city. Where Charity could handle about 200 trauma patients, the new facility at Elmwood can only take 40.

For years now, New Orleans has been talking about rebooting its economy by building a state-of-the-art medical facility. Since the flood, that proposal has been expanded to a sixty-seven-acre, $2 billion complex. Though Louisiana's health care system has long been the lowest ranking in the nation, the new center would focus less on emergency room services for low-income, walk-in patients and more on the kind of research and upscale treatments that would jump-start a local bioscience industry. The same shift is going on in many American cities, but once again the floods have given New Orleans the opportunity to move more quickly and decisively. "Changing demographics" is how the state's secretary of health and hospitals explains it. ". . . A lot of people left. And a lot of the people who left are uninsured." It's a little like the logic of the chain stores: Charity Hospital stays closed because there are fewer low-income patients. There are fewer low-income patients returning to the city because they can't get dependable health care.

In Mark's case, he went from the trauma center to two and a half weeks in rehab. "I don't have a thing to complain about it. The treatment of the ambulance, the folks at Elmwood and St. John's Hospital and the staff, even the food was good!" But, he points out, that's because he has health insurance. "The system, I guess, works as long as it's oiled by money. And in this particular case, once you're in the door, you're in the door because somebody's paying." He pauses a moment. "The problem with our system is that a lot of people don't get to go in the door."

He returned home late yesterday afternoon. "At this point," he says, swaying slightly in the sun, it's "pretty challenging ..." A laugh. "I'm okay if I lie back real slow ... and I don't move a muscle, anywhere. Then I'm fine."

He makes his slow way across the street, up a set of stairs, and into his FEMA trailer. It's identical to Carolyn's, identical to thousands across the region. "If you're in here by yourself, wonderful." He looks around, barely moving his head, neck stiff. "If you're trying to live here with a family? Probably drive you batty. I mean, imagine this place with a wife and two kids! ... But for a single person, it's a godsend. A godsend."

Mark sits at the little built-in kitchen table, takes half a cigarette out of the ashtray, and lights it. "I've been fortunate," he says slowly, "in having a constitution that's pretty resilient. All my life it's been so. God willing it stays that way."

Mark was born in Poland and grew up in Minnesota. He came to New Orleans, he says, "because I realized I'd never have to be cold again." And to Holy Cross, "because this was the only place I could buy enough land to have a Volkswagen repair business." In 1980, when he bought it, the big house on the corner had been heavily fire-damaged. It only cost him $30,000, but he had to live in a VW van for four years while he re-built. He ran his repair business out on the street or in the side yard, moving his VWs behind the fence at night. It was totally illegal, he says, smiling. He had slowed down by the time the floods came, and then "the cars, all the parts ... [were under] salt water ... Just to replace all my tools and equipment would have been prohibitive." His driveway is stacked with rusting bumpers, hubcaps, crankshafts. "I was gonna spend the next couple months hauling this to Southern Scrap."

Outside his trailer, there's an occasional crash as Joe continues dumping his ruined electronic equipment. "He had the illusion," Mark says philosophically, "that he was sitting on a gold mine . . . You know how we are: we delude ourselves because we want to feel that the things we've done and things we've given our time to have been worthwhile." He lifts an eyebrow. "We don't want to feel like a bunch of fools. Who have wasted all of our effort and time . . ."

He gets up carefully, exits the trailers, and walks slowly through a gate into his side yard. "Virtually eighty percent of all my foliage—bushes, plants, all that stuff—died . . . I spent almost three weeks raking all the toxic mud, okay? Raked and raked and raked everywhere. I hauled it all out to the curb. But I never raked up all of it."

He points to a small tree. "This one was dead: killed by the storm. But this one," pointing to a similar tree, "put out new shoots. And then died within a month and a half!" He limps over to a nearby green bush that's fallen into the yard. "This was a beautiful bush. And then two or three months ago . . . it just collapsed . . . for no good reason. It just fell! So even stuff that seemed to have survived, didn't. The *Pyracantha* probably did better than most things." He points to a prickly, ten-foot-tall hedge that follows his property line. "Look at the top: how it's growing, growing, growing." He waves with his arm in a cast. "But you look at the bottom: the bottom two, three feet are dead!" His voice is high-pitched, amazed.

Mark turns to make his way back to the street. "You think you know what's happening, what's going on, but no. You don't. There's more of a price to be paid than you thought."

Kyrah's still on the porch just across the empty intersection. Her young voice bounces off the walls and echoes out into the neighborhood.

"You know what I find most insulting? The only things that are up and running in New Orleans are the tourist spots. The French Quarter's up and running; Uptown is up and running . . . [but] every *neighborhood* of New Orleanians is in shambles . . . It's not fair. It's not fair to the people here, and it's not fair to the kids. Because they don't have good schools to go to. And a lot of the kids in the Lower Ninth Ward are gonna suffer because the only good school we had here, they're moving across the canal." She's talking about MLK. "So the only beacon of light that the little kids had is gone. And I went to that elementary school, and it set us up real well for college . . . And they wonder why they always want to call the Ninth Ward the ghetto." She puts air quotes around the word *ghetto*. "As soon as the Ninth Ward tries to build things up, they take it away. Always."

Still, Kyrah says, the Lower Ninth is used to fighting back. She mentions an elderly woman just around the corner. "Eighty-nine years old! And this lady is in her house, gutting her own house out—"

"Come on!" Carolyn shouts from her chair. "She's ninety! I'm sixty! We had shovels." She swings an invisible one. "We bashed the walls! We're not gonna wait forever!" She laughs. "I would like to be in my house for Christmas. *In my home for Christmas.*" Her big body rocks. "With lights on it!"

Kyrah's eyes get big, and she starts giggling.

"That's why I came back," Carolyn continues. "... to be in my house—ten oh one Jourdan Avenue—for Christmas. I didn't care if I didn't have furniture. I'll just have lights on my house and lay on the floor!"

The image causes a peal of laughter, and Kyrah joins in, one hand over her mouth, doubled over.

"Long as I'm in my house for Christmas!" Carolyn declares. "... *I want to get in my house!*"

The New Normal

Time Is Not the Same

(August–October 2006)

"Welcome to our humble abode."

A soft-spoken woman unlocks the door, in a hall lined with doors, in a dormitory at the New Orleans Baptist Theological Seminary.

"It's a *room*," she adds, drawing out the last word. And she's right: it's little more than that. Immaculately clean, brightly lit, institutional, it has space for a chair and a bed, a small fridge, and not much else.

"This is where we're living," Pastor Mel explains. "And we're pleased and thankful that we have this. We got our own room."

He smiles at the soft-spoken woman, his bride. He calls her Miss Clara. They're living in this room because her house—their house—caught fire and burnt to the ground. It's an event Miss Clara seems to comprehend only in bits, slowly, by going back over it again and again.

Two years ago, she was a single woman, divorced, a certain amount of savings and a nice house in a nice part of town. She met Mel; they started dating. When the levees failed, they were talking about getting engaged. Her house, out in the New Orleans East neighborhood, only got about two feet of water, and Mel had gone there beforehand with some of his men and raised most of her possessions above that level. It was damaged but fixable, and they immediately started to rebuild. Four months later, they got married.

Miss Clara understands all that. What's harder to take in is that they're once again without a home.

She sits on the one chair, while her husband sits on the bed. Mel has managed to locate a bigger apartment out by Lake Pontchartrain, but they haven't been able to move in yet. "It's a deal at a thousand," he says. "Before the hurricane, you could get a decent two-bedroom apartment for five hundred dollars. Most places now, it's a thousand dollars . . . And a lot of poor people are just being thrown out. So we're fortunate. Very fortunate."

Miss Clara nods her agreement, quiet, hands folded properly in her lap. She has large brown eyes framed by straight dark hair. Laugh lines. She looks to be in her forties but is actually older, brown-skinned, a beauty mark on her right cheek. She dresses conservatively, stylishly, in a brown blouse and blue pants, small gold hoop earrings. There's a respectable, churchgoing air to her: a less stern Coretta Scott King.

"You know what I asked Melvin just today? 'Did you hear sirens when the fire engines came?' I don't remember sirens."

She looks at the walls of their little room, puzzled. "What I remember is him," she inhales deeply, "screaming for me to wake up and call the fire department." Her voice is pitched low as she talks; she searches the ceiling for words. "I can't even scream it the way that he screamed it." She pauses. "The whole experience was strange. Especially of watching it and standing there with all the neighbors; everyone just standing there in the street and watching it." She describes the fire department coming: "It was like television; it was like the movies; it was huge." And then adds: "They got there in time not to save our home, but to save the neighborhood . . . Everyone is still rebuilding—"

"And *we're* gonna rebuild," Mel interrupts.

Clara takes her cue: "And we're going to, also."

Upbeat, decisive, Mel says a group is coming down from New Jersey "to do some missionary work," and they've offered to frame up the charred house. "It's gonna be different. And it's going to be nicer!"

Clara goes quiet when Mel speaks. She listens attentively, hands folded. When he's done, she offers a little history.

"This will be the *third* time working on this home. I came back to New Orleans in spring of 2004. Purchased the home. Made a decision: I would never learn another highway system; this was it!" She gives a serious look and then smiles. "My parents were here, my siblings, my son and his wife and the three grandchildren. I was just going to be in New Orleans. And I was single at the time. I was minding my business: this was my plan." Big-eyed. "So I bought the home and gutted the kitchen and redid some other parts . . ." Her gesture is both hands pushing stuff away from her chest. "I was on my way in 2004. And then 2005, it flooded. And 2006 . . . the fire. And for some reason," she raises a finger, "it's okay."

Mel jumps in: "Not for some reason. Because of our relationship with God."

"Yeah," Clara says tentatively. "Because I know that we're going to be fine. We just know it. We don't know the shape of it, but we know it. *I* know it because of where God has been in my life." She gains conviction as she goes along but still seems unsure, looking to her husband for confirmation.

Mel and Clara knew each other from their childhoods in Pontchartrain Park. Clara's family moved to the subdivision in 1961, when she was eleven. When she was fourteen, her mother died and, as she puts it, "our lives changed." She holds both hands up, turns them in the light, and adds: "You didn't live like a kid."

"Clara was a couple of years older," Mel says, "and I used to see her as a young man: fourteen, fifteen, sixteen years old . . . And she was cute. And she went out with the high school football stars."

Clara gives a small smile, then whispers, "Stop."

She went on to Southern University of New Orleans, within walking distance of Pontchartrain Park. She married, and she and her husband left the city in 1980. "And when I came back in '87, I had two elementary-age children." She became a substitute first-grade teacher at McDonogh #19 in the Lower Ninth. It had been one of the first two city schools to be integrated. Twenty-five years later, it was in "deplorable condition," Clara says. ". . . You were just furious. The system, once again, wasn't taking care of the children." She put her own kids in a parochial school, because "it was a quick move . . . I knew I could get their basics there." Then she started looking for a good public school. And was shocked.

"I called the superintendent's office . . . and I asked for a list of schools comparable to the schools in Champaign-Urbana, Illinois." She pauses, and then in a whisper: "They gave me a list. And see, there *shouldn't be* a list . . . They were magnet schools." The regular schools in New Orleans were far below what she was used to up north. To help change that, Clara went back and got her certificate to teach full-time.

Two decades later, when she and Mel re-met, they were both divorced, both with grown children. She was now a retired teacher, he was an ex-addict, but they had that shared beginning in Pontchartrain Park. "And our common interest," Mel declares, "was our relationship with God.

And putting that first." Clara nods agreement. "And we wound up me chasing her. And she finally giving in!"

"I did run," says Clara, smiling. "I had no intentions of . . . Well, I was just single. And I was gonna be single. I had my grandchildren; I had my family; I was back in New Orleans. And that was my plan . . . We met— when did we start this? It was '05. It was the week before Father's Day 2005. And we were married in January '06."

"Yup," says Mel, grinning. "God is good!" he adds, raising his voice.

"All the time," Clara adds in a whisper.

"All the time," Mel confirms.

It's a week after their house burned down, and Mel is stepping out of a white station wagon with GOD IS GOOD ALL THE TIME stenciled on its side. He's at his ministry, Bethel Colony South, which has grown again: it now serves some twenty-five men. There's a temporary meeting house at the back end of the courtyard, where Mel conducts morning services and the men receive work assignments. There's also a new gray office trailer to one side.

"We were rebuilding our house in New Orleans East," Mel explains, standing in the courtyard, "and we were two weeks away from moving in. One of our friends who does plumbing work, he was sweating pipes. And evidently a spark was left in the wall. Or something. We don't know exactly how it happened."

Mel and a new volunteer, Harry, are going to drive out and assess the damage. On the way, they'll visit Mel's parents' place. Harry is a tall white guy, six foot four or so, in a work shirt and blue jeans. He appears to be in his late thirties with a lean, construction worker's body. He doesn't say much, wears dark aviator glasses and a necklace with a large wooden cross.

"As you drive around the city," Mel offers, "you'll see that houses are still just the way they were a year ago." He measures a little space in mid-air with both his hands, as if measuring progress. "It's mostly faith-based organizations coming into town. We're still looking for the government help. They *say* they're doing what they need to be doing, but we don't see it . . . The community"—and now he cups his hands, holding a circle of air between them—"is coming together. And making its *own* plans, neighborhood by neighborhood." He reaches out to a few isolated spots. "And they're getting it done. But you're gonna see, a year after this, not a whole lot going on." He pauses. "Amen."

Mel drives away from the ministry, heading out through Gentilly Woods. His cell phone rings almost immediately. "Harry's gonna help us fix a couple of the vehicles," he explains into the receiver. ". . . Yeah . . . Harry's weighing whether or not he's gonna come and spend time with us in New Or-lee-ins . . . He's not a minister. But he knows the Word, loves the Lord. And he's got great talent in fixing things . . . We'll see what God does with that . . ."

Harry, looking out the window through his shades, mutters, "Lots of work."

Mel clicks off his cell and laughs. "Harry, there will be work here for ten years. For somebody that's reputable. Because a lot of people are getting beat by contractors."

Mel drives through the tree-lined streets of Gentilly Woods. "Look at all the houses that are still vacant." He points out the boarded-up windows, the overgrown lawns. The main change is the number of white FEMA trailers that dot the driveways. As if everyone had decided to buy the same model Winnebago.

By now, the federal agency has provided 120,000 trailers and mobile homes, 60,000 in New Orleans alone. Seven months after the flood, a family in Mississippi started complaining about respiratory problems: scratchy throats, difficulty breathing, runny and bleeding noses. Tests done by the Sierra Club revealed that over 80 percent of the trailers showed formaldehyde levels above the national safety standard. FEMA dismissed the findings and, a half year later, continues to downplay the problem. All people need to do, a spokesman advises, is "take steps to air out." Originally the agency was going to take back the trailers after eighteen months. But because rebuilding has gone so slowly, the deadline has been extended.

Mel crosses into Pontchartrain Park. "Marc Morial, one of our mayors, came from this community. Eddie Jordan, our district attorney, came from this community. Lot of legislators, congressmen, people who are now leading the city came from this community." He points out a boat still sitting high and dry on an unmowed lawn.

He stops in front of his parents' ranch house, the Virgin Mary out front, and pauses for a moment before going in.

"Our government is *failing us*." His voice is loud, insistent, as if he were speaking to someone in the distance. "We're still waiting—still waiting—for money to rebuild. And then they're telling us we're gonna have to raise our homes! We're gonna have to raise them three feet so that we can get flood insurance. Well," he almost shouts, "the water was ten feet! So, even if we raised it three feet, what would that do? We're still gonna be under seven feet of water. It's no difference."

Harry's quiet, shifting his weight, eyeing the building before him. Mel's voice drops.

"We got the willpower; we got the brainpower in America to do it. It's just . . . does America *value* its people enough, value the city of New Orleans enough?" Both hands open, he stands in the driveway. "What are we gonna do here?"

His cell phone rings at his belt. He cuts it off.

"Are we going to invest in our people? Or are we just going to say, 'Well, pull yourself up by your bootstraps. Do the best that you can'?" He raises his hands in the air as if surrendering. "We gotta help. The government's *gotta* help."

He looks at his cell phone, puts it back on his belt.

Bethel Colony, he continues, is based on the belief that "if you work hard, then—through God—all things are possible." But Mel believes in the helping hand of government, too. His family, after all, came up through the housing developments and took advantage of reduced-rate loans to move into Pontchartrain Park.

Mel steps through the front door of his parents' home, Harry behind him. "This is gutted, Harry. And this is a year after." The walls are framed out and wired, but there's still no sheetrock, no plumbing, no ceilings. Mel focuses on how much better it looks. "God has been good to us. When we first got in here . . . man! Man, man. Everything was just kinda tossed to and fro."

Harry is squatting, sunglasses off, taking a professional look at the foundation. "Some of these plates need to be replaced in here. Floor plates, stud plates. Some of them are pretty rough. And they're loose, too."

"Well, Harry, they're gonna rebuild." Mel says it like a vow. "They're gonna rebuild. And whatever it takes to rebuild, ya know, God is just going to send it."

Miss Clara shares her husband's faith. But she comes at the rebuilding from a different place. Mel is hands-on, helping the homeless, organizing his ex-addicts to gut buildings: his men depend on his practical optimism. Miss Clara's job since the flood has been to deal with the paperwork, the phone calls, the seemingly endless permissions.

She started the process during her six-week evacuation, when she and other family members were living out of a hotel room in Texas. She'd get on the phone with FEMA or with her insurance companies, trying to figure out which documents were needed and how to fill them out. "Of course, you were doing it long distance." Soon it became overwhelming, and she and her stepmother had to decide: "We either make phone calls in the a.m. or the p.m." pause ". . . for mental health purposes . . . Because you could literally be on the phone six hours a day."

Even Mel in his optimism admits: "We don't really know what's going to happen in New Orleans. With the hundred and fifty thousand dollars that Road Home said it was giving each homeowner to rebuild. That's not forthcoming just yet." He smiles. "They said they're going to have to interview each person individually. We don't know *how* long that's gonna take."

Often a homeowner will complete an application and then hear nothing for weeks. Reaching Road Home by phone can be difficult. When a caller does get through, their file may turn out to be inaccurate, or their application's been lost. There are months to wait before getting an interview. ICF, the private company hired to administrate Road Home, has instituted a policy that all communications will be verbal. So the homeowner has no written record of phone calls, corrections, promises given. After the interview, more months may pass. Finally, applicants deemed eligible receive a yellow award letter announcing how much they'll eventually receive. Then more weeks and months. As of fall 2006, some 34,000 homeowners have completed Road Home applications. The relief program has issued a total of thirteen checks.

Miss Clara tries to explain what this does to you. "Everything you need," she begins gently, "is going in slow motion." She lets that sink in a moment. "But you're moving real fast because you *need* so much. You need everything again! So you're trying to meet your every need that you may gradually meet over a lifetime." She drags both hands across an invisible horizon. "But now you're doing it all at one time?"

She knows it's hard to understand. She takes a deep breath and starts again.

"Mentally, you're moving very fast." She touches her forehead. "The system is moving very slow. Slow-ly." Again, a hand dragged across the horizon. "So . . ." She struggles for the words. "Your time is all mixed up. It's not normal. Not regular . . ."

If time seemed to speed up with the floods—and then come almost to a stop afterward—this is something different. Clara gropes to express what feels like a profound truth. She looks to the ceiling for the right words.

"Even if the home had not burned down, we would have still been *in* the process." Both hands go from head to chest: a gesture of working things through, of digesting. She and Mel had moved faster than most, she explains. "I have one girlfriend on the block, Dianne. She finished . . . and she's in her home. She's the only one on—no! Carol and Lewis. I think they're in their home now. I think there were two people who were already in their homes by the time ours burned. Everyone was still working on it."

She looks to the ceiling, again, tries another way to say it.

"Time *is* different. Time is not the same." Pause. "Because it's not like you're writing out your list and getting up and running your errands. Before I can make a move, I may have to get on the phone and call"—she starts counting them off on her fingers—"Entergy, the Sewage and Water Board, my insurance company. And then," voice dropping to a near whisper, "I might have to wait for them to call me back. I might have to call them again."

It's a whisper of shock, the same whisper she used to describe the New Orleans schools. It's not, she implies, how the world is supposed to work. She's an educated woman, a professional, and she's used to knowing how the system functions, to having her phone calls answered. But now . . . she can't describe it.

"If you're rebuilding—ordering things—that also makes time different . . . Because"—and she says this next sentence with a big smile, having finally hit upon what seems like an explanation and wanting to emphasize it, spacing each word—"*everybody has the same needs at the same time*." Pause. "So it's just not regular."

Mel and Harry now head toward New Orleans East and the burnt house. But driving out of Pontchartrain Park, Mel spots an old acquaintance and stops to talk. A black man in a green shirt with a blue handkerchief over his hair and a white dust mask stops working on his house and steps into the driveway to greet the pastor. They embrace.

"You getting it together, huh?"

"Well," the man answers, "I'm trying to get it right so I can get it on line—and get on out of here!"

They chat a little about old times. Mel remembers when he used to "witness" to this guy's baby brother. The baby brother who eventually relapsed and died of an overdose. "Oh, he knew," the man comments, "he knew. But that's the path he chose, bra. Look, ain't nothin' happen to us that we don't know about. 'Cause He brings it to your attention . . . He'll let you know where you're slippin'—and where you can pick yourself up at." The man grins.

Mel nods, smiles, and then disagrees. "I'll tell you, I *couldn't* pick myself up. Only the Lord did it. I couldn't do it, man!" Both laugh. In Mel's universe, friends can help; government can and should help; but it comes back to God. "That dope had me," Mel says. "It had me. It *had* me."

The guy nods. They chat a little longer, then hug goodbye. Mel and Harry get back in their GOD IS GOOD ALL THE TIME station wagon.

"He and I used to fight when we were kids," Mel explains as they drive off. "But we never ran together. He avoided the dope. For some reason, he avoided the dope. He just told me: 'I saw what it did to people.'" Pause. "*I* saw what it did to people, too. But I didn't think it was going to do it to me. I thought I was bigger and badder." A half laugh. "But that wasn't the case."

The car is passing through washed-out, gutted neighborhoods, open under the bright sun. It's as if this was the landscape of addiction, as if the city had been on something and, now, wasted, has to figure out its recovery.

"I never thought—the first time that I used drugs—that I would wind up addicted. And living on the streets. It's just like those beer commercials . . . you see pretty girls, you see the sparkling liquor, and it just make it all look pretty . . . They don't allow you to see the bondage side of it."

He crosses the Industrial Canal and enters the neighborhood known as New Orleans East.

"As you can see, there's hardly any traffic. Businesses still not being rebuilt . . . The Winn-Dixie's not open yet. Wendy's . . . Kirschman's, a furniture store. The dentist over here, he's not back yet. It was busy, Harry . . . This was a vibrant area. Louisiana Seafood: these were all places that were up and running and profitable businesses before Katrina. And now we've got a situation where nothing's here. *Nothing.* Absolutely nothing."

They pass a big, low blue building out in a green field. On its side, a cartoon of a rabbit and in huge block letters: BUNNY BREAD. Nearby, a group of modern-looking, attached condominiums stand in too-tall grass, their windows out. It's not clear if the flooding did this or the pre-disaster economy. If this is a landscape of addiction, how far back does it date?

Mel drives for a while in silence.

"I hate to say this, but there's a different level of business in the black community and the white community here in New Or-lee-ins. In the African American communities, you can look at the Sav-A-Center on Franklin Avenue, mostly used by members of the African American community. And the Sav-A-Center that's on Carrollton Avenue. Totally different situation." Mel says the Franklin Avenue supermarket was "dirty," with higher prices, fewer products. That's how the old New Orleans worked, and he doesn't want that part rebuilt. "I don't know the answer . . . Except for the black community to say, 'We're just not gonna accept it,' and not buy till the businesses bring it up to standard . . . Maybe it's still a throwback to slavery. Maybe we're still suffering from that. But I will not myself, personally, buy from the one on Franklin Avenue."

They turn and cut under an overpass. Above them is I-10, the interstate that made New Orleans East possible, that enabled this landscape.

In the first half of the twentieth century, black and poor people left rural America for the cities in what's been called the Great Migration. The subsequent large-scale abandonment of those cities by white people might be called the Great Escape. It was possible partly because of the Interstate Highway Act of 1956, which helped build 40,000 miles of roads like I-10. Along with highway construction came government-guaranteed housing bonds, housing acts, and long-term mortgages that included tax-deductible interest. This combination of federal laws has been described as "a great subsidy for the middle class." It was also a massive economic stimulus, as the country proceeded to build rings of suburbs around its older inner cities.

Here in New Orleans, the completion of Interstate 10 in 1972 created new developments to the west, cut through and destroyed the city's black commercial district on Claiborne Avenue, and helped make possible new suburbs north of Lake Pontchartrain. It also opened the way to the city's eastern section, then mostly marsh.

The fifty square miles that would become New Orleans East contained some of the lowest land in the metropolitan area. But it equaled a quarter of the city's total acreage and had been designated the "logical growth corridor." In the early seventies, a developer proposed turning the swamp into a "totally planned community where two hundred and fifty thousand people will eventually live, work, and play." The idea was to construct a suburb within the city: a middle-class neighborhood for whites only.

But around 1974, the city's racial balance began to tip, and in 1977 New

Orleans elected its first African American mayor: Pontchartrain Park's own Ernest "Dutch" Morial. Cleveland, Detroit, Atlanta also had black leaders by then, and like them, Morial inherited a city with a falling tax base and a failing infrastructure. Jobs were leaving, and the federal government was cutting its support of city programs. Over the next decade, for example, the U.S. budget for housing and urban development was halved.

New Orleans East still might have been built as planned, but then came the oil crash of the mid-eighties. If one of the nation's addictions was to cheap energy, Louisiana helped lead the way. The number of refineries on the lower Mississippi had grown from 175 in 1947 to 255 by 1967. And the number of petrochemical plants had gone from 6 to 60, helping to create Cancer Alley. Dependence only increased, and oil prices continued to rise through the gasoline shortage of 1973, the Iranian Revolution of 1979, the Iran-Iraq War of 1980, and the savings and loan crisis of 1984. In those years, the cost of a barrel of oil went from three dollars to over thirty. Then the bubble burst. In less than a year, crude oil prices fell by more than 60 percent. New Orleans was hit particularly hard. Credit dried up; housing starts slowed. The developer of New Orleans East pulled out, and the former swampland sat idle, drained and divided into lots, grass growing through concrete slabs. Almost as if it had been hit by a flood.

In the end, the subdivision was built, but not as originally planned. "This is predominantly African American," Mel says, pointing to neat two-story houses. "You can see these were hundred-and-fifty-thousand dollar homes. Some of them two hundred thousand, two hundred and fifty. People that have taken care of their families and invested in their community." By 2004, when Miss Clara bought here, New Orleans East looked like a modern version of Pontchartrain Park: middle-class, respectable, and 75 percent black. Before the floods, sections like this had fewer poor people, fewer blighted houses, and more people with jobs than the metropolitan area as a whole.

"This is our street," Mel suddenly announces. "A pretty decent community." Modern three- and four-bedroom brick homes sit on small lots. White FEMA trailers block driveways, but even with blue tarps covering most of the roofs, hedges are trimmed, bushes cut back. "This is Dianne's," Mel says, tapping on the car glass. "Dianne has redone hers."

He stops midway down the block in front of a brick ranch with pink shutters. A sign stuck in the front lawn reads: HOPE FOR A BETTER

LOUISIANA. Mel gets out, leaving his keys in the ignition, and strides to the front entrance. "This is my home. Burned last Thursday."

Inside, it's a disaster. The walls are slumped, waterlogged from the fire hoses. The ceilings are gone, blue sky shows through charred beams. The floor has disappeared under a knee-high mess of wet insulation, bubbled wood, wires. "You can see some things are still in boxes," Mel says. "Those are cabinets to be installed. Everything was new: the sheetrock, the roof, all of the wiring. Everything was new." He points across the ravaged room to a fuse box. "You can see the wiring still hanging."

As he moves in farther, stepping gingerly over the debris, it smells of wet charcoal and burnt-out electrics. "This was the living room." He points to a French door, wrenched open. "As you can see, we're adding on a patio in the back." He corrects himself: "We *were* putting down a patio in the back. I had enlarged the kitchen for the wife." He points to a blackened hole that shows no signs of ever having been a kitchen. "We recovered from the flood—rebuilt our house from the flood—and now we got to contend with the fire."

Mel tells it like a modern Bible story: how God woke him in the middle of the night to see flames sprouting from their new roof. "I was trying to put it out with a garden hose," he says, smiling a little, "and I wasn't able to . . . And I called the men at the ministry. And I said, 'Brothers, you got to start praying for Pastor, his house is burning down.' In fifteen minutes, the twenty-five brothers from the ministry was here! The fire department pulled up; they started putting the fire out. And we joined hands, and we prayed."

Mel stands in the middle of the wreckage, head down, his arms outstretched to both sides: holding hands with invisible partners. His white shirt stands out against the blackened beams.

"And we started singing! Harry, we started singing: 'I thank you Lord / I thank you Lord / I thank you Lord.'" Mel's clapping on the offbeat, singing out loud in his former living room. "'For your goodness to me / I thank you Lord.'" He's grinning. "In the middle of the fire!" he shouts, then launches into the next verse: "'He's been so good / He's been so good / He's been so good.'" Mel keeps clapping. "In the middle of the fire, Harry, we singing and praising Him! Giving the glory to God even in the midst of the situation."

Harry takes off his sunglasses and, unsmiling, scans the ruined house with a contractor's eye. Mel claps and laughs.

"And Harry, as we circled around singing, the neighbors—they were wondering if we were crazy." Harry grins at that, takes a sip from the Coke in his hand. "And the firemen: they *knew* we were plumb crazy. But we still gonna give God glory."

"Amen," Harry says quietly.

Mel raises one finger for emphasis, his voice in that brassy preacher's mode. "'Cause you see on the side of the truck 'God Is Good *All* the Time'? He's good in the bad time—"

Harry says the rest with Mel: "He's good in the good time."

"Don't make a difference what it is," Mel continues. "God's good all the time. And *He* knew this was going to happen. Why God didn't stop it, I don't know." Harry paces off a way, still inspecting. "Why a spark started it? I don't know. But I know what: God is in it with us. Through us. And we're going to rebuild."

"Amen," Harry says again.

"Amen," Mel echoes back, then pauses. "I just get charged up," he adds in a more normal voice. "People expect me to be crying and 'Oh, woe is me.' Man, that's foolishness."

He heads out what was once the back door, then walks quickly around his home, pointing out the ruined air-conditioning unit and where his library was going to be. Harry looks like he wants to stay and figure out where repairs should start. But while Mel sees God's plan in what's happened, he doesn't want to stick around. As Harry stares up at the black roof beams, Mel's back in the car, ready to go.

"What I know has made a difference for my family," Clara is saying in her quiet voice, "is where we were *prior* to the hurricane. In terms of our support for each other and our interactions with each other. And where you were *financially* prior to the hurricane. Not so much that you had to have a lot of money . . . but the way that you functioned? Made a difference in the outcome for you."

She's picking her words carefully. Her husband, after all, works every day with men who might be considered nonfunctional, with no financial base, and they're fighting to come back, too. She's not condemning anyone; she's just trying to identify what made a difference to her family. She believes there's a reason she and Mel were recovering from the flood— and will now recover from the fire. And it isn't solely a matter of faith.

"I think the young families with the young children—" pause "were more *impacted* than the older ones. My dad and Estelle, they're retired. So that steady check is coming in for them." Her hands circle, gather. "Even though they still had to get everything all over again, they had an identified income." Among the evacuees across the Gulf Coast, only about half of the nineteen- to twenty-five-year-olds have returned so far, compared to about three-quarters of those fifty-five and older. That goes against many predictions. "If you were already retired or," Clara smiles, "close to retirement age—'cause that's pretty much where I am—and if you don't have little children, you could ease into it in a different way. But those young families. With the little children. Having lost the home. And the employment . . ."

She pauses. She's speaking carefully, going from phrase to phrase as if she were stepping through ruins.

"Children don't tend to have the words to express their feeling. So it'll come out in their behavior? But most adults, you know, they aren't screaming. Well, sometimes we *are* screaming. Sometimes we have choice words. Or no words." She looks to Mel, sitting across the tiny room from her. "And sometimes it's a lot of hysterical laughter . . ." They exchange a glance. "I don't think you can get bored," she adds, raising her eyebrows, "because nothing's regular."

"You can get a little wacky sometimes," is how Mel puts it.

"Yeah," Clara says, smiling, then shoots him a look: *You mean me?* Mel laughs.

"Some of us are coming back," she continues quietly. "I am. Because I am married to Melvin." She looks from her chair across to where he sits on the bed. "That is why. Because I am married to Melvin. Right?"

"Yeah." Mel laughs again, a little nervous.

"I do look forward to normal," Clara says, "but it's"—and both she and Mel say the words at the same time—"a new normal."

Driving away from his charred home, heading back toward his ministry, Mel talks about the ruined landscape around him.

"Has the government failed us in New Orleans and Louisiana? I would say yes. But has God failed us? No. And I think that's gonna be the witness of this whole tragedy: the government is not the one you're gonna be able to turn to. Only God is the one you're gonna be able to turn to."

He rounds a corner and climbs the Danziger Bridge back over the Industrial Canal.

"You know I've had some devastating things happen to me in life. There've been times when Momma couldn't help; Daddy couldn't help me; wife couldn't console me; brothers and sisters couldn't help me; *nobody* could help me. Where do you go in those times? What do you *do* in those times? . . . When I was struggling with drug addiction, nobody could help me."

He's fallen into the cadence of a short sermon, complete with pauses and repetitions. He continues as he drives over the bridge into an industrial area: open space, railroad tracks, an occasional factory.

"People would tell me, 'Pull yourself up by your bootstraps. Get on with life! Help yourself.' Well, I *couldn't* help myself." Pause. "And I didn't know why. And I'm not a weak man, or a give-up kind of man."

His profile against the landscape is hawk-like: beaked nose, tough jaw, bald dome. "But I'd given up. Drugs had beaten me down so bad that I had given up. The *only* one you can turn to when you lose a child, when you have a heart attack, when you have cancer: you know, everybody gets real religious then. But that's it! That time the *only* one that can help you is God. And God helped me."

He swallows, gets his breath.

"So, no matter what I come through—lots of people with this Katrina thing will struggle. They lost their home; they lost this; they lost that. Well, I lived for three years on the street. Homeless. God taught me during that time that the value is not in the things, but in your relationship. *God values people.* The Bible says, 'God so loved the world that He gave his only begotten son.' He so loved the world? Who's the world? The world is people."

Instead of heading back to the ministry, Mel decides to take Harry down toward Backatown. He crosses a flat, man-made landscape hacked out of a dead cypress swamp. He slows to point out where MR-GO meets the Industrial Canal: the juncture where the surge from the Gulf overwhelmed the city. They're driving the same route the flood took.

"That whole ship canal should be shut down," Mel declares. Before it was built, the U.S. Department of Interior warned that digging MR-GO would result in "widespread ecological consequences," funneling saltwater into the bayou's freshwater swamps. By the time the Army Corps of Engineers finished in 1965, the canal had destroyed an estimated 20,000 acres of marshland. And it ended up barely helping the economy: on average, it was used by no more than one ship a day. After the oil crisis, in 1988, the St. Bernard Parish Council unanimously passed a resolution to close it altogether but got nowhere. Then Katrina hit, and MR-GO acted as kind of accelerator. At the height of the flood, Lake Pontchartrain was up ten feet and the Industrial Canal fifteen, while MR-GO was cresting at eighteen feet above normal.

Mel glances at the now-calm surface of the canal. "Because of people like Bollinger Shipyard and other wealthy people who have their shipyard business there, they won't allow the government—and notice I said they won't *allow* the government—to shut it down. They're so powerful—" He leaves the sentence there.

From the time it was first proposed, MR-GO pitted business needs—providing for the shipyards and a nearby Lockheed Martin plant—against environmental and residential ones. Business triumphed. The founder of the shipyard, Donald Bollinger, was known as "the Happy Republican." A leading party fund-raiser and a delegate to the national convention, Bollinger "believed in the American way," according to the company website. "He believed that each of us as individuals has the opportunity for the pursuit of happiness . . . He believed that it was critically important to be involved in politics." As Mel sees it, this particular American way—this pursuit of happiness—helped create the route that the floodwaters took to the city.

After the disaster, "Boysie" Bollinger, son of the founder, sat on Mayor Nagin's Bring New Orleans Back Commission—the one that advocated for a smaller footprint, a boutique city. He agreed with President Bush that entrepreneurship was the key to recovery. The Christmas after Katrina, Boysie dined with the president and proclaimed him "probably the best friend Louisiana has."

But in the wake of the floods, the public has begun to mistrust business as usual. As the city's main newspaper, the *Times-Picayune*, puts it, there's suddenly "widespread sympathy in arguing people's lives should trump economics." A spokesperson for Bollinger has warned that closing the canal would mean losing some 300 jobs: "Bollinger Gulf Repair would probably cease to exist." But in the new normal, that threat has less potency. Today, as Mel slows to look over MR-GO, Congress is in the process of requesting a plan to fill and close the canal for good.

That still leaves the question of how the city's post-flood economy is going to recover. This part of the Upper Ninth that Mel and Harry are driving through has gone from swamp to city dump to poor people's housing and now stands in ruins.

Harry looks out at the high grass, the abandoned buildings, the closed factories. "Doesn't look real busy, does it?"

"No," Mel answers. "National Linen Service . . . that serviced the hotels and restaurants—they were back here." The station wagon bucks on the bad road. "This is an area I used to buy drugs in. This little place right here across the street." He nods toward a blank, two-story storefront on a stretch of empty sidewalk.

A little farther on, Mel points to a few duplexes sitting isolated and empty. "They used to have what was called the Desire housing project right behind this row of housing. But they've torn that down." Desire (named after nearby Desire Street) opened in 1956: one of the city's last and largest attempts at postwar urban renewal. It replaced twelve blocks of workers' houses, tenements, and small businesses, including the Hideaway Club, where Fats Domino got his start. In their place, the city built a monolithic project consisting of 262 buildings with more than 1,800 apartments. Desire was a world unto itself, a world mostly of poor black children: over 10,500 residents, 75 percent of them under twenty-one. Government-designed and -run, deliberately isolated from the rest of the city, Desire amounted to a new definition of home.

It wasn't long before this home was known as the "Dirty D": sewers leaked, garbage collection was slow, there were high levels of rape and assault.

"They started tearing it down before the flood," Mel explains. "It was infiltrated with drugs . . . It was time." In its place, he points out, "they have some new housing coming up. But they're gonna destroy that, because they want the commercial property. The business people want that land; it's right next to the shipping canal."

"They sure ain't gonna rebuild most of this," Harry says, peering out from behind his dark glasses.

"Destruction, destruction, destruction," is Mel's response.

Their car drops in and out of a pothole, then drives over railroad tracks. Mel nods toward an empty park. "No children. That's something else you notice, looking around. You don't see any children . . ."

"Do they even have schools open here?" Harry asks.

"Very few . . . You just go and go and go, and you don't see people, and you don't see children."

Mel swings onto the Claiborne Avenue Bridge, looking down on Backatown. He keeps returning to these ruined blocks as if they could somehow explain what's happening to his city.

"There were businesses that stood here. Now they're just gone. Those are driveways that led to homes. Look at this house here, Harry! Just taken from its foundation, turned to its side." The emptiness affects both of them. "Levee break happened right here, Harry."

A silence.

Mel arrives at the blue house. "This is a group called Common Ground. A group of young people who've come into town when they heard the government was going to start taking people's land. They came in, and they started helping us here." He says it with some pride. This, too, is part of the new normal.

I Want to Keep Fighting Till . . .

(October 2006)

This sunny fall morning, Brandon steps out of Common Ground's blue house. He's got on a flannel shirt, open a couple of buttons, and is carrying a white Styrofoam coffee cup. With his dark hair cropped short, sunglasses pushed up on his head, a handsome five o'clock shadow, he looks much the same. But this isn't home anymore. He no longer has an official position at Common Ground.

As he crosses the raggedy front lawn, he looks over the hand-painted signs stuck there. "I remember it was a big deal for us: we put a sign out, and it said 'Eminent Domain for Who?' And it was supposed to be 'for Whom.' And we had this huge argument 'cause it sounded pretentious to say 'for Whom.'" He grins and shakes his head: at the tiny issues Common Ground debated, at the process of collective decision making, at the time that's passed since his early days here.

On the corner, he takes a right and starts walking the short block to the levee. He points across the street to a small white church, caved in along one side and barely standing. "One of the things that helped protect us was the commander. That was her husband's church."

He stops and considers.

"The majority of the New Orleans Police Department hated us. And the federal government hated us. 'Cause of what we are as activists and organizers, the stances we take." He licks his red, chapped lips. The exception was "the cops from this area . . . It was their grandmothers and their mothers and their babies who were left to have to wade through toxic water, ya know? So they were kinda renegade in terms of how they treated us . . .'"

If anything, NOPD's reputation got even worse during and immediately after Katrina. Some 250 officers deserted the flooded city. Malik and others reported incidents of cops shooting unarmed citizens. A month later, the Associated Press videotaped police beating a defenseless sixty-year-old African American in the French Quarter. By then, the chief had already resigned. In the shake-up that followed, Captain Bernadine Kelly, a black woman, was appointed commander of the district that includes Backatown.

"I remember when this started, I went in to Captain Kelly . . . and I said, 'Well, I'm gonna be moving into the Lower Ninth Ward in this house.' And she said, 'I know about it.' And I said, 'Okay. Well, I'm not moving in there with guns. And we're not fortifying it. If you want to come in and arrest me, you can just come in. There's no door, actually, so you don't have to send a SWAT team. It doesn't have to be like that. We can be civil to each other.'"

Brandon's Texas twang slides toward New Orleans.

"And she said, 'Well, if you move in there, and you're there between four p.m. and eight in the morning, we're gonna arrest you.'" He nods slightly, acknowledging that this was her next logical move.

"And I said, 'But you have to understand: there are like forty-two attorneys that want you to arrest me!' We didn't have forty-two attorneys, but we did have a bunch of attorneys helping." He smiles.

"And I said, 'But if you *don't* arrest me, you have to understand, you're gonna have a hard time explaining why a white guy, who's lived there for three days, is allowed . . . and you're arresting elderly black men that have been living in that community for fifty years. So either way that curfew's gonna have to go, ya know?'"

He remembers the police commander saying, "'Okay, Brandon, you do what you have to do. And I'm gonna do what I have to do . . .' And I said, 'Okay.' And she said, 'Just so you know, my husband's church is right there across the street from you.' And she winked at me!"

Brandon grins some more and nods toward the ruined church.

"It was different then, though." He takes a sip from his coffee, looks out over Backatown. "There was a lot of debris around." Now there's an occasional abandoned house but mostly acres of tall grass and weed.

"We had to make this rule," Brandon remembers, "that only twenty activists from Common Ground could be working over here. Because something we learned was that when you go into an affected community and you want to organize, and you want to provide space for a marginalized community to get involved in their own recovery efforts, rather than doing the traditional," he puts air quotes around the word, "which is a very white, Western imperialist approach—go in and be white saviors or something . . ."

He takes a breath and decides to start over.

"We realized in the *Upper* Ninth Ward, one of the mistakes we'd made is we got the community kitchen rolling. And everything that needed to be done was being done by outside volunteers." This was in their original center at the Mount Carmel Baptist Church.

In contrast, when the organization moved to Backatown, it tried to stick closer to its motto, "Solidarity Not Charity." Brandon helped set up a tool library so returning homeowners could borrow pry bars, dust masks, respirators. "If the residents want to gut each other's houses, then here are the tools, ya know? . . . And if the residents want to have a community kitchen, here are the pots and pans, and here's the food. But you'all gotta figure out who's cooking it. 'Cause if *you* don't do it, it's gonna end up being some vegan dish with curry and—and *ginger*." He grimaces. "A lot of ginger. Which I don't eat anymore, because at this point it makes me sick." A quick smile.

Brandon walks past a pair of abandoned cars and approaches the spot where the levee breached. Except he can't find it. And he isn't sure when the levee got repaired or how long it's taken the contractors to clear Backatown. He stops at an empty lot marked off with yellow emergency tape. Inside is a set of stairs that rises to nowhere. He takes off his sunglasses, puts down his coffee cup, and sits.

"There was this company here called ECC," he begins. It's the same California-based corporation that the dump truck driver railed against—the one, Brandon points out, that had a number of U.S. government debris-removal contracts in Iraq and Afghanistan. "There was this whole thing where they were trying to bulldoze homes *without* people's permission. Keep in mind that there were still residents—dead elderly black people's bones—in a lot of these homes."

He gestures behind as if Backatown were still a smashed landscape. He's motioning toward emptiness.

Common Ground believed ECC's bulldozing was the first step toward the city seizing property. The confrontation, in Brandon's words, "got very intense." One day a man showed up at the blue house: "a finisher," Brandon calls him. "He does negotiations in tense political situations . . . He came, and he said, 'All we want to do is a debris removal. So let's work out some way in which we can do the debris removal, and we won't have thousands of activists, like, knocking our bulldozers over. Or burning our equipment or something.'"

Again, Brandon nods at the expected, logical move.

"And I was like, 'Well we can talk about it.' So we set up this meeting. And then he calls before this meeting, and he says he has some friends from Homeland Security who want to be there." Brandon's gray eyes sharpen. "And I was, like, okay. So I call my friends who are videographers. So when they came in the house, we had videographers on it." He mimes a camera turning and grins.

As Brandon recalls the conversation, he told the ECC man, "The mere fact that I'm sitting here in a community that's 99.8 percent African American—or was before you allowed them to be decimated and sent across the country—yet, you're meeting with the one white dude . . . instead of meeting with any of the black community leaders." He takes a breath. "There's something wrong with that. You're trying to work a deal with me. There's something off here."

But the pattern continued. "This guy starts inviting me to these meetings after that: with FEMA, the Army Corps of Engineers, and the city folks. Everybody would meet and try to determine how to start to get the work done in this area. 'Cause they couldn't do it because of all the activists and the revolutionaries."

One of the proposals was for ECC to bring in a security firm. "Put up a chain-link fence and have Blackwater guard the area. And I was: 'You really shouldn't do that. 'Cause this is what the activist community is going to do. You have the folks on the left concerned about the marginalized community. You have the folks on the right wing—most of them are armed—and they're concerned about private property rights . . . So you really shouldn't do that. It's gonna turn really ugly. And then I'm gonna go to prison'—he points to his chest—'and we're gonna have all these issues.'" His voice is low, precise, a little dangerous.

Instead, Brandon says, they finally came to an agreement. "'If you want to make the money doing the debris removal, there's enough people that want the debris removal done on their property to keep you'all busy. Just tell the city you're not gonna do it to houses that don't have permission.'"

But even with permission, Brandon adds, they didn't plan to check for remains. "They were just gonna scoop it up as debris." He remembers threatening ECC with a media campaign. "You're gonna get scapegoated," he told the finisher, "and lose your job. So why don't you just start doing it right?'" He licks his lips, a breeze tugging at his blue flannel shirt. "And so they did . . . And since that they've found—as of two or three months ago—they found seventeen more individual remains here." He points down the length of the levee.

Brandon, in his early thirties, talks about these victories like some war veteran: weary, proud, a little confused.

"It's been a struggle *the entire way*. Every nice thing that the government has helped with—whether it be the city, the state, or the federal government—has been fought for tooth and nail. Ya know? Tooth and nail! And it gets tiring."

Sitting in the empty lot, he looks down at his scuffed boots.

"A lot of us had this problem. When the Upper Ninth Ward project started, they'd come by once or twice a night and pull us out . . . It was miserable." He's licking his lips, blinking his eyes. "You got to where, in a position of leadership, you couldn't take your fucking clothes off. 'Cause you didn't have any time. So people would do security shifts. And you'd lay there at night." He demonstrates by lying back on the concrete stoop, covering his eyes with his hands. "And you'd start to doze off. And then: 'Brandon, Brandon!'" He pounds his own thigh with one hand. "'National Guard! National Guard! National Guard!' And you're like, 'Oh fuck, man. Okay.'"

He sits up, then stands.

"And you get to the door"—he walks from the stoop into the dirt street—"and it's like, 'Boom, boom boom: National Guard!'" He hits his palm with a fist. "'Boom, boom, boom: National Guard!' 'I'm coming, man, I just woke up. Let me put on my shirt.' 'National Guard, open up! I'm coming in.'

"The twenty other activists in this house are, like, twenty years old. They've never experienced anything like this, never been arrested. So I better get out of the house so these guys don't come in with their guns.

"And you're so angry you just want to kill the guy." He raises both hands and shakes them, as if strangling someone. "But you can't kill these guys 'cause they would . . . kill you." He laughs and moves his hands to his close-cropped head, holding it. "There are also moral attachments," he says, wide-eyed, "to why it's not good to kill people . . .

"But that happened *all the time*. That's what it was like initially. So a lot of us, we leave here"—he strides purposefully down the beat-up road, miming his departure—"go back home, and you're like, 'You can drink tap water? You *have* tap water? You can take a shower?!' . . . Your perspective's totally different. And then you go to bed at night and you take your boots off, and you're like, 'You know? I can't sleep without my boots on!' So you keep your boots on."

He's suddenly come to the end of a run of words. He squats back on the stoop, lights a cigarette, scratches his short beard.

"I left to go to Venezuela. To ask Hugo Chavez for money. For the Ninth Ward residents." He laughs a little, sips some coffee. "I guess it was April or March." By then, Common Ground was a national and international phenomenon: a radical, volunteer collective trying to change the course of the city's recovery. Some say the trip to Venezuela was to get money for rebuilding; some say it was part of Brandon's dream to create a guerrilla movement in the swamps of Louisiana.

"You know, when I went to Venezuela, I was so excited about that government." His voice is soft. "I was so excited about Fidel Castro. And I was so excited when I heard stories about how the Panthers went to Algeria and fled the United States."

He puts out his cigarette, carefully G.I.-ing the butt, then picks up a long blade of grass.

"So I was in Venezuela, and I started realizing that there were faults with what was happening there, too. I started realizing there were some faults with Cuba." He nods, still soft-spoken. "And then I met someone who the Cubans had turned over to the CIA, that was a U.S. revolutionary . . . and I really had to start looking at power."

He plays with the blade of grass, studying it.

According to Brandon, "someone in the Venezuelan government" told him that seeking funds from Chavez might be illegal—that when he tried to reenter the United States, he could be arrested for treason. The trip was, by all accounts, a failure, and when Brandon returned, he was a changed man. As he now puts it, he started "looking at power dynamics."

With Malik off fund-raising, Brandon had often functioned as his second-in-command. Though the collective believed decisions should be arrived at through consensus—even decisions as small as the grammar on a sign—here in Backatown, Brandon had been something of a lone wolf: camping out with only a few others, dodging the National Guard, negotiating with the police.

"It's nice to have the notoriety. Initially, it was very important that we had a spokesperson, a co-founder that was laying out the message . . . Name recognition helps to get access to resources, to help people; it helps to protect you." But, he says, it can also lead to "celebrity trips."

When he came back from Venezuela, he wanted to change that, change what he calls "a white strongman in leadership." There had to be a way the collective—made up predominantly of white out-of-towners, including himself—could "share power and share decision making" with black residents.

Some of the young anarchists and feminists were eager for Brandon to step away. To them, he'd become the personification of what had gone wrong with Common Ground. Instead of modeling how a just society might work, it had turned "hierarchical" and "authoritarian."

"There was a time when I was running things," Brandon says, "and I was running things . . ." He holds his hands up like blinders on each side of his head. "I was doing it for good reasons. But then there came a time to shed that . . . and allow more people to have access to decision making . . . And Common Ground," shakes his head, "became so big."

During spring break 2006, Common Ground hosted 2,800 students from 275 colleges. The volunteers needed to be fed, housed, organized into work groups, kept safe. Costs began to run over $70,000 a month. The skills the collective needed were becoming less revolutionary, more administrative.

It made Brandon restless. He lobbied Malik to send him to Lebanon to apply the Common Ground model to what was happening in the Middle East. But to Malik, Brandon wasn't just changed; he'd had a nervous breakdown. "When he came back, he was messed up in the head." The ex-Panther told Brandon, "You need to go home, stay at home, get your mind together, and *then* come back."

So Brandon's been living in Austin for the past few months. Though he needed the break, he feels guilty about it, sees it as more evidence of his own white privilege. He launches into a description of what the people in the Lower Ninth have endured historically, starting with slavery, through sugar plantations and prisons, right up to the failed school system and the conditions at the Superdome. His point is that when they get depressed or burn out, they can't go home. "[But] I can . . . And I can go through three months of therapy, go through my PTSD stuff, and finally get to a point where I can take my boots off at night and sleep without my boots on."

He looks down, tongue flicking chapped lips.

"It's really weird to go from where four or five people want to inter-view you a day to a place where I just want to plant a garden. Plant a fucking garden! And go fish. And have a relationship.

"I was at a point, because of what I saw, where I wanted to take up arms and start—yeah—fomenting some change. That's where I was at. And a lot of people were there. And it sounds funny; I realize it kinda is. And it sounds so foreign." He jerks his thumb at the empty blocks of Backatown. "We know that our government is corrupt . . . How do you stop it?" He speaks carefully. "You don't use violence; I wouldn't do that. Nor is it necessary to do that . . . [Common Ground] used something called 'service-oriented direct action.' We saw a hole where people's needs weren't being met. And we filled that hole . . . by any means nec-essary. That was our logo at first: 'Humanitarian Aid by Any Means Necessary.' "

It's an adaptation of the Malcolm X phrase, and in many ways, Com-mon Ground has modeled itself on that activist era. As one of Brandon's co-founders puts it, they took ideas like the Panthers' free breakfast pro-gram and started "mixing those concepts with modern anarchist in-terpretations." Cleaning out the MLK school, organizing community kitchens, offering medical services: the Panthers used to call these kinds of actions "survival programs pending revolution."

According to its own data, Common Ground has helped gut a thou-sand houses in the past year and set up nine distribution centers. Bran-don is modest about his role in all this, though clearly proud of the accomplishments. And he sees what's happened in New Orleans as a model for a new kind of radical organizing. But it hasn't satisfied him. Or his anger.

"I have definitely gotten more radical. It feels like in this country—and excuse my analogy—but it feels like there's a woman being raped right here." He points to the dusty, rutted road in front of him. "And I'm like, 'Hey, this woman's being raped. Let's stop this guy.' " He stares at the spot on the road. "And you guys are all like, 'Well, bro, hold on. Why don't we talk about it and just ask him to stop?' And I'm like, 'Okay.' " He sits back, pretending to relax slightly. "So we ask him to stop for a while, and," clears his throat, "he doesn't stop. And I'm like, 'Okay! I don't give a shit what you'all say: that has to stop! I'm not gonna talk about how I don't like it; I'm not gonna hold up a sign; I'm gonna *stop that.*' You know?" He's back to staring at the imaginary rape in the road, all focused intensity.

"There's nothing *wrong* with me stopping that from happening. Physically stopping it."

He's a muscular guy, and there's a pent-up fury to this speech. He's trembling slightly.

"I feel like that's what's happening. We're in this country, and because there's so much privilege, there're all these women being raped right here. And we're all *talking* about it!" He spreads his hands and sits upright in disbelief. "We have to reevaluate. As much as it sounds radical, we have to reevaluate what we're doing . . . If it doesn't stop the rape, it's nothing more than some form of alleviating our own guilt. And making us feel better."

He stares down the sunny road, eyes blurred, then exhales slowly.

Common Ground "was radical," Brandon says; "Now it's not. It's radically different and challenging and helping and inspiring to a lot of people. But—" He picks another blade of grass and considers the collective from his present position as a retired member.

"It was radical when it first started. To have a stand-down with the government." Breaking the curfew, confronting ECC: these were stand-downs. But Common Ground's new normal is housing college kids and sending them out to clean storm drains. It's not that different from other volunteer groups like ACORN, or Habitat for Humanity, or the Catholic Charities. As Brandon sees Common Ground, "[It's] been effective for a percentage of the population . . . ten to fifteen percent of the population. That's being helped here and otherwise wouldn't have had any help. But there's still a big percentage of the population that *isn't* getting helped.

"It's been effective in the sense that it's a very large manifestation of the radical left doing something." He chops the air with one hand. "Of human beings doing something when their government fails. But is it effective overall? Does it change the system that created this in the first place?"

He shakes his head no.

"Is that levee," points, "that was built to the same standards . . . gonna [fail] again? Yeah! Are these people?" Stands up. "Look around: you see FEMA trailers here? I don't see any . . ."

A breeze moves through the acres of weeds.

"These are all little *lots*. Not fields or football fields. These are fucking people's homes! Everybody else got a fucking FEMA trailer." He's standing and pointing. "They're sitting in a FEMA trailer, and their house is getting rebuilt . . . But not these people. So, is it successful?"

He shakes his head again and paces a little ways down the road, then back.

"It's successful for some people. But it's not changing anything. It's not *challenging* anything! . . . Their system will just go on and on and continue doing the same thing. Unless we, as people, don't accept it."

Pacing, spinning, he seems like he has nowhere to go, nowhere to spend himself.

What's needed, he says, is to "truly figure out ways to stop these folks from doing this. This is a decision." He points out over the emptiness of Backatown. "This is a choice."

The next day, across the Industrial Canal in the Tremé neighborhood, another early organizer of Common Ground, Suncere, stands in front of a Catholic church. He's wearing baggy chino shorts that reach to midcalf, a gray and white camouflage shirt, a blue jacket. On the jacket, a pin with the Black Panther logo of a crouching black cat.

Suncere's still got his goatee and a faint moustache, that tattoo of the African continent under his left eye. But he doesn't look well. He's put on weight—even bigger across the chest and in the face—his black skin ashy, his dreads tangled and uncared for.

"This the whole history," he's saying. He nods toward a twelve-foot-long metal cross propped in the church courtyard. Iron slave shackles are welded to it; smaller crosses stick up nearby. Suncere reads from a bronze plaque embedded in the church wall:

> *The Tomb of the Unknown Slave* . . . This St. Augustine/Tremé shrine honors all slaves buried throughout the United States and those in particular who lie beneath the ground of Tremé in unmarked, unknown graves. There is no doubt that the campus of St. Augustine Church sits astride the blood, sweat, tears, and some of the mortal remains of unknown slaves . . . In other words, the Tomb of the Unknown Slave is a constant reminder that we are walking on holy ground.

Back when Brandon was having stand-downs in the Lower Ninth, Suncere was doing less dramatic work: organizing Common Ground distribution centers. "I would have to travel from Houma"—he pronounces it Homer—"pick up ten volunteers, stuff them in that little truck, take 'em down there, do the work, feed 'em, make sure they had water, turn around, bring 'em back to New Orleans after the workday, then turn around and go *back* to Houma 'cause that's where I was stationed at." The collective, Suncere says, is a miracle. "But it's a hard-ass working miracle. Common Ground didn't come together by magic. We had dedicated people who could do five things at one time." He estimates he put about 1,400 miles on his truck each week. Twice he dozed off at the wheel. One time he pulled into a McDonald's, only to fall asleep in the parking lot from eight-thirty till one in the morning, "the car still running!" He woke long enough to get a hotel room; then "I slept for two days."

Suncere starts talking about the red pickup he drove down from North Carolina. "It's a 1977 Scottsdale," he says proudly. "A classic. And I named it after Harriet Tubman, the great general Harriet Tubman . . . It's a 400 V8: big block! It's not a joke . . . I bought this truck with my dad's insurance money. When he passed away . . ." After Suncere made his two-year commitment to Malik, he stenciled the Common Ground logo on the truck's door. Instead of transporting black people out of the city—Suncere's original plan—it spent months ferrying young white volunteers into broken neighborhoods. And then it was stolen.

"I was breaking up a fight Sunday morning and left the keys in the damn thing. And this drunk white man jumped in my truck and drove off! I was crushed. Everything I talked about, I done in this truck: St. Bernard's, Plaquemines, Houma—all in this truck. You *know* NOPD ain't gonna look for a Common Ground truck, too! I felt like a stone about to crack."

Without a vehicle, he had to stop supervising the distro centers. In some ways, that may have been a good thing. By then it was March, spring break had begun, and Common Ground's core organizers were trying to deal with the influx of volunteers. Suncere ended up exhausted and broke.

"Being an activist, there's not a lot of money involved in it. Often no money at all. So my partner at the time, at Common Ground, felt sorry for me and got me involved with this AmeriCorps program, which pays you a stipend for doing mediation. 'Cause we were doing it anyway," shrugs, "so why not get paid for it? It's like a two-hundred-and-fifty-dollar stipend you get every two weeks."

During his training, Suncere got to talking with his AmeriCorps supervisor and heard about some problems over at a church called St. Augustine. The archdiocese wanted to close it and move its popular priest, Father Jerome LeDoux, out of the neighborhood.

Like many other organizations, the Catholic archdiocese saw the floods as an opportunity. In the mid-twentieth century, New Orleans had a white Catholic majority and was considered "unique" for its large percentage of black Catholics. By the time of the floods, the metropolitan area was still home to nearly half a million members of the faith, but that number was declining, and congregations were more and more made up of poor people. Nationally, the Catholic Church had been closing or clustering urban congregations for decades; sex abuse scandals and subsequent financial settlements had only made the situation worse. After the floods, the Archdiocese of New Orleans estimated it would face an additional 25 to 30 percent drop in congregants. Plus, it had a $40 million budget deficit—and storm damage to two-thirds of its buildings. Without giving specifics, the archdiocese announced a "post-Katrina realignment" that would "close damaged churches, dissolve struggling parishes and re-assign priests."

The question was which congregations would be realigned. That was determined, in part, by the new normal: the city had fewer black people and fewer poor people. In February, when the archbishop called Father LeDoux to tell him St. Augustine would be closing, the reason given wasn't flood damage: the nineteenth-century building had come through all right. Instead, the archdiocese cited the "small number of baptisms, first Communions, confessions and confirmations." In a subsequent letter, the archbishop wrote: "As we move toward the Easter season, let us pray that these changes will bring new life to the church."

To St. Augustine's congregants and other Tremé residents, it looked more like the end of a proud tradition. St. Augustine was founded in 1841 by the city's *gens de couleur libres*. In what's been called "an unprecedented social, political, and religious move," these free people of color also bought pews for slaves. With whites, free blacks, and slaves worshipping together, St. Augustine became arguably the most integrated congregation in pre–Civil War America. Its cherished Afrocentric tradition had been renewed right before the floods, when the jazz-loving, dashiki-wearing Father LeDoux dedicated the Tomb of the Unknown Slave.

The archdiocese maintained that the closing of St. Augustine was "purely administrative." But a church chaplain reflected the feelings of many of the congregants: "First they said it was financial. After that, it was the [attendance] numbers—and our numbers are up high, high. And after that, it was the administrative piece, and we disproved that." He accused the archdiocese of "racism, ethnic cleansing, and land grabbing." As one reverend put it, "Archbishop Hughes kept saying the plan wasn't about race, but it was."

When Suncere's supervisor filled him in, his first instinct was to take action. "I was like, 'Oh! They're not listening? Well, all you need is a drop squad to get their attention.' And she's like, 'What's a drop squad?' And I explained to her, and she seemed really interested." His serious expression folds into a grin.

Suncere went to a couple of meetings and suggested that if the archdiocese went ahead with its plan, a small group of activists—a drop squad—should occupy the church. "They was dead against a takeover," he remembers. "I mean, these people are *devout* Catholics. They are *not* rebellious people. Especially against the archdiocese. So it almost didn't happen."

Then Suncere offered up a counterargument. "Not pretending to know the Bible backwards and forwards or nothin', but I remembered a story about Jesus going into the temple and turning over the tables." His voice rises a little. "And I was like, 'Believe it or not, that's a form of protest. And I'm not saying we run up into the governor's mansion and do that, but we have to take a stand. 'Cause once this time has passed, you're going to be sitting home miserable for the rest of your lives. 'Cause you didn't move. 'Cause you didn't exhaust'"—he says this next part slowly and carefully,—"'every avenue possible to keep this church.'

"They thought about it—and they gave me the okay. I always kinda knew they was gonna give it anyway." He smiles. After months of service-oriented direct action, here at last was a stand-down.

"Originally I wanted to take four or five black people with me. But it didn't happen like that. I took a few white college students with me because I had to get them together at a drop of a hat. We didn't know exactly when Father LeDoux was leaving. We had to do it behind Father LeDoux's back. Because LeDoux was dedicated to the church: he wouldn't have done anything against the archdiocese or the order. We had to wait until LeDoux left."

On March 15, 2006, the notice came that St. Augustine would be officially closed. Father LeDoux celebrated his final mass March 19 and the next day left quietly. "It was comical," Suncere says. "Because as soon as he got in his car and drove off, we went right in the doorway behind him. He didn't even see us! Nailed the doors up and everything and began our sit-in."

Twelve people, two of them parishioners, occupied the church—Suncere calls them the "St. Augustine Twelve." "I think the people I took in there were selected by God himself. It wasn't an accident; it was a miracle that we stayed in there that long." Smiling, suddenly animated, he adds: "It woulda been a mess if they'd have charged that building . . . because when I tell you we had a national movement on our doorsteps, we had one *comin'*!" Nodding his head for emphasis. "We was havin' people come from all over the United States. To sit in here. It was probably one of the best experiences I ever had as an organizer. This whole area"—he gestures at the courtyard out in front of the Tomb—"was full of people every single day.

"They fed the hell out of us! I think I put on another twenty pounds—a pound a day—sitting in there. I mean they would cook for us: jambalaya, gumbo, them good doughnuts from Henry's every morning." He laughs. "And socks, drawers, mouthwash, toothpaste. 'Cause we had to take the building immediately. We didn't have time to pack."

The protest brought media attention; that was part of the plan. Suncere enlisted the head of Common Ground's tree removal team as his "stuntman. He's the one climbed on top of the church with his gear and dropped our banner . . . That was cool! . . . That banner was like a key piece, like planting our flag."

Professionally made, blue letters on white, the banner read:

MANY COLORS . . . MANY RACES . . .
SAVE ST. AUGUSTINE PARISH

In smaller letters was a quote from Pope John Paul II's visit here in 1987: "All churches should be like St. Augustine."

"We had everybody in that rectory with us," Suncere says. "John, he was a parishioner. We had a sister that was like twenty-one years old . . . When they were trying to paint us as these crusty outsiders . . . I was like, 'No, we need a press conference. And put her in front of them.' And we had another comrade of mine, Jimmy, who's raised in Jehovah's Witness! . . .

"All the right-wing radio stations was against us, but with us calling in—one thing you have to be able to do is counter the enemy's attacks." He grins. "And that's what they didn't count on: that we had good strategies. And the second—I didn't wait—the *second* they put some more craziness about us in the paper, bam! We responded. Bam! We responded. We had to counteract all that craziness. And we beat 'em back! Right-wing radio stations, the type Rush Limbaugh would be on, was

like: 'I don't know, folks. I'm kinda on the side of the parishioners now.'"
Suncere cocks his head. "It was breakin' their back."

The sit-in went on for nineteen days. Suncere's about to explain how
they lasted that long when he spots a middle-aged woman crossing the
street. She has short black hair, tobacco-colored skin, a striped shirt, red
eyeglasses, a big smile. "Hey now!" he shouts. When she comes over, he
gives her a bear hug. She launches right in.

"Both my children were christened in this church. So I wasn't about
ready to give it up. And my mother was buried through this church, so I
wasn't giving it up. And that brought me back to church. So God works
in strange ways."

"Strange and mysterious ways," Suncere chimes in.

"I was taking my daily walk," the woman explains. "I saw a kid I grew
up with." She corrects herself: "Kid? We ain't no kids: we're in our fifties!
And he told me what was going on. And I had no idea because . . . I'd just
come out of the hospital from having a stroke . . . So I told my daughter
what I was going to do: I was gonna come over here and sit with them
during the day. 'Cause I wasn't working or anything . . . So I come out
here every day, and we had fellowship with the church members and
these young people that were here from Common Ground . . . That's why
the archbishop don't like Common Ground now."

Suncere nods, beaming. "That's right." He suddenly looks stronger,
healthier.

"It's coming back," the woman continues, "slowly but surely. You know
we got our priest? He seems to be a young Father LeDoux."

"Get out of here!" Suncere throws one arm in the air, smiling, laughing. His square, thick body does a victory dance. "These people went
down *swinging*. They got back up and knocked them *out*." He giggles.

In the six months since, the woman explains, "we've gotten more parishioners. And that's a good thing. And old sinners like me come back
to the church? *That's* a good thing."

Suncere giggles some more. His whole face opens up, relaxes.

"But we couldn't have done it without them," the woman says. "Him
and his buddies—"

"Sorry about that mass," Suncere interrupts. He holds a straight face
for a moment, then dissolves into laughter.

The Sunday after Father LeDoux's departure, the archdiocese sent an
outside priest to conduct mass. He arrived accompanied by ten security

guards, some of them armed. During the service, protesters walked up and down the aisles with signs: OBEY GOD, NOT MONEY. The priest kept being interrupted, and finally, when the protestors led the congregation in singing—"Like a tree planted by the river / We shall not be moved"—he cancelled the mass and left.

The day after, the archbishop accused the demonstrators of "sacrilege," ordered them to "vacate the premises immediately," then removed the holy sacrament and closed the church "for the foreseeable future."

"Yeah," Suncere nods, "they took the sacred sacrament. And what little money the church had, they went into the safe and took that, too . . . saying we decimated the church."

"Desecrated," the woman gently corrects. "That *we* desecrated the church. But we didn't desecrate the church 'cause nobody had a gun . . . Yes, we did have outside help, but you can't always do it by yourself."

"Where there's injustice," Suncere says, "there is no boundaries."

"Right."

The protesters kept gaining support and national media attention, until on April 8 the archbishop backed down. His letter read, in part: "We have been able with humility and honesty to acknowledge deficiencies in St. Augustine's Parish and unfortunate missteps on the part of the archdiocese." The church was reconsecrated and reopened. Father LeDoux came back as a visiting priest for a Palm Sunday "victory mass."

The woman has to go. She gives Suncere a farewell hug and heads back down the street.

The victory mass, Suncere continues, was "one of the most beautiful things I ever been a part of." At the same time, he appreciated the irony: a self-professed revolutionary leading a drop squad to keep a church open.

"I was sitting there in the middle of this mass, and I'm talking to God." Suncere grins. "All this is going on around me—celebration, singing—and I'm looking at the ceiling, and I'm like: 'Look, God, this people got their goddamn church back. Can I get my fucking truck back now? I know you took it from me so I could do this damn action. Right?'" He's pointing into the air with one finger. "I didn't realize I had my phone on silent. The minute I said that, somebody called me and told me they'd found my truck."

He smiles, pauses.

"Believe that or not . . . I talk to God a lot. 'Cause we got a personal relationship. He uses me and knows me. He understands me."' Suncere's big arms are raised as he speaks. "I know I sound like a heathen, but . . . that's the relationship we got."

The victory here at St. Augustine, he explains, was "about human beings. How strong and dedicated human beings are. It's definitely not about me. It's also an example of what put Common Ground together: people who are willing to make great sacrifices . . . including the community here. These are *great* people in New Orleans. They always talking about the drugs and the violence, but you gonna have that. These are *beautiful* people."

He then points out a further irony: the stand-down was done behind Malik's back. "I was sworn to secrecy, so I couldn't even tell him I was going to do it. So he thought I was in Houma. And he cut on the news, and I was in the rectory!" Grins. "So to try to get him off my back . . . I would sneak out the rectory, go down to Houma, talk to my folks . . . a couple times a week . . . I went back and forth down there until we won it."

After the victory, Suncere took part in a two-week Common Ground fund-raising tour. "And my god, I barely got out of twelfth grade, but I was in Berkeley! Giving a talk! I was like, wow." Laughs.

Then, with his truck returned, it was back to the grinding drives to the distro centers. He'd sometimes sleep on the floor of the Common Ground office: no bed, no shower. Suncere says it was about a month ago that he cracked.

"I was thinking in my mind: 'I finally done lost it.' And I was crying. I couldn't stop crying. Snot. Shaking! It was like—man!—some kind of convalescent. [My partner at the time] kept talking to me, held my hands, telling me to come back. 'Come back. Everything's going to be okay.' About six o'clock that morning, I went to sleep. Woke up two hours later. I was still . . . screwed up." His eyes go red. "I think thanks to her, she saved me. She saved me. Because I was about that close to killing myself, too. She saw that in my eye. Stayed with me the whole time. Brought me back." A breath. "It ain't easy. It ain't easy. A lot of work, not a lot of reward. I guess you do it 'cause you *know* it's the right thing to do. 'Cause everybody ain't cut out for this."

He pauses to consider, standing on the curb outside St. Augustine.

"I don't have too much family. I'm not married; I don't have kids. The only reason I don't go back home is I think there's only one solution. That's why I'm scared to go back home."

Home for Suncere is Washington, D.C. "Four out of five—every child in Washington right now—will be incarcerated before they're eighteen.

Male and female. Our life expectancy is second [lowest] to Haiti's. Our infant mortality is second [highest] to Haiti's. Four emergency rooms have been closed, and that's before I left." He barely pauses for a breath. "There're over six hundred and forty NGOs for homelessness in Washington alone, yet we still have a nation of homeless. We have over four hundred NGOs for juvenile justice, yet those conditions still exist."

Rolling out these facts seems to give him a little burst of energy. But they're also why he hasn't gone home for rest and therapy the way Brandon has. Suncere's home has all the same issues as New Orleans. If he returns there having made no headway here, he's scared of what he might resort to.

"What am I gonna do? Sit there and talk to 'em? I can't theorize this shit out of 'em. I think the education is really important . . . but I can get you to really feel me, and the police can come in this community"—he gestures at the quiet residential street—"and shoot a twenty-four-year-old woman with two kids. What good is my words then? And I can't do shit about it! . . . What good am I? I can move you, but I can't move you to do anything about that. I can't even protect the women in my community."

His face is now a fixed mask, his voice soft and sad. He walks away from the church, his square body streaked with shadows from the tree limbs above. "I got to reevaluate and reassess what direction I want to go in to."

Now standing by the car door, he manages a thin smile. "What's gonna happen to the people of New Orleans? Coming from Washington, D.C. . . . I've seen gentrification . . ." Nods a little. "I've seen protests. I've seen people chain themselves to hospitals that's supposed to be closed. And yet and still, when the sun goes down, the government wins out." Nods again. "I believe that's what the National Guard's doing back here: to make sure the bankers' interest is being protected. I like to be optimistic, but I think we're gonna lose."

He says it almost without affect, as if it were a well-known fact.

"We've made a lot of history." Pause. "But I question that history if we lose. What good did we do if we lose? A lot of coaches would say, 'What's the intent of steppin' on the field if the intent is not to win? We rushed for three hundred and sixty-five yards today, but we lost.'" He sticks his chin out. "You know? 'Our wide receiver is going to Canton, Ohio, but we lost.' And that's how I kinda feel about it. It *can* be saved; there's still time. But if the American people," rolling his head from side to side, "don't look at the folks in New Orleans and the surrounding Gulf Coast and don't see themselves in their place, we're gonna lose." Nods for emphasis. "And we're losin'."

Pause.

"Me myself? All I ever really wanted to be—and I know it sound kinda mushy—all I ever wanted to be was a servant of the people. Especially after I came out of doing my little thing on the corner. I did a lot of bad things. But I did a lot of good things to try and make up for that. For me—I call it the Whirlwind; some people call it God—as long as the Whirlwind can use me in any capacity, I will continue to fight." Shrugs a little. "If I'm there, I'm gonna help ya. Might have to go through my little burnout phase to get my head back, to get right again. But I want to keep fighting till the day I die."

His voice has dropped.

"Not just for us, but for poor people all over the world. 'Cause it's an international fight . . . And I don't give a damn if nobody doesn't believe in it anymore. Like Che say, if I have to be the sole revolutionary, then so be it. 'Cause they really don't give you too many options any damn way. You gonna die any damn way."

Pause.

"Malik is probably one of *the* greatest visionaries I ever been around. I think the Whirlwind has selected him to run Common Ground the way he has . . . I think Malik's whole vision is to use the relief effort to build a collective effort in the community. And he's done that. The brother is employing forty-one people from the neighborhood! In Algiers. Right now!"

In April, Common Ground took over the management of a derelict apartment complex in Algiers. After freezing rents, it's begun what it estimates as a million-dollar improvement, training and hiring local residents to do the work, with the understanding that the owner will sell the building to Common Ground as soon as the repairs are done. The structure, near Malik's home, has become key to the cooperative's hopes: an alternative to business as usual, an answer to the question of how the city might move forward.

"[Malik] wants to build a community where there's black barbershops and this type of thing, but with a conscience. To rebuild this community back up again." Suncere says it in a loud voice. And then softer, looking away: "I think he knows we gonna lose. But he want to save as many people as he can. And I think he's doing a great job."

Nothing (Nothing) Has Been Decided (Has Been Decided)

(October 2006–January 2007)

Lathan has come a long way. He's sheet-rocked, spackled, and painted the bungalow on Burgundy. "I'm about to change the windows out," he says, as eager and nervously energetic as ever. "I have to go back to the original windows—wooden windows—because of the historic society. It's a little bit more money, but . . ."

He's changed his plans. Instead of moving in here himself, he and his son are turning it into a rental, meanwhile rehabbing his third house, a dozen blocks west, for the family to live in. It's his wife's idea; in fact, she's staying in Baton Rouge until it's finished. Lathan says the third house "has a lot more charm . . . I bought it [from] an old guy. And he's too old to do this again." It had water damage four feet up its interior walls, and Lathan was able to get it for just $35,000. He's had the electrical rewired and is now waiting for the power company to install a meter.

Meanwhile, his fourplex here on Burgundy is taking longer than he thought. A worker comes out of it, and Lathan waves and shouts: "Say hey, Mushie! Say hey!" Mushie laughs, and Lathan strides over to see how the ground-floor apartment is coming. It's clean and sheetrocked. Sunlight bounces off the new walls; a radio plays somewhere.

In the back room, Lathan points out his lawn mowers and yard equipment. "I got to keep them kinda close to me. 'Cause that's my third set, ya know?" He grins. "They got me. Oh yeah, they got me. The lawn mowers, the lawn equipment . . . clothes, tools. Now that we're here—I guess 'cause they see the cars here now—I haven't had any problems. But beforehand, man . . . I used to hate to leave."

Big-eyed, Lathan is pacing through the apartment as he talks. The National Guard is still in Holy Cross, but he's no longer sure they're helping much. "I was telling the police, 'I need you to patrol *this* area' . . . I think they're too damn busy in the French area." There's a flash of anger. "Awwww, man, the French Quarter!" He spreads his arms and casts a squinty look upward. "Didn't even shut it *down*! I'll tell you," laughs, "I'm sitting in my uncle's house, watching this catastrophic event, watching it on TV. 'Geez, look at my neighborhood!' And I'm looking at people walking their *dogs* in the French Quarter! . . . And I'm thinking, I lost everything. And that fuc—" censors himself. "Walking his dog! Yes, indeed. Yes, indeed. And a couple blocks away they got floating bodies. You know?

"It's tourism. And I'm a bartender. Been a bartender all my life. And I understand that. But you gotta wake up. Come on, man! This ain't funny. I really don't want to see him walking his dog. If he—" Lathan cuts himself off with a shake of his head and a brusque laugh. He keeps moving, heading out of the fourplex and back out on the street.

Once there, he nods toward his trailer. The electricity has never worked, and an inspector finally confirmed it shouldn't have passed inspection. "The wiring in there is fried." He's been calling since May to get someone to come pick it up.

"Yea," he says, "that's how FEMA helped me." He lets loose a belly laugh. "This was *my* money." He points to the bungalow. "My house was insured. So my insurance paid me. After beggin'." He smiles and shifts his attention to the fourplex. "Well, this is considered luxury. Rental property, a second home. They say they don't help out with that. I understand that."

Getting enough together to rebuild hasn't been easy. "The price has *doubled*. For material and contractors. Over*night* the price double!" In this new economy, plumbers and electricians are in high demand, and average weekly wages in the city are now up across the board. Workers like Lathan's former handyman, who used to help with the rental properties, have gone out on their own. "He got a newer truck than me! *Bigger* truck. He says best thing happened to him was Katrina. You know? He came back here and overbidded this shit. I said, 'Man, you got to help me out. You know how I helped you out before, when you didn't have?'" Lathan laughs, then gives a groan of disgust. "Our friendship went with the waters. . . ."

Sixteen months after the flood, the number of permits issued for new housing exceeds pre-Katrina levels. Homes are going up, but with the construction boom have come hustlers and operators. There's the plumber who ripped off Lathan, the one he vowed he'd catch.

"I caught him. Back in there in Chalmette, St. Bernard's Parish. I put that pistol in his face . . . I said, 'Get in my car.' He brung me to the bank, got me my money. Then he start cryin': 'Oh, I don't do this.' And I explained: 'You had more than enough time to call me and tell me.' 'Lathan, this happened: da da da da. I'm in a situation,' and all this. I said, 'I had to look for *you* . . .' And from what I heard—this what made me more angry with him—he was braggin' that he was making twenty grand a week gettin' people like that. That's what he was doin'; that was his racket! Halfway plumbing, twenty grand a week."

For Lathan, anyway, the local economy has changed. The French Quarter bar where he worked hasn't reopened. "My job went under with the storm," he says. His livelihood has shifted to rebuilding and managing his properties. He's in the real estate business full-time.

Nationally, home prices are reaching new peaks. Here in New Orleans, rents are still rising, and realtors report that while the upper-end market is soft, sales in working-class neighborhoods like Holy Cross "have begun to move briskly."

Lathan applied to the Small Business Administration to fix up his properties. "And they said, 'You don't have a job to support a loan. How you gonna pay back a loan if you don't have a job?'" He laughs at the circularity of it all. "That's it. Everybody got their . . . situations. Luckily, my situation is just that: it's not a problem; it's a situation. I'm coming through it. I got my family."

He seems momentarily reassured but then starts walking rapidly down the street. "Man, man, man!" he mutters. ". . . I don't know . . . I'm *trying* to come back. And I'm trying to put together affordable housing for the people." He motions towards the fourplex. "To help *them* come back." He bulges his eyes in exasperation, then blows out a mouthful of air. He looks across the street where there's nothing but boarded-up homes. One middle-aged white woman lives in a trailer at the end of the block; otherwise, Lathan seems to be the only resident here.

"You know what? I really don't think they want us back."

For the first time, his speech slows. He stops pacing.

"Because the help just isn't there. If it is, I'm not finding it. I really *don't* think they want us back."

Over 40 percent of Holy Cross residents were homeowners before the floods; almost 60 percent of those held mortgages. For a year now, the Department of Housing and Urban Development (HUD) has had an emergency moratorium on foreclosures, and it's been possible to get by on FEMA aid, unemployment, and food stamps. But the moratorium ended this August. In the first quarter of 2007, foreclosures in Louisiana jump 450 percent from the year before.

"*I'm* back," Lathan says, animated again, pointing to the upstairs apartment where he and his son, Ethan, are living. "I'm up here, gettin' them together, gettin' them together . . . Every day I do a little somethin'. And they say a little somethin' is better than a whole lot of nothin'." Laughs.

He's almost ready for his first renters. "I got some people now that are on a waiting list. A prescreening. I don't want to just rent it to anybody . . . I'm not gonna put it on a Section 8. That's what a *lot* of people are doing now with their houses. And it definitely ruins the integrity of the neighborhood." He shrugs. "I give it to the lady that's trying on her own, ya know? Fightin' like I'm fightin'."

If Lathan believes in the individual, in fighting on his own, he's also betting that Holy Cross will come back as a neighborhood. Otherwise, his real estate won't be worth much.

"You heard about the Greenola project with Brad Pitt?" Out of the passenger seat of his pickup, he grabs a laminated proposal. "It's around the corner here. They're modular homes."

A month ago, Pitt announced the winner of his design competition. Now he's planning to erect six single-family homes, a twelve-unit multifamily building, and a community center, all about a half mile from where Lathan is standing. The buildings will use solar and geothermal power as well as recycled materials to achieve "net-zero" energy consumption. Because it aims to make NOLA green—and maybe because it has a gentrifying, granola-crowd feel to it—the project has been dubbed "Greenola."

Lathan flips through the prospectus: colorful architectural sketches of postmodern buildings rising above the floodplain. One design looks like three trailers stacked unevenly on top of each other; all feature solar panels and lots of glass. "It's gonna be nice . . ." Lathan says. Then adds, still smiling: "I don't know, man. I would think they'd open up the schools first."

He tosses the prospectus back in the front seat of his truck.

"You know what, though?" hands on hips, in front of his truck.

"Anything to improve the neighborhood. I'd rather condos over there—" nods in the direction of Pitt's project—"than all this Section 8." Gestures to his own block, then spreads his arms full width. "I'm sorry." Laughs. "Low-income housing? I'm sorry." Laughs again. In this new economy, he's a landlord, a landowner. "If they add value around there, it's definitely gonna trickle down to me."

Bordering Lathan's property toward the levee, 905 Sister Street still has a naked Ken and Barbie riding on its chain-link fence. Beneath is a sign: UNITED WE STAND. There's also a graying piece of plywood that reads: 905/DEMO.

The house is a low-slung, single-story brick ranch. Ron, the owner, is a middle-aged white man with what seems like a perpetual grin.

"I'm an ex-Vietnam vet who has seen—" He pauses. "Quite a few things. You know, when you're in a war zone, you're amazed that people in those areas live like this for years and years. They have no electricity, no running water . . . We've had a taste of that here." He nods at his block. "I think a lot of folks here realize what happens in a war zone."

His house faces the green rise of the levee. It looks fine in front: an intact roof held up by white ironwork with a narrow, cluttered porch. Then he strides around back to reveal that it's a facade: the front intact, the rear heavily damaged.

Grinning, Ron steps into what must have been his daughter's bedroom: bright red walls with a life-sized, hand-drawn mural of the rock-&-roller Jimmy Page. "That wall there is eat up with termites. That's one of the biggest problems now, is that the house is eat up with termites." In the front room, there are still mirrors and pictures hanging, a TV with a couple of wineglasses sitting on top of it. In the kitchen, white curtains frame the windows. But the ceiling's down, and the roof beams are riddled. "Nothing but a hive for Formosan termites." Ron looks around. "What is there to save at this point?"

His plan is to build a new house on the site. "Hopefully, like a lot of folks, go up with cinder blocks till I'm above flood level." But first he needs the city to demolish his old one. He put his name on the list in October, a year ago, and has spent the time since "just waiting on the bulldozer.

"He actually came last week!" Ron's eyes light up. "And he stopped . . . and then he went to another house! I asked him why. And he said, 'Well, I've never been to anybody's house to bulldoze where they had cut the lawn.'" Ron laughs. Out of the city's now-estimated 75,000 seriously damaged buildings, only 4,000 or so have been demolished. The rest, like this one, sit.

Still, Ron is determinedly upbeat. And thankful for what help Holy Cross has received. First, the military, "who were on top of these big bulldozers, pushing things around, trying to clear the streets and make way for people." And since then, he says, "Thank God we have Mexicans!" Laughs. "We have about twenty thousand Mexicans that came into our community and, hey . . . they get it! They really *are* good workers; most of them are real pleasant. And I'm sure they're looking to make this their home." He even has thanks, if a little grudgingly, for Brad Pitt. "We, of course, appreciate any and all help and assistance we're getting. Money and otherwise. And he is helping . . . [Along with] the millions of other people who are down on the Gulf Coast . . . the thousands of churches who came down here, the—"

He's interrupted by Lathan, coming around the corner in his pickup, waving.

"My neighbor," Ron explains. "Now, this man's got it together. He's already flipping houses in the neighborhood, making money. He's a smart cookie. He really is."

After the storm, he and Lathan limbed the big sycamore that grows on their shared property line. Yes, the block is working together, Ron grins. It's just that the money is so slow. And the termites so fast.

Next to Ron's, a small bungalow has been put back on its concrete pad. A black mom and her two teenage daughters, fifteen and twelve, are renting it. They've just gotten back into town after a year in Houston—still home to some 68,000 former New Orleanians. The kids are registered for school, but the mom says, "They got no stores, no nothing, on this side." She means this side of the Industrial Canal. "We manage. But it's rough."

Past the bungalow is a modern A-frame, a blue tarp serving as its roof, no sign of work being done on it. At the foot of the levee, on the corner of Sister Street and North Rampart, a small tree grows next to a telephone pole. It's been decorated with Christmas balls, and beside it stands a dwarf Santa Claus. It's part of Patsy's effort to brighten the neighborhood— like her plastic flowers, her wind chimes, her tire full of stuffed animals.

This January morning, Patsy's come to the corner with one of her dogs. She's in a long burgundy coat, bright green pants, and a black blouse with a colorful abstract pattern. Her short hair is held by two red clips.

The dog turns out to be Buddy, the dark mutt that was sleeping in the middle of the street months ago. Though he survived by begging house to house, he wouldn't let anyone touch him. "When I finally got him," Patsy says, "he wanted to sleep right there, in front of that crape myrtle tree." About a month ago, when they had what she calls some freezing spells, she finally convinced the dog to come inside. Gradually she was able to pet him and, finally, bring him to the vet. Patsy tells the story like it's proof that there really is such a thing as recovery.

As Buddy sniffs around, Patsy seats her large frame in a white plastic chair by the curb. In the seat next to her is a teddy bear. Behind is her son's house. Like Ron's place, it looks pulled together from the front: a shotgun with a small porch supported by three white pillars. But behind that, it's just framing: an empty shell under a blue roof tarp.

As Patsy begins to list all Buddy's ailments, she notices someone walking down the empty street. "Hey!" she shouts in her squeaky, high-pitched voice. "Come on down!"

It's Mark. His motorcycle accident has left him slightly stooped and twisted. He's wearing a wine-colored watch cap and a bright red sweat-shirt, his gray moustache trimmed. He looks fit—except for the dirty bandage wrapped around his right hand.

Patsy watches him approach with a careful, amused expression. Then, nodding at the bandage, she announces: "He put it in the lawn mower while the lawn mower was—"

"Running!" Mark guffaws, his wide face creasing.

"An electric lawn mower," Patsy explains. "He's laughing about it now. You should have seen him a week ago."

"Yeah, it was not a fun thing. Patsy, fortunately, made her car into an ambulance. Applied pressure and drove me to the hospital."

"Naw. My son—"

"Just the tips," Mark says, raising his bandaged hand a little. "Between the joints and the ends of my fingers—"

"Is gone," Patsy clarifies.

"Is gone," Mark agrees. "But the joints are all still there. So, it's not, you know, really critical."

"We tried," Patsy allows in her sincere, social worker's voice. "My son actually went back to the scene of the crime."

"Yeah! He picked up the tips . . . But they told us because they were chopped badly by the mower, they couldn't align the vein and the nerve properly enough to try and reattach it. So."

"You know," Patsy begins to say, "how there's usually a—"

Mark interrupts: "He got a snack there."

"Huh?" Patsy isn't following.

"Buddy," Mark says, motioning to the dog. "He got my fingertip."

"Oh," Patsy gulps. And both laugh.

Mark offers to get some coffee and walks back up the street to his house: a slightly bent, elderly white man with a determined stride. "You should have seen us when this happened," Patsy continues, her voice grainy. "He came down the street screaming, and then I—" She shakes both hands. ". . . And then when I found out what happened"—she shuts her eyes and raises both big arms above her head—"I was screaming! I was screaming! But the lucky thing is," talking rapidly, "he didn't bleed on the way there? The way everything kinda got chopped," she makes blurring motions on her own fingers, "it kinda sealed up, almost like cauterized them . . ."

The city's medical system isn't much better now than it was five months ago when Mark had his motorcycle accident. Only one of the seven general hospitals is operating at pre-Katrina level. Four, including Charity, are still closed. And the proposed downtown medical complex remains just a proposal. In pre-flood New Orleans, health care was the third-largest private employer, after tourism and retail. Since then, the number of medical-related jobs in the area has dropped by more than a quarter. Not only is it harder to get care, but the loss of jobs adds to the post-Katrina anxiety—which contributes to more accidents like Mark's.

Patsy takes a moment to consider what progress the city has made.

"Not very much at all. I mean, we got more people coming back into this area right here." She looks down her block. In Holy Cross, permits for electrical installations have more than doubled over the past few months, the biggest jump of any city neighborhood. It's a sign that people like Lathan are trying to rebuild. But that still accounts for less than 15 percent of the houses. Most of the rest remain without power. Across the city, more than 33,000 have asked for electrical permits. But the city's population is still barely over half of what it was pre-flood.

No, Patsy announces, here's the only progress she's made: "I finally learned how to get out of the FEMA trailer bathtub without breaking my face!" She grins. "I got stuck in it for about a half hour one time. 'Cause I'm like really big? And I have these bad knees. And to fit in it, you just about have to get into a fetal position." She demonstrates, chin to knees, sitting on her plastic chair. "I got *in* it. But when it got time to get out—I couldn't lift the load out." Grinning wider, her hands balled up to her eyes. "And I'm like, no! Don't tell me I'm gonna have to call somebody to get my fat, naked behind out of the FEMA trailer bathtub!"

Like others, she's grateful for the trailer—and eager to get rid of it. "We're just getting finished with the gutting and all." She sighs and looks into the cold breeze. Her side yard is still full of ruined possessions. "A lot of people are just kinda waiting for that monetary help from the Road Home. And we still don't know what people are going to do."

Road Home's promise of $150,000 per house now has a hollow ring to it. In November, Governor Blanco ordered ICF, the private firm administering the money, to "calculate ten thousand awards" by the end of the month. But when December came—six months after Road Home was approved—it had only gone from thirteen to ninety-two issued checks. That left 80,000 applications unanswered. At this rate, the payments will take more than thirteen years to complete. ICF's response: "The Road Home program never established a specific goal for closings."

Once money finally is paid out, the average grant is now projected to be closer to $68,000. Homeowners knew that Road Home was subtracting all insurance payments from the amount of its closings. But they've now discovered it's calculating maximum payments by comparing what a house was worth pre-flood to what it will cost to rebuild—and taking the lower figure. That means people in poorer neighborhoods, like the Lower Ninth, will get less money and still have to pay the post-flood, jacked-up repair costs. The average homeowner is now expected to receive some $50,000 less than what will actually be needed to rebuild. Which helps explain the quiet on this block, from Joe and Linda's empty home to Ron's termite-riddled one to the three boarded-up houses across the street from Patsy's.

Down on the far corner, Mark's small figure reappears, carefully balancing coffee in white mugs. When he arrives, Patsy puts the question to him: what kind of progress has he noticed?

"I don't know. It's so marginal. Small steps here and there. Like, you see a Burger King open? . . . But then you see a gas station torn down. Gone forever. And another building torn down. And just bare ground. To me, it's almost like we're marking time, you know? We're not going back; we're not going forward; we're just churning in the same place."

Patsy's watching Mark intently.

"I don't know what the story's going to be. I have no idea at all . . . The pace is slowing down as far as houses and stuff. There's not as much impact anymore from the trash hauling. Or people gutting houses . . . Now everybody's waiting for Road Home. Who knows what Road Home is going to do?"

"Right," says Patsy. "And to decide if they're gonna let them buy them out." That's the option Joe and Linda took; vines are starting to grow up their empty house. It's still a possibility for Patsy.

"Anybody's guess," Mark adds. "Anybody's guess."

Patsy stands. As if on cue, Buddy rises up on his hind legs and puts his front paws in her hands. "Oh!" she murmurs in her childlike voice, "you wanna dance?" Then she sways a little, side to side, two-stepping with her dog on the sidewalk.

When Buddy drops back to the ground, Patsy reminds Mark: "This solar energy company called Sharp Solar has donated solar units to people. And we're having a lottery." The "we" is the Holy Cross Neighborhood Association; Patsy's on the board.

"That right? Free solar units?"

Along with Pitt's Greenola project, Holy Cross has declared that it wants to become the focus for what it calls "sustainable restoration." "We believe," as a member of the neighborhood association put it, "we can cause a ripple effect throughout New Orleans and the Gulf Coast to make this region climate-neutral." The Sharp Solar lottery is part of that. If all goes well, the company will provide solar panels for nine Holy Cross homes. Looking out across the ruins, nine isn't much of a ripple. But Patsy tries to be optimistic.

"Things like that are happening. There is a historical grant—" she begins.

Mark interrupts. "They're gonna give you up to fifty thousand dollars if your house is legitimately historic, located in a legitimately historic area. I got two like that. And you keep on reading, keep on reading, and down at the bottom it says, 'We will not pay for any work already completed.'"

"Right," Patsy agrees.

"My work's eighty-five percent completed. So what possible—" Mark begins.

Before he can finish, Buddy is yanking at his leash, and Patsy is getting pulled back toward her house, saying, "He's pretty strong," before disappearing behind her front gate. Mark barely blinks.

Like Lathan around the corner, Mark's been doing most of his rebuilding on his own. Early on, he ducked the National Guard to work on his houses, and he's continued despite his accidents: hauling away scrap metal, supervising construction crews, mowing, painting. "My apartment building's coming back." One of the four rental units is already filled.

"It's definitely better than it was six months ago. Definitely. At least you can drive around the block and see faces. And a trailer. Some people in a house." Mark smiles. "It's big change, big change . . . Nowhere near like it was when people were living here. But at least it's in the right direction."

Still, he's worried that his independent, entrepreneurial spirit won't be enough, that without government help his neighborhood is, as he says, "giving up . . . I can only hope that Road Home's Louisiana program *will* give the people some money to come back." He looks thoughtfully down the street. "They haven't come back yet. That was ostensibly the reason they haven't."

The morning news this January reports the latest Road Home figures: 98,000 applications, 117 checks issued. Mark bursts out laughing.

"Louisiana," he manages to gasp. "Don't you love it?"

Kitty-corner from Mark's house, Carolyn has decided to fry some whole chickens. She's got a big stew pot set up on her portable propane stove, the stove she cooked on for months while she camped in her double shotgun. Her Christmas deadline for getting back home has come and gone. She's still in her FEMA trailer, and its kitchen isn't nearly big enough, so she's put the stove on the little porch outside the trailer. Now, steam and smells waft over Holy Cross and drift up into the winter sky.

Carolyn sits on an overturned white plastic bucket, a fork in each hand, peering into the pot. Her round black body is in an orange sweatshirt and chino pants. Earlier, she took a big hypodermic needle, filled it with "mixed seasonings . . . greens . . . spices . . . everything . . . dill pickle juice . . ." and injected it under the skin of the two fryers. Then she dropped them into a couple inches of bubbling peanut oil. "The way I cook is my grandmother. She taught me how to cook with whatever you have . . . Make something out of it!"

Her grandmother lived over in Backatown, when the cypress swamp was still wild, and used to cook muskrat, rabbit, coon, "even the nutra rats," Carolyn says. "We used to skin them . . . and do with the bacon and sweet potato." She grins, wind blowing back her hair, eyes alert. "A lot of people say, 'Oooo, you ate rat?!'"

She leans sideways as she laughs.

Sometimes her grandmother "would get, like, some birds—she'd take the bird brain—and put it in the gumbo." She makes a mincing movement with her thick fingers. "That's supposed to feed your stamina... Basically, that's how I learned how to cook anything."

Carolyn ended up a chef, beginning her career in 1969, the year she got married. She was twenty-two. "I don't know why I married him," she says as an aside, "but I did. Back in those days, if you didn't get married when you were twenty-one, you were the old maid." She pokes at the chicken. "That was stupid... I was going good by myself...

"I was a regular cook," she continues, "... like a scratch cook. I didn't need a recipe: whatever you wanted, I fixed it... Maybe I was born to do it; I don't know." As a child, in a family of twelve, "I was the rice person. And before I know it, I got to be the bean person. And I was this little short girl that's stirring in this big pot." She rocks with laughter. "I always had that gift of doing something... I think it's true: seventh child is born with love. I am my mother's seventh child."

She worked at hotels in the French Quarter and downtown, finally retiring in 1995. "One thing led to the other, and I said it must be time for me to go... I had a mild stroke anyway. And a heart attack. One after the other." In the past decade, she's been surviving mostly on disability and social security.

"I can say whatever it is I wanted to do in my life, I was able to do it... It's like with this house... Everyone asked me when I first came back here, 'Miss Parker, why *did* you come back?' ... I said, 'Because I wanted to come *home*. This is *home*... I want to step on this *ground*; I want to sit on this *porch*.' " At the end of each sentence, she drops her hand on her thigh, underlining. "And I want to just look around and *breathe*." She's peering to all sides, bright-eyed, dark-browed.

"I mean, my house could have been gone like all the other houses the other side of Claiborne. But it didn't. And I feel to believe that it was intended to be here. God does things for a reason. And I think that reason," considering for a moment, "was to get us back here. To—to—" her hands circle, reaching, "to grasp whatever it is that was left. And only bring it *up*..." Both palms rise. "I felt that, had I left, then nobody else would be down here. Somebody has to stand."

She extends a fork into the steam, pokes. "See, they just about done." Two women walk by on the street, and Carolyn shouts: "I notice you'all keep passing?"

The women wave. "It smells good!"

"Yeah," Carolyn shouts back, grinning. "I'm deep-frying these chicken."

Now she lifts them into a plastic container, scrapes the crisp bits from the bottom of the pot, and limps into the trailer. Her walking is worse. She was scheduled for a double knee operation this month, but it's been postponed. Maybe in the spring.

Inside, she begins to carve quickly, carefully. There are sides of greens, sweet potato, and rice. She gets out some plain white plates and then stands to say a prayer with Rahsaan. "You don't say half of the grace," she explains when her son hesitates. "You say all of it. Then you won't choke on half your food." Chuckles.

Her daughter, Kyrah, Carolyn explains, decided not to return to Syracuse. "She's going to UNO [University of New Orleans]. She's majoring in education." Carolyn's now sitting on the bed, a plate of food on her lap.

At the moment, Rahsaan adds, Kyrah's having a "crisis": UNO doesn't want to accept her previous credits. Plus there seems to be no way to transfer her scholarship. So Carolyn has ended up paying the first installment of tuition with the emergency relief money from FEMA. That'll further delay repairs on the house. But as Carolyn says: "[Kyrah] really want to teach kindergarten through fourth grade. To catch the babies before they get too old."

This past fall, Kyrah explained her decision. "My mom doesn't want me to go [to Syracuse] . . . My mom has been my biggest fan for everything . . . always there pushing me when I want to give up . . . I guess because of that, I feel like I'm indebted to my mom for the rest of my life. So, I figure, why not come back and help her?"

Still, she's determined to leave New Orleans eventually. "Everybody's poor . . . Even the bus drivers are mad at everybody. What's even sadder is we were pretty much in the same exact position *before* the hurricane . . . I mean . . . the school district was in a shambles before."

The issue of neighborhoods being "non-viable" has been quietly dropped since the mayoral election. Rather than putting forward an alternative proposal, Mayor Nagin has maintained the public position of having no plan. Let the market determine the recovery. But with progress so slow and his voter base frustrated, he decided a month ago to appoint a "recovery czar." Dr. Edward Blakely, an African American academic and author, had managed the recoveries in San Francisco after its 1989 earthquake and in Oakland after the fires of 1991. Blakely arrived in New Orleans and declared its problems began with ignorance. "There are only about six people in the world who have done this, and I'm one of them." Mayor Nagin, he added, "had no idea where to start."

The czar began his job with a non-negotiable demand: to control any and all recovery money coming into the city. "If I don't have it, I go home—I quit." Now that he holds the purse strings, he's begun reviewing the various master plans—the mayor's, the city council's, and the most recent, called the Unified New Orleans Plan, funded by the Rockefeller Foundation. From these, he'll cull the ideas he likes and decide how to go forward. "Everybody should be allowed to rebuild," he says, echoing the mayor's free market approach. "But that doesn't necessarily mean everyone should be allowed to rebuild in exactly the same place they built before."

From nineteen-year-old Kyrah's perspective, none of this planning amounts to much until something changes on the street. And nothing has. Referring to the *veves* still on most houses: "It's kind of like a depressing mark on everything. It still looks like the same disaster area we came back to *last* Christmas."

What progress her family has made is mostly thanks to nonprofits. A sign stuck outside their front gate reads: TCA. MINOR HOME REPAIR. TCA, Total Community Action, is a New Orleans social service agency founded in the mid-sixties. It's provided workers to rip off the double shotgun's old roof and lay on a new, dark green one. Now the house is at least secured from the weather, and they can think about new electricity and plumbing.

But the estimate for the electrical work is $10,000. They don't have anything like that. Before the flood, as Kyrah has explained, they were surviving on "seven hundred dollars a month for food. And to pay bills and everything. We only got nine thousand dollars a year. To live off." Even if Road Home comes through, they'll still have to worry about "these contractors who take half of the money and never come back... Or you have the contractors, electricians, and roofers who *cannot do* any of the things they say they can."

The family's convinced that if Kyrah's father were still alive, their house would already be done. "My dad was a roofer for the poor people... Used to charge them a lot less than what he should... He was like the Ninth Ward Santa Claus." He and Carolyn knew each other from Backatown and got reacquainted after Carolyn divorced Rahsaan's father. Kyrah was born sixteen years after her brother. When she was twelve, her father was murdered. "He got in a fight and got killed... This guy... he had a two-by-four with a nail in it. And hit my dad in the head a couple of times..." It happened right nearby, on the St.

Claude Avenue Bridge. "Ever since then, it's been me and my mom. Strictly."

Sitting on her bed in the trailer, a plate of chicken on her lap, Carolyn remains hopeful that things are about to get better. She says she was one of the first to apply for Road Home, and they promised her the process would be accelerated. Her mortgage was paid off a decade ago. And Carolyn adds, smiling, "They didn't have to worry about fighting over no insurance, because no insurance was there . . ."

At that, she puts her plate of chicken to the side and lifts her chin.

"They didn't want us back. They *don't* want us back. But we *are* back."

They're almost exactly Lathan's words. But where he's fighting for his home by doing his own repairs, investing in real estate, Carolyn's strategy has to be different. "We have the patience of Job," she says. "We gonna wait. And *they* gonna see. And we gonna," she pauses between each word: "*still be here.*"

It's like a siege: ruined houses, poor medical care, few schools, the delay in relief money. Plus FEMA recently declared its new deadline: it will start repossessing trailers early this spring. Against these obstacles, Carolyn sees her only real weapon as the ability to wait. To pray and to wait.

Right now, she's especially disturbed by the latest addition to the siege: the threat to her church. As part of its post-Katrina realignment, the Catholic archdiocese has announced that its two congregations in the Lower Ninth will have to merge. They'll worship at either St. Maurice or the building where Carolyn married and baptized her children, St. David.

St. Maurice is bigger, older, more ornate, with marble pillars and a high cathedral vault. It's always been the neighborhood's white church. In the sixties, its congregation included prominent leaders of the segregationist Citizens Council. When she was a child, Carolyn remembers, "[though] we were supposed to be going to church to praise God . . . blacks had to go *upstairs*. To the balcony. And to the *back* . . ." Her eyes glint, the rest of her face unmoving. "You just took their communion and *got out*. You couldn't even stay there to go to mass." That, she explains, is the reason St. David was built. "Because of St. Maurice's attitude. They didn't want us there."

Though most of St. Maurice's congregation has moved out to the suburbs, the archdiocese announced at a recent community meeting that it would resolve the issue through "dialogue." "Where do people want to worship?" a soft-spoken priest had asked. A white man with a northern accent, he had instructed the mostly black congregation to repeat twice after him: "Nothing (Nothing) has been decided (has been decided). Nothing . . ."

Carolyn stood and spoke at the meeting. "St. Maurice, this is *your* home. I'm visiting you. . . . St. David is *my* home . . . *I want to go home.*" Now, in her trailer, she says the archdiocese has gone out of its way to close "all the black Catholic churches." Her speech slows; her eyes flare. "[It's] bringing us back to a place—a very uncomfortable place—that I really don't want to revisit . . . Nobody wants to revisit segregation."

As far as she's concerned, the threatened closing is a call to arms. But she's worried that people Kyrah's and Rahsaan's ages don't recognize that. "I hate to say this, but it look like our younger generation don't fight strong enough. Look like they just let people turn them around." She has a perplexed expression. "And you know, we came up with that 'Don't let nobody turn you around.'" Smiles at the old hymn lyric and civil rights slogan. ". . . I'm sorry: I can't just sit still and let you promise me you're gonna do something, and then you don't do it."

It's why, she says, pointing to her silent, flickering TV, she supports the latest protests. This week, on Martin Luther King Day, residents marched on the St. Bernard housing development in midcity. It's one of the Big Four that HUD closed after the floods. Now it's been announced that it's scheduled for demolition. In response, protestors circled the complex, found an opening in the fence, and broke in: a drop squad. As Carolyn speaks, they're still occupying a number of apartments, demanding the development be reopened.

"They're gonna stay in there," Carolyn says, "until HUD decides to either fix them, or fix something for them to move into. And I think that's a *good* idea." It's the same strategy she's using: to wait. "'Cause if they didn't, HUD's not gonna worry about you . . . What the city wants to do and HUD wants to do is tell them it's unlivable. But they told me the same thing." She gives a triumphant grin toward her double shotgun. "I'm still alive!"

To Carolyn, the fight for home goes way back. "I'm a lady of action," she explains. "I believe in action . . . the NAACP, the National Urban League. I got hooked up with the late great Reverend Avery Alexander." In 1960, at the time of the sit-ins that changed the South, Carolyn was in junior high, and the Reverend Alexander was helping to organize the Consumers' League of Greater New Orleans. "You see him maybe when they show the civil rights in New Orleans? He's the old man that they're dragging down the steps of city hall." She stops and stares over her plate of chicken. "Uh-huh! Beating his head on the pavement—uh-uh-uh—as he goes down the steps." She bobs her head, mouth open. "That was the man that taught me, really, about life and about civil rights."

During an Easter break when she was in high school, she became the first black to work at the Elmer Candy factory. Carolyn says she was hired "'cause I was *passant blanc*: very, very fair. With long hair." She speaks slowly, like she's revealing a secret. "Long curly hair. Like creole. So they couldn't tell." She worked there for three days making Heavenly Hash and Gold Brick chocolates. "When they found out I was black, they was really, really peeved." Her oval eyes open wide. "I went from sitting at the table, eating—to outside in the back!" She rocks sideways with laughter. "I said [to Rev. Alexander], 'I had to eat my lunch outside! And it's raining out here. And you know I don't like getting wet.'"

A few years later, Carolyn went over to the Desire housing project, "[to] see what that Panther stuff was all about . . ." The Black Panthers had set up their headquarters at the Dirty D. "So the meeting was going fine," Carolyn recalls, "until for some reason, the police decided to come . . . And they just started a fight with the Panthers. And calling people 'niggers' and all kind of stuff." She lowers her head and gives a stern look. "Yes, I was one of them that turned over the police cars in the Desire housing project. That was not a good thing," she announces, "but it was a good thing in a way . . . The police was beating this boy with billies, and I couldn't stand it. And the boy didn't do nothing! They was just beating him to be beating him . . . If God wanted us to be beaten," her voice rising in indignation, "we would have been an animal . . ." She snorts a laugh. "My grandmother was *really* shocked with that one. They all thought I was gonna be a nun!"

She's done with her meal. It's gotten dark out, and the trailer only has a dim overhead light. Carolyn sits on the edge of the bed, facing the tiny kitchen and Rahsaan.

"My grandmother was fair," she explains, stroking her own cheek, "but you could still see she was black. But I was fair, and you couldn't tell." At age three and four, she says, she was "just like a little white girl." One day she got on a city bus with her grandmother. The driver saw the elderly black woman and the light-skinned toddler and "thought that she was my—" A breath, and then with emphasis: "*Mammy*. 'Cause that's what they called them back then."

At the time, buses in New Orleans had screens to segregate white riders from black. "I didn't know nothing about a screen . . . So I went and took me a seat in the front." As more whites entered, her grand-mother "had to go way to the back . . ." A grimace. "Then I got up be-cause I wanted to go sit with my grandmother. And this white lady said, 'Come on, I'll hold you, baby.'" A look of amazement. "And I said, 'No. I want to go with my grandmother.' Ooo, Lord! When I said that!? Them people!?"

She laughs again, falling to the side, then stops. "Children don't know nothin' about this. But from a baby, they made me realize it. In the worst way . . ." She gathers herself. "I felt that everybody should have been able to sit down on that bus. And I think that stayed in me, from a little girl. 'Cause ever since that, I been like—well, some say like an activist." Caro-lyn rolls her eyes. "But I'm not an activist: I'm just a person who don't like things going the way I been seeing it being done." She shrugs. "And I just like to see it change. I like to see somebody be treated fairly."

It's time to wash and dry the dishes. Rahsaan is about to head off to his restaurant job. But Carolyn needs to make one last point. "We are a mixture of people," she says, ". . . and we're family. Even though some of us act stupid . . ." She laughs. "My momma is some from Jamaica, some from this one, some from that." Her father, she says, revealing another secret, was Mexican. "That's why I was comfortable when [the roofers] came here . . . A lot of them when they see me," she assumes a look of careful inspection. "'Yeah, I'm looking at her eyebrows. Yeah!'" She laughs and brushes her thick, arched eyebrows. Kyrah, she continues, "had Mexican from my side, and Cherokee from her daddy's side. I'm telling you, the people here in New Orleans are mixed."

She grins: a big woman perched on a small bed in a dark trailer.

Then, in what seems like a switch of subject, she starts talking about the dinner she just cooked. "You had the blend: you had the Black, you had the Indian, and then you had the Cajun . . . 'Cause the chicken was Cajun, the potatoes were Indian, and the greens were Black." She cocks her head with a big smile. "Oh, I forgot about the rice! Your Asian." She bursts out laughing, slapping her hands together. "That's how we cook down here."

On the Rise

Still So Much Work

(January 2007)

Almost no time has passed. Yet as Carolyn waits and Lathan hangs
sheetrock, Common Ground has a different sense of urgency, enters a
new phase.

Suncere is sitting in the back of a building in the Ninth Ward. It's
painted an extravagant mix of yellow, green, and red, and the sign over
the entrance reads: WELCOME TO THE COMMON GROUND HOUSE OF EXCEL-
LENCE MEDIA CENTER . . . FREE COMPUTER, FREE PHONE, FREE LAWYERS
AND NOTARIES. The inside is a warren of small rooms full of college-
age volunteers answering phones, typing on keyboards, conferring in
corners.

Suncere sits in a tired-looking armchair. He's even bigger than three
months ago: thick thighs and legs in unwashed blue jeans, his chest bulg-
ing a raggedy black parka. His hair is matted into a couple of big dreadlocks.

He often sleeps here, in Common Ground's House of Excellence,
though he no longer has a job in the collective. Harriet, his beloved red
truck, has broken down. "Last time I was out in St. Bernard," he calcu-
lates, "was February. It's almost been a year. 'Cause I was so burnt-out, I
felt . . . that I really couldn't help them."

Today he's decided to go back and visit Mike. He follows the same
route over the Claiborne Avenue bridge and out Judge Perez Drive.

"I used to be going two-twenty-five," he says as rain spots the wind-shield. "Now I'm about five. I can barely feed the cat." He gives a slight smile. "I can barely be responsible enough to feed the cat." His voice is steady, but the emotion is washed out of it. He has a low-grade, persistent cough. "My 2007 plan is to take my time and rebuild Suncere better. Hopefully, at age thirty-six, I can learn from the lessons of a past."

He nods out the car window. "This used to be scary as shit. Riding up and down these roads out here? I did *not* like it. 'Cause this was where the Klan live . . . They'd start shit with me, say shit to me, make me want to fight. And then the next thing I know, they on the cell phone calling the sheriff on me and shit. It's scary." He coughs. "Here I'm supposed to be this big, bad, thorough man, and these motherfuckers just call a whole police force on me . . ."

When he reaches Violet, Suncere turns down Mike's block, still a jumble of FEMA trailers, condemned homes, empty lots. "Nothing has really changed here . . . That's sad . . . All this time we been here. Seventeen months!" Suncere lifts both big hands and sighs. ". . . Nuthin'."

The car pulls to a stop in front of Mike's flagpole. The only flag flying today is the Stars and Stripes. A man and boy come out, the man with a little beer gut, salt-and-pepper beard, work clothes. He introduces himself as Mike's younger brother, Charlie. The boy is ten or so, chunky, known as CJ.

"Everything's so slow." Charlie's bayou twang is less pronounced than his brother's. "Federal government should be doin' somethin' other than what they're doin'." He shrugs, standing by his pickup's open door. "They go to Third World countries, spend millions of dollars, and it's like we're forgotten about . . . They don't care. Long as they line their pockets with all them governmental contracts." He says the last two words like a complicated curse. "They forgot about the average person."

Suncere faces him, nodding his big head.

"I don't see things getting better," Charlie says. ". . . I live down the road a little ways . . . My house has been gutted, and it's been blasted with baking soda." Like Mike, he got help from Project Hope. Unlike Mike, he hasn't gotten much further than that. "I got electrical to do and flooring to do and all the plumbing." He and his family have been staying in a trailer provided by his employer. Now he has to return it, and he's having trouble getting a FEMA replacement.

"I been bit by a rat," he adds, as if he just remembered.

"He was on CNN!" CJ chimes in.

His father gives him a smile. Then, in a low, steady tone: "I lost my wife in September. Eighteen years." He looks at CJ. "That just added to the nerve deal, you know? Makes you that much more on edge."

Charlie says his wife got sick, no sign of it being life-threatening. She went into the hospital and died. There doesn't seem to be anything else to say. "Well, I'm gonna go and get my gas line going." He gets into his truck, leans back out the window. "If I can get it turned on."

As the pickup pulls off, Suncere turns and takes a closer look at Mike's home. The lawn is mowed. There's a white mailbox out front with the street number on it. A border of white gravel has been laid around the foundation.

"He got rid of the trailer!" Suncere almost shouts. "They're in the house! . . . Oh, my God, look at this house! I don't believe it . . . He's really back!"

Suncere walks past a three-foot-tall Virgin Mary and rings the front bell. A red *veve* is still on the brick between the new door and windows.

"Hey, Suncere! Long time no see, buddy!" Mike seems only mildly surprised, as if old friends wander in and out all the time.

Suncere settles into a sofa while Mike and Kim wrestle to get a foam cushion back into its slipcover. Mike looks good: gray beard neatly trimmed, pressed green shirt. Kim still seems thin, fragile: a cancer patient.

"You've done an incredible job!" Suncere glances up at the ceiling fan, nods toward the new kitchen counters.

"I still got a little to do," Mike answers modestly. "Lot a work in da neighborhood's still gotta be done."

"I sit here and complain," Kim adds cheerfully, "about what we have to do. But then I turn around and look out there," points to the picture window behind her, "and think, 'Man, at least I'm in my house, and everything's done.'" She smiles her toothy smile. The window is streaked with raindrops. The view is of a FEMA trailer with another empty red-brick house behind it.

Suncere catches them up on what he's been doing: the drop squad at St. Augustine, the speaking tour in California, then another stint down in Houma. "I was so fried," he says, "I couldn't deal with much of anything."

Mike mentions that they invited Project Hope volunteers over for a Christmas meal and missed him.

"I was just in such a bad mental state," Suncere explains, "I didn't want to see anybody."

"Yeah." Mike nods. "I was like that for a little."

"We know what's that like." Kim nods at her husband. "He ended up in the hospital for a while."

When Suncere says he's felt guilty about not coming by sooner, Mike interrupts. "You have no reason to feel guilty, brother. What you started down here is still going! And strong."

Suncere finds a smile.

"[Project Hope] cleaned up some houses out here last week," says Mike. "And they were raunchy. I mean *raunchy*. When da windows are broken and da rain gets in . . . it ain't too bad. When dey been locked up and boarded up? Ohhh!" Mike rocks on the sofa.

The conversation falls into an awkward silence. Mike's settled in a big armchair. Kim's on the sofa, and their teenage daughter has joined them. Facing them from across the way, Suncere has slumped down in his seat and extended his thick legs. He looks like he's about to slide onto the floor.

"I just got to chill out a while," he finally says. "It's incredible, but it looks like I'm well on to that two-year commitment I put down . . ." He talks a little about the pledge he made to Malik and his time out in Houma, the mosquitoes down in the bayous, the shrimp barbeques, how welcoming the people were.

That gets Mike reminiscing about one of his first jobs. "Drudgin' for shrimp," he says, grinning. "See, what I like about dat—workin' on a drudge boat, or trawlin', or whatever like dat—it's peaceful."

"Yeah," says Suncere softly.

"It's steady work, but it's peaceful. Like no other type of work in da world. I mean, everybody has a job they love."

Kim reminds him that, with his health, "you can't do that no more."

"I know, but . . ." Mike won't be stopped. "Like when I used to work in da Gulf. On a double-rigger, man! Grab you a six-pack of Bud, you go on up top da cabin, got your little kickback spot dere, look at da stars, just reach up and grab dem out da sky! I mean, dey right *dere* in your face."

Again Suncere mutters a soft "Yeah."

"It's quiet. Them seagulls howling and whatever . . . It's just—it's just . . . nerve-calming."

There's another stretch of silence.

It's broken by a tall black man in a hoodie who walks in the front door without knocking. Suncere greets him with a surprised "Hey, brother."

Mike makes introductions: "Dat's my daughter's boyfriend."

As daughter and boyfriend move to the kitchen, Suncere barely hides his amazement. Is this the same home that flew the Confederate flag?

The door opens again, and Mike's brother Charlie returns with CJ. As Kim explains that her daughter's graduating from Chalmette Unified High School this year, the blond granddaughter, now five, wanders in with her little brother. He's now a redheaded toddler taking some of his first, tentative steps. A small black dog adds to the hubbub.

Two and three conversations start going simultaneously. Suncere tells a story about the time he "lost his cool" at Common Ground headquarters, cussing and kicking over chairs when he couldn't get volunteers for Houma. "I knew then it was time for me to pull out."

Mike won't let Suncere criticize himself. "You gotta light a fire under dem!" He compares it to the recent housing protests that he, like Carolyn, has been following on TV. "Dey tried to shut everybody out! Because dey was buyin' [the projects] and turnin' dem into condominiums. All dese people lived up dere before dis started! You can't just tell dese people, 'Now you don't have a home. We gonna tear all dis down.'"

Kim agrees. "They went in there to *clean up*! They feel like we feel: that's their home."

"Well, Common Ground helped organize that," Suncere says proudly. "The night before—actually the last three days—we was sending crews at night. And we would sneak in there, and . . . we cut a hole in the fence. 'Cause we had planned an action: we was gonna take over a dwelling . . . The police was surprised that the fence could be removed so quickly . . ."

Now it's Mike's turn to mutter a soft "Yeah," adding: "They can't just shut dem people out."

"Naw, man! Not when you're telling people to come home, and you got nowhere to put 'em."

Mike spreads his tattooed arms to take in his house and family. He compares what he has here to those kept out of public housing—or, for that matter, still in trailers. "Dey miserable. Dere's my little nephew right dere." He points to CJ. "You can ask him . . . It makes you stir-crazy, man. I mean, I picked up the TV, trew it through the frickin' door! . . . I had a nervous break—" Mike begins, then simplifies. "I just went frickin' ballistic."

Still slumped, Suncere halfheartedly launches into what sounds like a memorized speech. "There's still so many Americans don't have a *clue* about what's happening down here. We need to get the information out to them, same they need to pay attention . . . Real Americans got to stand up. And take it back from these corporations. They gonna kill us."

"Well, dey doin' a good job!" Mike laughs, and his brother Charlie joins in.

Charlie's been standing near Suncere, mostly listening, but now he says how FEMA shouldn't have put money into blue tarps and trailers. They should have just given it directly to the homeowners. "This place would be up and running by now!"

They try to have a conversation in the chaos of the room. Mike shouts out his belief that the government doesn't trust the citizens it represents, is scared to give them money directly. Because they'd take it, he says, and "be movin' out of da state. To get away from da water and da chance of it ever happenin' again."

He turns to his wife. "How much we got in dis house?"

"All our money we had," says Kim with a big smile: "Seventy thousand dollars."

"And I only paid eighteen thousand for the house when I bought it."

The noise level is rising. Kim's got her blond granddaughter on her lap; the baby's playing with a toy cell phone; CJ is eating candy on a stick; his father has lit a cigarette. Kim's other daughter, the mother of the kids, comes in and out, refilling juice bottles and picking up toys.

Suncere looks around, delighted and a little out of place. Maybe it doesn't equal a revolution, but isn't this part of what he and Common Ground have been fighting for?

Finally he hoists himself off the sofa and, after hugging everyone good-bye, heads outside. It's still rainy and cold. Mike and his family wave from the door, then go back into the warmth. Suncere hesitates before getting in the car. His mood darkens.

"It's sad," he says, looking past Mike's house and down the block, "to come back and see that with all the work we done here, there's still so much work to *be* done."

Suncere's plan is to leave New Orleans in the next few days and go back up to Asheville, North Carolina, for what he calls a two-week break. "Ohhh yeah!" he says with a big grin. "I'm gonna have a good ol' time when I get there." Then his face goes suddenly sober. "I'll come back and help out."

He says the last like even he doesn't believe it.

Back in the Upper Ninth, out toward the site of the old Desire housing project, the streets are still mostly empty. But a row of cars with out-of-state plates is parked outside one three-story brick building. It's St. Mary of the Angels Catholic School, the current housing for Common Ground's volunteers.

A guitar player strums in the abandoned playground. A woman sits on a little kindergarten-sized chair getting her hair cut. And on the broad front stairs, in a clean white T-shirt, is Brandon. He's back as interim director of the collective.

"It's like you're a surgeon," is his explanation. "You just want to chill out, so you become a dishwasher. But then you see a guy with his leg shot up, and you gotta become a surgeon again, right? You sew him up."

Last month, Malik called Brandon back from Texas because he felt the organization needed help. The collective had continued to shift away from stand-downs and toward more personal politics. "Because of our activist culture, how we work in this country," Brandon says, "people tend to focus on each other. So organizing became organizing *within* the volunteer base." He pretends to pull at his own insides. "[Instead of] walking up the streets asking what [the community] wanted." In a decision unpopular with some of Common Ground's organizers, Malik turned to Brandon to reinvigorate the organization, put it back in touch with locals, reconnect it to its radical beginnings. One of Brandon's first moves was to push for and help arrange the recent occupation of public housing.

"It's nice to see a demonstration in New Orleans, and the majority of the people in the demonstration are residents." Brandon smiles. He's still got his hair buzzed short and that movie star stubble. "It's nice that people come and struggle in solidarity, but it's nicer to see *residents* doing it. People are coming back, and they're like, 'You know what? No!' They realize the government isn't helping them . . . You can imagine . . . what sort of *rage* people are going through. So it's nice to see people standing up for themselves. And joining together to do it."

A step down from him, a young woman listens with a look of near adoration.

Brandon says he understands why HUD wants to tear down St. Bernard and the other, older developments. "I mean, the place was hell. But not as big a hell as a prison cell. Or not as big a hell as not having anywhere to go. You got to remember these projects—people say don't call them that, but I *do* call them that: *projects*. The government started these *projects* to put people in housing and then have resources for job training, skills . . . Then halfway through the *project*"—Brandon chops the air with one hand—"the government cut the money."

In the seventies, President Nixon declared a moratorium on all federal housing assistance. In the eighties, under President Reagan, HUD's budget fell from $36 million a year to $18 million. And in the nineties, President Clinton helped implement HOPE VI, a plan to raze "distressed public housing" and replace it with "mixed-income developments." It was touted as a way to get rid of decrepit projects, but HOPE VI doesn't require that the same number of units be rebuilt. As a result, the nation now has 10 percent fewer subsidized, low-income apartments.

Here in New Orleans, the housing authority had already cut back, but it used the occasion of the floods to "just put fences up," Brandon says. "Told everybody, 'Sorry, you can't get your stuff . . . [Or you can] get your stuff if you call this number' and then that number doesn't work."

His voice is low-pitched, speedy. What rest and therapy he got in Texas seems to have worn off. He keeps nervously flipping his cell phone open and closed with one hand.

Now and then there's a boyish smile, like when he tells a nearby volunteer, "The police are gonna be intense tonight." Another round of housing protest is scheduled for later this evening. "If you got arrested, wouldn't that be a big deal?" he asks.

Brandon got arrested a couple of nights ago, but it wasn't for protesting. "The basic gist of it is, there's a local drug dealer, and he kept coming up with a gun . . . punched a couple of volunteers in the face. And people tried to talk with him, and he kept coming and doing it. So I got in a situation where I tried to detain him till law enforcement got there." He nods to himself, as if confirming that this was the right thing to do. "And when law enforcement got there, they were friends with him! They knew him." His dark eyebrows go up in surprise. "So they arrested me . . . I think what it was . . . it was a crooked cop wanting to get some protection money."

He spent the night before last in the Orleans Parish Prison. "I watched, um, three fights: six grown men beat each other. I watched the guards bet on the fights. It was nasty; it was really ugly." He stood in the corner of his cell and "every time somebody bumped into me, I'd go, 'Hey.'" He drops his voice to rough macho, then laughs. "I was kinda scared, but I got out. I'm okay."

The woman on the step below listens, rapt.

Brandon is hoping his arrest can become a rallying point, a way to refocus Common Ground. Later this evening, he's going to meet with leadership about how to tie the arrest to larger issues: corruption in the police force, the city's ongoing crime wave, the court system's "way of exploiting low-income African Americans."

He's about to go on when a black SUV pulls up. Out of the passenger side steps a black man with gray dreadlocks halfway down his back. Brandon smiles.

"Hey, Malik!" he calls. "What's happenin'?"

"All right!" the black man shouts back.

Malik's arrival is an event. Most of Common Ground's volunteers have only heard of him, never met him. The small group on the steps of St. Mary stands, eager to get a look at the founder of their organization.

Malik seems not so much larger than life as brighter, more in focus. His face is small between white beard and moustache, eyes tired with pronounced bags under them, small black birthmarks dotting his brown skin. But these details get lost in the drama of the bulky body, the mass of dreads, his big welcoming smile. Hugging and repeating, "All right! All right!" he makes his way up the steps and into the building.

Inside, it still looks like a school. But the table out front, where security guards would sit, is manned by young volunteers. On one wall is a whiteboard listing the various work crews and their daily assignments. The other wall has a chart with snapshots of Common Ground's main organizers, their functions and telephone numbers. Brandon is listed as interim director: "Any Questions, Suggestions, Concerns, Get In Touch With Him!!" Arranged around his picture are a dozen others: "Business Administrator," "Site Coordinator," "Media Coordinator," "Queer and Trans," "Outreach Coordinator," "Sexual Violence Awareness Advocate." All are young and white.

The passing volunteers—two girls bringing in their laundry, a curly-haired boy with a backpack—greet Malik with awe and surprise.

"How many people you have here now?" he asks Brandon.

Brandon says they're sleeping and feeding between 300 and 350 a night. Mostly the volunteers are gutting houses in the Upper and Lower

Ninth, but they're also cleaning out storm drains. "[And] walking up the streets with brooms and shovels, picking up everybody's trash and bagging it."

"And how," Malik asks, "has the community taken that?"

"Cool. Real cool. It's just been a little bit of time."

Malik nods his gray head and starts fixing a cup of coffee.

"All people want to know in this community," Brandon says, his voice rising, "is that there's *one* person they can call in case something goes wrong. They don't want to call and have ten different people each time and never know who to talk to." All questions go to Brandon. He's the strongman again, at least temporarily.

Community relations have suffered, Brandon acknowledges, because Common Ground volunteers are predominantly white, young, and from out of town. But, he says, "If it was young African American men and women doing this work, like the sixties and seventies when the Panthers were doing—"

Malik, stirring his coffee, cuts in: "We'd be dead."

"We'd be dead," Brandon echoes.

He leads Malik and a small group of followers down the old school's green-tiled main hall. In a side room that looks like it was once the nurse's, there's a small dispensary: the only place in the Ninth Ward, Brandon says, where people can come when they cut themselves, need to have their blood sugar tested, or want other minor medical attention.

"It's past criminal," Malik interjects. "It's immoral . . . We have a state-of-the-art health clinic right on St. Claude . . . that they won't allow us to open." He says he plans to visit there later.

As a guest of the Catholic Church, Common Ground is allowed to rig additional lighting in St. Mary, set up a kitchen, convert classrooms into bunk rooms for volunteers. But the archdiocese has made clear that it doesn't want the building to become even a temporary homeless shelter. Now Brandon opens the door to a room full of cots and explains it's for "local people that, um, their homes have been destroyed. It's not a shelter," straight-faced. "It's a *volunteer* space for locals-who-don't-have-to-go-out-on-work-crews . . . That's how we do around that."

Back out in the main hall, Malik stops again to make a point. "The city refused to give us any kind of support. City, state, federal government refused to give us any support. *All* the work that we are doing, we are able to do it simply because of the contributions that are coming to us."

Here's the four-stall bathroom that serves all 300-and-some volunteers. Yeah, Brandon says, "[it's] pretty rough . . . but we're living better than a lot of residents around here. If that means anything . . ."

They pass through the school gymnasium. Three times a day, it's transformed into a communal dining area. Out the side door is a narrow yard where tools are stored. Brandon shows off the stacks of stepladders, wheelbarrows, rakes, hoes, shovels, brooms "that we use to clean the community. Since the city won't clean the community." Near by are plastic milk crates full of hammers, scrapers, saws, pry bars. "They're real basic," says Brandon, Malik nodding, "but we can't really afford to buy a whole lot." Another area around the corner is for respirators, Tyvek suits, and work gloves. It's like the original setup they had at the Greater Mount Carmel Baptist church, but larger and better organized.

"Now if we can do this," Malik stops to say, "why can't FEMA do it? Why couldn't FEMA offer returning residents that's coming into their house a wheelbarrow that they could use? Hammers? Just the basics. They *refuse* to supply! And the only reason they refuse is that the only person who's in dire need of it—is the poor. And the disenfranchised. And those are the people they don't want back in New Orleans."

It's the same conclusion Lathan and Carolyn and Pastor Mel have reached. Malik declares it with no surprise, as if he knew it long before the floods.

The ex-Panther talks like someone used to public speaking: carefully paced, short phrases, his New Orleans accent sweetening the tough words. Brandon watches and listens hard—the way the young woman on the stairs listened to him. Malik's cadence, his barely suppressed anger, certain phrases: Brandon has adopted all of these. It's like finally meeting someone's father.

Malik explains why he isn't around Common Ground much. "Every month we have to raise almost a hundred thousand dollars to keep our operation going." Most of that "goes in direct service . . . and the other ten percent . . . go to me to go out on speaking tours to raise that money . . . That's all I'm doing is going to an airport, to a hotel, to a speaking engagement, back to a hotel, back to an airport." That's why Brandon is showing him around, why he's not sure how many are housed here, why the volunteers seem startled to see him.

They pass a refrigeration truck humming in a back alley, a kitchen tent that volunteers erected, a big school bus converted into living quarters. When they reenter the school, Brandon and Malik start up to the second floor for the strategy meeting. On the stairs, a small red sign reads: ALL VISITORS REPORT TO PRINCIPAL'S OFFICE.

The meeting room is an old classroom complete with a teacher's desk, blackboards, and peeling yellow paint. Brandon takes what was once the teacher's seat behind the main desk. Even if he's informal about it—instead of sitting, he squats, boots on the office chair—he's clearly running the meeting. Malik and a couple of other men face him in a row of small, student seats. Toward the back of the room are a half dozen young white women in their twenties and thirties.

Brandon begins by describing his arrest. "While I was spending the night in jail, I decided we needed to do something about it, make a statement about it. So one of the things we've come up with is, we're gonna have an 800 number . . . to report corruption in the police department." He wants to announce this initiative the day after tomorrow at a press conference, where he also plans to challenge the legality of his arrest and "point out to the mayor's office that what's needed is not longer jail sentences and prison sentences. But what's needed is for the crime *in the police department* to be fought."

If anything, violence in New Orleans has increased. In recent, separate incidents, a well-known black male musician and a white female filmmaker were murdered. All told, there have been nine killings in the first ten days of 2007. The mayor's response has been to once again call for a curfew. And the governor's announcement of a "crack down on criminals" is also familiar. Frustrated, scared, angry, 5,000 residents marched on city hall last week, protesting the murders, demanding better police protection, jeering Mayor Nagin. One sign read: ANOTHER HURRICANE'S HERE! . . . THIS TIME IT'S RAINING BULLETS.

"This is just a continuation, a constant," Malik says to the group. In his opinion, Brandon's arrest is part of a pattern that includes harassment of volunteers and police surveillance of Common Ground buildings. If there's going to be a press conference, Malik declares, it has to address the root cause of crime.

"What they done at St. Bernard by locking people out of public housing?" The founder pauses, looks around. "I'm gonna tell you: to be in a city that you can't *get in* your house—your kids don't understand the politics of it. All they understand is, 'Hey! I'm not in my house.'" Homelessness leads to crime, he says: robbery, prostitution, drug dealing. The state's solution has been to throw kids—especially young black males—into prison. In 2005, the United States had the highest incarceration rate in the world, and

New Orleans had the highest rate in the United States: double that of any other large city. Ultimately, Malik says, the crime can be traced back to unemployment. "With all this reconstruction going on in the Ninth Ward . . . that's what creates the rage." It's the word Brandon used earlier. "They're sitting around in their community, watching everybody else working."

A woman in the back—short dyed-blond hair and a white peasant blouse—suggests Brandon first file a police complaint. "I don't think you should have a press conference," she says. "To me, instead of coming out really aggressive right off the bat . . . go through what they ask you to do." Then, if the police don't respond—"and I think a lot of the people in this room don't have a lot of confidence [that they will]—then use that." She turns out to be Brandon's lawyer.

"We have to start holding them all accountable," Malik interjects.

The lawyer worries about Common Ground's reputation. And about too much of the focus being on Brandon. Another woman asks who's going to set up this 800 number for police complaints and who's going to answer it and respond.

"It's me," says Brandon, "that's going to be answering . . . I'm gonna be encouraging everybody to come and talk to me personally."

Malik now seems unsure about the press conference—and even less sure that it should center on Brandon. He keeps bringing the conversation back to broad solutions. "I've found that the best deterrent to crime," pause, "is some employment at a livable wage . . . If the government won't start no training program, we need to." Malik's voice starts to rise. "If they won't start an ex-offenders program, we need to." Now he's standing, excited, pivoting to speak to the whole room. "If they won't start housing people, we need to!" That's what a Common Ground press conference should focus on. "Make it clear: we a peaceful organization, but we're addressing some hard, violent issues."

Brandon squats on the teacher's chair, listening.

Malik may not manage Common Ground's day-to-day operation, but he's the inspiration, the one who convinced people like Brandon and Suncere to leave their homes and come work in New Orleans. The next day, outside the blue house in Backatown, he's in a red windbreaker against the raw weather, a black sweatshirt, a Black Panther's beret. He looks like an old warrior revisiting a battlefield.

"This area of the Lower Ninth is one that—" Malik pauses, looks around. "That's real dear to me. Many days I used to be right here," pointing to a boarded-up brick bungalow with a blue tarp roof. "'Cause I had family that lived all up and down this street."

Besides the blue house, the landscape has mostly been emptied. In the distance, down the mile or so of the levee, there's one pair of FEMA trailers and three or four gutted houses.

"One of the things that depresses me," Malik says, ". . . to the degree that I don't come over here that much . . . I'm always reminded of how it was." He speaks slowly, standing still in the cold. "How at this time of day, you would see children playing up here in the street." He stirs one arm toward the distance. "You would see families in their homes all up and down this block, sitting outside . . ." He taps off where the stoops once were, the homes set close together, porches almost touching.

He's in the middle of reminiscing about Backatown when he spots a crew of volunteers: a dozen young white women carrying shovels and hoes, their sweatshirts dirty. "All right!" he greets them. "What y'all been doin'?"

"Cleaning storm drains," one woman says.

"All right." Malik grins. "What school y'all from?"

"Swarthmore College . . . We're with Common Ground."

When they discover they're talking to its founder, they gush. And Malik laughs. "I thank you for what you'all are doing and the sacrifice you're making."

"Well, thank you for organizing this!" The students go on to explain they're staying at St. Mary. When Malik asks how long they have to wait to shower, they answer, "An hour . . . when there's hot water . . ." And the police, they volunteer, "are arresting people for trying to help out. Sometimes for no reason."

"So, you see what we been going through?" Malik shakes his gray dreads, thanks them again, hugs each of them goodbye.

He walks by one of the few standing buildings; on its cinder-block first floor, someone's spray-painted BAGHDAD.

"We have been classified as enemies of the state. For doing what? Helping people? . . . We have served over a half million people . . . and we have raised one point eight million dollars . . . The government says they done spent billions of dollars, but they can't offer a resident back here a respirator! They can't even offer him a hammer or a wheelbarrow . . . And then they get mad on us 'cause *we're* offering it!" He's standing on a bare concrete slab, the remains of someone's house. "I'm not trying to set up no second government. I'd *love* to be able to work along with the government . . . We were told they didn't want no volunteers. Only thing we could do was leave the city. . . . We need to bridge this, learn from the mistakes we made; . . . make sure this *never* happen nowhere else again!"

Malik pauses and gazes around, as if to locate himself.

"Brandon should be classified an American hero!" It was Brandon, Malik says, who insisted on staying out here in Backatown, who tried "to make sure you get the opportunity to get back to your land . . . That's the reason why the Ninth Ward is open." He points at the cold emptiness. "If they make this a city only for the rich," Malik intones, "I hope the most high are destroyed. I hope another hurricane come through here and wipe New Orleans off the map." His voice is level, dispassionate. "But I believe we have a chance of transforming this. By working together."

Common Ground's plan to buy the apartment complex in Algiers has fallen through. After months of the collective running the building and making repairs on it, the owner suddenly refused to sell. Malik believes it's because of Common Ground's politics and his own past. "Yeah, I was in the Panther Party. Yeah, I was in a shoot-out with the police. That was in 1970, you know?"

Malik was twenty-two in 1970. "Most of my family had some kind of presence in New Orleans all the way to slavery." He was born in Algiers, on the city's west bank. From an early age, he says, he was "caught up in the street. Drugs, violence, you know . . ." When he was twelve, he watched "sit-ins at lunch counters here in New Orleans with Reverend Avery Alexander. I watched him being dragged up and down the stairs of city hall, simply because he dared to sit at a lunch counter." At seventeen, Malik enlisted in the navy, partly to "get away from this." He served in Vietnam. After his honorable discharge and not long after returning to New Orleans, he joined the newly organized Louisiana chapter of the Black Panther Party. He was about the same age as many of the volunteers who have come down to join Common Ground.

The Panthers' headquarters was next to the Desire housing project. They had been invited there, Malik says, to reduce crime. With their free breakfast program, the Panthers were feeding 300 to 400 kids, as well as offering after-school tutoring. "It was easy for me to start a health clinic," Malik says of his Common Ground work, "because in the Panther Party, that's what we done. It was easy for me to start a distribution center, because that's another thing we done. It was easy for us to talk about an environmental cleanup program, because we done *this* in the Panther Party."

The other thing the Panthers did was carry weapons. "We believed that you had a right to defend yourself . . ." Nationwide, fifteen police officers and thirty-four Panthers had been killed by the time Malik joined the party. FBI director J. Edgar Hoover had declared the Panthers the "greatest threat to the internal security of the country" and was using a secret counterintelligence operation, COINTELPRO, to monitor and neutralize them. In New Orleans, Mayor "Moon" Landrieu's police department infiltrated Malik's group. The day after the Panthers discovered and roughed up two undercover cops, the police arrived at Desire in force.

"There was basically eleven of us in the party office at the time," Malik remembers, "and almost a hundred police with everything from a .60 caliber machine gun and armored cars down to their revolvers. We had about nine shotguns, and a couple of handguns, .357 revolvers . . ." Malik's wife and two small children were also there.

As Malik recalls it, the police "shot up in the office maybe twenty minutes straight . . . The firing was coming in so fast we literally had to pour water on the walls, because you could see the sheetrock expanding from the heat till you could touch it, and it would just pop."

When it stopped, Malik crawled from room to room to assess the damage. Amazingly, there were no major injuries. Malik and the others were taken to Orleans Parish Prison, where he was charged with attempted murder. While there he helped organize a hunger strike that led to the first and only prison chapter of the Black Panther Party. It was working for the release of members of that chapter—the Angola Three—that would eventually bring Malik and Brandon together.

After eleven months in jail, the Panthers from Desire were acquitted. Malik moved to California. "At the time, just like most black men, I was full of rage and felt like the movement had abandoned us, and we did some things we are no longer proud of . . ." In the seventies, he served a five-year term for armed robbery in Los Angeles. In the eighties, he converted to Islam. By the nineties, he was leading a tenants group opposing the demolition of low-income housing in San Francisco. A few years before Katrina, he came home to New Orleans where, with Sister Helen Prejean, he co-founded the anti-death-penalty group Pilgrimage for Life.

In the days after the flood, Malik saw history repeating itself. "A *so-called* African American mayor and a *so-called* African American police chief . . . sat here and allowed this governor to declare martial law on *African Americans*." In his neighborhood of Algiers, he heard that police had shot a black man, dumped his car by the levee, and set it on fire with the body inside. He watched armed vigilantes patrol the streets and, with police cooperation, keep black evacuees from entering white neighborhoods. Six days after Katrina, there were rumors that the NOPD had killed two black citizens and wounded four others on Danziger Bridge, one of the spans that crosses the Industrial Canal near Pastor Mel's mission. Witnesses swore that the victims were unarmed and innocent. But the police claimed to have found guns on the bodies and discounted these and other allegations as exaggerations: leftover political rhetoric from another era.

As he stands in Backatown, Malik insists what he saw was "blatant murder . . . The majority of the men who died in the storm . . . were black men who died of multiple gunshot wounds . . . That's the reason we formed Common Ground. 'Cause we saw people dying on the streets." And that's the reason, he maintains, that Common Ground is being harassed. Though it rejects violence, it shares the Panthers' fundamental mistrust of the government and their belief in a citizen's right to self-determination. The fight for home is, in Malik's view, a revolutionary one: a fight for justice.

"If Common Ground had been started as an all-black organization," Malik says again, "they would have killed us."

On St. Claude Avenue, not far from Carolyn and Patsy's block, a handicapped ramp leads up to what looks like a small house. Inside is a reception area with new chairs, new tiled floors, and children's artwork on the walls. Beyond are examining rooms fully equipped with tables, scales, blood pressure equipment, stethoscopes, medicine, filing cabinets, even stuffed animals for the kids.

"Everything is here," Malik almost shouts, "except for the patients. We had staff, we had doctors, we had nurses—that was willing to volunteer. In an area that needed health care more than any other area in New Orleans!"

Common Ground is already running a free health clinic in Algiers, and others have sprouted up across the city. With many of the big hospitals closed, the city—especially its low-income population—has come to rely on this network of community centers, often volunteer-run and on makeshift sites. The idea for this one was started by two nurses, both from the Lower Ninth. They knew the area had been underserved long before the floods, but the closing of Charity—where one of them had worked—just made it worse. So, while one woman donated her water-logged home here on St. Claude, the other—with the help of Common Ground—organized volunteers to gut and rebuild it. People across the country donated some $30,000, as well as medical equipment. Contractors worked for free.

The opening was scheduled for the first anniversary of the floods, nearly five months ago, but as one Common Ground volunteer explains: "The same day the clinic opened, they shut it down. Same day we were celebrating . . . they showed up. With a surprise that hurt everyone."

First, the New Orleans director of safety and permits cited the clinic as a commercial enterprise in a residential zone. Then the agency found other violations, like the need for a second guard rail on the handicapped ramp. "Every week that we would do what they tell us needed to be done," Malik says, "they'd give us something else."

As he tours the immaculate, unused rooms, he talks about how many kids he knows with Katrina cough. "And where they gonna go at? To get treatment? And this place is right here!" The city still has only a third of the hospital beds it did before the floods, and those are often far from low-income neighborhoods. Plus, more than a third of the city's residents—98,000—are living without health insurance. To Malik, keeping this clinic closed is another example of harassment.

Suddenly the whole thing seems to tire him out. He takes a seat in the pristine reception room. In his black beret and red windbreaker, he looks like a patient waiting for care.

"I haven't had a day off from this"—he gestures around—"since the hurricane. Not one day. In most cases, everywhere I go to try and raise money to do the work I'm doing, I got to relive a nightmare. 'Cause that's what they want to hear: 'What happened?' So, for the last year and a half, that's all I've been doing."

He tries to describe his average day. "Wake up in the morning to a threatening phone call. Go to bed in the evening with a threatening phone call. Spend all day where you gotta make sure that these hundreds of volunteers that come down here is *safe*. You know? Deal with the racists who come in to Common Ground and go into the showers and the bathroom defecating. Deal with the ones who come here telling our volunteers that they don't have no business in this community . . . Deal with the blacks that call me all kind of Uncle Toms"—his eyebrows lift— "for having whites in our community. No, I don't get no peace 'cause I catch it on all ends."

He had a heart attack in November, two months after the floods. He went to the temporary medical clinic run by the military in the Convention Center, got treated, and went right back to work. "I don't even have time to read . . . If I pick up something and start," miming a book in his hand, "here go the phones . . . Either a person is dead, a person is in jail. 'I want to come back home.' 'Can you help me come back home?' 'Can you help my family?'" He's thrusting one arm down, then the other, picking up phone call after phone call. "'Can you gut out my house?' 'We need food.' And the hardest thing to tell a person is, 'No, I can't help you.'"

"I'm fifty-nine years old," Malik continues. "I've outlived most of my peers . . . I have twenty-one grandkids: I've been truly blessed . . . I don't live no perfect life, and I'm far from being the perfect human being. But I know what: every evening before I close my eyes, I beg forgiveness for what I done. And every morning I thank Him for allowing me the opportunity to help somebody." He looks around the reception room, then out the dark windows. "I'm gonna fight this injustice . . . Whatever I can do, I'm willing to make that sacrifice. Do I like it?" His small eyes focus. "No. I *hate* coming over here." Pause. "I hate going to St. Mary's. I hate to have to leave those kids living in that cold building at night . . ."

Outside, a steady drizzle has started. It's getting late.

In the pitch blackness of a second-floor classroom at St. Mary, a voice.

"We don't have enough electricity for the building. It's cold in here, and I've been sick, so we got a heater. One of those electric ones? So I put it on, and it blew something."

A grin flickers in the shadows. A body is outlined against a window streaked with rain. Outdoors are a few, distant security lights.

Suddenly the electricity pops back on, and there's Brandon. He's in jeans and a jean jacket, a black ski cap pulled down over his ears. "Somebody plugs in a hair dryer in this place," he chuckles, "and it blows a fuse."

The room, he explains, is not only where he chairs meetings, but where he sleeps: a mattress on the floor. "That's how we can do all the stuff we're doing, 'cause we don't use the money for ourselves."

He looks at the paperwork spread out on his desk.

"Today my schedule was crazy, man." In the morning, he appeared on a religious TV channel. "I don't go to church, really . . . I just appealed with them to please, please, please help with our shelter . . . And we're getting response. It's great! People are really working together."

Since his return, Brandon has started a project to set up homeless shelters in strategic parts of the city. "We're putting them in areas we believe there's a restriction on the restoration of services in order to not have people return . . ." He sees the potential for a series of stand-downs, with attendant publicity for the collective. "If the SWAT team wants to show up and kick out a bunch of single mothers with their little children, then, ya know, they can . . ."

Brandon flips a page of a spiral notebook. "Tomorrow I'm going to the mayor's office to meet with his staff about what we do and how we can assist them. It's kinda cool." Once again he's the head negotiator. He swivels in his teacher's chair and peers out the window into the night.

"So I'm feeling really confident. I feel confident that as long as we keep using creative models, this area is gonna stay in the hands of the people who lived here before the storm. And they're gonna be *better* off than they were before the storm." He grins. "And I'm feeling pretty good about the Lower Ninth Ward, too . . . Somehow or other, we're gonna get a house," he taps the desk, "on every block." He wants Common Ground to create its own jack-o'-lantern effect: one building per block to resist the bulldozers.

As Brandon considers a moment, the lights in the classroom once again flicker off. Then on.

"I think we're gonna win." He bobs his head in affirmation. "I think we *are* winning. The fact that we're *here* is winning." He licks his chapped lips. "And the fact that these communities are so involved . . . We have all these churches and synagogues and mosques, and everybody's working together." He looks down at his desk. "So naw, I don't think developers are gonna win this one. I really don't. I'm sorry it took this to get people working together . . . but they're really doing it! Definitely doing it . . . In the meantime, we just gotta make sure . . . we can keep meeting with everybody, keep volunteers coming, keep food and some shelter. And we'll be all right . . ."

He stands. "I've gotta go work on setting up a soup kitchen with Pastor Johnson. His congregation is on fire for doing something!" This is the pastor of Greater Mount Carmel, "where we had our community housing. They're gonna use [their] community center to feed people." He names some other ministers who are helping, then raises his hands and laces his fingers together. "Everything's kind of interconnected, working together. You know? We might not have the money the developers have, but man, we have some stuff they don't have. Ya know? We're on the side of right." He licks his lips. "We have a lot of heart. And we have all the culture and the heritage of New Orleans behind us. And I think that's gonna win in the end. I really do. We just gotta stick with it, ya know?"

Downstairs in the lobby, volunteers come and go. Outside, smokers stand in small groups. It's misty and cold, and the Upper Ninth is dark: the houses, the businesses, the FEMA trailers. Now and then, the lights go out in St. Mary, too. There's a brief hush among the volunteers. And then they start chattering again, waiting for the power to roll back on.

If You're Gonna Leave
Anybody Behind

(December 2007)

Almost a year has passed since the lights flickered off and on at St. Mary. The second anniversary of the floods has come and gone.

The entrance to Pastor Mel's ministry is crowded with vehicles: two vans, a panel truck, a couple of cars, a big white SUV with GOD IS GOOD ALL THE TIME on its side. There's a new, eight-foot-tall security gate. Beyond it, the main building now has a dark blue second floor: more sleeping quarters for the men, who helped frame, sheetrock, and side it. There've been other improvements. Yellow storage sheds now hug the building, and across from them, a narrow modular unit that houses two "quiet rooms." The ex-addicts can go here for Bible study or counseling. Another door leads to Pastor Mel's new office.

The pastor is busy elsewhere today. That leaves his lieutenant, Brother James, in charge. James is fifty: a short, black man in slightly crooked wire-rimmed glasses. He stands stiffly in the late morning heat, as if he's had a back injury. He uses a white washrag to mop his brow and dab at his eyes.

"It's hard to turn down people," James explains in his gentle voice, "even sometimes when we don't have beds." Right now, Bethel Colony South is home to fifty-four men—at and probably past its capacity. They crowd into the back courtyard, load vans out on the driveway, lift weights in the sun. "The guys are grateful," James says, "even if they just sleep in the hallway." Pause. "It's better than under the bridge. Around this time of year . . . it does get chilly sometimes. It's not a good time to be outside."

James knows about this firsthand. He was deep enough into crack that "at one time," he says, "[my sister] didn't want to see me. When I'd come to the house, she'd just shake her head. 'Look at ya! You're terrible looking. Don't ask me for no money; I ain't gonna give you no money.'" James enters his own small office, next to Mel's, and sits on the edge of his desk. He takes off his glasses, mops at his brow and eyes. There's a bright poster of a sailboat on the wall behind him and, stacked on a shelf, multiple copies of a book called *101 Ways to Reinvest Your Life*. "I waste a lot of *my* life," he sighs, "chasing drugs."

He offers a quick version: born and raised in New Orleans, went to church regularly till he was nineteen or so. "'88 got hooked on crack cocaine." Couldn't keep a job, stole and hustled. "I was able to talk to get whatever I wanted from people. If I talk to you long enough, I can get what's in your pocket." Entered a program eleven years ago, got out in '96. "I went to only one rehab program," he says, holding up a skinny finger, "and by the grace of God, I've been clean since." Came out wanting to do full-time service at a ministry but couldn't find an opening. "Last year, after the storm, Pastor Mel called me. And we talked, and I was available . . . I been here since August of last year. Full-time!" He claps his hands and beams.

The ministry has grown, James explains, because the need has. "Since the storm, we have a lot of people come to New Orleans for work . . . You can make a lot of money here in New Orleans if you're in contracting, roofing business, carpentry . . ." It's December 2007, and the population of city is only two-thirds what it was, but it's providing some 33,000 more construction jobs than before Katrina. And unemployment has dropped. The trouble, Brother James says, is that some of the workers "come with an addiction . . . Once they get down here, they been abandoned by contractors . . . [who] know these guys are on drugs. And they use them up, and they disappear on them."

James mops his brow and stares, nearsighted.

The drug of choice, he says, is still "crack cocaine." In his experience, "[it's] more like grass . . . can get a pretty good hold on you, but it's more of a mental thing." He touches his forehead. "You can get off it; I did . . . but heroin . . ." He pronounces it hare-on. "We have a lot of guys who come with that hare-on addiction, and we'll work with them. But if we see it's getting real bad, we'll send them to the hospital . . . We don't have that type of training or facility. You know, when it get that deep . . ."

One of James's responsibilities is to help with legal problems. "What happens with a lot of guys is they get arrested for trespassing 'cause they're sleeping in an abandoned house." James tries to help them through the system. "I go to court so often these days, I feel like Matlock and Perry Mason rolled into one." He grins.

The work often seems futile. Like all rehab programs, Bethel Colony South has a lot of men who can't make it, who relapse or just wander off. But James believes this particular program has an advantage. "God has a big plan for the ministry. Pastor Mel, he's the visionary . . . but I can see it, too . . . People come here, and they're blessed." As for his own future, "This is always where I was supposed to be: doing the will of God. And when you're doing the will of God? It never gets boring." He puts his glasses back on and stands in his stooped posture. "I always wondered why I couldn't get anywhere . . . [Now] I'm where God wants me to be. So I don't think I waste anything." He smiles. "I don't think so."

As James steps back outside, Pastor Mel comes walking down the length of the compound. He's wearing a clean white shirt, sharply pressed, and chino pants. "Praise God!" he says into his cell phone, chuckling. But when he gets off, he looks weary: his moustache grayer, his brown eyes tired. At the far end of the compound, some of the men are shooting hoops.

"We don't have any more room," Mel says. "We had to turn away a guy today. Turned away three last night." He points out a three-story structure next door: a former mini-mall, empty since the floods. He hopes to buy it and turn it into a 200-bed homeless shelter. He'd also like a separate ministry for women: he gets calls for help all the time but has nowhere to house them. And, he adds, there's a need for both a mental health facility and a medical clinic to treat "high blood pressure, diabetes . . . hopelessness . . ." He sounds like Malik: trying to provide basic services that the government hasn't. And like Malik, he's exhausted by it. "Where there's a need," he says, smiling a little, "we try to serve."

His big, athletic body moves toward the front gate. He nods his shaved head, greeting a volunteer, then makes sure of one of the men's work details. He gets into the GOD IS GOOD vehicle. He wants to check the progress on his and Clara's house in New Orleans East.

*   *   *

If he looks tired, Mel says—his profile sharp against the passing landscape—it's not just from running an overpopulated compound; it's how he spent the morning.

"A thing called deliverance. The Catholic Church calls it exorcism? One of the brothers, after class this morning, came to talk to me . . . This, um, demonic spirit started to reveal himself." Mel's voice is low. "In the Christian world, we know that we deal with spirits, powers and principalities, wickedness in high places. And God gives us tools to deal with that." A soft sigh, eyes on traffic. "When you are using drugs, you are opening yourself to the spirit realm . . . So brother came with that situation this morning. And we spent from nine-thirty to one-thirty praying over him, anointing him with oil, reading Bible verses to him. And in Jesus's name, challenging the forces of darkness that had taken over his life . . ." Mel glances down at his chest. "I've changed shirts. It gets very intense."

He's driving up the Danziger Bridge and across the Industrial Canal. The slowly recovering city passes outside: fewer FEMA trailers than a year ago, more open stores and houses. Still, the neighborhood he's leaving, Gentilly, has less than 40 percent of its pre-storm population. And New Orleans East, which he's entering, has only about a third.

The block he and Clara own a house on is bustling with activity. Their next-door neighbor, Mel explains, still has a trailer out front, but she's almost fixed up her house and has bought the one across the street for her daughter. The next down and the one opposite it are both renovated. Directly across from Mel and Clara's, a black man totes a sheet of plywood.

"Looking good, Tony!"

"Getting there, Mel. One man, one day at a time."

Tony, Mel explains, is a New Orleans homicide detective who's been gutting his home on his days off. There's the whir of a table saw and trucks coming and going. Farther down the block, a two-man crew is repairing a roof. That owner, Mel says, also bought the lot next door. Only one house on this side of the street and two on the other aren't occupied. "And ours," Mel says, turning. "And we're just about there."

It's been almost a year and a half since Mel and Clara's house burned down. It's now got a new roof and new windows and doors, and the exterior is wrapped in white Tyvek insulation, waiting to be re-covered.

Progress on this block has happened through individual initiative, without a master plan. Last spring, the city's recovery czar, Edward

Blakely, made an executive decision: he would focus on seventeen "recovery zones" designed to "spur activity from investors." By investors, he didn't mean homeowners like Mel or the homicide detective across the street. Instead, the city proposed spending over $1 billion of recovery money "to fuel investment from entrepreneurs and developers." Fifteen of the seventeen zones are on the less flooded, upriver side of the city: "redevelop" and "renew" zones. The two most severely damaged areas are called "rebuild" zones. One is in the Lower Ninth between Backatown and Holy Cross, the other not far from this block in New Orleans East.

The plan appears to take a step away from Mayor Nagin's hands-off style and toward committing to which parts of the city will get help when. The czar has announced his decision is final: if he gets in what he calls a "cat-fight" with the various neighborhoods, "they're going to come off the list." Blakely still supports a free market approach but feels there needs to be some direction, some authority imposed. He's worried that residents are "rebuilding their homes on their own, literally on their own with almost no government assistance at all." From his point of view, this pioneer attitude—what Common Ground might call grassroots anarchism—threatens the power of government. "Defiance is still in the air," Blakely says, "—that people want to do things on their own. And they don't trust the system that they elected, or they didn't elect but was in place."

He sees one example of that defiance in the "lower-income population . . . trapped outside the city." It still thinks it has the "right to return," which the czar dismisses; he declares there's no such right. He doubts the evacuees will ever come back and believes that's probably for the better. In an April interview, Blakely called New Orleans residents "buffoons," described their leaders as "insular," and announced he was looking forward to an influx of newcomers "without the same attitudes of the locals."

The recovery czar promised his new plan would take effect immediately, and there would be "cranes in the sky" by September. That date came and went two months ago, and there are no signs of any cranes. Another program he's endorsed, Lots Next Door, is also just a plan so far. It's supposed to help residents buy adjacent, blighted properties, but the homeowners here on Mel's block are still acting on their own. Mel and Clara, for example, have put down a deposit on an empty house a little farther up the street. Because real estate prices haven't bounced back, they were able to pick it up "very inexpensively," says Clara. And in what the recovery czar might categorize as a defiant tone, she adds, "It kind of gives you control on who moves in."

Clara's come to the front door of their house. Dressed neatly in a plain green sweater and slacks, she describes their progress as "step by step. But we're getting it done . . . Melvin and I," she says quietly, "are fortunate to have a neighborhood where people are trying to come back."

Mel's concern is that the recovery czar and the city in general will block what's gotten them this far: "one man, one day at a time." Properties that were tax delinquent before the storm are now coming on the market. And soon the city's Redevelopment Authority will auction off the estimated 7,000 abandoned houses it's bought through Road Home. The plan is to sell these properties in clusters to "non-profit and for-profit developers." Mel frowns. "I think they're gonna give to developers to pick first and allow them to go through and develop . . . Everybody should have the *same* opportunity, not give developers a better opportunity."

Clara murmurs a quiet "Yeah."

Mel figures part of what's kept large-scale developers out of New Orleans East is "[they're] concerned about the levees . . . the educational system, the business climate." Around here, Mel says, the levees are "basically nonexistent compared to what I see in the more affluent areas." And even though New Orleans East is "the largest area in the city, a hundred square miles . . . it's got the fewest [police] officers." Mel gives a rough laugh and looks down the street.

Across the way, workers are measuring lumber. Two women carry a new mattress wrapped in plastic. The rebuilding effort is stimulating the local economy; for the first time in decades the average per capita income in New Orleans is higher than the national figure. Part of that is who lives here now—and who doesn't.

"So, the city has changed," Mel says. "And changed forever. There was a time when black people had some power here. Some. Now that that's gone, it's a new day. I don't know if that's good or bad . . ." Population counts this summer found the metro area almost 60 percent white and about 30 percent black. And there are fewer poor people. The free market approach to recovery has started to produce that boutique city Mel feared from the start: smaller, richer, whiter.

"Things have to change," he declares, looking out over his block. "Because things weren't good before the storm. The school system was bad; the police department was struggling; hospitals were struggling . . ." But for those on the bottom, those trying to survive, he doesn't see the current situation as much of an improvement. "I think the city is getting darker. Crime is on the rise; drugs are on the rise; killing is on the rise. And they can't seem to get a handle on it." The solution? "It has to be a comprehensive thing. If you're gonna leave anybody behind, then everybody's gonna suffer . . . We're all citizens, trying to live a life that we can raise families and build on, so our children can have more than we had."

Down the street, a Latino worker slides a long plank off the back of a flatbed. At Mel and Clara's house, a storage bin sits on the front lawn near a port-o-potty; odd pieces of lumber are strewn about. "We got some friends who are coming down from Cornerstone Church up in New Jersey," Mel says, "that's gonna do the stucco work and the brick work . . . It was gonna be like eighteen thousand dollars, and it'll probably only cost us six. God is great! Only God."

He now walks up the path to the front door. "We're taking it a little bit at a time, 'cause we're getting money a little bit at a time. When we get it, we put it into the house." Behind the door, there's a small entryway with a glass-block dividing wall. It leads to a big, open, not-quite-finished living room. A stepladder has been left standing in about the spot where, under charred beams, Mel sang, "I thank you Lord / I thank you Lord / I thank you Lord." A ceiling fan now spins overhead, and the walls are various pastel shades.

"All Clara's design," Mel says. "I did the structural design, but she does all the decorating."

"With directions about structure," Clara puts in.

"Amen." Mel grins.

The living room blends into the kitchen, which has cabinets installed and a half-built work island in the center but no counters yet. There's a refrigerator, a dishwasher, and a microwave, not all hooked up. "Little by little by little," Mel says softly. "Little by little by little." Then he adds in a louder voice: "And it's a fine house if I should say so myself." Grins. "This is a resurrected house!"

The year-long resurrection has been partly due to volunteers coming down from the Jersey church, the men from Bethel Colony South, and a local architect who helped with some drawings. Plus, Clara says, they had "the assistance of an attorney," choosing her words carefully, "who *encouraged* the insurance company to give us the funds." She laughs. Then, with a thin smile, eyes unblinking, she grows serious.

"There's nothing the government has in place to protect its citizens.

You're just at the mercy . . ." She frowns a little, as if trying to understand this. Then in her sweet, schoolteacher's voice: "Most people do what they're supposed to do. You think you're okay when you follow the rules. But there's another reality." She's touched that reality, felt what it's like to be powerless, and won't forget. It's her new normal. "It's not just us; it's all of America. Because those insurance companies are nationwide. And we all have the same federal government."

Clara leads the way from the kitchen down a hall to the master bed-room. "We wanted to tear the house down completely. After the fire. Because there was so much damage. But when we went to the city regarding permits, they said if we tore it down, we were going to have to raise it three feet." She frowns. "And I said, 'Well, the damage is from fire, not from water.'"

FEMA's rules are that any new structure has to be three feet or more off the ground. So they rebuilt keeping the same footprint but changing the interior design. Off the kitchen, they've enclosed a sunroom; today, its floor is still piled with paint cans, rollers, new fixtures in cardboard boxes. They've put in a stairway to what was an upstairs attic and is now a living space for visitors and grandchildren. "So we'll hear the pitter-patter of many feet," says Clara as she climbs up into the whitewashed, narrow room.

Mel is explaining that they paid the men from his ministry to do a lot of the carpentry up here, when his cell phone buzzes. "Praise the Lord, brother. What you got?"

Mel listens, then puts the call on speaker phone. ". . . Seven thousand six hundred and forty dollars' worth!" an excited voice says.

"Praise God!" Mel answers, then explains. "That's something, huh? Man calls up this morning—and he's done other things for the ministry—and he just said, 'I'd like you to meet me at Sam's Wholesale Club . . . and I just want you to get what you want. Not what you need, what you want.' And I said, 'All right, I'll send some brothers from the kitchen' . . . So, this man bought *seven thousand dollars* worth of food for the ministry! That's how we survive . . . That's the way God blesses us . . ."

As they start back down the stairs, Mel's cell phone rings again. "Clean and sober?" Mel says into it. "That's great, Joe D . . . Yeah, yeah . . . Very soon."

Mel flips the phone closed, then explains that he keeps it on day and night. "Well, yea . . . What do you do when a man calls you at three o'clock in the morning and tells you, 'I'm tired of living; I'm tired of druggin'.

Please help me. I don't want to commit suicide'? What do you do? You talk to him. You know? You do whatever's necessary . . . 'Cause that may be the only time he cries out for help . . . So, you just do it." He looks Clara's way. "I'm glad I got a wife that understands it."

She smiles.

Back down in the kitchen, amid all the new appliances and the freshly painted walls, Mel again tries to explain what his morning's work was like. Men needing deliverance, he says, "speak in strange voices, howl like an animal, slither on the floor." At first, the subject feels out of place in this redone middle-class ranch house. But for Mel, addiction and homelessness are real; this shelter, like all others, is temporary.

He points off the entrance hall where his office will be. He'll counsel men there; maybe some will live in the renovated attic. "We want to try to be in by Christmas," he says. That's three weeks away. "I don't know if we're gonna be able to . . . but we're trying."

Mel's parents are home.

From the outside, in the winter dusk, it's hard to tell. The front of their house is lit by a hanging globe on each side of the main door, another at the end of the driveway, and there seem to be new, big windows. But the lawn is still ragged. And their statue of the Virgin Mary is gone: tire tracks end at the spot where it once stood. Mel explains that burglars came one night, backed a truck up, and carted it away. They also took the front door off the house across the street.

That house now belongs to Mel and Clara. The elderly woman who used to live there decided she was too old to return and sold it for not much money down. That means that, in addition to their own place, they now own two derelict buildings. The main reason they bought this one is to stabilize the neighborhood. That's also why Mel's sister has purchased the house on the corner, though she plans to live there. Together, the family has created a kind of security compound around Mel's elderly parents: an occupied circle in the continuing emptiness of Pontchartrain Park.

"Some people," Mayor Nagin recently declared, "are coming to the realization that the recovery is too hard, that they could move somewhere else." Pontchartrain Park has one of the lowest rates of return in the city. Though wages in the construction sector are rising, there are fewer white-collar jobs like the ones that many Park residents held. And higher-end homes still aren't selling. Realtors say it's temporary and blame the cost of homeowners insurance, which has tripled since the floods.

But it isn't just insurance, and it isn't just New Orleans. Over the past year, the number of houses sold nationwide dropped by 10 million. Back in February, one of the largest subprime mortgage lenders in the country filed for bankruptcy. In June, the brokerage and banking firm of Bear Stearns announced it was halting redemptions on two hedge funds that were backed by subprime investments. And in July, the U.S. supply of unsold homes reached a sixteen-year high. Experts are assuring the American public that the economy is fundamentally sound, but 3.5 million houses are now worth less than what's owed on them. The current term for these homes is that they're "underwater."

To many in New Orleans, the irony is obvious. It's as if the flood that began here is slowly creeping across the country.

Over the past year, Mel's parents' house has been transformed. The front room—little more than a concrete slab—has been sheetrocked and painted. On a long white couch up against one wall, Mel's father and two of Mel's sisters are watching football on a wide-screen TV. Where the water pipe was ruptured and dripping is now the kitchen: Mel's mother is in there arranging trays of food. Toward the back, where there were only shadows and mold, there are now a series of bedrooms.

"For us," says one of Mel's sisters, "it's a miracle. None of us are back in our house but our parents. We wanted them to be first . . . and they are." A proud smile. Here's the bedroom where she and her sisters used to sleep. The walls spotless, new doors hung, it's now a study for Mel's father. In the master bedroom, belongings are still stacked to the side. In the corner is a statue of the Virgin Mary that Mel's mother thinks may be *the* statue, stolen off her lawn and put up for resale at a local garden store. She's keeping it here in her bedroom till they can erect a pedestal for it in the yard. And till the neighborhood is a little safer.

Back in the front of the house, a new cut-through connects the kitchen to the dining room. "It's the same," says Mel's sister, "but it's different . . . Sometimes I sit here and I look at the house and, you know . . . this is the home we grew up in. And I'm so glad they're back," gesturing toward her parents, "but there's memories we lost. That we'll never get back."

Mel's mother is wearing a black-and-white print dress and red lipstick. While everyone else watches LSU on the wide-screen, she goes to a nearby curio case filled with what she calls "Katrina treasures." "Nothing much, but . . . come and see this, Melvin." Still in his pressed white shirt, Pastor Mel pulls away from the game.

"You remember that?" His mother points to an orange bowl.

"No," says Mel.

"You don't remember that?"

"No . . . it was a long time ago, Ma."

She reminds him that he bought it for her with the earnings from his first grass-cutting job. Then, she points out a doll-sized tea set. "Over fifty years old," she says. "Even before we moved in the Park. And Dad was able to salvage it." There's some glassware as well and, on a shelf behind the sofa, a line of ceramic frogs: all found in the mud and wreckage of their ruined house. Mel's mother beams at these reminders of the past. They now decorate the present: her grown children once again gathered in a functioning house, her husband watching the game, the smell of gumbo wafting in from the kitchen.

Mel calls across the room: "Daddy?"

"What?"

"You'all didn't get a Road Home check, did you?"

"Oh no."

"No," Mel explains. "What they did was borrow some money from the SBA—that they have to pay back—got a little bit of insurance money, and that's it. They've gone into their personal savings and done what is necessary . . . But a lot of people don't have those kind of resources."

At the start of the year, Road Home had nearly 106,000 applicants and had only issued a little over 500 checks. Since then, 60 percent of qualified applications have been paid out. On average, homeowners wanting to rebuild have had to wait 250 days. Many waited over a year. And those who decided to sell their property to the state are finding payments delayed another 100 days. Public anger at the slowness of Road Home— blamed on bureaucratic tangles and incompetence—has helped convince Governor Blanco that she can't be reelected. But as she left office this month, she increased the payment to ICF without consulting either the legislature or the voters. That brought the private firm's fee for administering Road Home to over $900 million. The state eventually fined ICF $1 million for "failure to meet performance standards," but the firm still managed to quadruple its annual revenue. "The mistakes for the Road Home program," a Senate oversight committee will conclude, "lie at many levels of government."

Pastor Mel would like to believe the government is doing the best it can.

Congress has, after all, set aside almost $17 billion to restore Gulf Coast housing. But by the second anniversary of the flood, 70 percent of that was still unused. "I think some of it's incompetence," he says, sitting at the dining room table in his parents' rebuilt home. "But I'm understanding now that people they think are *not* coming back are put on the bottom of the list . . . I can't say it's some wholesale strategy, but . . . they have a way of holding up money if they want to . . . And people get discouraged."

The pace of returnees has slowed. As Mel sees it, those who've come back—like his parents and his neighbors in New Orleans East—are "people getting it done, *not* the government. The government is *still* failing us." His voice gets hard. "Road Home is having to cover the losses that people incurred that *insurance companies* are not paying . . . The American people are having to pay!"

The Road Home delay has helped keep Pontchartrain Park empty. And that's encouraged thieves. "I see here, in the evening, all kinds of thugs," Mel's father says gently. "Walking around. I see them breaking into people's houses."

New Orleans not only continues to be the nation's murder capital, with more than 200 in the past year, but it now has the highest overall crime rate. Neither the NOPD's "crackdown" nor citizens' protests have made a difference. As far as Pastor Mel is concerned, there's no waiting for a government solution.

"Nobody else is going to bail us out of this one." He takes off his reading glasses and places them on the red tablecloth. "I'm sick and tired of blaming everybody else for the problems that are in our community . . . You step up and do it! And quit complaining about it."

He gestures out his parents' new picture window towards the darkness.

"The park needs to be cleaned? Buy a lawnmower and clean it. Bring some of your friends over." His voice is rising. "Pick up the paper; make a difference in your community. Quit depending on someone else to do it!" He raps the table with his knuckle. "Want the crime to stop? Men, let's step up! Want our families to be saved? Men, step up! . . . Want better schools? Men, step up!"

Mel pauses, controls himself.

"New Orleans is like the rest of the urban areas. And it's getting to be that way in the suburban areas, too . . . America," he concludes, "is in serious decline. And doesn't want to acknowledge it . . . America as a whole—and where we are as a people. And if we don't turn back to God, we're doomed." Pause. "And I don't see us turning back to God."

It's halftime in the football game. Everyone gathers in the dining room. All stand in a circle and hold hands. "Father, we thank you, Lord God," Mel begins, head bowed, "for this time—this fellowship . . . Father, we thank you for this food . . . And we pray, Father, for those who are downtown, sleeping on the streets, Father, in front of city hall, Lord God." About 200 homeless have been camping near city hall. That many again are under a nearby overpass. "We pray that You would send some-one to feed them, and, Father, we ask for housing for all of those who have been displaced. Redo our city, God, not in the old way that it was, but in a better way. We pray this in Jesus's name. Amen."

Amens echo around the table. The family goes into the kitchen to help themselves to gumbo. When the others are seated around the table, Mel goes back to get more shrimp. His mother and sister call it "dragging the bottom."

As he eats, Mel explains that the homeless have been congregating downtown for a while now.

"It's like a tent city," Clara adds.

"They got nowhere else to go," Mel says.

Mel's sister speaks over the bustle of dinner: "The homeless have just taken up residence. More and more and more. They have tents there. It's sad. It's really sad."

"They're trying to get them moved," Mel adds. This week, the state an-nounced that it planned to fence off the area near city hall to begin con-struction on a new, $80 million office building. "What you gonna do with several hundred people? No facilities to house them and—" His cell phone rings. It's Brother James; he'll be right over.

After the gumbo come stuffed peppers. Mel's mother promises bread pudding to follow. "We call it a poor people's dessert." She sits at the other end of the table from Mel and Clara. "When the kids were growing up," she says, "we had it every Sunday . . . We couldn't afford the whip-ping cream, so we'd beat the whites of eggs, put it back in the broiler, let it brown . . . He still loves it." She points to Mel, who has a bemused smile. The dessert story starts his mother back through family history: how Mel used to sneak into the cabinets at night and eat all the canned peaches, how her family grew their own food years ago.

Brother James arrives, gets a plate, and sits between Mel's mother and Clara. It's almost a party, almost the old normal. From the next room comes the buzz of the TV and the shout of the announcer's voice. Mel asks his father what's happening. "They're in the fourth quarter, two minutes and forty seconds left."

The bread pudding comes out, and there are compliments for Mel's mom. A can of Reddi-wip gets passed around. Now Clara begins to talk about the people who are just returning to the city after a couple years of evacuation. "When they come back, they're still challenged. They say they smell it."

Mel's mother nods her agreement, takes a bite of the pudding.

"They can't stand seeing blighted homes—I call them Katrina homes—where the grass hasn't been cut." Clara looks around the dining room table. "Everyone can't do this. Everyone can't come back into this and be sustained. It's not regular."

"That's true," Mel's mother murmurs.

The football game has ended; the news comes on. People pass in and out of the dining room.

"Well, I hope I live long enough," Mel's mother says in a quiet moment, "to see the community come back. It's not going to be the way it was," she adds.

"That's okay," Clara answers.

"But everybody knew everybody." Mel's mother sighs.

Mel reassures her. "It's gonna happen, Ma."

In a soft voice: "I know it will."

A family photo album is brought out. It's been reconstructed to replace what Mel's parents lost in the floods. There they are at their marriage ceremony, his dad in his Air Force uniform. There's a va-va-voom shot of Mel's mother when she was sixteen. Over a high school portrait of Mel, his mother says: "He came from good stock." And smiles.

Dishes are cleared, washed, put away. Then it's time for goodbyes. Mel hugs his mother. He's tired, and he still has a meeting at Bethel Colony later tonight. But before that, he's decided he wants to go downtown to one of the homeless camps to see if there's anything he can do. His mother stands under the only light on the block and waves goodbye.

It's now estimated that the number of homeless has nearly doubled since the floods. Nobody knows how many are sleeping in the city's thousands of vacant buildings. Public shelters have 600 fewer beds than they did before the storms, and many private agencies, including Mel's, are full. Overall, the percentage of homelessness in New Orleans is almost three times the next highest metropolitan area. "In a modern urban U.S. city," says one expert, "we've never seen it."

Mel drives through the dark, his headlights flashing off buildings, only sporadic street lights breaking the black. It's cold and damp this December night, and the streets are mostly empty. A red Walgreens sign rears up and then disappears.

Mel works his way into the Tremé neighborhood and down Claiborne Avenue. The I-10 freeway runs directly overhead and under it, in the shadows, are vague, humped shapes. That might be a tent, or a heaped pile of belongings, or a human. It's quiet except for the thump of traffic on the thruway above.

"That's people that have been left stranded since Katrina," Mel says softly. "People just trying to survive."

He slowly drives past.

"A lot of people," he finally says, "have come back looking for work. And they just don't have a place to live that's reasonable." Last month, the city's housing authority approved $30 million to demolish the Big Four low-income housing projects.

Mel parks his car across the street and walks under the overpass. As he approaches, silhouettes step forward: dark forms against the big concrete pillars that hold up the thruway.

"What did they tell you about the floods?" one man asks, his voice a little too loud. "What did they *tell you* about the floods? *I'm* gonna tell you." He believes the authorities deliberately blew the levees. "To save their precious tourism . . . And it caused a lot of tragedies. Because in the lower-income areas are a lot of poor people. Who *died*." He has a slight lisp, maybe some teeth missing. "My wife and I—well, not so much me, but my wife—still have that, how you call that? Flashbacks. If you'd have seen how many bodies that was floating around in this area . . . from the Lafitte Project to Tulane and Claiborne, all the way Uptown. It was a mess. Nobody cared about us then—not our mayor, not our governor, not our president. Not even our congressmen. So if they didn't care about us then, why should they care about us now?"

There's the irregular thump of cars overhead. When headlights swing by, colors flare up for a moment: a white sheet, a striped blue blanket, someone's red hat. Then, dark again. The profile of a man with his cap on backward drinks from a paper bag, his arm around someone else.

Mel spots a familiar face and steps farther into the shadows. He hugs a man who used to be at Bethel Colony South. Most of the people in this camp, it turns out, are not out-of-towners, not immigrants, but locals. They've either been left homeless by the floods or were living in the streets long before the disaster.

"I have to watch my back every day," the man tells Mel in a slurred, slow voice. "I didn't choose to be out here." Pause. "I don't have the kind of money to pay rent for one bedroom: six hundred dollars deposit." Pause. "I don't have that." Pause. "This man been knowing me a long time." Pause, gesture toward Mel. "I used to live with him." Pause. "And I messed up." Pause. "He didn't mess up on me; *I* messed up." Pause. "But he never stopped loving me for what I was." Pause. "Never." Pause. "And he never will." Pause. "You have to choose a life."

The man talks about his high blood pressure, about his niece stealing his welfare check, how he won't be eligible again till next June. "So I *have* to work just to keep me goin'."

"Amen," Mel says. "Call me. Call me right away." He hands the man a card.

"I will." Pause. "The only day I have off" pause, thinks. "Is on Wednesday."

"Call me Wednesday morning."

"Because, Pastor, I'm at the point—"

"I see."

"I don't even trust nobody."

"I know. You got to call me."

"I will. Oh, I will. I will call you."

Mel's white shirt stands out as he moves among the shadows. He starts talking to a short woman in an oversized knit cap.

"Can't get in a shelter," says the man beside her. "'Cause, you know, you got to have a job."

"Ain't no shelters," Mel answers.

Another guy comes over, shakes Mel's hand, introduces himself as Roger. "I'm just out here, uh, still struggling. I can't fool you."

All Mel says is: "Out of control."

"It's a very sad situation," the first man says.

"What's the greatest need?" Mel asks. "We'll come down . . . What's the greatest need?"

The outline of the man shrugs. The flash of headlights shows he's short, gray-haired, African American. "Greatest need? The greatest need is for someone to get us out of this hell. It ain't hit you yet, but it's coming . . ."

At that, Mel goes still. Then, he rallies, organizes a prayer circle, everyone holding hands.

"O God, times like this, I don't know what to say. Father God, I'm gonna ask You for a solution to this . . . Be with brother Roger as he sleeps tonight. We ask You to protect him and camp Your angels around him."

Mel's voice rises.

"I don't have the answer, but I know that You do. Help us to help in whatever way . . . And we know that Your heart weeps, Father, for the struggle that the brothers and sisters are going through here. So, Father, I lift them up to You, in Jesus's name. Amen."

There's a murmured amen.

"I *will* see you again," Mel says to Roger.

"They got to have a solution somewhere," Roger answers. Then he and the others blend back into the dark.

The Lucky Ones Still Standing

(December 2007)

It's not much past dawn, December 2007. A pale yellow light strikes both the St. Claude Avenue Bridge and the emerald top of the levee, but leaves the sunken surface of the Industrial Canal a dark that's almost purple. On the Holy Cross side of the avenue, four of the first ten houses appear to be occupied, four look abandoned, and two have FEMA trailers in front. Then comes a square block completely empty except for foot-long grass and a couple of concrete slabs. Current estimates place Holy Cross at less than a third of its former population.

The playing fields at the Holy Cross Catholic school have been kept up, but the main building is still abandoned. What look like big trailers remain tacked out front. As to what's going to happen to these seventeen acres, the chair of the school's redevelopment committee said recently: "No decision has been made on the land use. This is a blank canvas."

Around the school property, most lawns have been mowed, and there don't seem to be demolition notices, but many houses are boarded up, and there's the occasional blue tarp still serving as a roof. The pink brick home with the TO GOD BE THE GLORY sign has a spotless front yard and a new roof and paint job, but there's still a FEMA trailer between it and the street.

Two years and two months after Katrina, Carolyn's double shotgun remains a beat-up green with a slash of red *veves* in front and a trailer out back. What's changed is the rear porch. It's been completely reframed, windows and doors removed, a fresh plywood floor installed.

Across the way, the abandoned Semmes elementary school has had most of its windows knocked out.

Next to it, Joe and Linda's is barely discernable. Thick green vines smother the front fence and porch, climbing all the way to an open attic window. There, a brown tabby cat stretches in a jungle of red blossoms.

Next door, a trailer and a van are parked outside Patsy's yellow house, with a FEMA trailer just inside the fence. Not a sound breaks the early morning quiet.

Patsy's son's house is still open from the front stoop clear to the back. It's got new two-by-four framing, but left out in the elements, that's already starting to gray.

At the foot of the levee, the dwarf Santa has been turned into a dwarf Indian. Thanksgiving was ten days ago.

Down the levee, at 905 Sister Street, Ron's termite-infested home is gone; the city finally demolished it. There's only a cleared space with a trailer to one side. Ken and Barbie still ride the front fence.

On Burgundy, opposite Lathan's properties, other houses now have ladders propped on roofs and dumpsters at the curb, but no one seems to be home.

And coming back down Jourdan toward Carolyn's, it's a patchwork of recovery: the first house abandoned, the next redone and occupied, the next being worked on, the next redone but unoccupied, then three small cottages with people in them. An elderly woman in her bathrobe comes out of one and picks the morning paper up off the drive.

Carolyn's is quiet. At the intersection, a black kid in baggy pants waits for his school bus. He says he's a freshman at George Washington Carver. Carver High is across the canal, near where Desire used to be. Carolyn went there, as did Pastor Mel's wife, Clara. In bad shape before the floods, it still hasn't been rebuilt. For the second year, the students assigned to it are going, instead, to the temporary classrooms tacked onto the Holy Cross School. "We're in the same trailers and stuff," the baggy pants kid says. "That ain't right." Condition there have been described as "terrible."

Slowly more kids trickle to the corner. Hoods pulled up, headphones on, they don't talk much but give off the faint murmur of hip-hop beats. When a boy in a red sweatshirt steps out of a white van, it stays: his mother wants to make sure the bus shows.

"We went away for about three years," she says. Hers is a big, round, brown face, with a scar over one eyebrow. "It was kinda hard getting back, had to go through a little proper channels . . . but this is my home. I'm thirty-seven years old . . . This where we live, we breathe, we eat; get along." She launches a stream of happy words: "crawfish, crab, gumbo, Mardi Gras, the works! I mean, heyyy! This is five-oh-four [the city's area code].

"My son"—she looks toward the teenager on the corner—"he's autistic, and he experienced some of the stress . . . You take him out of his environment, and in his mind, it's like, 'Why aren't we going back home?' And I had to constantly explain to my child: 'We goin' home soon; we goin' home soon.'"

Part of the reason they waited, she says, was his education. After the floods, there were no schools. Last fall, the city's educational system reopened with about a third the number of pre-flood students. During this, the second fall of operation, the student population is up to about half what it used to be, but the number of schools has increased to nearly two-thirds the pre-storm level. That includes state-run, city-run, and privately run programs. To this mother, it seemed enough like a functioning system to finally come home.

But here in the Lower Ninth, the new era of school choice isn't offering many options. "When we came back, that's all the school they had open for right now: Carver and a couple of other . . ." More critically, the city hasn't been providing the kind of instruction her son needs. Many charters aren't accepting students with disabilities. Last year, 2,000 students in need of special instruction couldn't find a place in any city school.

Still, she's delighted to be in New Orleans again. "When we got back here?" A grin splits her round face. "Couldn't wait! I was, like"—her voice goes high—"ba-a-a-by! It was like living in the land of Oz. Like Dorothy? That's what it was . . . We gone these different places; we seen all these strange things." A slight wrinkle on her smooth brow, "and then like when the little tornado, cyclone, brings the child home? We got back home and say, 'I wish I was home. Thank God we come back home.' It's like they say: there's no place like home . . . Here, you walk where you want to go. You feel a sense of freedom."

A yellow bus comes down Jourdan and stops at the intersection. The kids pile in. As the driver turns up North Rampart, the mother pulls away, too, and the block drops back into stillness.

Down the street, the door to Patsy's trailer slowly swings open. Patsy's big body steps out to greet the morning. She stands so only her head can be seen above the top of the fence. Her face is creased with sleep, her blond shoulder-length hair disheveled. The tip of one freckled shoulder peeks out of her nightgown: a long white T-shirt that reads SAVE NEW ORLEANS, END GLOBAL WARMING.

"My house isn't ready," she reports. ". . . The whole downstairs has been gutted. We had to do a lot of, um, chopping up the concrete to get to the pipes underneath . . . Now it's to the point where a ce-ment guy is coming just to lay the ce-ment down . . . Yesterday, my son had a central air/heat guy come over and give his estimate on doing that. So it's slowly coming together. We're pecking at it. Like little woodpeckers." Both big hands emerge over the top of the fence to illustrate: "Doop-doop-doop! Just pecking away." Smile.

Before the flood, she used her first floor for storage. It was so packed— with her grown son's baby toys, her sixties record collection, old books— she could barely get around. "Years ago, in the eighties, I got robbed three times. Actually," circling her arm, "everybody around here who worked got robbed about three times. In a two-month period. They'd rob you and give you a little time to get your new stuff from insurance," laugh, "and then they'd come back and get that! So we had a lot of doors all boarded up down there. But when I was walking down there the other day, it was like, 'Ahhh! I didn't think my house was this big! I didn't even *know* I had a door over there.'

"I used to always worry . . . about what was going to happen when I died. The main thing was, who's gonna go through all that stuff?" She laughs and hides her face in embarrassment. "Well, Katrina helped us with that." Deeper laughter. "Anyway, [the house] is pretty big right now, and I have *vowed*," pause, "to take hold of my sickness, my pack-rat syndrome."

She's still in her FEMA trailer. The deadline to take them away was extended this past February and then again in July. Now, neighboring Jefferson Parish has set March 1, 2008, as a firm date for removal. Here in New Orleans, the 15,000 families still in trailers worry they're next. "The recertification people came . . ." Patsy thinks a moment. "Last week. To see how far along we were. To see if I can keep the trailer longer. I can't keep this one," she adds sweetly, "because this is one of the ones that had the high formaldehyde content."

FEMA has continued to downplay any problems. Meanwhile, the Department of Health has declared it can't "predict the consequences" of having lived two years in a contaminated trailer.

"I," Patsy says, stuttering a little, "I kept the air-conditioning going and windows open and doors open just about the entire time I've had it. So I can't smell it there anymore. Initially I could . . . before they were even coming out with the formaldehyde notice . . . If you talk to people who work at a shipyard—you know they wear masks when they're doing the fiberglass." One hand comes up over the fence to cover her face while her other hand paints the air, ". . . That's how this was in the beginning. So they're trying to find me an alternate living space." She thinks Mark across the street might have an apartment to rent. That would be "do-able," she says, "because the dogs can still have the yard here. And I can bring them in at night with me . . ."

One of her dogs is beside her now, down behind the fence. There's a scuffling. "Oh, Beau!" she says, looking down. "He catches rats all day long. That's his thing . . ." Sunshine is starting to cascade down her block.

"At this point, I think we kinda don't know any better. It's kinda like you've adjusted to it. And this is the way life is. You just do little bits at a time." She shakes her blond head as if trying to wake up. "But if it weren't for all the volunteer groups? . . . All those people coming down to help us in whatever way they can, even if it's yard work or," pause, "just any-thing. *Anything!* I mean, they've certainly helped physically . . . but emotionally—just to know that somebody *cares* is the important thing." She thickens each syllable with her twang: caa-ares.

"A lot of people are rebuilding themselves 'cause they can't afford the contractors, you know." That's what her son next door is trying to do, but he's come full stop. "It's bad! He ran out of money, and he's fighting with the Road Home people right now. And—" The phone rings in her trailer; she disappears to answer.

When she returns, her blond hair has been brushed into a neat page-boy, and she's put on a long green blouse over her T-shirt. Moving slowly, she makes her way out of her driveway, calling, "Here kitty, kitty, kitty! Here kitty, kitty, kitty!" She feeds the stray cats, she explains, pointing to the big plastic buckets of dry food. The tabby comes down out of the tan-gle that covers Joe and Linda's.

The street is still. Across the way, the yellow bungalow has had its rail-ing pulled off and construction permits taped beside its *veve*. Patsy says Joe and Linda sold it to Mark. They kept its sister house next door to store "whatever they think they can save." It's been nailed shut for more than a year.

Patsy is putting out cat food, admiring her curbside garden, when she spots a figure at the end of the block. "Here comes the doctor!" she shouts.

It's Mark—gray, fit—in an old white lab coat that reaches to mid-thigh, a blue and black knit cap, sandals over socks. "Another beautiful day!" he yells, and heads off.

"You're not coming over?" she yells back.

Mark dutifully reverses course. "You look," she says as he comes up, "like Marcus the Magnificent today."

"This is my father's lab coat," Mark explains. His father was a vet back in Minnesota. Mark's dingy, dimly professional appearance sets both of them giggling like kids.

"It looks like you got snow on top of your hat."

"White paint," Mark answers. Patsy puts one big arm around his skinny shoulders. "That tree," he says, pointing toward the tree at the foot of the levee. "What do you have on there?"

"The tree?" Patsy asks in her innocent voice. "That's just garlands and stuff. Remember he was an Indian for Thanksgiving?"

"Right."

"But he's got to come out the closet, so to say, for Christmas. And be himself . . ." Patsy laughs. For Halloween, she explains, the dwarf figure was an orange witch with a pumpkin for a head. "On St. Patrick's Day, he was a leprechaun, all in green, and the tree was all in green . . . He was an Easter bunny with buck teeth." She brings her fingers to her mouth and wiggles them. "And big ears," pulls at the air above her head. "The kids liked it at Easter 'cause I dug out my change, and I put it in the Easter eggs . . . I don't know who the smart one was to figure it out first." Laughs.

"I think you did a magnificent job over here," Mark says. He points to the curbside garden in front of Patsy's son's house. It's thick with vines, white lilies giving off a deep perfume, yellow and orange nasturtiums, and a single bright red poppy.

"All I did was take all my seeds and mix them up in a bag together."

"Just beautiful."

"That's a poppy, an *unreal* poppy . . . When I plant seeds, I get ants in my pants," Patsy scrunches up her shoulders, ". . . and I just can't wait for them to grow. So I go and get silk flowers and stick them in the ground . . . So I'll have something to look at while I wait."

Mark marvels at all her efforts to spruce up the block. "I can hardly keep the grass cut."

"Well, that's why I did this: so I wouldn't have to cut the grass." Which reminds her that she's supposed to be working this morning with the Holy Cross Neighborhood Association: "I gotta get back to the garden."

She excuses herself, opens the door to her van, and moves a big folded sign from the driver's seat. It says: HOLD THE CORPS ACCOUNTABLE. She gets in, then waves as she pulls away.

"And I got to get back to painting." Mark disappears down his driveway.

The block goes quiet again. The red top of a big barge floats past the levee.

Across Jourdan Avenue, workers start arriving at Carolyn's double shot-gun. A Latino stands on a ladder and sawzalls under the eaves of the back porch; another unwinds a power cord. The third worker is African American, round with a bald head and a dark black beard, in his forties maybe. He's the head contractor.

"In this area here, I got three jobs that's gonna be going on." He doesn't speak like a local; it turns out he's from California. "I got this one. And then I got another one down in Arabi. And then I'm building a new home on one of those slabs over there on Forstall Street." Forstall is in Backatown; it happens to be the street Carolyn grew up on.

"I came down January '06," he continues. "I came down to work on the levees. 'Cause I have dump trucks . . ." He was doing construction work on the West Coast when he heard about the job opportunities post-Katrina. But, he quickly explains, it was more than that. "My grandfa-ther is from New Orleans . . . All his family is here . . . So I got deep roots here in the Ninth Ward." He calls Holy Cross "prime property" and talks about how he wants "to come back here and retire." Rebuilding the neighborhood, he says in his deep voice, "makes me feel real good. When I talk about it, it brings tears to my eyes." Like in California, he says, when he dresses up as Santa each year and hands out free presents: "Giv-ing back and everything: that's a beautiful thing."

Carolyn has finally gotten some money for repairs. It isn't from Road Home—she's still waiting for that—but from the historic preservation grants that Mark and Patsy mentioned almost a year ago. "I was lucky," Carolyn will explain later. "I received a phone call from Preservation . . . saying that we being in a historic neighborhood, they might be able to help me." Using matching federal funds and collaborating with the local Preservation Resource Center, the state was offering around $45,000 per historic home. Mark didn't qualify for his main house because he'd already done most of the work, but he got a grant for the bungalow he bought from Joe and Linda. Lathan got one. Patsy and her son each received a full $45,000. "By the time they got to me," Carolyn will say, "it went down to twenty-six. I thank God for the twenty-six!"

Historic Preservation earmarked Carolyn's grant to restore the back porch with its distinctive, sideways-opening "wing" windows. She could also use some of it for foundation work, plumbing, and electrical.

It was Carolyn's son, Rahsaan, who found this contractor a few weeks ago. "I just happened to meet them across the bridge at a corner store . . . They were having lunch. And I said, 'Hold up a second! Are you a contractor?' He said, 'Yeah. Yeah, I'm a contractor.' I said, 'Well, what kind of work you do?' He said, 'We do everything.'"

The family took the historic grant and what savings it had and paid for the work up front. With builders in New Orleans at a premium, that's become common practice.

"This guy," Rahsaan continues, "when he started work, he would knock on that trailer door. And he would ask me to come out and take a look real quick. And he showed me where some of those beams were not good . . . It would've hurt him to his heart if we'd told him to fix just [the porch] and left the rest of it. Because Ma's house would've collapsed in six months' time . . . I got myself a good contractor . . . He didn't gouge us or anything . . . We're sitting pretty."

This early morning, the contractor explains what his plans are.

"Since this is a historical home, it has to be put back historical. The original windows, they're wooden." He's stacked them on the porch: multipaned, side-hinged. "So I'm gonna refinish those myself. Replace all the glass panes I need to replace, build custom framing, and set them in here," indicating the new porch walls. "I'm doing the foundation," he goes on. "New seals, everything . . . Siding. We're trying not to replace too many pieces because this wood here is hard to find." He's talking about the cypress planking that many Holy Cross homes were built with in the nineteenth century. Often they were cut from nearby swamps, used on the river barges till the boats were decommissioned, then reused to build houses. "They don't make it anymore. You can nail into some of this wood, and your nail bends!" Jovial belly laugh.

"We're doing it in stages; they wanted it in stages . . . Floor, windows, sheetrock—everything that she wants done in here, I'm gonna do . . . So, she can get back in her house. And get out of this FEMA." He calls a March 1 deadline for removing trailers "not realistic." He believes most of Holy Cross won't be ready. But for Carolyn? "They can come pick it up in March. Yes. 'Cause she will *be here* in this home!"

Rahsaan has been trying to supervise the work when he isn't at his restaurant job. Kyrah is also keeping an eye on things, but she's a full-time student. So the other day, the contractor says, Carolyn did her own inspection. This despite having finally gone through with her double knee surgery. Carolyn's position is clear: "I want them to finish everything we agreed to. I paid them for it; I want that finished . . . You got my money; you got the material; now let's move!" She came out, the contractor continues, with "no stick, no thing! That woman got a will there. She is definitely blessed . . ." She walked a slow tour the entire way around the house. "[The neighbors] see her, and that makes them drive even harder. And that's a beautiful thing . . ." The contractor gives his deep laugh. "I better not mess up."

A little later, Kyrah emerges from the trailer. When she can afford to, she boards at college. More often, she's sharing a bed with her mother in these cramped, possibly toxic quarters. She often wakes with a clogged nose. "I will buy it," she says of their FEMA trailer, "to burn it."

This morning she's in a gray hoodie over a yellow T-shirt. She looks sleepy. She waves to the workers, then avoids the construction by cutting through the cinder-block garage out back. She's headed to MLK, her old elementary school. "I haven't seen them since before the hurricane."

Now twenty, Kyrah has given up the idea of going back to Syracuse. She's done a fall semester at the University of New Orleans, taken last winter off to work, returned to UNO for the past summer and fall. It's hard putting together the tuition, and she's thinking of taking another year off to make some money as a beautician. Once she graduates, she says, she wants to teach at MLK, but "probably . . . for a short amount of time. 'Cause I don't want to stay in the New Orleans school system too long."

Kyrah starts down Jourdan. The house next door is still abandoned. The one after, Kyrah says, the owner is rebuilding on his own, "all day and all night." He was one of the winners of the solar panel lottery; the new technology gleams from the roof of his still-unoccupied house.

On St. Claude Avenue, the only stores that have opened are a gas station and a taco stand. This area was supposed to be one of the recovery czar's development zones, but there are still no cranes in the sky. Kyrah says she'd like to see the Lower Ninth get a supermarket and "maybe some malls and coffee shops." But there are still only a couple thousand people this side of the canal. "It's kinda confusing," she says, looking at the abandoned blocks. "'Cause you want to know what they're going to do with all the houses. Can't just leave them there, gutted out." She shrugs sleepily. "Who knows?"

She passes Louis Armstrong Elementary School. Formerly known as McDonough #19, this was one of the first two schools integrated back in 1960. It's where Miss Clara taught in the late eighties, finding it in "deplorable condition." Now, it's boarded up and, as Kyrah says with a laugh, "very closed."

Another half dozen blocks, on the edge of Backatown, she comes to MLK's yellow and purple building. Its parking lot is full of cars; kids enter through the rear entrance.

MLK is home.

As its name suggests, the school is a product of the civil rights era. "When it opened," Kyrah says, "it was the school for all of the kids in the Lower Ninth Ward . . . That's when everybody found out we could achieve more than the kids who get everything they want . . . Most of us ended up going to four-year universities."

Principal Hicks had always resisted making MLK a magnet school: she wanted to educate neighborhood kids, not the city's best and brightest. As to becoming a charter, "we actually thought charters were the demise of education." But the first year after Katrina, thirty of the city's forty-seven schools reopened as charters. And this spring the state brought in a new superintendent, Paul Vallas. In his previous jobs in Chicago and Philadelphia, Vallas championed what's been called "market-driven education": closing schools with low test results, eliminating local school boards and teachers unions, bringing in outside management and staff, encouraging the switch to privately run operations. This year, half the city's 1,100 teachers are new hires, many of them recent college grads without experience. Two dozen new principals have been trained to follow a centralized "managed curriculum." The instructional day has been extended by an hour and a half. And New Orleans continues to be the only city in the nation with the majority of its students in charters.

"We have an opportunity here," as one of the city's new principals puts it, "to create a model that works, so we can say to other schools, other districts, and other cities and states, . . . 'This is how we give all students a quality education.'" New Orleans may have been heading this direction before the floods, but as Vallas has said, now there are no "institutional obstacles . . . No one tells me how long my school day should be or my school year should be. Nobody tells me who to hire or who not to hire."

More than the recovery czar or the Catholic archdiocese, more than the mayor himself, the new superintendent of schools has been able to transform the city's post-Katrina landscape. The federal government is encouraging the switch to charters, providing start-up money on top of local school taxes. The state is waiving national guidelines and allowing charters to select their students through admission tests. Kids can apply from anywhere in the city—and students with learning problems don't have to be admitted. As of this fall, almost 20 percent of the city's charter school kids are labeled "talented and gifted," compared to barely 1 percent in the so-called regular schools. It's a formula for higher standardized test scores, a guarantee that the experiment will, on some levels anyway, succeed.

But with charters skimming off the gifted and most of the city's white students continuing to go to religious and private academies, the Recovery District is left running what are widely seen as "schools of last resort." And, as Kyrah says, "not doing a very good job. At first they were feeding people frozen lunches. And they didn't really care if the kids had books." The Recovery District—with a third of its former student population and more than 90 percent of those officially in poverty—is sending children to buildings Kyrah calls "raggedy, rat-infested, broken. Falling-apart bathrooms with no stalls." By the end of the last school year, fewer than half its students were bothering to show up for class.

"[It's] all part of this strange scheme," Kyrah says, "where they're trying to keep everybody out. They put you in a public school—give you this terrible, raggedy building—and tell you, 'If you don't like it, then leave.' You can't exactly put your kid in a private school, because you don't have the money for it. So it's kinda like the whole housing situation: . . . if you can't afford it, don't come back."

Faced with having MLK turn into a school of last resort—and with the Lower Ninth continuing to be so empty that there weren't enough neighborhood kids to fill her school—Dr. Hicks saw little choice. She decided the charter option was "the only way that we could reopen." As Kyrah puts it, "The parents, the principal, and the school staff . . . didn't care for how the Recovery School District was running things. And they decided they wanted to run their own school. They know what they need, so they take care of it." This August, MLK came home to its old building. But it returned as a charter school, the only one in Louisiana managed not by an outside company but by its own board of directors.

The day has turned cold and overcast. Kyrah walks the length of MLK till she finds a side entrance that's open. Inside, where the flood line once ran like a dirty graph, the cinder-block walls are now painted turquoise. Teachers are busy taping up kids' pictures and displays. Down the hall, a banner proclaims PROUD AMERICANS GLAD TO BE HOME. Beneath it are crayoned self-portraits of kindergarteners.

A teacher recognizes Kyrah and shouts, "She's a King baby!" Another gives her a big hug. "So what are you doing now?" she asks.

"Going to school," Kyrah answers, "and, um, working."

"Well, that's all right," the teacher says with a big smile. "You sound disappointed?"

Kyrah—the honor student at MLK, the triumphant grad who'd made it out of the city with a full scholarship—is now at a local college, struggling to come up with tuition. "I just had a job at a day care," she explains, "but I quit it. So I'm just working on my degree."

She stops to peek in a class. The walls are clustered with projects, the shelves full of books, there's a low hum as teams of five- and six-year-olds work together. "Same teachers, same quality," is Kyrah's reaction. ". . . Teachers that love to teach." By turning charter, MLK was able to control hiring: it brought back nearly all of its staff, most of whom have more than twenty years' experience.

The 650 students here are still overwhelmingly poor and black, but they now come from all over the city. The boys dress in dark pants, the girls in green checked skirts; all wear clean white shirts with the school name printed above the pencil pocket. MLK is being profiled in national publications as an example of the city's recovery and the new market-driven approach to education. Its test scores remain high, but that may be due, in part, to its percentage of students with disabilities being among the lowest in the system. On the second anniversary of Katrina, President Bush chose to have MLK as his backdrop when he declared, "This town's coming back."

Kyrah now approaches the principal's office. A big HOME SWEET HOME sign hangs on one wall of the waiting room, and there's a life-sized black Santa in the corner. "Home indeed," Kyrah says. "I spent too much time here. I spent more time here than I did at home . . . My principal," she'll add later, "doesn't want nothing less than the best for her kids and her teachers. Ever."

When Dr. Hicks emerges with a "Hey!" Kyrah answers "Hey," suddenly a little shy. The principal is a tall woman with a dark brown, big-featured face, deep-set eyes. She looks at Kyrah with amusement: "How are you? What's going on? Where are you in school?" Kyrah explains she's at UNO. When she adds that she's majoring in education, Dr. Hicks looks shocked. "Really! Are you serious? How's your family?"

"Momma's all right," Kyrah answers. "She got knee surgery."

They talk about where Kyrah's classmates are at college and how many have gotten back in their homes. Thirty-five MLK families were in the flood and "did not," in Dr. Hicks's words, "make it out."

Then Kyrah brings up maybe coming back to MLK to teach someday. Dr. Hicks's response is to start teasing her. "You'all put more gray hairs in my head than anyone . . . You'all were disgusting!"

Kyrah laughs; the secretary laughs. It's not exactly a job offer. Then Dr. Hicks, a busy woman, has to go. "All right, Boo," she says. "Thanks for coming in."

A hug. Kyrah exits past the HOME SWEET HOME sign.

On Sunday, Carolyn decides to go to church. She wears a black-and-white print dress and carries a black leather purse in one hand, a cane in the other. As she limps slowly out of her trailer, Kyrah follows, all dressed up in a tight white T-shirt, purple jeans, and black high heels.

When they reach the car, it's hard for Carolyn to get in. First she sits on the backseat, then scoots inside till just her lower legs dangle, then turns and grabs her legs and pulls them. As she does, her skirt rides up to show four-inch scars from the top of each kneecap down toward the shin.

The operation, a couple days before Easter, didn't go well. They put her under and then, in Carolyn's words, "in the middle of surgery, while they was dealing with one leg—getting ready to deal with the other—who wakes up?" She laughs. ". . . They shot me with something to knock me back out . . . They was all upset because they said that wasn't supposed to happen . . . They shot me like an elephant!"

Kyrah takes up the story: "She literally could not wake up . . . They overloaded everything trying to knock her out. To the point where . . . she was all loopy and crazy."

"My heart stopped," Carolyn explains.

"She stopped breathing," Kyrah confirms. Soon the family had gathered to pay their last respects.

Carolyn tries to explain how it felt. "Within your mind, your brain, it's like a clock . . . like a movie." During surgery, "I decided to take a trip to memory lane. Like, go backwards. Visit the dead instead of coming to the living . . ." She says she stopped in the sixties, "back there with all the old-school music." She laughs. She saw her mother, her brothers; it was like going home. "Then, I had to realize I wouldn't see my children." And she gradually floated back to consciousness. When she did, she was singing "Louie Louie."

Carolyn spent a week in the hospital and has hardly been out of her trailer since. She looks older, grayer, heavier. Among other things, she's missed going to church.

As they pull away from their house, Kyrah announces the good news: "We got St. David back!" The authorities have yet to make an official statement, but the parishioners of the smaller, African American congregation appear to have won the realignment fight.

"I guess the archdiocese figured out that it would be cheaper for us to go back to St. David," says Carolyn, "instead of trying to redo everything at St. Maurice." The auxiliary bishop of New Orleans calls the reopening a "beacon of hope in this community."

St. David is home.

It's a small brick building off St. Claude. The white sign out front says ESTABLISHED 1937, STAFFED BY JOSEPHITE FATHERS. Carolyn eases her way out of the car and slowly mounts the front steps. To her left is a stained glass window of Noah's ark coming to rest after the flood.

The inside is still unfinished: raw plywood floors, fresh sheetrock down one aisle, insulation piled near the new glass entry doors. The congregation is a couple of hundred people, from infants in their mothers' arms to elders who need help getting down the aisle. All join in the hymns. At the end of the service, Father Joe offers a closing prayer: "Let us go in the peace and joy of Christ."

Afterward, the crowd takes its time filing out: men in blue suits with red ties and matching handkerchiefs, women in big hats and elaborate hairdos, teenagers in jeans and sport shirts and flat-brimmed baseball caps. Here's a nearly seven-foot-tall man in a striped leisure suit; there's a tiny elderly lady, her yellow-gray hair in a tight bun.

The sunny front courtyard comes alive with talking and joking: "Hey baby, how you been?" Hugs and handshakes go round in circles. "I went to school over here from elementary up to sixth grade," one woman says, "and I'm back home . . . It's a blessing." The seven-foot man explains that the church is "just waiting on the electrician . . . And after that, we're gonna start hanging sheetrock . . . We'll be in there soon. We in there now!" Father Joe in his black and purple vestments is greeting people at the foot of the stairs.

Carolyn is one of the last to come out, walking carefully on her cane. Father Joe asks Kyrah, "Is she dancing yet?" Carolyn shoots him a look of amused contempt.

"No," Kyrah answers, "but she be dancing inside."

Carolyn, grinning, starts the slow process of getting into the car. "This is a big butt," she announces. "It's not that easy." And when she's finally made it: "See! That's how it is. I'm like a puzzle."

As they drive away, mother and daughter decide that instead of going straight back to Jourdan Avenue, they'll take a look at Backatown. They want to visit the 2400 block of Forstall, "the house where I was born," Carolyn says. ". . . my grandmother's. Who gave it to my mother . . . for generations and generations . . ."

Kyrah spent a lot of her childhood there. "My summers especially, when my mom was working full-time as a chef . . . It would always be me, my grandmother, and Didi the cat . . . Then if I got bored and my grandmother fell asleep, I would go to [my cousin's across the street]. Honestly," she continues, "[Backatown] was more active than Holy Cross. Holy Cross was kinda like the neighborhood where everybody stayed inside, stayed to themselves. But then on *this* side, everybody's sitting on porches, having block parties, braidin' hair on the porch, cookin' food on the porch! The neighborhood was really, really close-knit . . . Half the people had broken air conditioners, so they'd just sit outside, drinking beer, minding other people's business . . . Everybody knew everybody."

Carolyn reminisces about when Backatown had "apple trees, peach trees, fig trees . . . When we was hungry, you didn't have to worry about anything." She stops herself. "We don't have no house no more . . . Our house just went flying down the street."

"Like so many others," Kyrah agrees. Both grow still.

Carolyn hasn't been to Backatown since the floods. She points to where a barbershop used to be. "Most of these houses," she enunciates, pausing between almost every word, "were historic." Now many are draped in vines, open to the elements. Or they're gone entirely: a concrete pad with a house number spray-painted on the curb in front. "These are the ones who are waiting for Road Home," Carolyn says slowly. "To give them the funds that they need to come back. Just like I am."

As they drive closer to where the levee breached, they get even quieter. "See, all this was houses," Carolyn says in a monotone.

Kyrah: "It's nothing but grass now."

"That's because they used the demolition people to come through here. They wanted to have just flat land . . . In other words, if they tore the houses down and destroy everything, they figure that these people have nowhere else to go. And then they could do whatever it is they have planned . . ."

They stop talking and fall back into a deep silence. It's like people driving through a cemetery.

Their car reaches their old neighborhood. "Is this Forstall?" Carolyn asks. There are no houses, no street signs, just waist-high grass and a few saplings scattered here and there.

"Yea, this is Forstall," Kyrah answers, pointing. "Auntie's house was on that block."

"No, we're further back if that's—" Carolyn peers out, trying to iden-tify some landmark.

"I think it was in this block . . ." Kyrah reads the house numbers painted on the curb: "That's twenty-four twenty-eight."

"Twenty-four sixteen is further up."

"It's back that way." Kyrah hitches her thumb; they turn around.

"That's it there," says Carolyn, motioning to a patch of grass.

"No, that's twenty-four oh-eight . . . I don't see it."

"Well, it just ain't no more," Carolyn finally declares. "I know that. It's just an empty lot."

Silence. The wind blows through the high weeds; the white scar of the new levee cuts across the horizon.

"The thing is," Carolyn finally says, ". . . I don't know if I would have came back if I knew it was like this." They listen to the wind. "You have to admit, it's really depressing. Let's get out of here!"

A nervous laugh, another pause as they pull away.

"A lot of these people"—Carolyn has trouble finding the words—"are not even here. A lot of these just put their houses up for sale, and they're selling their land . . . What I'm saying is not that people don't want to come back, 'cause a lot of people really want to . . . but what you coming back to?"

Kyrah begins to talk about how high rents have gone, when her mother interrupts her: "What are these little things?"

Outside the car window, she's caught sight of a jumble of bright pink geometric shapes.

"What is this?" Kyrah asks. "This pink stuff?" Rectangles and squares and triangles, maybe fifteen to twenty feet long, are scattered like giant pink blocks across Backatown's empty lots.

Carolyn is getting excited. "Yeah, what is all of this? This is something new . . . What is this!?"

Bands of workers are building and placing the day-glo pink shapes. Camera crews follow the work; small groups of officials hurry by. Carolyn zips down her window and calls out: "Excuse me? What is this?"

A tall, stylish white man bends down to look into the car. He's in a very clean white shirt, and his long brown hair cascades over the collar. "Ve're trying to build a hundred-and-fifty homes for the people here." He speaks with the remains of a German accent, unsmiling and a little confused by this large black woman and her pretty daughter.

"Oh, bless you!" Carolyn squeals. "Come and get a kiss!" She opens both hands, and he laughs, leans in the window, gets his kiss.

"I know it looks veird," he says in his sincere voice. ". . . Ve need vorld attention back here because—"

Carolyn, excited, speaks over him: "I know, baby, because I'm that lady—"

"—Brad Pitt with us," he continues, ". . . it vas his idea to do an art installation."

"—on television, saying they could get that land over my dead body?"

The young man pauses, looks confused, backs a little away from the car.

"I didn't mean over my dead body," Carolyn explains. "It was just the idea: people need their houses. I mean, all these houses were unique."

"Right," he says hesitantly. "The art installation is basically to bring attention back here." He nods at the big pink shapes. "So Brad's gonna be with Larry King. He's gonna be on *USA Today* Monday morning. Talking about this problem. These people have been forgotten; they've been wronged."

Carolyn just nods.

"So, ve invented this nonprofit organization, Make It Right . . . To give houses to the people on their properties . . ." By the end of today, there will be some 400 pink shapes, spread out over fourteen square blocks.

It's a fund-raising idea, the man explains. "Any time a donation is [enough to build] one house, ve vill assemble one of the pink houses."

Carolyn keeps saying "God bless you" and "That's so sweet!"

The man identifies himself as one of the architects working on the project. Different teams, he explains, will create different designs, and the owners will be able to choose which one they want. The idea is to raise enough money so a three-bedroom house will cost no more than $150,000.

"I'm in one of them historic doubles," Carolyn cuts in.

"All the architects," the man continues, "had the same floor plan and square footage to verk vit—"

"I'm just starting to repair mine. I have one of those big French doubles? In Holy Cross."

"Ya, Holy Cross: that's where Brad started—with the Global Green competition. He—"

"I know."

Pitt's original Greenola project is moving slowly. The first structure was completed this summer, and work has begun on others, but no one is living there; it's more of a showcase. Instead, the actor has swung his attention over to Backatown, which he's called "the hardest-hit spot of the hardest-hit area, the icon of all that was wrong with the recovery." He's put up an initial $5 million; a movie producer friend has pledged to match that; this pink art installation is designed to raise millions more.

If Backatown is an icon for the failures of the recovery, this is a very specific kind of alternative. Celebrity-driven, funded and run mostly from out of state, Make It Right is a high-end charity, filling the governmental void with star power.

"It's really not easy," the architect continues, talking faster. "The construction is not back here . . . it's more expensive to build. But somebody has to start. I—" His cell phone rings. ". . . I actually have to run . . . Ve are all trying to do the same thing, right?"

He gives a boyish grin, and Carolyn grins back.

"God bless you, sweetheart. Like I say, I'm gonna still keep fighting . . . because this is my neighborhood. I've been down here—"

"Ya," the architect interrupts, polite but trying to get away. "Ve really want this neighborhood to come back. And safe. Look at the designs . . . All the houses are raised to eight feet . . . Ve're trying to rebuild smart. Going to be sustainable. Going to be green houses with the right materials . . . And still, hopefully, affordable . . ."

"Thank you," says Carolyn from the darkness of the car.

"Thank you," the architect answers. "Ciao."

Past the bustle of pink shapes is Common Ground's blue house. Except now it's white, covered with newly installed insulation, and it isn't Common Ground's anymore. Standing out front is the tiny elderly lady from church, the one with her yellow-gray hair in a tight bun.

"Miss Cager?"

Miss Cager peers into the car, birdlike. She has a small face behind thick glasses and very soft, pale brown skin.

"They fixing your house?" Carolyn asks. There's still a Common Ground sign out front: LEND US AN EAR, GIVE US A HAND, DONATIONS NEEDED.

"Yep, my folks are fixing it up." Miss Cager looks over the pink-strewn landscape. "Yeah. Almost three years." Her voice is gentle. She says she let Common Ground camp here because, "well, I couldn't get in it. So, you know, it made it useful." The organization, she tells Carolyn, has moved down the block into one of the few other houses still standing; the one that had BAGHDAD spray-painted on it. As to when she'll get back in her home, "it'll take time."

"Mine, too . . ." Carolyn answers. "Then, they don't give you enough money to—"

"No, they don't. Yeah."

Road Home, Carolyn declares, has promised her "but a little forty something."

"That's all they gave me," Miss Cager says. ". . . It ain't right, but thank God we got that."

The two women chat a little longer: the one in the car, the other beside it. "Thank God," Carolyn says, "your house is still standing. 'Cause my momma's house on Forstall is gone."

"Yeah," Miss Cager answers, looking out across the bustle of Backatown: workers stretching pink plastic, camera crews, architects. In an empty field nearby, a flock of cattle egrets—white, long-necked birds—hunt among the high weeds.

"My sister's house next door, that's gone. My daddy's house is gone. My sister down there on Galvez? Her two houses gone." Miss Cager shrugs her small shoulders. "I was the only lucky one that's still standing up."

Back over in Holy Cross, before returning to their trailer, Kyrah and Carolyn make a slow tour of their block. As they drive toward the levee,

Mark happens out of his driveway. It's now cleared: his FEMA trailer and the pile of auto parts are gone, his big white house has been renovated.

Mark is home.

Despite his accidents, his rental buildings are coming along, too; he's even let out a few units. Like Mike in St. Bernard, he's finished well before the rest of his neighborhood. Now he leans in the car window to ask Carolyn how she's doing.

"Fine. You know I got both my knees replaced. That's why you didn't see me."

"Are they working better?"

"Oh, yes. I can even kick now . . . I'm gonna kick these FEMA people. And these Road Home." Her eyes flash. "That's why I got my knees done."

Mark chuckles behind his gray moustache. Asked how his hand is doing after getting caught in the mower, he pulls it out of his pocket and holds it up to the light. The tips of the first two fingers are gone, but he clenches and unclenches it. "Working fine."

They've been driving around, Carolyn explains, seeing how Holy Cross is doing. Mark laughs. "This is probably the best block you've seen, huh?"

Carolyn grins proudly. "You see they've started on mine?"

"You're looking pretty good over there." He points past Carolyn's. "Now, when you go out that way . . . it's a lot worse, right?"

"You know Brad Pitt over there?' Carolyn asks.

"Yeah. Right, right." Mark nods his head, chin on chest, and thinks a moment: the philosopher, the entrepreneur. "See, what I'm afraid of is, the people that used to live over here, they're not coming back. If they haven't come back in two years, they're not coming back."

"I just been saying the same thing."

"It's very, very disheartening," Mark goes on. "'Cause we don't have the population growth, either, to buy these places and fix them up. There's some rental pressure, but not that many people want to buy houses here. I hate to think that five years from now, we'll still be driving through the same thing."

Carolyn pauses. "We're in better shape than some of the neighborhoods." It's half statement, half question.

"Oh, yeah! A lot better."

Kyrah and Carolyn continue past Patsy's and the other empty houses, take a turn at the dwarf Indian by the levee, go along Sister Street past

Ron's empty lot, and then head up Lathan's silent block. When they get back to their own house, Carolyn opens the car door but can't move her legs. They've gone stiff, she says.

She slowly turns till she's almost lying in the backseat. "I'm gonna get out, baby. It just takes me a while." Then, counting to herself—"one, two, three!"—she heaves up and is standing. With her cane supporting her, she balances for a moment. Then, face stern, she starts dancing in place, shaking her big hips and lifting one hand to the sky.

Kyrah giggles.

"No, seriously," Carolyn says. "That get them loose." Then she grins, too.

Conclusions

We Fall Down, But We Get Up

(February–October 2008)

Time speeds back up.

Or maybe what happens in 2008 is that New Orleans stabilizes. And as it does, events no longer drop one by one into limbo, but connect. Press forward.

The city is now around 310,000 people—70 percent its former size—and holding. In the first year after the floods, the population bounced back by 40 percent, but in 2008 it only increased by 4 percent. "The sense of urgency," as one local demographer puts it, "is past."

The new New Orleans is smaller and has proportionately fewer kids. Its center of density has shifted from black neighborhoods like New Orleans East and the Ninth Ward to less flooded, whiter areas like Uptown and the Garden District. Unemployment is low—around 3 percent—but a quarter of the city's residents are living in poverty. Cooks, health care providers, bus and truck drivers are averaging less than $35,000 a year. Once wages like that allowed people to live on the "happy plantation," but monthly rents are still up more than 40 percent since the floods. That puts them only $100 lower than New York City's.

The city is running fewer than 20 percent of its pre-Katrina buses. In parts of the Ninth, Gentilly, and other areas, basic infrastructure like sewage and water still waits for repair. FEMA allocated more than $6 billion toward solving these problems, but the state has only spent about half that.

By 2008, it's become evident that New Orleans is trying to recover within a national economy that has become, as one observer puts it, "unhinged." Across the country, the decades-long real estate boom has ended. Almost 2 million mortgages are in default, at a cost of some $5 billion. National unemployment has climbed to above 5 percent. In the spring, the collapse was being called a credit crisis or banking crisis. By the end of the year, it will be officially declared a recession.

In some ways, the recovering city is actually doing better than the country. As the national economy collapses, Road Home money has finally kicked in. By the third anniversary of the flood, close to 115,000 homeowners—some two-thirds of those eligible—have received their grants. That $6.5 billion has begun to function as a local stimulus program. It's as if New Orleans is that homeowner whose house is finally getting repaired—only to look up and realize the rest of the neighborhood is falling apart.

On Palm Sunday 2008, Carolyn and Kyrah are returning from services at St. David. Kyrah's giggling about the moment Father Joe asked if anyone had an anniversary to acknowledge. She was worried her mother was going to announce, "This time last year I almost died."

"Uh-uh," her mother corrects her. "You don't do that with death." She pronounces it det. "You don't be playing with det . . . Det will be standing around the corner there, waiting for you to slip down."

As they approach Jourdan Avenue, Carolyn crows, "Look at my house! Look at it!" The exterior of her double shotgun has been painted a deep turquoise blue with searing yellow trim. The front porch is off-pink.

The car stops, but mother and daughter don't get out. First they admire the new paint job. Then they point out that the FEMA trailer is still here. And that the back porch still has its windows stacked to one side. "Because of that contractor," says Carolyn.

Palm frond in one hand, she brings the other to her breastbone. "I'm not a terrible person. I'm a sweet person . . . He kept telling everybody he was a preacher. And 'Don't worry, Miss Parker. You don't have to worry about me 'cause I'm gonna do what I say I'm gonna do.' And then when he got the money, he figured, 'I don't have to do it.'"

Carolyn gestures toward the porch.

"This particular morning, I seen those back windows were upside down and backwards . . . They don't close like they're supposed to . . . The little guy he had putting in those back windows couldn't get it quite right. So . . . the contractor told him, 'Just do it any kind of way.'"

Carolyn's eyes go big.

"I stayed in there," pointing to her trailer, "and I'm listening . . . And I said, 'What do you *mean*, do it any kind of way? When you accepted my money, you didn't do *that* any kind of way! You gonna do what you say you gonna do on this contract. Or you give me my money back.'"

Carolyn deepens her voice and scrunches up her face to play the contractor. "'Let me tell you something, old lady.' That's what he said! He said"—she raises one finger and tick-tocks it back and forth with each syllable—"'old la-dy.' A bell goes in a lady's head when you call her 'old la-dy.' And then to tell me I'm not getting anything—after you have my money!?"

She'd paid him not only her Historic Preservation grant but part of the Road Home money they'd finally received. All of it up front.

"'I'll get somebody else to do it if you can't do it . . . And apparently you *can't* do it. You been at this since November . . . this is February . . .' Took my money and then called me a disgusting old lady? I told him, 'I'll show you disgusting.'

"I called 911 and said: . . . 'You got exactly ten minutes to get here, or you gonna be pickin' up somebody' . . . And then before I could get the phone hung up properly, there were two cars . . . zip! zip! . . . I mean, what they thought I had? A machine gun or what?"

Kyrah tries to hide her giggles.

"They was some National Guard or something . . . Anyway, he was trying to talk to them and trying to make it look like I was just old and didn't understand."

Carolyn had been taking photos of the work site all along, and now she showed them to the officers. "This is what he found; this is what he did; this is what he messed up. And this is today . . . Does this look like he done any forty-six thousand dollars' worth of work?" The female officer told the contractor to come around the property fence and put his hands behind his back. "When she said that"—Carolyn's voice is high and full of delight—"that man's face just—whop!" She drops both arms to her lap. "He was just in *shock*."

Now, once again, all she can do is wait. Wait on a trial and a chance to get her money back. And hope for help from volunteers.

"This," Carolyn motions toward her gleaming house, "wasn't done by the contractor. This was done by Catholic Charities."

"Alleluia gutted it out," Kyrah explains. "Catholic Charities painted it."

"And these people right here"—Carolyn indicates a big white van pulled up to her curb—". . . they're the one put the sheetrock in. They with Preservation?"

"No," says Kyrah.

"Who they with? I got people in my house, and I don't even know!" She laughs and waves her palm frond. "I just say God sent me a bunch of angels."

A thin, middle-aged white man ambles up the sidewalk. He owns the big white van with the capitalized writing on it:

JEFF OF ALL TRADES
IN CASE OF NUCLEAR OR TERRORIST ATTACK
THE BAN ON PRAYER IN SCHOOL WILL BE
IMMEDIATELY LIFTED

Jeff was headed to Florida when he stopped in New Orleans to volunteer. "I got hooked up with OnSite Relief," he explains. "It's a young couple out of Canada. Fantastic people! They have a true heart of volunteering . . . They got, like, six jobs they're doing."

"He's like an angel," Carolyn says. She's gotten out of the car to greet him and is now standing by her fence, waving her palm frond and grinning. "He flies around!"

"Don't put me too high," Jeff laughs. "Because it's just farther I got to fall down."

Carolyn's grin gets bigger. "We fall down, but we get up."

She tells Jeff about her near-death experience in the hospital. Now she can walk; she even gets to church. "Today was almost an anniversary for being alive again." The wind blows her blue dress. Behind is her freshly painted blue and yellow house. She nods to it and to the rosebushes she and Kyrah have planted in their side yard. "This is pretty good, huh?"

Last week, under pressure from a frustrated public, the recovery czar Edward Blakely announced that he'd soon be stepping down. He claims to have 400 projects in the works, but after two years, there are still no cranes in the sky. "I think we've moved beyond recovery now," he announced, "and it's embedded in normal operations." Normal operations on this block include the gutted and empty Semmes school, windows broken and glass strewn over the playground. Mark's white house is pulled together, but Joe and Linda's is covered by vines and rotting in place. Patsy's FEMA trailer is gone, but her yard is still a jumble of wrecked possessions. And her son's house next door remains a see-through shell.

Carolyn credits volunteers for what progress she's made. As she and Jeff talk outside, a college student is block-sanding the spackled walls of her kitchen. In what will be Kyrah's bedroom, a blond high school girl is rolling primer on the walls. "This is our first day," her mother explains in a thick drawl. "We came down from Birmingham, Alabama, for spring break." Her daughter's getting community service credits.

Down the street in the big empty lot behind Patsy's, three girls are mixing cement in an orange wheelbarrow. Inexperienced, eager to please, they giggle as they try to open a cement bag with the tines of a rake. One says they're from Philly: "First time down." "I never realized how bad it is," says another. "And how slow," says the third. They're high school students. "Our rabbis organized it through the Jewish Funds for Justice."

Patsy's son, Adrian, threads his way toward them through the piles of old windows, plastic PVC pipe, bits of fencing. He's in a green WE ARE BACK AND REBUILDING HOLY CROSS T-shirt. The girls smile as he holds a level to a four-by-four fence post; then they shovel the concrete around its base and try to stomp it down.

Behind them, a woman steps out of Patsy's back door. Her orange sweatshirt reads CENTER OF JEWISH LEARNING. "We have hundreds of kids down here now," she explains. "We take people—Jewish people— from all over, for Katrina recovery as well as urban renewal work . . . Our mission is to create a more just and compassionate America."

Judging by this block, that new America is mostly young white volunteers doing work homeowners can't and the government hasn't. On the third anniversary of Katrina, President Bush notes that the federal government has spent $126 billion on the Gulf Coast. But what he emphasizes is the $3.5 billion in private donations and the 14 million hours of volunteer labor. "The greatest reason for hope," the president says, "is the people who are making this recovery possible." Especially those who are "called to come to New Orleans . . . to help spread the entrepreneurial spirit."

All together, the federal, charitable, and private insurance money that has come into the Gulf Coast equals less than half the cost of the damages sustained.

Inside Patsy's, volunteers have gutted her first floor down to bare studs. Work lights are set up; a hammer echoes. But there are still piles of wooden furniture, a red plastic milk crate full of her vinyl records, and, against one wall, a bookcase stuffed with moldy books and magazines, hopelessly stuck together.

Patsy has moved across the street into apartment A in Mark's brick building. The walls of her rental are draped in red and blue fabric. Her big body is in a leopard print dress. Her blond-gray hair has been combed.

"Everything's gutted," she says. "With the exception of a double bookshelf . . ." Sighs. "I'm just trying to figure out a proper dis-po-sal," three long syllables, "for them. I don't know if I want to bury them, or burn them, or what . . . That's the last of what I've got to get rid of: the books." She shrugs. "Slowly, slowly, we're pecking at it like a little wood-pecker." Again, one hand pecks the air.

"What I'm starting to do now," she says in her cheerful voice, "they pulled the fence down off of Joe and Linda's . . . I'm clearing it up so I can plant some things there, at least *use* that earth before they bulldoze the house down." She smiles. "Put some herbs and tomatoes and different things like that. 'Cause it gets full sun. A good place to plant. That's the next job."

Patsy still has no definite date for getting back into her house. The only one on the block who's home is Mark. Ron's lot on Sister Street remains empty. Around the corner on Burgundy, Lathan has finished rehabbing and is renting his two houses, but he's still fixing up his residence on Chartres.

The only other person on Burgundy was the middle-aged white woman who lived alone in her trailer near the levee. One day this June, Patsy noticed the woman's van hadn't moved in a while. "We knocked and didn't get any answer . . . Nobody had seen her, so we called the police." They broke in to find the woman lying in her bathroom in a pool of blood. NOPD ruled it death from natural causes; the neighborhood is convinced she was killed. "She was on her back," Patsy says, "with her legs open and one left out of her panties . . . You would have thought rape or attempted rape." While 2008 has seen an overall drop in crime, New Orleans remains the nation's murder capital. That, too, is "embedded in normal operations."

In the fall, the block had to evacuate again. Three years and a day after Katrina, Mayor Nagin announced a voluntary evacuation in the face of Hurricane Gustav. The next day, he made it mandatory, adding a dusk-to-dawn curfew. Some 2 million people left southern Louisiana, and this time, thousands were provided with public buses and trains. "It's smooth," the mayor said of the evacuation, "it's effective, and it's getting the job done."

Before leaving, Patsy placed a sign on the dwarf Santa Claus: GUSTAV with a red slash through it. She tapped the statue on the head: "You be good while we're gone." Mark packed a truck and parked it on high ground in case he decided to go. Lathan hugged Patsy goodbye, then left in his pickup.

Carolyn, Rahsaan, and Kyrah drove to Alexandria, Louisiana. "Like we did last time," Carolyn explains. She only agreed to leave after hearing the police chief promise to "blanket" the city to prevent looting. "They said they were going to have National Guards as well as police. And they were going door-to-door and making sure that everybody leave. But before we got to Alexander, we listen over the radio and hear that everybody didn't leave New Orleans." Pause. "That didn't make any sense."

The hurricane was a Category 2 resulting in seven deaths. "There wasn't no damage here," Carolyn says. "Minor damages . . . We came back the day before they told us to return. When I came back . . . I didn't see a police anywhere. I didn't see *anybody* anywhere . . . We came back, and nobody stopped us . . . We got out the car . . . and first we spotted the stuff all over the place and the cinder block . . ." She points to a chunk of cinder block that's come to rest inside the trailer. Someone threw it through the door, trying to break in.

"Ain't nothing but them junkies . . ." Rahsaan explains. "They watch everybody's house . . ." It didn't help that there had been a power outage in the Lower Ninth, leaving the evacuated homes even more vulnerable. "The guy across the street over here? His house got looted twice . . . They raided his vanity, looking for prescription drugs. Raided his twin daughters' piggy bank."

"When the police finally did come to me," Carolyn says, speaking slowly, eyes black with anger, "which was about seven hours later . . . [I told them,] 'If I didn't know better, I'd say you'all was getting a cut out of this. That you'all left people here so they could go in people's houses and get whatever they wanted!'"

Rahsaan simply says, "The mayor's a slap-head! There shouldn't have been a single soul back here. *That's* a mandatory evacuation . . . The evacuation program was a success, and the levees held: that's all they were concerned about."

To many, Gustav showed that New Orleans could survive a hurricane, that rebuilding here wasn't as foolish as some thought. But to Rahsaan, it meant something different. "The city of New Orleans has *proved* to the Lower Ninth Ward that they don't give a damn."

"It wasn't just the Ninth Ward," Carolyn interjects. "It was city-wide."

"I'm just saying: from our neighborhood's standpoint, we're always *last* with everything . . . We were last to get security . . . We were last to get our power on . . . It's just ridiculous . . . From now on, the neighborhood is going to get backup generators and *stay*. Like we used to . . . 'Cause we have no more confidence in the NOPD or the National Guard . . . I'm not going nowheres."

His mother, furious, agrees: "We're staying!"

A month after Gustav, the roses Carolyn and Kyrah planted in the side yard are blooming. And there's a single pear on the small, new pear tree. But the FEMA trailer still sits in back, the deadline for its removal extended yet again. Three years and two months since the floods, Carolyn is still waiting to get back in her double shotgun.

She steps inside to show how far it's come. There are walls up, and the walls are painted. The kitchen is now a rich orange, its door trim lime green. "At first I didn't think that was gonna clash like that," Carolyn says, ". . . but I *liked* the way it clashed. To me, if it don't say something inside, it's gonna be boring." The next room is Kyrah's: a glowing pink with a yellowish trim. Then comes Carolyn's bedroom, paler pink with navy blue glass doors separating it from the front living room. "I don't want everything white," Carolyn says, straight-faced, "'cause I'm not in the White House." There's still no electricity, and paint cans and tarps are scattered over the floor.

Carolyn crosses to the other half of the shotgun. Rahsaan's room is a deep blue, then comes a bathroom with big gray ceramic tiles, another bedroom—Easter purple with pale yellow trim—and then what was the other half of the kitchen: yellow-orange and blue.

"Isn't she big?" Carolyn grins, standing on her back porch. It's a light blue with white trim and bright yellow windows. She and her children have been doing the painting. "I can't do over my head," she says. "But like that?" She makes brushing motions side to side, swinging her hips. "And with my music on? I be gone!"

She looks around. "This is my favorite room . . . These windows," she says, "was like butterfly wings. They open just like butterflies." Both hands go to her chest, then spread out to illustrate. The contractor reinstalled them upside down, and the volunteers couldn't get it right, either. There's a gap between some; others butt together but won't lock. "They're gonna fit . . . because Carolyn's gonna *sand* them. And help them find their way to be butterfly wings all over again . . ." Her hands return to her chest.

"I'm not gonna stand here and lie and say that I'm not happy," Carolyn announces. "Because I *am* happy! I'm full of joy . . . The man, he's coming to hook up the electricity next week . . . And the plumber is supposed to be coming to hook up the bathtub and other plumbing . . . I think I would be *in* my house for November."

But for all the progress she's made in 2008—for all that time has sped up—Carolyn admits her patience is finally running out. "You know what this is like? You ever waited for a birthday cake? . . . I'm not worried about perfection. All I'm worrying about," and she uncharacteristically sighs, "is being able to go in my room, put my brass bed together, and lay on that sucker! That's all I want." Right now, her bed is in parts in a white storage container on her front lawn. "It's gonna happen. Even if I have to do it myself and piece by piece. It's gonna happen."

The change that's come to Backatown in 2008 is more radical. In mid-March, as Carolyn and Kyrah are going to Palm Sunday services, there's a celebration near the new Common Ground headquarters. A pair of big buses have pulled over. Milling around them is a crowd of volunteers in black T-shirts that read MAKE A DIFFERENCE. They've been given brand-new wheelbarrows, new rakes, new work gloves. "We're here," one young white woman says, "to clean the sidewalks."

There aren't any sidewalks. Brad Pitt's "pink project" is over, and Backatown has returned to empty lots: some mowed, some with chest-high grass. But there's a big sign strung over one street: MAKE IT RIGHT WELCOMES THE CLINTON BUSH GLOBAL INITIATIVE. Cars are parked all over, a CNN truck is off in a field, and tourist buses keep pulling in and dropping off visitors. Outside Common Ground headquarters, a brass band is warming up: tuba, saxophone, trumpets flashing in the morning light.

On the street with the sign strung over it, volunteers stand in groups holding their brand-new tools. Brad Pitt comes striding down among them. The actor is in a tight white shirt, jeans, and a white newsboy cap. He has a compact body and a big handsome face, incredibly familiar. As he stops to talk to an advisor, a police-led string of SUVs pulls up and out steps former president Bill Clinton: a crop of white hair, a red sports shirt, an equally familiar face. Clinton is a head taller than Pitt and bends down when the two speak.

They start walking up the block, stopping to talk with volunteers and pose for photographs. The procession will culminate in an official groundbreaking. Make It Right hopes to have a half-dozen new houses ready by the third anniversary of Katrina, five months from now. "This to me," Pitt will say, "is a social-justice issue."

A block over, on a second-floor porch, Malik and Brandon observe the commotion. The dreadlocked, graying black man and the nervous, handsome white man sit side by side. Brandon has put on some weight, and his hairline is receding at the temples, but overall he seems rested and healthy. Malik appears unchanged: long matted dreads, bags under his smiling watchful eyes.

"I thank Brad Pitt," Malik is saying. "Even though we don't communicate that much . . . I thank him every day for what he has done. Because I know there's no way in the world we'd get this many people . . . without him." Brandon nods in agreement. "I be kind of suspect," Malik adds, grinning, "when it happen only around election time . . ."

It's the middle of the 2008 presidential primaries. Candidate Barack Obama came to town last month, declaring that the botched Katrina response had broken "a trust . . . a promise that our government will be prepared, will protect us, and will respond in a catastrophe." His main rival for the Democratic nomination is Clinton's wife, Hillary. "But if I'm hungry," Malik insists, "regardless of what time it is, if you feed me, you're okay with me . . . This is a hungry community, and at least he [Clinton] brought bread."

The brass band is playing in the distance. More people are arriving.

"I'll never forget when he came to my house," Malik nods at Brandon, "and we started talking about opening up this place. And the things he went through . . ." The founder shakes his head. "I'm gonna tell you: if we'd have had this much support, in this area, in January '06?" jabbing home his point with one finger. "Right now we would not be celebrating the *start* of construction; we'd be celebrating the *end* of construction."

But today isn't Common Ground's celebration. And Brandon isn't with the collective anymore. His stint as interim director didn't end well. If he thought at the time that his job was to re-radicalize operations, he now says he was there "to shut down St. Mary's and kind of decentralize the effort . . . It almost destroyed the organization." He's since gone back to Texas to live in a small town. "One hundred and nineteen people," he says. "And I have six chickens and a rooster."

As New Orleans has stabilized, Common Ground has had to shift priorities. Instead of emergency relief, it's begun to focus on the less dramatic mission of long-term rebuilding. In 2008, it has fewer volunteers, fewer high-profile stand-downs, fewer donations. The Lower Ninth Ward Health Clinic finally opened in the spring, but other major projects, like the police hotline and the string of homeless shelters, fell away. Key organizers left, including Suncere, who never returned from his two-week vacation. As St. Mary shut down, Brandon went, too.

"I did leave in tears," he says now in a quiet voice. "I felt betrayed. Bear in mind that doesn't mean I *was* betrayed. And I felt hurt. And somewhat helpless . . ." He doesn't give any details, simply adding: "I'd never really had time to heal after Katrina."

It's hard to talk over the crowds and music, so Malik and Brandon move inside. Common Ground has rehabbed this two-story building over the past few months, and they settle in a freshly sheetrocked office. Together, they launch into a description of what's happened to New Orleans in general and Backatown in particular.

"All the social safety nets that the government should be providing," Malik says, "was *never* provided in this community. It was neighbors helping neighbors . . ." There used to be rent parties, he says, and dances held to pay off second mortgages. "I've seen many times when people back here gave suppers. That's how this community is built."

After the floods, Brandon continues, when TV covered the Uptown neighborhood or St. Bernard, "it was always people talking about rebuilding their homes—"

"Or even the Holy Cross area," Malik interjects.

"But when it was this area, it was always a white guy in a suit talking—from Baton Rouge!—about what was going to happen here. It was never the residents."

Malik and Brandon speak in tandem, connecting Backatown's history to Common Ground's. Today's groundbreaking, they argue, is a kind of happy ending, and both have made a point of being here for the occasion.

"You get all kinds of rumors about what Brad Pitt is doing," Malik says. "But if it wasn't for Brad Pitt . . ." He ends the sentence by gesturing out the window. "Look back here! This is the last area to get electricity . . . You can't tell me that by now you shouldn't have a high school open in this area! You can't tell me why you don't have faith-based institutions, the parks that are needed for these kids. There's no reason for none of this not to exist here . . ." Voice rising, in public speaking mode, Malik sums up the city's attitude toward Backatown: "These ain't nothing but poor folks." The government wasn't bringing the neighborhood back, and, in the end, Common Ground couldn't. Which leaves charity—and Brad Pitt.

With Malik around, Brandon tends to defer. Later, when the hoopla is over and the crowds have started to leave, he takes a walk. At the former blue house, now Ms. Cager's, he squats by the curb.

"Groundbreaking day," he says in his soft Texas twang, "and they didn't acknowledge the efforts of the grassroots organizations that were here." A grin and a shrug. As to the celebrity-driven aspect of Make It Right: "They have a figurehead, but we do, too. Everybody does, even if they don't mean to."

Brandon points out that Make It Right isn't going to help Ms. Cager. Or anyone trying to rebuild. On the other hand, the new Pitt houses seem like the best bet for the neighborhood as a whole. "I know that on these few blocks—if residents can come back—I know that canal can't be expanded." Brandon hooks a thumb toward the levee. "And I know that if that canal can't be expanded, then big-money interests can't do what it wants down here . . . So I think any efforts are good efforts. And I haven't heard a lot of residents with negative statements. I've heard a lot of anarchists . . ." He lets the sentence dangle.

"But I think it's just the natural progress of effort in this particular system. What happens is you challenge"—he brings one hand down, whack, on an empty palm—"and the government steps in . . . And if you challenge back"—another whack—"and you're lucky . . . ultimately, they co-opt your concept. It's co-opted by the mainstream. And that's not necessarily a bad thing, you know?"

Brandon lights a cigarette, takes a puff.

"Pitt is focused on this area . . . I appreciate that . . . And I think the residents do . . . But it's not radical anymore."

He starts to walk toward the levee, coffee cup in one hand, cigarette in the other.

"I'm glad it happened. I'd do it again. Some of it I'd do differently, but . . . most of it I couldn't have done differently. And I think the majority of us feel the same . . . I wish we had been more inclusive, though . . . When what you focus on is the rights of others, it's real easy in this country to get pretty radical. When you realize the connections between systems that are oppressive and unfair."

He mentions his and Suncere's commitments to Malik: neither ended up staying as long as they'd promised. "That's worked out differently."

Brandon is now sitting in the blue shade of the levee wall, back against the rough concrete, looking out over Backatown.

"You can't always do what you want to do . . ." He licks the corner of his mouth. "I've heard it said a moral decision is not between a right and a wrong; that's easy. It's between a wrong and a wrong. So you have the ideal of what you'd like to see, and then you have the reality of what's going to happen . . . We really thought that the residents would come back. And the government would continue to be neglectful. And we would have an autonomous zone. And we would appeal to foreign governments for aid. Or something . . ."

He drags on his cigarette.

"When the residents came back, we discovered that's not what a lot of the residents wanted . . . People just wanted roofs . . . They just wanted their communities back. They didn't want all the big, lofty, we-thought-this-up-in-a-café-in-France ideals."

He's sitting right near the spot where he once compared daily life in America to a woman being raped. "At this point, I would like to think I would still involve myself to stop it, but I wouldn't be cursing while I did it . . ." He smiles a little. "To put it simply, at thirty-one the world is not as cut-and-dried, as black and white, as it was a few years ago . . . I have a daughter now," Brandon reveals, grinning. He's helping to raise her back in Texas. "And I love my daughter."

He still sees Common Ground as having been "born out of a very radical concept: let's oppose this land grab." In addition, it was a "challenge . . . [to the] politics that's prevalent in radical left movements." Focusing on service-oriented direct action was a "huge change. [We're] no longer a vocal group of people who don't do anything. I think we've grown into a vocal group of people who can put their words into actions . . ." He estimates 15,000 volunteers have passed through Common Ground. "And then they go back to their own communities and tell people . . . I think that's a really good thing.

"It's nice to have been involved in the—the—" His hands circle groping for the word. "The creation of that effort: that life . . . I'm honored that I was able to do that . . . We didn't accomplish all we meant to accomplish—"

Brandon leans back against the levee, his breath suddenly gone, his eyes red.

"But we did accomplish something. We have done good . . ."

He inhales slowly.

Six months pass.

In the fall of 2008, a middle-aged white man is standing outside Common Ground headquarters. Easygoing, with a background in real estate and a polished, business-like way of talking, Thom is the collective's new director.

"Malik's in the hospital," he explains. "A little heart thing. He's okay . . . a little numbness in his feet." And Brandon is back in Texas after a stint in Minnesota protesting at the Republican National Convention. As the organization they helped found has turned into a more "traditional non-profit," they've had less and less to do with it.

Thom says Common Ground has been helping Make It Right, "providing them with the names of a lot of residents whose homes we had gutted and who had been working with us. So, of these first six houses, four or five of them are people that we had originally presented to them."

He points across the empty block. There, in the wasteland of Backatown, are a half dozen postmodern buildings with long, swerving rooflines and shimmering, brightly colored walls.

The Pitt houses would be eye-catching anywhere, but they're particularly so in this flat, grassy landscape. They're all raised a story above the flood plain. From there, they extend into the air in swoops and flares. Here's a purple-blue double shotgun set on eight-foot concrete posts, its roofline aslant, its raised front porch yellow, its entrance triple-insulated sliding glass doors. There's a pale block of a house with big concrete steps leading to a second floor dominated by porch railings pressed into cartoony shapes. One large peach-orange house looks like a McMansion from New Jersey or Beverly Hills, with a gleaming, solar-paneled roof. Nearby is a three-story house with a trellis up one side. As soon as the newly planted vines grow, it will form a foundation-to-roof wall of green against the hot New Orleans summers.

Laid out on the horizon, the houses look like expensive sculptures. It's as if a small section of Backatown had been invaded by millionaires—millionaires determined to live not on the street, where social life used to be, but a story up in the air.

Beyond these two or three showcase blocks stretch the same un-mowed lots thick with swamp grass. In the Lower Ninth, only about 10 percent of the families have made it back. Thom points down the street to a bright orange number spray-painted on the curb. It's the city's newest kind of *veve*, signaling a property that has been sold to Road Home. "Every day you drive around, you see one more marking. That's what we're frightened of." He estimates there're 220 lots like this between here and Holy Cross: a growing emptiness.

Citywide, about a tenth of the homeowners who've gotten Road Home money have decided to sell rather than rebuild. But across the Lower Ninth, it's more like a fifth. In all, the New Orleans Redevelopment Authority (NORA) will soon control between 4,000 and 7,000 properties. Not since the oil bust of the eighties has the government owned so much of the city's real estate. Though 10,000 houses have now been demolished, the latest estimate says that leaves almost 72,000 vacant, ruined, or unoccupied. In the remains of the industrial north, Detroit and Flint, Michigan, now have nearly 20 percent blight. But New Orleans leads the nation: a third of all its buildings are considered beyond repair.

What Common Ground is worried about, Thom explains, is that the city is still planning to bundle these lots, making it easier for developers to buy them. To block that, the collective has made an offer to purchase some of the bundles. "So that we can . . . begin building duplexes and fourplexes. For people who are coming out of Section 8 vouchers." He smiles, runs a hand through his thinning blond hair. "We're hoping to go ahead and get into cooperative housing."

It's like the earlier attempt to buy the apartment complex in Algiers. But this effort would involve working with a construction firm, taking out loans, becoming one of Backatown's major landowners. Some see the potential for co-optation: radicals turned landlords. But Common Ground considers it getting to the root of the problem: sooner or later, if the fight for home is going to change anything, the collective has to challenge the basic concept of private property. Cooperative, low-income housing is a first step.

The goal, Thom says, is to "repopulate this area as quickly as we can . . . [We're] trying to make it attractive so people want to come back here; that's our big thing now . . ." He points at the dusty roads, still potholed, some impassable. "The big problem that we have here is infrastructure. We have this huge broken water main here . . . We do need to get some control over this area to make sure it's a little . . ." He looks for the right word. "Pristine. The problem that we're running into," he adds, "with more and more people coming back, is we have a small rat problem . . ." A grin. "But we've come a long way. This time last year, the grass was twelve feet high. You couldn't even see across the street. It's getting, slowly, better."

A breeze blows through Backatown, moving the weeds, humming off the new buildings.

"Quite frankly, this thing that Brad did is the first—nobody has done it; the city hadn't done it—this is the first concrete thing..." Thom smiles and gestures out at the lots around him. "We can't mow this forever."

For New Orleans East, 2008 has produced different stages of recovery. Overall, about half the suburban-looking streets are still unoccupied, which means it has the largest number of vacant buildings of any district in the city. The corner house on Pastor Mel and Clara's block is almost obscured by weeds. But down their street, just about every house has been rebuilt, and there's only one FEMA trailer left.

Mel and Clara are home.

Their living room has been furnished in beige: sofas, armchairs, an ottoman. There are new hardwood floors. Twin bookcases are each topped with a bronze, three-dimensional sign, one saying PEACE, the other FORGIVE. They're full of books: *The Spiritual Life Guide*, *The Encyclopedia of Bible Facts*, lots of black history. A flat-screen TV hangs on the opposite wall.

Clara, smiling, stands at the kitchen island preparing a salad. She's quick to say there's still some painting left to do. "Melvin designed the house. He says God designed it, but... Melvin and God designed the house."

Mel's mother, seated on one of the sofas, laughs.

"And I decorated," Clara goes on. "All the colors and fixtures." She points to a recessed alcove in the living room. There, surrounded by photographs of family members, is a quiet still-life of fruits and flowers and shells. She bought it, she says, up in Minnesota, at a low point in her life, and she's used it not only as a focus of regular meditation but as a color guide for their new home. The neutral of a shell was taken for trim; the blue from the rim of a bowl became the walls of the master bedroom.

Touring the house, Clara can't get over "the perfection" that the men from Mel's ministry put into the work—from the floor moldings to the paint job. "They weren't serving Melvin; Melvin couldn't motivate them to do this... God's presence influenced this perfection." The furnishing is still sparse—a big double bed in the master bedroom and not much else, an exercise bike and a couple of chairs in the sunroom—but Mel and Clara have been living here now for a month and a half.

It's still hard for Clara to believe. "Melvin and I stand," she says, and then pauses, hands by her sides: a small brown-skinned woman in a dark blouse and blue jeans. "We stand." She lets another moment tick by, smiles as if listening to something. "We stand. And we look. And we say, 'Uh-huh!'" Clara giggles. ". . . It's a home. This is our first home together."

Pastor Mel, in a crisp white sports shirt, sits at the kitchen island with his hands folded before him. His parents are in the connected living room along with a visitor: his and Clara's nephew Tim. He's a leukemia patient living with them during treatment. That, Clara explains, is why they built a big house: to have room for family and friends and people in need.

Mel is talking about the racial problems that have cropped up at the ministry lately. Whites think they're better than blacks; blacks think they're better than Latinos. "Or even the alcoholic who thinks he's better than the crackhead . . . Or the crackhead who thinks he's better than the heroin addict. We all in the same place," he adds quietly. "We wind up broken, broke down. It's just all of us trying to find some way that we're not as bad as somebody else."

The subject of race is in the air today. They've just watched candidate Obama deliver his "More Perfect Union" speech about the nation's legacy of discrimination, about the "anger" in both black and white communities, about a feeling of "dreams slipping away in an era of stagnant wages and global competition."

"The points Obama made," Clara says, passing out plates for lunch, "just rang so clearly with me . . . That's just America." She recalls the prejudice she's faced in her life. "That's the truth of living in America. I think it's important to acknowledge the truths . . . [We] have disabled America by not acknowledging them . . ."

As people eat, the talk gradually shifts to the city's recovery. "It's happening," Clara says, "but there're going to be large areas where there are no people. You can see that happening now." She mentions an older woman she met at the supermarket. The woman has rebuilt her house and moved in, but no one else on the block has come back. "I am so afraid," she told Clara.

Mel's mother nods; Pontchartrain Park is the same. A lot of her former neighbors, she says, "just can't face coming back."

Clara declares softly, "Some people can't pull this off."

Mel's mother places some of the blame on Road Home. "It was just frustrating, frustrating . . ." Now that checks are being issued, more people are returning, but "slowly, slowly . . . On my side of the street," she pauses to think, "we're gonna have just about everybody . . ." Still, by late 2008, only 40 percent of Pontchartrain Park's residents have returned.

Clara mentions the overgrown house on the corner of this block. "That really impacts the whole neighborhood . . . Knowing the way the city is functioning, we're gonna end up—"

"We're gonna end up cleaning them up ourselves," Mel's mother cuts in. She's neatly dressed, her hair coiffed, wearing dark red lipstick, and angry. "Road Home's buying some of them," she adds.

"And that's not a good thing," says Clara. "We can't rely on them. They don't put anything in place to protect the citizens. And we're living with a lot of that."

Sighing, Mel's mother comes back to the condition of Pontchartrain Park. "One notch up," she says, "but very slow. We don't have street signs in our neighborhood. Every time we call, they say it's next on the list . . ." There are plans for redoing the golf course but no progress. And one in every nine houses has been abandoned and sold to NORA.

In the Park, as in Backatown, a celebrity-driven not-for-profit is trying to lead the recovery. Actor Wendell Pierce is known for his role in the TV series *The Wire* and now *Treme*. He was born and raised in Pontchartrain Park and has set up a community development corporation; it's put in a bid on 114 NORA properties. Pierce is promising to stop outside developers, rebuild "green," and return the Park to its middle-class prosperity. "We're exercising our right to self-determination."

"It just baffles me," Mel's mother says, "that a country as rich as we're supposed to be . . . that they haven't been able to move faster. We still have people in trailers . . . people sick from the formaldehyde . . . homeless people still out there . . . Three years. Three years! . . . Still quibbling about the public housing projects . . ."

The last seems to particularly bother her. The final vote on razing the Big Four came just before Christmas. Protestors, some organized by Common Ground, stormed city hall, leading to confrontations with the police, injuries, and arrests. Despite the opposition, the city council ended up voting unanimously for demolition. Now only Lafitte—where Mel's mother once lived—remains standing. "That was built strong," she says. "I would have thought that some of them could have been preserved." Instead, HUD's plan for mixed-income developments will reduce the city's number of low-income units by a third.

The conversation is interrupted by the arrival of a redheaded white woman in a New Orleans Saints jersey. Mel introduces her as his daughter-in-law. Tumbling through the door with her are two blond children. Mel swings the five-year-old boy up into his arms while crowing at the boy's sister: "That's Paw-Paw's girl! That's Paw-Paw's girl!" Mel's mother bends to kiss the boy, as he declares, "You could never catch me!" "No," the seventy-five-year-old replies, "I couldn't."

Outside, a little later, Mel explains. "These are two of my grandchildren. I've got eleven of them. That's . . . my son's wife. He's in New Orleans . . . but he's still angry with me. About all the things that happened . . ." Mel looks across his rebuilt suburban block. "When I first started using drugs," he says slowly, "[my son] was in high school . . . All he saw was me and his mom fussing and fighting . . . Then all the money leaving . . ." He stares at the rows of brick ranch houses as if they weren't there. Or as if they were there, but could just as easily disappear.

Through 2008, Mel's ministry has continued to grow. Bethel Colony South now houses sixty homeless ex-addicts. On a bright early morning, they pack the meeting room, sitting at long tables, Bibles and notebooks before them. The members range from teenagers to old men and seem to be about equally divided between black and white, with fewer Latinos than in the past.

"What is done in the dark," Mel is telling them, "will come to the light." He's talking about twenty-five dollars that got stolen last night, but instead of trying to find out who did it, Mel declares the devil "a great deceiver" and moves on. First he singles out a man who dropped out of the rehab program two months ago and has now returned. "There's a humility I have not seen before in you. So, you're gonna make it . . . The brokenness that you came in with this time? I hope that's what's necessary for you to grab hold . . . Brothers," he continues, "when you'all came in, you made a six-month commitment. That six-month commitment is not to me. It's to God . . . God don't tell you after you made a commitment to Him that you can leave early!"

The men laugh, but they know many don't make it through the program.

Now Mel turns to a young black man in his twenties who's been missing appointments. "Son," says Mel in a harsh voice, his index finger in the air, "there *is* no more chances. The next time I get any kind of bad report on you," his finger cutting small slices in the air, "we're sending you home to Momma. 'Cause if you're not right in your relationship to us and to God, you're wasting your time. And you're wasting ours."

Mel takes off his reading glasses. "As far as Nick leaving last night, Nick left because Nick wanted to leave. All right?" Amens. "When you are here, you keep your focus on *you* and nobody else.

"And brothers who complain about this program? Who say it's falling apart, and the pastor's falling apart?" Mel lifts his voice toward its brassy range, brow furrowed. "Ain't *nothing* falling apart! You know why? You know why?" A wave of applause sweeps through the room. "Because God takes *care* of this ministry! If I were to die, Brother James steps up." James is in the corner, shoulders hunched, peering over his crooked glasses. "And . . . you'all have a nice party for me."

There's a release and laughter. Then one of the men reveals it's Mel's birthday and presents him with a card signed by everyone. "Amen, brothers. Thank you all. See," Mel says over more applause, "this means something to me." Yes, they face obstacles, he says: a three-thousand-dollar electric bill, a two-thousand-dollar water bill. "[But] the electricity's never gone off. The water's never gone off since we been in the ministry. That's the way God provides . . ."

The men "amen" and then Mel gives them their work assignments.

"Attitude check?" he shouts.

"Praise the Lord!"

After the room clears, Mel consults with James and some of his section leaders. "We started having a lot of murders here. In this community. Right behind us . . . One night we heard thirteen shots . . . We've had an influx of drug dealers and an influx of prostitution in the area. So neighbors started calling us, and we alerted the police . . .

"These are all spiritual issues," he goes on. ". . . We started doing what we call our Jericho Journeys. Six Saturdays we walked the entire community: prayer and praising God. And on the seventh Saturday, we did it seven times. And we have seen a break in the crime: the drug dealers are being pushed out. Because we're dealing with a spiritual problem with a spiritual solution.

"And," he adds, "that's one of the reasons government can never fix it all." He shakes his gleaming, shaved head. "Government can't legislate morality . . . That's why this works . . . Because we're doing it God's way, not man's way . . . If you notice, the times are getting more evil and darker." He sits forward and ticks off his evidence: greed, war, rape in Africa, the spread of nuclear weapons. "We see man that is only focused on their desires . . ." And it will lead, he says almost matter-of-factly, to

"the war of all wars . . . Armageddon . . . This whole experiment, or . . ."
He looks to ceiling for the right word. "Journey of man can't end any
other way . . ."

As he speaks, the stock market has just finished a five-day stretch during which it lost almost a quarter of its value. Unemployment nationwide
is now past 6 percent and rising, and real estate values have plummeted.
In an emergency measure, President Bush has approved the Troubled
Asset Relief Program, TARP. Like the blue tarps that covered so many
roofs in New Orleans. Except in this disaster, the $700 billion in relief
will go to rescue banks and other big businesses.

Mel, who's left the compound and is now walking down the block,
maintains that "the global crisis that's going on right now . . . [has] not
affected us . . . Because God has given us a unique way of funding this
ministry . . . All sixty men work . . . There's a lot of work to do, still, because of the hurricane. So we're able to paint houses; we're able to cut
grass; we're able to clean houses." Harry, the contractor who toured the
city with Mel, is now helping to run work crews.

Given the financial times, Mel adds, "we know that alcoholism and
drug abuse is going to increase." The camps under I-10 and near city hall
have been cleared out, but the number of homeless in the city has stayed
high. The need for his ministry only grows.

Halfway down the block, Mel points out a gas station that's reopened
and a soul food restaurant that's about to. "It's real interesting what's
happening in New Orleans right now. It seems that we're always opposite
of what's happening nationally." The collapsing economy has hit urban
centers particularly hard. This year, Milwaukee will lose 10,000 jobs,
Tampa 23,000, Atlanta 34,000, and Los Angeles 83,000. New Orleans,
meanwhile, will gain 8,000 jobs.

Mel pauses to consider, "Things are—not bad here . . . There still seems
to be money . . . The Road Home situation is *now* starting to make available properties . . . You have a situation where government is *starting* to
work. It's been long and slow, but it's starting to work." He grins, walks
past Kim's Food Store, stops.

In front of him is a large black-and-white sign: GOD IS GOOD CAR WASH.

"It took us," he says, "about two and a half, three years to get it open.
Because we needed to have the right tanks in the ground . . . We black-
topped the parking lot here; we put the tents up; we built the little
buildings . . . This property used to be an icehouse." Mel points left. "A

little bar here, and on the end," points right, "a little all-night bar called Rich's. And a lot of drug dealing and prostitution was happening here."

Now, Mel says, the car wash is helping to keep the ministry open. All the workers are ex-addicts. They gather among the white open tents wearing yellow slicker pants. Some hose down cars, others wait with towels. There're about a dozen of them, and that goes up to twenty or so on Saturdays. They wash an average of seventy cars a day at fifteen dollars a car, twenty-five with a wax job.

Mel stands in the fine spray that bounces off the pavement. "A man's supposed to provide for his family," he declares. With this business, "the men get back in the habit of work, meeting schedules, being up on time . . . That's all part of the recovery." And as the men recover—and the city recovers—the hope is that the nation's economy will, too.

On the walk back to the ministry, Mel outlines his plans to open a women's compound. He stops at the empty, two-story mini-mall next to Bethel Colony South. An old sign says this was once a health club and a nail salon. Mel's still hoping to turn it into a neighborhood medical clinic. "And along the back side, put a couple more stories on and put a homeless shelter in. That's the vision . . ."

He looks up at the building.

"We've been praying on it."

The Future Is What We Got
in Front of Us

(August 2009)

Close to the fourth anniversary of Katrina, Malik is sitting on a stool in the kitchen of his house in Algiers. It's the room where Common Ground was founded. "Right here at this table," Malik says.

He's in an orange cut-off sweatshirt that exposes his strong arms; he looks healthy. In the dark paneled kitchen, his different personae seem to merge: Vietnam vet, ex–Black Panther, ex-convict, father and grandfather. He's still an activist: in late 2008, he made an unsuccessful run for Congress as a Green Party candidate. But he now has even less to do with Common Ground.

The organization, he says, is diminished. Its plan to buy land in Backatown hasn't progressed. It's working on a program to train local residents to rebuild homes, but that hasn't gotten off the ground, either. It does have volunteers replanting cord grass in ruined cypress swamps, and there's a move to do more community farming in Backatown. But according to Malik, the organization no longer has the space or the funds to house many volunteers.

Over the past four years, he says, the collective raised $4 million and attracted 22,000 volunteers. ("I would go on to say 21,000 was white.") It typically accommodated some 400 to 700 at a time. But recently, with St. Mary gone, "we had to trim everything down . . . Now, we could house maybe forty people."

In explaining Common Ground's difficulties, Malik no longer cites police harassment or fallout from his own radical past. Instead, he blames one person. "That's why Common Ground almost closed—because of Brandon. The reason we had to get rid of our women's center is because of Brandon. The reason we were kicked out of St. Mary's was because of Brandon . . . It was sabotage."

The news broke eight months ago, but Malik is still in shock. On December 29, 2008, Brandon responded to what he called "allegations in the media" with an open letter. It began "To All Concerned . . . The simple truth is that I have chosen to work with the Federal Bureau of Investigation." He signed it, "In Solidarity."

As Brandon explained his decision, he began his involvement with the FBI in November 2007. That would have been after he left Common Ground in tears and just before he came to New Orleans for the Pitt/ Clinton groundbreaking. "I began to feel that we as a radical, radical left," he told a reporter, "because of the way we pseudo-governed, I started to feel like we were a little silly, critiquing the U.S. government, when we had so many faults of our own." So when Brandon was looking out over Backatown, saying that a true moral decision was between a wrong and a wrong, he'd already begun collaborating with the federal agency.

Then, he says, when he went to the Republican National Convention, he suspected that "a small select group of people [among the protestors there] had bad intentions, and I felt the need to do something about it . . ." He provided the FBI with information that led to the arrest of two men on the charge of making and possessing Molotov cocktails. They would eventually plead guilty.

To many in and around Common Ground, this meant Brandon was a "snitch"—and probably had been from the very beginning. One organizer accused Brandon of being an agent provocateur who brought weapons to Malik's house and deliberately led the collective into militant stand-downs. She maintains he was responsible for the "discord" with other relief organizations, that he "demanded a chain of command with him on top," that his focus when he returned as interim director was "to dismantle the primarily women and queer leadership team at the St. Mary volunteer site." A group of organizers in Austin claims to have evidence suggesting Brandon had been working with the FBI since "2006 or earlier." Many current and former members of Common Ground have publicly denounced him, including Suncere.

Brandon has repeatedly denied these allegations. He does admit to on-going differences with the collective. He saw Common Ground as a way of "helping people, [of] getting things done . . . [not] creating a little anarchist utopia." But he insists his work with the government began after New Orleans. "Honestly to God, I never did anything with the FBI while I was with Common Ground . . . I worked my butt off, just like everybody else did, for that city . . . And I don't appreciate being told I was out to destroy [the organization]."

Malik's sense of betrayal remains. "I knew there were informers here . . . but we couldn't put our hand on where was this coming from . . . I mean, this was COINTELPRO that far supersede what we went through within the Panther Party . . . [I was] the laughing stock of the city. 'Cause I was supporting and training *Brandon* to detect who was the informer."

He strides through his kitchen to an adjoining bathroom and points to a flyer taped over the toilet. He says he keeps it there as a reminder and then reads it aloud: ENOUGH IS ENOUGH! LET'S SOLVE THIS. REPORT PO-LICE CORRUPTION. CALL BRANDON . . . 1-888-396-5236. "If a person called, what you think happened to them? . . . What happened when he turned that information over to the police?" Malik pauses, eyes bright and fixed. "He have ruined *lives* here!" Again, Brandon vehemently denies this.

Malik shakes his large head. "I supported Brandon all the way. Until he openly came out and stated that he was working for the federal government . . . My son and I—that's my oldest child—we stopped speak-ing because of Brandon." Pause. "My son told me, he said, 'Pops, listen. This man is an agent . . .'" But Malik sided with Brandon. Now, he says, "I don't ever even want to see him again in life. Nuthin' broke my heart the way he did. Because I know he didn't *have* to. Brandon was—" Malik collects his thoughts. "Brandon was classified in the progressive move-ment in America as a hero . . ."

While denying Malik's accusations, Brandon refuses to criticize the ex-Panther. "Everything I know I learned from Malik: . . . how to speak, how to act . . . and how, when people attack you, to let it go . . ."

Their now-broken friendship goes back to the early days after Katrina. Algiers, across the Mississippi from downtown New Orleans, didn't flood. Officials established a temporary city hall here, as well as a police headquarters and evacuation center. Meanwhile, Malik was running into bands of armed white vigilantes attacking black evacuees. "The first confrontation I had," he says now, "was right around that corner." He's left his house, gotten in a car, and driven a block or so toward the river.

"The second was right in front of that brown truck." It's a quiet, residential street with fenced-in yards. "And it was after the second one that I made a call for assistance."

Brandon, Suncere, and others rallied around him. Malik told them of cops shooting unarmed victims, burning bodies, destroying evidence. He believed the police were helping to cordon off streets so blacks fleeing New Orleans couldn't enter the nearby town of Gretna. "American-born citizens that was denied access to another part of America simply because of the color of their skin." He counted "nineteen young men, who we saw—who I saw—that was killed by multiple gunshot wounds . . ." These stories were largely dismissed or ignored: "When I told the police about it, they told me those vigilantes had a right to protect their community!"

But Brandon appeared to be among those who believed him. And more than that, he saw the same pattern of injustice that Malik saw. It's why Common Ground was founded. Now that Brandon's revealed his work with the FBI—no matter when it began—it's like denying that any of this happened. Just recently, the U.S. Justice Department launched a full-scale investigation of NOPD actions during and after the floods, including the possibilities of murder and of an official cover-up. To Malik, driving through Algiers on this hot August day, it's too little too late. "The FBI has came to me, but I refused to even talk to them. 'Cause my thing is: justice delayed is justice denied . . ."

In the end, Malik remains more concerned with the future. Despite continual opposition, Common Ground still exists. Malik says it's the first time since Reconstruction that a large white presence has been in the black community "for anything other than oppression or exploitation." He sees the collective as part of a larger, older, ongoing fight. To demonstrate what he means, Malik drives through a low-income section of Algiers to what he calls a "sanctuary for those who cannot find work."

It's a run-down commercial building, white cinder block, with a couple of big live oaks in the backyard. Under their shade, a dozen black men and women sit around a small yellow table. A group of four slaps dominoes down; others look on. Malik introduces the group as the "formerly incarcerated"; he says he spends a lot of time with them.

"Does anybody here have a job?"

Malik poses the question like a TV interviewer. All shake their heads no. A man in a white undershirt says he's been a house painter "for over twenty-one years . . . Can't find work now. I ain't worked since last year, man." Another ex-offender—in a Saints hat, a handkerchief thrown over one shoulder—says he worked recently. Malik asks if the government helped him find the job. "Hell, no! How I get work? I seek and destroy! I *search* for my rations."

The woman sitting behind him cracks up at that. Then she answers: "No, the government don't help me."

"They don't help me, either," says a younger, clean-cut domino player, "and I'm a disabled veteran."

"Well, you must be hooked on drugs?" Malik asks, his voice all sarcasm.

"No, no . . ."

"You mean you don't smoke no weed?"

"Nope. I don't smoke weed or cigarettes."

"You got to be on *somethin'* that they don't want to help you." Malik smiles. ". . . You mean to say that you being a veteran, and they're building Federal City on the old Navy Base, they won't even hire you?" Work has begun on turning a nearby, century-old military installation into a modern residential development that will house 1,400 residents. Federal City has a billion-dollar budget, and the developers estimate the project will create 10,000 jobs.

"They not going to hire me," the vet says, unsmiling.

Away from the table sits a gray-haired man who's missing his left leg from the knee down. "I ain't saying the government's not trying to help," he offers, "but it's all tied up . . . The majority [of the money] still isn't here. Got politicians going to jail."

Just a few days ago, the former congressman representing New Orleans, William Jefferson, was found guilty of eleven corruption charges that dated back to 2000. It was his seat that Malik ran for.

The domino game ends. There's a reshuffling that sounds like bones on rocks. Then new hands are dealt. The young vet says he's lived in a nearby project called Christopher Park since 1978. "They got, what? One hundred thirty-four units. Only eighty-eight of them is available . . . They refuse to rebuild. Or fix the roofs. Or renovate them . . . Because they want to do something else: they fixin' that up for when Federal City comes through here."

Malik decides his next stop will be Christopher Park. Once he's left the domino game, he starts talking about organizing a Common Ground "rehabilitation network." It would provide ex-offenders like these with job training and a family support system. "If you can sell drugs, you can sell socks, you can sell pants . . . We're not telling you that you need to stop hustling," smiles, "but maybe you need to change the manner of your hustling."

Malik now points out Woodlands, the apartment complex Common Ground was trying to buy and turn into affordable housing. Since the owner backed away from the deal, it's stayed empty. Nearby is the site for a new high school. It's part of what the New Orleans superintendent calls "the largest school construction program in the city's history" costing over a billion dollars, mostly federal money. Malik wipes a sheen of sweat off his forehead. "Nobody from the community is working at it."

Around the corner, Christopher Park is a series of connected, two-story apartments built like a suburban subdivision: 1971's version of urban renewal. At the time, its mix of condominiums and rent-to-own apartments was hailed as "a model of what can be done in public housing." Now most of the windows are boarded over, the grass is uncut, and the few remaining residents seem to be sitting out on the stoop, waiting.

In his orange sweatshirt, Malik walks between the closed buildings. Steel plates cover first-story windows; white graffiti on red brick reads RIP MISS D. To one side, someone's backyard barbeque sits locked behind a twelve-foot-high security fence. To the other side, the brick facade of the buildings has been yanked off, revealing composition board and charred framing.

Part of Christopher Park was in the city's "scatter-site" program: homes and apartments that were supposed to offer poor families a "foothold . . . [in] moderate-income, less segregated neighborhoods." Last winter, the housing authority approved the sale or demolition of 500 scatter-sites, including 50 here. Dozens were closed in Gentilly near Pastor Mel's ministry, hundreds near Mel's house in the eastern part of the city, and hundreds in the Lower Ninth. Those areas flooded. But the real problem, Malik argues, was that the program was undermined from the start. He points past a ruined playground to ripped-open houses. "That wasn't Katrina. That was already like that. That was Hurricane Corruption. That came *before* Katrina."

He crosses to Christopher Park's community center. Its exterior walls are a faded pink, its iron entrance gate buckled. Malik steps inside to a trashed room full of broken computers and piles of garbage. The slashed walls reveal webs of electrical wiring. In a former Section 8 office, file cabinets have been left with their drawers sprung; manila envelopes and computer printouts cover the floor.

"This is everybody's files," Malik says, face cold. "None of it was even important enough for them to pick up . . . It got their social security number, their work history, their address . . ." Malik waves at the mess. "This is our federal government here."

A man and woman approach. The man has a black, pockmarked face and walks with a cane, his eyes a cloudy gray. The woman wears a pink, low-cut dress against her deep ebony skin. Her hair's a mess, there are dark circles under her eyes, she stares ahead expressionless.

"What is going on?" she asks in a slurred voice. "Why ain't the city coming out and looking at what we're living in? . . . Ain't nobody got no reason to live like this here." Her head juts forward, her neck muscles straining, while her lower body stays slumped and passive. "I mean, we didn't ask for this. We didn't ask for none of this. I ask for it to be *peaceful*. To have a quiet and neat neighborhood. Where I can come out my door and be comfortable." She reaches up to brush at her hair; there's no fixing it.

Malik asks her how long Christopher Park has been like this.

She stares across the ruined office, past the overgrown playing field, to the slumping houses. "Oh . . . for months and months." She says only twenty-five homeowners are left on-site.

"See, they gave them vouchers," the man explains. "To move out. To leave us stuck out. And let the grass grow."

"Everybody talk about the Ninth Ward," Malik says, "but look at this here. This is forgotten! . . . And this wasn't flooded . . . This came from pure neglect and corruption. 'Cause they wanted people out of here, and they want the land . . . They keep it like this here 'cause they know, eventually, ain't nobody going to want to stay here."

The woman looks around with dulled eyes. "This," she says, "is very discrimination back here."

Malik can only raise his hands in the air.

Near Common Ground headquarters in Backatown, Make It Right has added nine more zero-net-energy houses in the past ten months. Sited fairly close together, they make these few blocks feel almost crowded.

The owner of one of the Pitt homes is standing at its second floor entrance. A middle-aged black man, he has a gray beard and a solid belly. His blue T-shirt reads: ALL FOR ONE/HOME FOR ALL. His family lived on this block before the floods. When the levee breached, his home was torn off its foundation, and he watched his mother and one of his granddaughters drown. There's a small memorial plaque out front: TIL THE END OF TIME WE MISS AND LOVE YOU BOTH.

Until a couple weeks ago, the surviving family lived in a pair of FEMA trailers next door. Now they've moved into this pale blue structure, three stories high, suspended over a gravel parking area. "It's a lot bigger than what we had," he says with a grin, some bottom teeth missing. "A lot newer than what we had. And a lot different than what we had." The main room is a combined family space and kitchen that rises twenty feet to a peaked ceiling. On a nearby wall is a battery of thermostats and energy monitors. The master bedroom features a spiral staircase leading to an exterior balcony. Being in a house lifted in the air, he says, "gives us a way to see the neighborhood . . . in a way we never saw it before. Because now we're so high up."

He mentions how the first thing his granddaughter asked was: "Can I run through the house?" A puzzled face. "So they ran from the front door to the back door." Now a smile. "It was like that was freedom that they never had for a long time . . . the freedom to be able to continue what we had before."

He walks past three other bedrooms, then steps onto the raised back porch. "In the winter, we're gonna spend a lot of time out here." He gestures past another Pitt home with its roof armored in solar panels, past the new Common Ground headquarters and the old blue house, all the way to the Claiborne Bridge. Four years ago, this was a smashed-together landscape, the world turned inside-out. "Sometimes you'll come outside," he says, "and see a house springing up that you didn't see the day before."

He still can't quite believe it. He says he wakes some nights to discover, "Oh! The trailers are over there. And I'm inside the house . . ." Laughs. "It's almost as if Katrina didn't happen. And that's what we really want. We want to move forward . . . 'Cause basically that's the past. And the future is what we got in front of us."

An estimated 4,000 homes were lost in the Lower Ninth. Compared to that, Brad Pitt says, his effort is "just scratching the surface." Beyond the few blocks of high-tech houses, grass and weeds take over, ending in a levee and, behind it, an old cypress swamp.

This is where Carolyn used to catch catfish and muskrats when she was a girl, then bring them back to her grandmother to cook. By the late sixties, MR-GO had helped channel saltwater into this freshwater swamp, and now the bayou is pocked with broken white "cypress ghosts." Last month, the final 352,000 tons of fill were dumped, and MR-GO was officially closed. Still, a sign posted here says the Mississippi River delta is continuing to lose thirty square miles of marsh a year, weakening the storm barrier, making another flood that much more likely. The city has proposed restoring this bayou; Common Ground volunteers have floated little trial patches of swamp grass in the dead-looking water.

Today, a black man is digging in the grass along the levee. Trailing behind him is a teenager in dreads and a toddler. When the man looks up, it turns out to be Lathan, the owner of the bungalow and fourplex on Burgundy. And that's his son, Ethan, and grandson, Majestic. They've come over from Holy Cross to fish; first, they're digging worms.

Lathan looks older, rounder, maybe a little slowed down. He says he used to get crabs out of this bayou, baskets of them, and he's here to teach his grandson how to fish. "Though people say the water's toxic." He rolls his eyes and laughs. He still paces around as he talks.

His bartending job never came back. He's surviving off the rent on his two Burgundy Street houses. And, he adds, "I'm waiting on Road Home." He makes a face and laughs again. Road Home is closing. Around 124,000 homeowners have received a total of over $8 billion, with nine out of ten saying they'll use the money to rebuild. Some 27,000 eligible homeowners are still waiting for their checks. Meanwhile, a group has filed suit against the federal government saying the program was prejudicial, that their payments couldn't cover repairs because they were based on the lower home values in black neighborhoods.

Lathan announces in a loud voice that Ethan has graduated from high school and is thinking of going to college. Ethan just smiles, then wanders off to play with Majestic. In a much softer voice, Lathan says that Ethan was shot last Christmas. In the back. No, it didn't happen in New Orleans; it happened in Washington State, when Ethan was visiting his grandmother. He woke up in his cousin's house to find a man with a gun demanding money; the rest is unclear. New Orleans may be the murder capital, but the violence is everywhere. "Bullet's still in him . . . right near the spine. Doctors out there said he wouldn't walk again . . . So we brought him back here . . ." Ethan spent two months in the hospital.

Lathan has done what he calls a "rush job" on the house on Chartres Street. He put the money he got from Historic Preservation toward restoring the bungalow's hardwood floors and fourteen-foot-high ceilings.

Lathan is home.

But Ethan came back in a wheelchair. After months of rehab, he's finally walking again. "He played football in high school . . . and I saw him where he couldn't keep up playing soccer with my grandson." Lathan shakes his head.

He had invested in two more buildings in Holy Cross but has had to sell them; his son was his main helper and partner. After he was shot, Lathan says, "Everything just stopped."

The farther out Claiborne Avenue toward St. Bernard Parish, the more fixed-up the buildings look. Judge Perez Drive has begun to turn back into a string of Walgreens, Shell stations, Burger Kings. Chalmette almost looks like a city again. While the parish has had to back off its ordinance requiring landlords to rent to relatives only, it recently passed a law banning all apartment buildings: another attempt to "maintain demographics." That, too, has been found to be racially discriminatory.

Farther down the highway, in Violet, there're no chain stores and little construction, just small businesses boarded up. Near Daniel Park, Mike and Kim's home now has a pair of concrete lions guarding the front path. A big metal garage has gone up in the backyard. There are no flags flying.

Kim is sitting on her leather TV chair, her legs covered by a Saints blanket. Her thin brown hair is in bangs, and she wears glasses. Most of what you see of her face is her big, toothy smile. Mike is on the couch. His round head and round arms stick out of a T-shirt that says UNIVERSAL X-L STREET TEAM. He's barefoot, in shorts, with a neatly trimmed salt-and-pepper beard, perpetually red faced.

"It seemed like it took *forever*," Kim is saying, "for people to start coming back in here. And they trickled"—she wiggles her fingers— "little by little . . . Last month, the last FEMA trailer was pulled out."

"Yeah, it's getting better," Mike says in his raspy smoker's voice. But the neighborhood is still a dumping ground. He recently caught a truck pouring raw sewage into the closed treatment plant behind their house.

Their granddaughter—seven or eight now—prances through the room in a spangly wig. Her little brother is in day care, and there's a new baby. Both Kim's grown daughters are working as waitresses at a casino truck stop. "What dey make?" Mike asks. "Two-somethin' an hour? . . . Plus tips."

A couple of supermarkets have opened in Chalmette, but the prices are outrageous. "I mean, I buy some Lipton tea—" Mike begins.

"Five dollars," Kim finishes.

"You go across da river—"

"You get two boxes for that."

Mike's mother's lot is still empty to one side of their house; on the other, two homes have been torn down. Parked on the empty land is a little black trailer with PROJECT HOPE stenciled on the side, all that's left of the Common Ground spin-off. "I haven't seen any of dem," Mike says. He remains grateful for their help. As to the government, "I still don't tink dey did what dey shoulda did . . ." And the closing of MR-GO, he adds, is "good, but it's too late."

"Should have done it years ago," Kim puts in.

"All da marshland's gone from around it." Mike grunts. "It's too late! It's gonna take a lot to get it back." Pause. "Long time."

Slipping on flip-flops, Mike makes a quick driving tour of the neighborhood. The next street past his looks tidied up: suburban homes with basketball hoops in driveways and air conditioners humming. But on the street behind his place, the houses are still mostly empty: roofs gaping, fences lumped under vines. Unlike New Orleans, St. Bernard Parish had almost no vacant buildings before the flood. Today, nearly 60 percent of its structures are blighted, worse than in the city. Where New Orleans has been relatively slow to demolish, St. Bernard has been aggressive, using FEMA dollars to tear down a third of its pre-flood housing.

"You could probably buy one of dese . . ." Mike says, looking out at low ranch, "for eight to twelve to fifteen thousand dollars. It's just ridiculous." Between the houses are big piles of trash: tires, old sheetrock, beat-up sofas and chairs. "People tink it's da dump . . . I mean, you can't blame dis on da government. You gotta blame dis on da people. Da people dat own dese properties, da people dat are redoing dese . . ." A lot of them are owned, he says, by "landlords who didn't get da money . . . didn't have insurance or what have you. Den you have people who were able to buy dem dirt cheap—are just sittin' on 'em."

Mike's been back in his home for three years. It's gotten to the point where either the neighborhood improves, he says, or "I'll be out of here! . . . I don't want to, but if it doesn't get any better, dat's the only choice I have . . .

"Den you have da drug issue," he adds. It's returned as strong or stronger than before. "I see young kids right here on dis corner sellin' crack. Standin' here like dey own it. It's gettin' . . . out of hand."

He turns and drives back down his street. He points out where the Vietnam vet lived; the house has been pulled down. "And dere was one after dis one . . . he's gone . . . Dey come back, and dey gutted dere houses and seen da things going on . . . like wit da drugs, and said, 'Best to just keep goin'.'"

Back in his home, he feels better. It looks normal; his family's here. He and Kim agree they aren't actually leaving.

"It's changed for the better," Kim insists. ". . . It took this hurricane to make people realize that . . . We all need each other around here."

"It's been a *long* time comin'," Mike adds.

Kim speaks over him: "This neighborhood's not supposed to be the best in the parish."

"For everybody to open dere eyes and not look at da color of somebody's skin—"

"This street ain't no different than any street up the road—"

"I don't care if you're white, black, green, or yellow—"

"—it ain't no different than anywhere else!"

"—if you hit da drugs or you a thief, you a thief!"

Mike steps back outside a final time. Under the empty flagpole, he kicks at the lawn. "Still trying to get da grass to grow." His cackle of a laugh. "It's comin', but it's slow."

In the November 2008 presidential election, Obama loses Louisiana by a 40-60 margin but takes New Orleans with 80 percent of the vote. In February 2009, Congress passes and President Obama signs the American Recovery and Reinvestment Act. The stimulus package includes $288 billion in tax cuts, a $224 billion increase in funding for education, health care, and unemployment benefits, and $275 billion in federal contracts, grants, and loans. By the fourth quarter of 2009, the president's advisors believe the stimulus has provided up to 2 million jobs, reduced taxes, and helped raise the country's gross domestic product.

The National Bureau of Economics declares the recession officially over in June 2009, but as one economist puts it, "We're still clawing our way back." The foreclosure rate is the highest in decades as more and more people lose their homes. Unemployment is at 9.5 percent, with 5 million people declared "long-term unemployed." What jobs can be found are mostly in the service sector—and barely pay above the poverty level. In the new economic landscape, the question is recovery: how—or if—the nation comes back.

Nothing seems to have changed at the Holy Cross School. Real estate prices remain low, and the authorities are apparently in no rush to make a decision. So these seventeen acres sit. Opposite the school, the pink-trimmed TO GOD BE THE GLORY house has a new fence. Then comes a double shotgun, like Carolyn's, except no one's touched this one. It sags toward the ground. The two-story brick apartment building next to it is boarded up. And there's a FOR SALE sign outside the small wooden bungalow directly behind Carolyn's.

Compared to the rest of the city, Holy Cross ranks low both in the median price of homes and in the volume of houses selling. Last year, it had some 1,200 blighted or empty residential lots, part of the more than 5,200 across the Lower Ninth. New Orleans as a whole still has the highest percentage of blight in the nation, but cities that never flooded are dealing with similar problems. Flint, Michigan, has started bulldozing whole neighborhoods. And the U.S. government is considering doing the same in fifty others, including Detroit, Philadelphia, Pittsburgh, Baltimore, and Memphis.

In front of Mark's house, hung from the limb of his pecan tree, there's a new three-foot-long sign: GURU. Mark comes out of his driveway pushing a red lawn mower. He's hunched from his motorcycle accident, gray-haired, in work pants and a paint-stained blue T-shirt.

"Working my butt off, as usual." He smiles. His house and his rentals are finished. "We got some Road Home money; that helped. And we got the flood insurance, of course. That was the biggest help of all. So, moneywise, I was only short about twenty grand." He laughs. The harsh August sun makes him look old. He wipes his forehead with the hand missing fingertips.

"I look around me, and I just thank God for the shape I'm in—in comparison. You go in this neighborhood four years later, and half of it is still *desolate*." He throws both hands forward for emphasis. "What worries me is that the people who used to live here—old Ninth Ward, basically poor people, low-income—they all *worked* here." St. Claude Avenue once had gas stations, dry cleaners, hardware stores, fast-food joints. It's still almost totally shuttered. "If those jobs aren't here, people aren't gonna come back here to live."

Last year, Road Home money provided a stimulus: all told, the city gained back some 91,000 of the 175,000 jobs it lost after the floods. But in 2009, the national recession is taking its toll. The city is losing jobs again, if not as quickly as the rest of the country. Today, New Orleans barely offers more work than it did during the oil bust of the eighties.

"My own personal opinion," Mark continues, "is that so many of these people who evacuated, they ended up in Ohio and Kentucky and Texas and Pennsylvania and all that, and they got *more money*. They're getting paid at least a buck or two or three more in their pocket than they used to get here . . . And the schools are head and shoulders—anywhere!— over what we had here . . . If you're looking at it logically, from the think-ing man's standpoint—of what's good for you and your family—" His voice drops to a whisper. "Why come back?"

Pause. Gnats circle his gray head.

"I don't say that aloud too often 'cause it's—" Another pause. "Unpa-triotic." He cracks a white-toothed smile and backs away, laughing.

Turning in a slow circle, Mark starts to survey the block. There's his own big white house on the corner, a solar panel on the south roof, a big hedge once again surrounding the property. "Some of the stuff never came back," he says of his plantings. ". . . I've got less variety, but I've got maybe the same amount of foliage." Next door is his set-back brick apartment building, where Patsy was staying last year. Its four units are occupied by young white kids. "There's a couple in construction, there's one in electronics, one works in a library . . . pretty much low-income." Mark says he charges $600 for a two-bedroom: "You're not gonna find that anywhere in the city." Average rent in New Orleans remains consid-erably higher than the national average.

Next comes the yellow cottage that Mark bought from Joe and Linda. There's a sign out front: THIS HOUSE IS BEING CARED FOR . . . DO NOT DE-MOLISH THIS HOME! Mark thinks it was built around 1870 and says he bought it partly because it was eligible for one of the historic grants. To qualify, he needed to rebuild with the "old-fashioned gutters, tongue-and-groove on the porch, the right kind of New Orleans brick for the piers. Had to do all that shit. But for forty-five grand? It's worth it. I bought the place for forty, put five in my pocket, and started working."

Adrian, Patsy's son, has purchased the sister bungalow next door, even though he's still working on his own. Adrian's plan is to tear it down, Mark says, and hold on to the building lot. The house on the end of the street closest to the levee has been boarded up since the floods. "I got no idea what's going to happen. Every once in a while somebody comes by and cuts the grass."

Back at the top of the street, opposite Mark's, no progress has been made on Semmes School other than fresh plywood over the broken windows. Along its fence line, banana trees have grown, their big leaves like elephant ears. The property next to it is the surprise: instead of Joe and Linda's house, there's an empty lot.

Next door, high up in the blue sky, two men are silhouetted on Patsy's roof. She's asleep, one yells down. "She usually sleeps till about eleven . . ." She's staying on the first floor, he shouts.

Patsy is home.

And she's buying that lot, the roofer goes on, pointing to where Joe and Linda's house used to be. "It was about to fall on her!" Patsy's getting the land through the city's Lot Next Door program. It finally got started last summer, with the goal of eventually selling some 5,000 properties to next-door neighbors.

"Patsy got a grant," the roofer shouts, "from the historical society. That's why we're doing it in slate . . ." He points and grins. "We're putting a heart-with-wings design up here." It looks like a cartoon: big red hearts flying across the roofline.

The neighborhood is a patchwork of abandoned houses and empty lots. Mark, the entrepreneur, sees this as an opportunity. "It appears that the city [will] auction them off. And if the price is right, why not buy a used-to-be fifty-thousand-dollar house for ten? I mean, even if you just buy it to sit on it for five years."

He pauses, sharp-eyed, to let that sink in.

"The one I think is attractive—just for me personally—is that little brown A-frame behind these." He points around the corner to Sister Street. The A-frame is one of the few houses that still has a blue tarp covering its roof. Next to it is the rented bungalow, then Ron's still empty lot, with Ken and Barbie riding the fence. Beyond that is the bungalow where the middle-aged woman was murdered. Ron recently bought it. "Twenty-five grand," Mark says. "That's all it went for! That cute, darling little cottage. Brick. With that big pecan tree and all."

Road Home grants, Mark continues, "took so goddamn long . . . I think people just got disgusted . . . [But] the historic grant is making a hell of a difference." All told, some 125 homeowners in Holy Cross got historic preservation grants. Between that and the Lot Next Door program, the neighborhood is consolidating: fewer people, but they own more land. Mark, Lathan, Patsy, Adrian, Ron: all now have two or more lots. It's as if time were reversing, as if Holy Cross was heading back to the era when a single family owned a whole block.

Instead of smart growth, New Orleans city planners have begun talking about "smart decline." That seems to include cutting the amount of low-income housing. So HANO is rebuilding the Big Four with fewer units, is leaving 4,000 federally subsidized apartments unrepaired, and is refusing to rent apartments that it's fixed up. Since the floods, the city's housing authority hasn't offered a home to anyone on its waiting list, which is now thousands of families long.

Mark's survey of the block ends with his own GURU sign. "That's there," he explains, "hoping that someone will actually look into the, uh, ramifications of a guru." He thought people might stop in and ask him for a "slightly different view on their life, on their ambition, on their hopes . . . But, unfortunately, no takers." He laughs deeply. "I don't think there's gonna be. It's been up there three months."

He shrugs and, limping slightly, gets back to pushing the red lawn mower across the green grass in front of his pink bungalow.

Down the block and across the street, the trailer is gone from behind the double shotgun.

Carolyn is home.

"When did I move in?" she asks Kyrah. "Was Mother's Day, huh?"

Kyrah thinks for a minute. "It was before Mother's Day, so it had to be, like, early May . . . We weren't in here for Easter."

They were sure they'd be back in their home last fall, only to spend another six months in the FEMA trailer, waiting. Carolyn starts in on how it was actually kind of cozy. Kyrah won't hear it. "I hated that trailer . . . [And] as soon as they said that the walls were up on the house, she was rushin' me and my brother to hurry up and take stuff out of the trailer and put it in the house." On and off, mother and daughter had been sharing a double bed for almost three years.

Kyrah has transferred from UNO to Tulane. "Majoring in English. Not sure what I'm gonna do with it . . . I don't know if I'm gonna teach, write, go into journalism . . ." She's upset with MLK Elementary for letting her favorite music teacher go. And she fantasizes "all the time," she says, about her life if she'd stayed at Syracuse. "Most of my friends have graduated . . . They have, like, real jobs."

She came back to Holy Cross, Kyrah now says, "because I was home-sick, and I wanted to help my mom . . ." Kyrah is scheduled to get her diploma by the spring of 2011. And then "I really need to get *out* of New Orleans . . . So many people have gotten complacent . . . Everything is pulling together in some areas . . . [but] you have some places where, okay, it looks the way it did after Katrina hit . . ." Her brother, Rahsaan, is also hoping to get a job somewhere outside the city, maybe outside the country.

The court hearing to recover Carolyn's money from the contractor still hasn't been scheduled. In a separate case, he's pleaded guilty and paid a fine for "acting as a home improvement contractor without being registered." Carolyn wants more than a fine. "I want from him what he took from me! I want all my damn money . . ." And, she adds, "We have thousands of people that have been defrauded like I was. Thousands!"

One reason she's vague about when they got home is that they're not quite. Until she can recover her money, she says "[I'm] in this position where I really can't move . . . Because my house is still not completed . . . There are still some repairs that have to be done. Which is the plumbing. And, hopefully, we'll have that done this week." When the plumber arrives, they can finally hook up the air-conditioning: they've been without it through the spring and into the stifling summer heat. "I mean, it's been, what? Four years almost? . . . I'm not saying I'm not grateful and don't thank God. 'Cause there are people in worse shape than I could ever be in. But . . ."

Carolyn's brass bed is finally installed; it sits in front of a small TV. There's hardly any other furniture, but the bare wooden floors have been refinished and shine darkly. A new ceiling fan spins overhead.

"For now this works," Kyrah says. ". . . We make do with what we have . . ." Her room has a mattress under a cone of mosquito netting, a small fan turned toward it. There's a single table in the kitchen, the china waiting to be put back in the china hutch, no chairs.

"Don't get me wrong," Kyrah says, sounding like her mom, "it was nice of the volunteers to come and do it." But it was charity, not the professional job they might have had if there had been money to pay certified contractors. Kyrah points to the gaps around the windows and over the doors. During termite season, "[they] were just coming from out of nowhere . . . And now we're walking around with spray all the time." The butterfly windows on the back porch still don't close; the bathroom next to Kyrah's room leaks; the new tiles are pulling off the floor.

Carolyn settles on her front porch, waving to Mark across the street. "It's still a happy ending for me," she says. " 'Cause I'm in my home. I'm not in the trailer. That was the most important thing I wanted. Not only to come home to New Orleans but to continue living in my home."

She pauses.

"I don't think I would have survived as easily in this condition if it wasn't for my children coming to live with me." They helped her through her knee operation, then rehab; they still help her get to church and make the long bus ride to get groceries. Which reminds her: "We're tryin' to get us a supermarket . . . We need stores."

"We were fightin' for this *before* the hurricane," Kyrah puts in. "And that's the problem. We were always the kind of people—in the Lower Ninth—who were on their own."

Carolyn puts some of the blame on her now-convicted congressman. He visited Holy Cross after the floods, she says, and was "standing right here—right there! . . . Right in my yard! . . . and said, 'Don't worry . . . I'm gonna work on it and see what we can do' . . . So, how am I supposed to feel? I'm on a fixed income."

Kyrah says most politicians take money. Carolyn stares out at the block, quiet.

After a pause, Carolyn mentions a neighbor and her daughter who died in the flood. "None of these politicians can erase that . . ." her voice soft. "They're gone . . ."

Another pause.

"Now, maybe this is the reason why I drive, and I push, and I am the way I am." Both her big hands are in fists. "'Cause, like Father Joe say, 'You never released it.'" Her hands open, and she leans quickly forward. "'Carol, you never cried. You need to cry . . .' I said," her voice low, "'Because I was taught not to cry.'"

Longer pause.

"And I don't cry . . . This is not just the hurricane . . . When [Kyrah's father] died, I don't think I cried very much . . . There's just something about crying . . . And when you're dealing with the NAACP—and I was fighting with all this racism and the civil rights stuff—you gotta be strong."

A last pause as the sun fades and the mosquitoes start coming on.

"Crying is not part of it."

Down from Pastor Mel's ministry, a bunch of mom-and-pop businesses have now opened: a brake alignment shop, a laundromat, the soul food restaurant. His GOD IS GOOD car wash fits right in.

At the ministry, the driveway is packed with used trucks and vans. One white one still has PRISON showing dimly beneath a new coat of paint. Inside the compound, there's been yet more construction: another living area has been piled on top of the main building, plus additional offices have gone up. The main entranceway has been reduced to an alley.

Bethel Colony South now serves some ninety men. They overflow the meeting room, singing along to a three-piece gospel band: "Open the eyes of my heart, Lord . . . I want to see You . . ." A white guy with a ponytail stands to lead a prayer. He prays the ministry "will develop a fine relationship with the fire department."

Across the way, in an upstairs room, Pastor Mel meets with a dozen crew leaders, deciding who'll be cutting grass, painting, in the kitchen, working the car wash. Mel's in his usual crisp white shirt, cleanly shaved, reading through gold-framed glasses.

Also at the table is a large black woman whom Mel introduces as Sister Shonda. She, he explains, will be "helping with setting up the women's ministry . . . So many times we have women calling for help. And you've just got a couple of ministries in town that are helping women . . . Depression is a major issue. Anxiety. Hopelessness." Sister Shonda, he adds, has experienced both addiction and prostitution. "So she is equipped to help women who are struggling through that."

Mel is convinced that the women's ministry will end up in his original building, the one with the damp cinder-block meeting room. "God has step by step prevented the gentleman who, uh, reneged on his promise to sell us [that]; God has worked it out so he can't do anything else with the building . . ." Anticipating the day, Mel has asked LSU architecture students to design a new, six-bedroom women's dorm.

Plus, the ministry has bought a home across the street from there; Harry, the contractor, is living in it with two others. "It's part of another transition," Mel says with a two-handed swooping gesture, for ". . . guys who've stayed here a year . . . The community back here, we're envisioning as a healing community . . . [for] men who are committed to God. Who are coming out of jail and need a place . . . where they're not ostracized, where they can find a job and people will welcome them."

Mel heads over to the prayer meeting. An older white guy in a wheelchair—oxygen tubes in his nostrils—is thanking God for the ministry's "beautiful buildings . . . We didn't have the funds, Lord, but You came through . . . We built this building, and we did it for Your edification, not ours."

A visiting pastor steps forward and presents Mel with a small statue. It's Cain, he explains; he rebelled against God and murdered his brother, so he represents what's going on in New Orleans: "a lot of worthless killing." The visiting pastor then rallies the men, assuring them that they aren't just ex-addicts but "kingdom builders . . . We have to flip the world upside down!"

After the closing prayer, Mel yells, "Attitude check?"

"Praise the Lord!"

As the men head for their jobs, Mel once again drives through Gentilly Woods. The neighborhood looks more pulled-together now: cars in driveways, lawns mowed. Real estate prices here are about the same as in the Lower Ninth, but houses are selling twice as fast. Once Mel crosses over into Pontchartrain Park, the number of empty lots increases noticeably. Landscaping has begun on the park and the golf course, and there are now some usable baseball diamonds. But the median house price is below $45,000.

Outside Mel's family's home, a clipped hedge grows each side of the front door. There's a birdbath by the curb, multicolored wreaths on both doors, and a statue of the Virgin Mary has been reinstalled in the garden. Mel and Clara haven't had the time or money to renovate the house they bought across the street, but neighbors all around have moved back in, and Wendell Pierce's Pontchartrain Park Community Development has picked up a house down the block.

Mel's mother stands outside in a white blouse and pale pink pants. "Many of our neighbors," she says in her gentle voice, "are unable to come back. So many of them are still fighting with insurance companies and haven't gotten their money . . . It's not the same," she says, looking out at her block. And adds: "It won't be the same. We have to adjust to change."

She counts off the houses surrounding hers: one neighbor has died, another is back, then three or four in a row are occupied. "Because everyone wants to come home, you know? Some of the parents have died and willed their houses to their children. They're living in it, and they love it out here. We just can't wait"—spreading both hands in front of her—"to get it back where everything is going to look really nice. And clean. And manicured lawns. And children playing." As if realizing how far away that is, she gives a sad, red lipstick smile. "The stress that it took on people's lives . . . It's taken its toll on me; I feel the effects. But I'm going to fight it!" She manages a laugh. ". . . I want to see my grandchildren grow."

Inside, Mel's father sits in an armchair in the back bedroom that's now his "prayer room." He has thick eyeglasses, close-cropped gray hair, a soft face and voice. "I'd say less than fifty percent of the people who originally lived in this whole area," he moves one finger in a circle over his head, "are back." This room—praying and reading in it—gives him comfort, he says. "As the years have gone by since the storm, I've accepted [God's will] even more."

He picks up the current issue of a local Catholic newspaper and reads aloud from the obituary of a priest. "He had to struggle to help bring back the people in the parish . . . Not only did they rebuild the church, but they rebuilt the community . . ." Mel's father cites the article as an example of how the archdiocese has helped the recovery. It turns out to be the priest who let Common Ground use St. Mary's school. "As long as . . . you love your neighbor as yourself," he says softly, "you'll be all right."

From Pontchartrain Park, there's a quick stop at Mel and Clara's house in New Orleans East. Clara's nephew, Tim, is still fighting leukemia, and he's down to eighty-eight pounds. "Even in that situation," Mel says, "he has joy." Clara is helping with the day care for his young kids. "We are praying for a miracle," she says.

Out on their block, house after suburban house is finished: the lawns manicured, hedges clipped, religious statues carefully replaced. But the city's changed. Ninety-three percent of the white population has returned, but only 83 percent of the black. The past fall's elections produced—for the first time in decades—a white majority on both the city council and the parish school board.

The same vote includes an amendment to give the city's new master plan force of law—even though the plan still hasn't been written. The amendment is put forward as reform legislation, a first step toward strengthening zoning and ending graft. It passes with heavy white support. But here in New Orleans East and in the Ninth Ward, black voters overwhelmingly reject it. Many worry that once the master plan is written, it will once again "green-dot" their homes for demolition, and there'll be no way to fight it.

The director of the city's finance authority calls that "paranoia." A spokesman for the Boston-based firm hired to create the master plan expresses his concern about "doubts and suspicions . . . We need their trust." Recovery czar Blakely, still in office, won't comment.

While continuing to say that the recovery needs to be based on "intelligent free market decisions on where to come back," both Blakely and Mayor Nagin are supporting a major public-private development project called Reinventing the Crescent. Set along a downtown stretch of the Mississippi, it would mix high-priced condominiums, subsidized housing, parks, and shopping malls. As his last term comes to a close, the mayor is proposing transferring millions of dollars in federal block grants from the inner city and applying it to this front-of-town project.

Reinventing the Crescent follows the new urban demographic: some of the nation's fastest-growing cities are being spurred by the return of young white families and retirees. At the same time, the black and the poor are being priced out, often evacuating to the now-aging suburbs. If the trend continues for the next decade, Washington, Atlanta, and other urban centers are projected to become majority white.

When Pastor Mel gets back to the ministry, he and Brother James decide to take a walking tour of the block. "We appreciate what the government does," Mel says, "and the government is for the welfare of the people. But we, the people, can do more, too. It doesn't require the government doing everything..." Mel heads down the sidewalk back straight, James a little hunched, both in their crisp white shirts.

They pause outside the empty mini-mall next door. It now has a FOR SALE sign out front. "We pray that anybody who got the building," Mel says, "would be people who want to help people . . . We're still praying . . ."

Next they move to an empty brick apartment complex. "There is a developer who bought it for two hundred thousand dollars from a city agency..." Mel laughs. "*We'd* have bought it for two hundred thousand dollars!" The ministry doesn't have the money, but "if God wants it to happen . . . God will make available somebody who will call us up and say, 'God told me you needed some money . . .'" He cites a financial advisor to the seminary who just wrote the ministry a $10,000 check—and then added $10,000 for Mel's retirement account. "That's the way God does stuff!"

Brother James, standing in the sun, mops his forehead with a white handkerchief.

Farther down the street, Mel points out where a motel is about to open. A sno-ball stand and a sandwich shop are already in business, and there's a day care center coming soon. The city's Redevelopment Authority has bought the nearby mall, still boarded up. "We don't have a dry cleaners," Mel adds. "We don't have medical clinics."

At the end of the block, Mel and James stop at an empty building with red roof and trim. "This is the place," Mel announces, "they were going to open the daiquiri shop at."

A gray car is parked in front, and a white man leans up against it, cigarette in hand. Mel stands maybe fifteen yards from him and begins to speak in a loud voice.

"We talked to the guys who were going to open it: nice guys. But we don't want a daiquiri shop . . ." In Louisiana, it's legal to serve mixed drinks-to-go as long as they're in a sealed container. A daiquiri shop is basically a drive-through bar. "One of the owners, before the storm, owned a daiquiri shop down the street. And they had drugs coming out of it; they had shootings; they had prostitution . . ."

Mel went to the city council and asked it to reject the application. "Which they did," he continues. "After this happened, the state fire marshal—" pause "—the sewage and water board—the department of environmental quality—" pause, "descended upon our ministry."

Brother James listens, nodding his agreement. Behind them, the white guy has gotten on his cell phone, and he, too, is talking loudly. Now and then, he kicks a yellow ball with the tip of his sneaker, and a little black-and-white dog runs across the empty parking lot to retrieve it.

Mel was worried about opposing the daiquiri shop. "I really thought," he says, "that I was going to walk by the ministry one morning and I was going to get shot . . . But you gotta take a stand in the community." His voice rises toward his preaching style. "To build a community, we have to build a community together. *Not* just take the profit out and go back to our own little comfortable community." Right now, he adds, the ministry is "under the burden of a fire watch. They say because we don't have a sprinkler system . . . So we are spending two hundred and fifty dollars a day to pay the fire department to do a twelve-hour watch." His voice has reached a shout and echoes on the quiet street. "Whoever did it, they're dealing with God!"

"That's right!" Brother James murmurs.

Then, quietly, Mel adds: "And the brother behind us is one of them."

The black-and-white dog has started barking repeatedly, a high-pitched yelp as the man looks down at the yellow ball and refuses to kick it.

"If you fight for the community," Mel continues, "and have a master plan—a sustainable plan where you've got family-oriented businesses— then you're gonna grow families. So, we as the church, we at Bethel Colony South Transformational Ministry"—his voice high again—"that take men that others don't want, and God changes their life; they're renewed and restored—*they* go back! And *they* sustain community!" His words rise above the empty parking lot.

"So, we're gonna fight. No matter what the cost. We will be here!" He clenches both hands and shakes them for emphasis. "No matter what! No matter what." He points to the cracked asphalt beneath his feet. ". . . We're gonna meet the challenge. We're gonna stand firm in the Lord! And we will not," he insists, "will *not* be moved."

Epilogue

(August 2009–October 2011)

On February 6, 2010, Mitch Landrieu wins a landslide victory for mayor of New Orleans, garnering 70 percent of the majority-white precincts and over 60 percent of the black. It makes him the first white to hold that office since his father, Moon Landrieu, left in 1979.

The city still has a 60 percent African American majority, but that's 5 percent below pre-flood numbers. Housing segregation has increased: many white neighborhoods have gotten "dramatically" whiter, while areas like Pastor Mel's Gentilly and eastern New Orleans are blacker. In many white sections, home prices are up, sparking talk of a turnaround. But real estate in neighborhoods like the Ninth Ward continues to lose value, as it does in the metro region as a whole. The increase in home values that occurred right after Katrina has been erased by four years of declines.

Two weeks before Mitch Landrieu's inauguration, the *Deepwater Horizon* oil rig explodes off the Gulf Coast, killing eleven and eventually dumping almost 5 million barrels of oil along the Louisiana coast. It's the worst maritime oil accident in U.S. history, shutting down further drilling, fishing, shrimping, oystering, and a section of the tourist industry.

Kim calls it a "double whammy": first the floods, then the oil. Mike blames British Petroleum, owner of the rig, who "worked dere way around dis,

dat, and da other . . . da safety tings dat should have been implemented."
It's been good for his repair business: the big metal garage and his
mother's lot next door are full of boats. But he worries about continuing
contamination from both the oil and the dispersant that was sprayed to
get rid of it. "When you cut him open," Mike says of fish caught since
the explosion, "and you get to his liver and kidneys . . . dey gonna be
oily . . . His gills gonna be all brown-lookin'." And there will be more
spills, Mike predicts, "until dey get off da oil habit. Which is never gonna
happen."

Mike's mom has decided not to return to Violet. He's bought her lot
and, on the opposite side of the house, two others that Habitat for Humanity owned. "Dey couldn't get anybody to move in back here—because
of da neighborhood . . ." The double lots are now fenced in and planted
with grass for the grandkids to play on.

St. Bernard's population is still down almost 40 percent, and the parish has 16,000 blighted homes. New jobs tend to be low-wage: in 2011,
over 40 percent of St. Bernard's workforce can't afford to pay market
rent.

"I don't think it's gonna change any more than what it is," Kim says.
". . . There's more drug activity than there was before. And it was bad."

"I think you're looking at," Mike concludes, "as good as it's gonna get."

On his visit commemorating the fifth anniversary of Katrina, President
Obama declares, "This city has become a symbol of resilience and of
community and of the fundamental responsibility that we have to one
another . . . Ultimately, that must be the legacy of Katrina: not one of neglect, but of action; not one of indifference, but of empathy; not of abandonment, but of a community working together to meet shared challenges."

New Orleans has 344,000 inhabitants, three-quarters its pre-flood
population. It's about the size it was a hundred years ago.

Lathan leans against the tailgate of his pickup. He's parked outside his
home in eastern Holy Cross. His son, Ethan, still recovering from being
shot, is going to community college now and has just been promoted to
manager at McDonald's. Lathan drives his grandson, Majestic, to school
five days a week. "When he wants to go to the playground, I let everything else go. You're on!"

He's kept his rentals on Burgundy, but "people over there are sitting on their money." On the other hand, this new neighborhood—near Chartres Street—he calls "a gold mine." Houses are being bought and flipped for good profits. Who's buying? "Whites. I got to tell the truth."

Holy Cross still has fewer than half the people it did before the storm.

The Holy Cross School has announced that its seventeen-acre property is on the market for some $2 million. The school is proposing three scenarios, all of which involve converting the main building into upscale condos overlooking the river.

Burgundy Street hasn't changed much: one house opposite Lathan's is occupied, one is being fixed up, two look abandoned.

Ron's lot on Sister Street remains empty, his bungalow on Burgundy unoccupied.

By the levee, the dwarf Santa is gone, hauled off by the sanitation department. A group of neighbors went downtown and salvaged it from the landfill but, Patsy reports, "he had an arm missing . . . I've got his head in a bag . . . He's been in intensive care for some time."

Mark's new home is an old parts shed from his Volkswagen business. He's moved it onto his driveway where his trailer used to be. "I had the experience of living in the FEMA trailer, and it wasn't bad. I thought, 'I can live in this! It's big enough for me, one person.'"

He's renting out his big white house and, meantime, has bought and is fixing up the A-frame around the corner. He says he got it because "it was so damn cute," but he won't live there. "Too big!" he laughs.

In his opinion, the city was starting to come back, especially the tourist industry. "Then this oil spill came up, and the oysters got shot in the ass . . . It seems like someone's got it in for us."

Mark is now seventy. He's recently had a growth removed from his back: "Damn thing took thirteen stitches!" He's being treated in St. Bernard at a medical center still in temporary trailers. The parish is accepting bids on a new three-story building. And by the summer of 2011, there's also an urgent-care center out near Pastor Mel and Clara's home in New Orleans East. It's the first all-hours medical service to open east of the Industrial Canal since Katrina.

Evictions and demolition have begun for the medical "superblock" that will replace Charity Hospital, but construction is still pending.

* * *

Mark crosses the street to Patsy's. Her house is a new peach color with a pale green trim. Joe and Linda's former lot has been turned into a community garden with raised vegetable and flower beds, a sunken rain garden, a variety of old chairs set out in the shade of big green umbrellas. The young people who rent from Mark hang out here and help with maintenance. They call Patsy "Momma Patsy."

As Mark enters her backyard, he has to step past a broken ice cream maker next to a crushed pond liner, overflowing garbage bags, empty animal cages, a refrigerator, a sink, puddles of dog crap, a broken plastic hobby horse. "When you look at this," Mark grins, "you can tell Katrina never left."

Patsy comes to the back door. She looks thinner, her long gray hair pinned up. She's carrying three live chickens under one arm and is followed by her three big dogs. They're all living in the redone half of her bottom floor, which still doesn't have a working kitchen.

"My house is way not ready," she says. "The upstairs has not been touched." She's not even sure what's stored up there. "I'm such a junkaholic. I got junk everywhere."

"You could grow old," Mark says, "trying to find something worth stealing." They both laugh.

Patsy's knees are worse, and there's a walker abandoned in the garden. This past spring, she broke her arm and had a "huge chunk" taken out of her leg trying to stop her dogs from fighting. "It wasn't an attack. I tripped on their leashes, and when I went down, I went down in the middle of them, and *zzzt!*"

When a breeze comes up, there's the tinkle of her wind chimes.

Directly behind Patsy's, beside the St. Claude Avenue Bridge, backhoes are taking down a line of vacant buildings. In the fall of 2010, a sixteen-year-old girl was raped here. According to the NOPD, "a man came out from an area of tall grass in front of an abandoned house, grabbed her and pulled her inside."

"The community just went nuts," Patsy says. "They started to have rallies . . . Landrieu right now is trying to crack down on the blight—crackheads squatting in the houses, people setting fires . . . Anyway, the city just went on a rampage, started tearing the houses down."

Mark thinks it's a good thing. "After five years, a lot of these places have bad roofs. And the water gets inside that house, it goes quick. Really goes quick."

Citywide, a quarter of all residences are blighted. "I'm very fearful," says the Louisiana Speaker of the House, "that we'll end up being like Detroit."

Patsy's son Adrian has painted his home a pale green and put on a new, diamond-pattern roof, but he still isn't living there. He's rewired twice; both times looters got in. "They clipped it from the box all the way up to the attic . . ." Patsy says. "A week after the electric was stolen the second time, somebody stole three of the crape myrtle trees . . . Three seven-foot trees!"

Across the street, Adrian's put in a demo request for the house he bought from Joe and Linda. Mark's renting its twin to a young mom with a toddler. The house at the end of the street hasn't been touched. Neither has Semmes school.

Carolyn's double shotgun finally has plumbing and air-conditioning. She's sitting in the dining room, smiling.

Before Katrina, she says, "I was the homeowner of a house that was still in need of repairs . . ." Now the gutting and rebuilding have brought it up to code. It has a new roof. And her children are living with her. Even with the money she lost to the contractor ("I'll never see that . . .") and the years of waiting, if the question is whether she's better off than before the floods, her answer is a quick smile, a nod, and a drawn-out "Yesss!"

Kyrah has put on some weight, let her hair grow out into a round Afro. She looks more comfortable, more settled, more like her mother. She's once again pushed back her schedule for finishing college and is wondering if getting a degree still makes sense. In this economy, it doesn't seem to guarantee a "real" job, and she's deeper and deeper in debt from student loans. When Carolyn says her children have fewer opportunities than she did, less chance to improve themselves, Kyrah doesn't argue.

In September 2011, management changes, and Rahsaan loses his job at the downtown restaurant. Master's degree in hand, he goes looking for work—and finds a position in another restaurant.

*   *   *

Father Joe has been reassigned. There's now a Haitian priest at St. David, which seems to be thriving.

One Sunday after services, Carolyn returns to Backatown, the first time she's been since Brad Pitt's "pink project." There are now some fifty Make It Right houses. The sewage and water in the neighborhood have been fixed, though there are still acres of empty lots, many of them sold to Road Home. On some of the properties that Backatown residents have managed to hold on to, there are signs of rebuilding.

Carolyn says the landscape doesn't produce the same "disappointment and disgust" it did last time. She stops at the empty site of her grandmother's house, looks out on the weeds, and says a silent prayer. Later, she'll reveal it: "I'm here. I'm a little disappointed, but I love and miss you all. I'll never forget you. And I want you to rest in peace."

In 2011, the city proposes a new high school in Backatown. Mayor Landrieu says it will "anchor" the area and "send a message loud and clear that we are addressing the inequities of the past."

Student enrollment in the city's public schools is still only 60 percent of what it was pre-flood. There are fewer kids in New Orleans in general, especially in the neighborhoods where the big housing projects have been taken down.

In early 2010, the U.S. Secretary of Education calls Katrina "the best thing that happened to New Orleans education. That education system was a disaster . . ." He quickly apologizes.

By the 2010–11 school year, there are sixty-one charter schools in the city. When Superintendent Vallas tells a mostly African American audience that charters are doing "a heck of a job," he's jeered. A month before the fifth anniversary of Katrina, parents and advocacy groups file a complaint with the Louisiana Department of Education alleging a "systemic failure to ensure that students with disabilities have equal access to educational services and are protected from discrimination."

Vallas leaves in April 2011. A month later, the new superintendent announces that a charter school will be moved into McDonogh 35 High School, from which Ethan graduated. The old public school is scheduled to be closed.

MLK school continues to be a symbol of the city's new, privatized education system. It's the first stop on President Obama's first visit to New Orleans after his election. On a patch of ground behind its purple and yellow building, Common Ground has helped set up the Garden of Eatin' Food Science and Nutrition Program. Principal Hicks has become a member of Common Ground's board of directors.

A billboard just off the Claiborne Avenue Bridge proclaims in big red letters: AFFORDABLE CUSTOM HOMES BUILT ON YOUR LOT! FREE HOUSE RAISING WITH HMGP GRANT! Below is a contact number for Common Ground.

Thom, the operations director, says Common Ground has dropped the idea of getting into real estate. "That would be crazy for us . . . It's scary out there." Instead, he's setting up a home construction program. The collective has erected a model house next to its headquarters, and Thom says they already have contracts to build four new homes and elevate thirteen.

To provide crews, Common Ground is training locals in the construction trade and recruiting "better-skilled, more highly motivated volunteers." Not only do volunteers lower the cost of labor, but the collective is now charging them twenty dollars a day for room and board. "We have forty volunteers a day; it's like four thousand dollars a week . . ."

Thom no longer has much patience for what he calls "free radicals." He tells the story of a FEMA official who was around during Brandon's era, how she remembers volunteers yelling "all sorts of stuff" at her. When she returned recently, Thom reassured her: "The anarchists are here, but they now have manners."

Malik, Thom adds, "in all honesty . . . hasn't really been involved in this for two years."

Common Ground's founder has been staying in Algiers. There, the Justice Department investigation has ended up largely supporting his version of what happened during and after the storm. More than a dozen police officers have been indicted, three have been found guilty of shooting and burning the body of an Algiers man, five have been convicted in the shootings of unarmed black citizens at Danziger Bridge, and at least nine other Katrina-related police actions are under investigation. The *New York Times* calls it a story of "rumor to fact" and quotes Malik: "We've been screaming it from the top of our lungs since those first days, but nobody wanted to listen."

In the fall of 2011, in Eugene, Oregon, Malik speaks to a crowd of young people protesting against financial inequities, part of the Occupy

Wall Street movement. "It was people like yourselves that saved New Orleans . . ." he announces to cheers. "In the same way that you saved New Orleans, you'll save the nation."

Brandon is once again a celebrity, though of a different sort. The *Austin Chronicle*'s cover story was entitled "The Informant: Revolutionary to Rat." The episode on Public Radio International's *This American Life* was called "Turncoat." During the sixth anniversary of Katrina, a documentary movie about his collaboration with the FBI plays on national PBS. Brandon still lives outside Austin, helping to raise his daughter and doing a lot of speaking to conservative and Tea Party groups.

Suncere has started the Sankofa Children's Free Breakfast Program in an apartment complex in West Asheville, North Carolina. "Within the last twelve weeks," he says, "I done put out seven hundred meals with no money at all . . ." As well as asking for donations of industrial-size grills and pots, Suncere says that to carry food and other supplies, "I need a pickup truck. An old pickup truck."

New Orleans has more than 9,000 homeless—the most of any city in the nation—with 3,000 to 6,000 squatting in abandoned buildings. A quarter of the city is living in poverty, 10 percent higher than the national rate. Of the families who used to live in the Big Four, about half have returned to the city, under 10 percent to the new replacement housing complexes.

Pastor Mel's ministry has continued to grow. In the summer of 2011, it's serving around a 115 men. He won the face-off with the daiquiri shop; it's been turned into a chicken wings outlet instead.

Bethel Colony South has been able to buy its former home. The building with the damp, cinder-block meeting room is now a women's center. It's added two dormitories on the property, and Sister Shonda is supervising thirty-five to forty women and their infants.

It's also bought the mini-mall next door. There's a thrift shop on the first floor, with housing and offices above. Across from the car wash, Mel's group has put a down payment on a small building it wants to make into a food store. All in all, real estate purchases have created some half a million dollars in debt, but the car wash, the income made by the men, and private donations are helping it keep up with payments. Mel and Clara have rehabbed the house they bought on their block in New Orleans East, and some of the profits from its sale will go to Bethel Colony South as well.

The ministry now amounts to a business, and Mel's role has changed to where it reminds him of his early days as a college-dropout entrepreneur. "It's a familiar feeling . . . but it's different now . . . I'm not doing it for me." He has a fifteen-person management team that includes Brother James. One result is that Mel spends less time with the men. "I don't like that, but it's necessary."

He tries not to answer every cell phone call. He tries to find more time for his own Bible study. His relationship to God, he says, is "always deeper."

Mel's parents continue to live in Pontchartrain Park. Its 2010 population is down almost 45 percent from 2000.

Actor Wendell Pierce's rebuilding plan for the Park has made little progress: only a handful of model homes have been completed by the summer of 2011. As Pierce explains it, being a nonprofit means the "interface with government can be tough." In September 2011, he teams up with out-of-state developers to propose a supermarket in Carolyn's neighborhood on the site of the Holy Cross School. This time, the actor says, the project will be entrepreneurial: "completely free market."

Nationwide, during 2010, banks repossess 1 million homes, 1.5 million people declare bankruptcy, and more than 20 million people remain unemployed. The number of people living below the official poverty line is the highest it's been in half a century. Black poverty is almost 30 percent, black unemployment double that of white.

The 2010 census reveals that majority-black urban centers including Chicago, Atlanta, Washington, Cleveland, and Philadelphia have a decreasing African American population. One commentator dubs this "The Whitening of Chocolate City."

The country has 150,000 fewer low-income units than it did fifteen years earlier. Meanwhile, a front-page article in the *New York Times* declares: "Public housing is falling apart around the country, as federal money has been unable to keep up with the repair needs of buildings more than half a century old."

The average price of a home is down almost 20 percent since the economy breached. By the end of 2010, nearly a quarter of the nation's homeowners are underwater.

Acknowledgments

This book exists because of and thanks to the people of New Orleans: their generosity, their extraordinary ability to tell a story, their courage.

Jonathan Demme helped conceive of this project, was my traveling companion throughout, and helped make these visits possible. If books had above-title credits, his would be on this one.

The family of Donald and Herreast Harrison helped this book enormously, especially with insights into New Orleans culture. For more information on them, see Al Kennedy's *Big Chief Harrison and the Mardi Gras Indians* (Pelican Press, 2010).

Many people advised, encouraged, and provided information along the way. They include Bethany Bultman, Dick Connette, Edwidge Danticat, Anne Giselson, the Greater New Orleans Community Data Center, Steve Elson, John Lipscomb, Dave Marsh, Nancy Nicholas, Alexander Shasko, Elena Stokes, Bob Taplin, the reporting staff of the *Times-Picayune* with special thanks to Katy Reckdahl, and Frank Wilkinson.

Rachel Mannheimer, Carrie Majer, and the rest of the folks at Bloomsbury helped make this happen, as did my agent David Black.

Finally, my thanks to my family—Marta, Amos, and Lorenzo—and especially to my father, Jesse Wolff, whose support was always above and beyond.

Notes

Like a Tree Planted by the Rivers

4 "Blessed *is* the man . . ." King James version.

4 **evacuation** Cooper and Block, *Disaster: Hurricane Katrina and the Failure of Homeland Security*, 172.

5 **National Hurricane Center** Cooper and Block, 133.

5 **By early Monday morning** See Cooper and Block.

6 **FEMA** Jacob Vigdor, "The Economic Aftermath of Hurricane Katrina," *Journal of Economic Perspectives* 22, 4 (Fall 2008).

6 **Its leadership** Saundra K. Schneider, "Administrative Breakdowns in the Governmental Response to Hurricane Katrina," Special Report 515, Michigan State University, http://polisci.msu.edu/schneider/Administrative%20Breakdowns.pdf.

6 **House and Senate committee** Cooper and Block, 172, 178, 242.

7 **fifty-one or older** "Most Katrina Deaths a Direct Result of Flooding, Study Finds." *Insurance Journal*, May 18, 2009, www.insurancejournal.com/news/southcentral/2009/05/18/100605.htm.

9 **death toll** See www.hurricanekatrinarelief.com.

9 **half the number** See Mike Davis, "Who Is Killing New Orleans," *Nation*, March 23, 2006.

10 **master plan** Bring New Orleans Back Commission, "Action Plan for New Orleans: The New American City," Urban Planning Committee, January 11, 2006.

11 **Latinos** Sam Quinones, "Migrants Find a Gold Rush in New Orleans," *Los Angeles Times*, April 4, 2006.

12 *Washington Post* Neal Peirce, "Katrina Paradox: Calamity but Fresh Ideas," *Washington Post*, January 29, 2006.

13 "... re-calibrate ..." Gordon Russell and Frank Donze, "Planners Anticipate a Better City," *Times-Picayune*, January 22, 2006.

13 the flood damaged Horne, *Breach of Faith: Hurricane Katrina and the Near Death of a Great American City*, 45.

14 In the nineties Wilson, *Cities and Race: America's New Black Ghetto*, 14, 75.

14 U.S. economy has declined U.S. Bureau of Economic Analysis, National Income and Product Accounts, Table 1.1.1.

14 *veves* Métraux, *Voodoo in Haiti*.

14 National Guard finally Cooper and Block, 204–22.

14 half of the city Leslie Williams, "Higher Ground," *Times-Picayune*, April 21, 2007, quoting the findings of Richard Campanella.

14 nexus Richard and Marina Campanella, *New Orleans Then and Now*, 10 [henceforth Campanellas].

15 "back-alley" pattern Campanella, *Bienville's Dilemma: A Historical Geography of New Orleans*, 179–80 [henceforth *Bienville's Dilemma*].

15 higher, drier ground Lewis, 50.

15 early twentieth century Campanellas, 23.

15 agents for racial segregation Colten, *An Unnatural Metropolis: Wrestling New Orleans from Nature*, 78.

15 David Duke Bridges, *The Rise of David Duke*, 5.

15 300,000 FEMA Marable, *Seeking Higher Ground: The Hurricane Katrina Crisis, Race, and Public Policy Reader*, 276.

15 in the papers the other day James Varney, "Somewhere Someone Is Making Millions on FEMA's Emergency Housing Trailers," *Times-Picayune*, January 21, 2006.

15 all black Greater New Orleans Community Data Center, "Pontchartrain Park Neighborhood: People & Household Characteristics," www.gnocdc.org/orleans/6/31/people.html.

16 about 1,000 families Ibid.

17 The city's population Lewis, 124; *Bienville's Dilemma*, 64.

17 Fifteen percent of its housing units Gordon Russell, "It's Time for New Orleans to Admit It's a Shrinking City, Some Say," *Times-Picayune*, November 22, 2008; Katy Reckdahl, "Lafitte Demolition Permit Unsigned," *Times-Picayune*, March 12, 2008.

17 median rent Alison Plyer, Elaine Ortiz, and Kathryn L. S. Pettit, "Optimizing Blight Strategies," Greater New Orleans Community Data Center, Annual Report, November 2010 [henceforth Plyer, Ortiz, and Pettit]; Vigdor.

17 **less than $25,000** Vigdor; O. Osei Robertson, "Property and Security, Political Characters, and Dysfunctional Regime: a New Orleans Story," 52, in Marable.

17 **below the poverty line** Kelley Beaucar Vlahos, "Katrina Renews Poverty Reality," Fox News, September 11, 2005.

17 **time sped up** Russell and Donze.

17 **lower than Atlanta's** Rabinowitz, 78, and Robertson, 52, in Marable.

18 **two-thirds white** Steinberg and Shields, eds., *What Is a City? Rethinking the Urban After Hurricane Katrina*, 105.

19 **not only black voters** See Robertson in Marable.

19 **as many white voters** Mike Longman and Jarret Murphy, "Shifting Winds: New Orleans Three Years Later," *City Limits* Special Edition, August 29, 2008.

19 **"a chocolate New Orleans . . ."** "Transcript of Nagin's speech," *Times-Picayune*, January 17, 2006.

Solidarity Not Charity

21 **about 12,000** Greater New Orleans Community Data Center, "St. Claude Neighborhood: People & Household Characteristics," www.gnocdc.org/orleans/7/23/people.html.

23 **"anti-apartheid and animal rights issues . . ."** Common Ground Relief Volunteer Handbook, January 2006.

23 **handbook** Ibid.

23 **mainstream media** David B. Grusky and Emily Ryo, "Did Katrina Recalibrate Attitudes Toward Poverty and Inequality?" *DuBois Review* 3, 1 (2006): 59–82.

23 **U.S. Census Bureau** Grusky and Ryo.

23 **watershed** Ibid.

23 **President Bush** Courte C. W. Voorhees, John Vick, and Douglas D. Perkins, " 'Come Hell and High Water': The Intersection of Hurricane Katrina, the News Media, Race and Poverty," *Journal of Community and Applied Social Psychology* 17 (2007): 415–29.

23 **". . . [economic] gains . . ."** Grusky and Ryo.

23 **second largest** "Gap Between U.S. Rich, Poor Is Widest in Atlanta," MSNBC.com news, October 26, 2011.

23 **handbook** Common Ground Relief Volunteer Handbook, January 2006.

24 close to 50,000 Ibid.

24 ". . . revolutionary transformation . . ." Ibid.

24 ". . . workers' cooperatives . . ." Ibid.

24 without a hierarchy crow, *Black Flags and Windmills: Hope, Anarchy, and the Common Ground Collective*, 63.

25 Before the flood Richard Campanella, "Urban Transformation in the Lower Ninth Ward," in Feireiss, *Architecture in Times of Need: Make It Right Rebuilding New Orleans' Lower Ninth Ward*, 77; Carol McMichael Reese, "From Field of Disaster to Field of Dreams: The Lower Ninth Ward," in Feireiss, 39.

25 ". . . the murder capital . . ." Juliette Landphair, " 'The Forgotten People of New Orleans': Community, Vulnerability, and the Lower Ninth Ward," *Journal of American History* 94, 3 (December 2007): 837–45.

25 three-quarters of its residents Greater New Orleans Community Data Center, "Lower Ninth Ward Neighborhood: People & Household Characteristics," www.gnocdc.org/orleans/8/22/people.html; see also Feireiss, 40–42.

25 60 percent Sarah Carr, "The Changing Face—and Faces—of New Orleans," *Times-Picayune*, August 23, 2009.

25 Five months ago Landphair.

25 largest number Ibid.

26 original master plan See Bring New Orleans Back Commission, "Action Plan for New Orleans."

26 "There's nothing . . ." Landphair.

27 Brandon and a friend See crow.

27 hampered Mark Sappenfield, "Katrina Poses Key Test for Stretched National Guard," *Christian Science Monitor*, September 2, 2005.

27 ICE agents U.S. Immigration and Customs Enforcement.

28 a core committee See crow, 97, 134.

28 tended to defer crow, 135.

31 President Bush . . . television interview Cooper and Block, 204.

31 governor Blanco BBC News, "New Orleans Rocked by Huge Blasts," September 2, 2005.

33 great flood of 1927 Barry, *Rising Tide, The Great Mississippi Flood of 1927 and How It Changed America*, 238–58.

34 big industry "History of St. Bernard Parish," www.stbernardparish.net/history.

34 considered closing Fairclough, *Race and Democracy: The Civil Rights Struggle in Louisiana, 1915–1972*, 235.

34 picked the Ninth Ward Baker, *The Second Battle of New Orleans: The Hundred-Year Struggle to Integrate the Schools*, 379.

34 "cheerleaders" Fairclough, 234, 244.

34 "Don't wait . . ." Baker, 415.

34 600 Ibid., 416.

34 more than 90 percent Lawyers' Committee for Civil Rights Under Law, "St. Bernard Parish Agrees to Halt Discriminatory Zoning Rule," press release, Washington, D.C., November 13, 2006.

34 three of St. Bernard's "Katrina Timeline," www.ominous-valve.com /katrina.html.

35 "complete destruction" Jonathan Rauch, "Struggling to Survive After Katrina: A Hard Year for the Big Easy," August 14, 2006, http:reason.com /archives/2006/08/14/struggling-to-survive-after-ka.

35 *Exxon Valdez* Miguel Llanos, "44 Oil Spills Found in Southeast Louisiana," MSNBC.com, September 19, 2005.

35 almost as empty Rauch.

35 treated for depression Ibid.

35 almost tripled See Steinberg and Shields, 54.

37 about 40 percent "Violet, Louisiana," www.city-data.com/city/Violet -Louisiana.html.

37 "blighted" Richard Slawsky, "St. Bernard Parish Housing Authority Would Work to Clean Up Slums," *New Orleans CityBusiness*, June 20, 2005.

A Walk Around the Block

42 5,500 Greater New Orleans Community Data Center, "Holy Cross: People & Neighborhood Characteristics," www.gnocdc.org/orleans/8/20/people.html.

42 Thomas J. Semmes Herman de Bachellé Seebold, *Old Louisiana Plantation Homes and Family Trees* (Gretna, LA: Pelican Press, 1941), 1:31.

42 not-for-profit Ariella Cohen, "Councilman Connected to Nine Blighted Buildings in the Lower 9th Ward Neighborhood," *Lens*, January 18, 2011, the lens.org/2011/01/19/johnson-blight_19_2/.

43 1859 "Holy Cross," Rebuilding Together, New Orleans, www.rtno.org /neighborhoods/holy-cross.

43 seventeen-acre campus "History," Holy Cross, www.holycrosstigers.com /History.

44 third-largest Campanellas, 18.

44 Ninety-nine percent *Bienville's*, 230.

44 busiest slave market See Woods, *Development Arrested: The Blues and Plantation Power in the Mississippi Delta*, especially 6; *Bienville's Dilemma*, 201.

44 twenty-five auction Campanellas, 18.

44 as collateral Johnson, *Soul by Soul: Life Inside the Antebellum Slave Market*, 16.

44 "poised on the brink . . ." Ibid., 1.

44 doubling the black population *Bienville's Dilemma*, 180–82.

44 In 1869 Medley, *We as Freeman: Plessy v. Ferguson*, 25, 81.

44 Semmes Ibid., 209.

45 German immigrant Ibid.

45 "Broadway of New Orleans . . ." See Brothers, *Louis Armstrong's New Orleans*, 80.

45 For history of Rampart Street, see Sublette, *The World That Made New Orleans: From Spanish Silver to Congo Square*, 119; Brothers; Sublette, *The Year Before the Flood: A Story of New Orleans*, 52.

45 former plantation owners Campanella in Feireiss, 71; Earth Search, Inc. "Archaeological Survey and Testing in the Holy Cross Historic District, New Orleans, Louisiana."

47 1880 to 1936 and National Historic Register Greater New Orleans Community Data Center, "Holy Cross Neighborhood Snapshot," www.gnocdc.org /Orleans/8/20/snapshot.html.

48 Speaker of the U.S. House See Jack Shafer, "Don't Refloat," *Slate*, September 7, 2005.

48 the average house value Cassidy, *How Markets Fail: The Logic of Economic Calamities*, 236–38.

48 highest rate Zandi, 48.

48 home construction Ibid., 139, 132.

48 wasn't benefiting Cassidy, 236.

48 home prices dropped Ivan J. Miestchovich, "New Orleans Economy & Real Estate Market: Redevelopment and Rebuilding the University of New Orleans," www.norpc.org/assets/pdfs/eda-conf-2008/ivan_miestchovich_web .pdf.

48 one realtor Kathy Chu, "New Orleans Home Seller Struggle," *USA Today*, July 27, 2007; Deon Roberts, "University of New Orleans Real Estate Report Offers Mixed News," *New Orleans City Business*, June 7, 2006.

48 ". . . in the real estate business" For Baker Bill see Adam Nossiter, "A

Big Government Fix-It Plan for New Orleans," *New York Times*, January 5, 2006; Bill Walsh, "White House Deals Blow to Baker 'Buy-Out' Plan," *Times-Picayune*, January 24, 2006.

49 more police per After the storm, the NOPD lost 300 officers from a force of 1,700. See Mathieu Deflem and Suzanne Sutphin, "Policing Katrina: Managing Law Enforcement in New Orleans," *Policing* 3, 1 (2009): 41–49.

50 shotgun For a detailed study of the shotgun house, its history, and its development, see Vlatch, *By the Work of Their Hands: Studies in Afro-American Folklife*, especially 181–213.

51 1875 map Earth Search, Vol. II.

52 racially fluid *Bienville's Dilemma*, 33, 164.

52 dotted with them Ibid., 144.

52 "an architecture of defiance" See Vlatch.

54 Allelulia Group See www.yeslord.com.

They've Not Done What They Needed

60 a lobbyist Eric Lipton and Ron Nixon, "Many Contracts for Storm Work Raise Questions," *New York Times*, September 26, 2005.

60 blue tarps Aaron C. Davis, "U.S. Paying a Premium to Cover Storm-Damaged Roofs," Knight Ridder, September 30, 2005.

60 Sixty percent Blaine Harden, "A City's Changing Face," *Washington Post*, May 17, 2006.

61 absentee ballots "Killing the Black Vote," Color of Change.org, http://orig.colorofchange.org/voting/message.html.

61 The results showed Harden; Bill Quigley, "Eight Months After Katrina," CommonDreams.org, April 26, 2006.

61 40 percent Brian Thevenot, "Flood-Ravaged Neighborhoods May Lose Clout," *Times-Picayune*, May 2, 2006.

61 strategy paid off Dan Glaister, "New Orleans Mayor Wins Surprise Re-election," *Guardian*, May 22, 2006.

61 Landrieu Robertson in Manning, 50–51.

61 ". . . zones of concentrated poverty" David Brooks, quoted in Adolph Reed and Stephen Steinberg, "Liberal Bad Faith in the Wake of Hurricane Katrina," *Black Commentator* 182, May 4, 2006.

61 "and I'm not sure . . ." and **"We finally cleaned up . . ."** Reed and Steinberg.

61 just over half Rachel E. Luft with Shana Griffin, "A Status Report on

Housing in New Orleans After Katrina: An Intersectional Analysis," in Beth Willinger, ed., *Katrina and the Women of New Orleans*.

61 140,000 Quigley, "Eight Months After Katrina."

62 More than half Lewis Wallace, "First Came Katrina, then Came HUD," *In These Times*, January 16, 2008; DeMond Shondell Miller and Jason David Rivera, "Landscapes of Disaster and Place Orientation in the Aftermath of Hurricane Katrina," in Brunsman, Overfelt, and Pico, eds., *The Sociology of Katrina: Perspectives on a Modern Catastrophe*.

62 rents have gone up Quigley, "Eight Months After Katrina."

62 almost in half Ibid.

62 a third of the apartments Katy Reckdahl, "Lafitte Demolition Permit," *Times-Picayune*, March 12, 2008.

62 "Big Four" Ibid.

62 already targeted Nicolai Ouroussoff, "History vs. Homogeneity in New Orleans Housing Fight," *New York Times*, February 22, 2007.

62 decades of segregated housing Wilson, 24.

66 ". . . as quickly as possible" David Giner, "Stranded and Squandered: Lost on the Road Home," *Seattle Journal for Social Justice* 7, 1 (2008).

68 Around 1940 Martha Mahoney, "Law and Racial Geography: Public Housing and the Economy in New Orleans," *Stanford Law Review* 42, 5 (May 1990): 1251–90.

68 Franklin Roosevelt's Rabinowitz, *Urban Economies and Land Use in America: The Transformation of Cities in the Twentieth Century*, 122.

68 450 developments Wilson, 25.

68 shaded by oaks Nicolai Ouroussoff, "All Fall Down," *New York Times*, November 19, 2006.

68 Most American cities Mahoney.

68 second-busiest port *Bienville's Dilemma*, 25.

68 With veterans returning Mahoney.

68 first to be ratified "New Orleans Was a Pioneer in Public Housing," Doug McCash, *Times-Picayune*, February 13, 2011; Ouroussoff, November 19, 2006.

68 tile roofs Ouroussoff, November 19, 2006.

68 9,000 new Geoffrey S. Wiggins, "The Power and the People: Race and the New Orleans Housing Crisis, 1946–61," College of Urban and Public Affairs, University of New Orleans, www.urbancentre.utoronto.ca/pdfs/housing conference/Wiggins_Power_People_NewOrl.pdf.

68 Twenty percent Mahoney.

69 "stopped cold . . ." Maurice d'Arlan Needham, *Negro Orleanian: Status and Stake in a City's Economy and Housing*, 172.

69 ". . . poor for generations" Rabinowitz, 126.

69 "federal ghettoes" Mahoney.

70 "Housing is the one . . ." See Needham, especially 127–28, 163.

70 30 percent black www.pbs.org/wgbh/amex/neworleans/peopleevents/e_integration.html.

70 appease white voters Fairclough, 152.

70 exclusively black Wiggins.

70 The city built Mahoney.

70 underwritten Chakara Watson, "Pontchartrain Park 1955: One Woman's Story," in *New Orleans Unmasked*, http://cat.xula.edu/unmasked/articles/419.

71 whites only www.denisetrowbridge.com/portfolio/stories/pontchartrain beach.html.

71 maintenance fell off Denise Trowbridge, "Pontchartrain Park Amusement Park," *Liquid Weekly*, September 2001, www.denisetrowbridge.com/2008/12/pontchartrain-b.html.

73 fifty or older Greater New Orleans Data Center, Pontchartrain Park Neighborhood: People and Household Characteristics, from 2000 census, www.gnocdc.org/orleans/6/31/people.html.

74 city council *City Limits* Special Edition, August 29, 2008.

74 story about HUD Donna White, "HUD Outlines Aggressive Plan to Bring Families Back to New Orleans' Public Housing," http://archives.gov/news/2006/pro6-066.cfm.

74 State of the Union Horne, 347.

Got to Do What You Got to Do

76 fewer than 10 percent Karen Rowley, "GulfGov Reports; One Year Later," Public Affairs Research Council of Louisiana, 2006.

76 ExxonMobil Ibid.

77 1,600 Bill Quigley, "Trying to Make It Home: New Orleans a Year After Katrina," *Counterpunch*, www.counterpunch.org/quigley08222006.html.

77 "a mixture of . . ." Arianne Wiltse, "Unity of the Spirit," *Gambit Weekly*, May 30, 2006.

77 less than a third Wiltse and Rauch, "Struggling to Survive."

78 a federal judge Associated Press, "Katrina Victims and Insurers Square Off in a Courtroom," July 11, 2006.

79 ICF International See the ICF website, www.icfi.com.

79 board of ethics Davida Finger, "Stranded and Squandered: Lost on the Road Home," *Seattle Journal for Social Justice* 7, 1 (2008).

79 No checks have been issued Michelle Krupa, "Road Home Isn't Easy Street," *Times-Picayune*, October 7, 2006; Bill Quigley, "Eight Months After Katrina."

82 privatizing, too Renae Merle, "Storm-Wracked Parish Considers Hired Guns," *Washington Post*, March 14, 2006.

84 Chalmette www.city-data.com/city/Chalmette-Louisiana.html.

86 new regulations Associated Press, "FEMA: Louisiana Homes Must Be Raised off Ground," *USA Today*, April 13, 2006.

86 ". . . enable people . . ." J. Robert Hunter, "False Claims," *New York Times*, May 2, 2006.

87 given ten days Bruce Eggler, "Task Force to Uphold Home-Gutting Rules," *Times-Picayune*, August 3, 2006.

87 Good Neighbor Plan Rauch.

88 Section 8 became code Jonathan P. Hooks, "St. Bernard Parish Agrees to Halt Discriminatory Ruling," press release from Lawyers' Committee for Civil Rights Under Law, November 13, 2006.

89 the parish admitted Ibid.

90 "Mortgage holders have . . ." Walsh.

We Sitting Here Waiting

92 4,000 linear feet Cajun Industries, Inc. Projects, www.cajunusa.com /CATSUBCAT/CatSubCatDisplay.asp?P9=CSC2&P1=728&P7=0; Wells, *The Good Pirates of the Forgotten Bayou: Fighting to Save a Way of Life in the Wake of Hurricane Katrina*.

94 "formally admitted . . ." Levee.org, "New Study Faults Army Corps for New Orleans Levee Failures," compiled from a National Science Foundation report, May 22, 2006; Charles C. Mann, "The Long, Strange Resurrection of New Orleans," *Fortune*, August 29, 2006.

95 ECC Tommy Santora, "Debris Removal and Demolition Work Progressing," *New Orleans City Business*, February 27, 2006, http://findarticles .com/p/articles/mi_qn4200/is_20060227/ai_n16198036/?tag=content;col1; Gulf Coast Commission on Reconstruction Equity, "Good Work and Fair Contracts: Making Gulf Coast Reconstruction Work for Local Residents and

Businesses," created by Interfaith Worker Justice and Good Jobs First, 2006.

95 A recent report Jordan Green, "Fraud, Scandal and Greed Have Crippled the Gulf Recovery—but Made Some Very Rich," in "One Year after Katrina: The State of New Orleans and the Gulf Coast," a report published by Gulf Coast Reconstruction Watch, a special project of Southern Exposure/Institute for Southern Studies, August 2006.

96 "heyday . . ." crow, 182, 186.

96 "driverless bus . . ." Ibid., 134.

97 a source of pride Amy Waldman, "Reading, Writing, Resurrection," *Atlantic*, January–February 2007, www.theatlantic.com/doc/200701/waldman -katrina.

97 opening day ceremonies Steve Ritea, "The Dream Team," *Times-Picayune*, August 1, 2006; Daniel Rible, "First School in Lower Ninth Reopened," *New America Media*, August 30, 2007.

97 as weak a school system Waldman.

97 Fewer than half Ibid.

97 student population Cowen Institute for Public Education Initiatives, "New Orleans Public Schools History: A Brief Overview," Tulane University, www .tulane.edu/cowen_institute/documents/NewOrleansSchoolHistory.doc.

97 "multiple instances . . ." "History of Schools in New Orleans," arch.co lumbia.edu/Studio/Spring2006/Marble/TC/Morgan.pdf.

97 70 percent BBC News, "US School Segregation Rises," July 18, 2001, http:// news.bbc.co.uk/go/em/fr/-/2/hi/americas/1445545.stm.

97 school resegregation Boger and Orfield, eds., *School Resegregation: Must the South Turn Back?*; Ryan, *Five Miles Away, A World Apart: One City, Two Schools, and the Story of Educational Opportunity in Modern America*, 157.

97 private accounting firm Ralph Adamo, "Squeezing Public Education: History and Ideology Gang Up in New Orleans," *Dissent*, July 8, 2009.

97 Recovery School District Ibid.

97 nearly 90 percent Cowen Institute for Public Education Initiatives.

97 Milton Friedman Naomi Klein, *The Shock Doctrine: The Rise of Disaster Capitalism* (New York: Metropolitan Books/Henry Holt, 2007).

97 ". . . once-in-a-lifetime . . ." Waldman.

97 fired all 7,500 Waldman; Adamo.

98 ". . . the school was back" Alicia Dennis, Susan Schindehette, "Kendall Goes Back to School," *People*, August 27, 2007.

98 ". . . do it ourselves." Ritea, "The Dream Team."

98 "... in an appropriate environment." Ibid.

98 FEMA had committed Steve Ritea, "Students Are Ready, but What About the Schools?" *Times-Picayune*, August 6, 2006.

98 staged a protest Valerie Facine, "MLK School Reopens in Lower 9th," *Times-Picayune*, June 10, 2007.

99 15,000 National Guard Brian Thevenot, "National Guard Leaves New Orleans, Ends Crime-Fighting Help," *Times-Picayune*, February 27, 2009.

99 crime-control tools Adam Nossiter, "New Orleans Crime Swept Away, with Most of the People," *New York Times*, November 9, 2006.

99 ... mid-year death toll Associated Press, "National Guard Sent to Patrol NOLA," June 19, 2006.

99 "arguably one of the ..." Moore, *Black Rage in New Orleans: Police Brutality and African American Activism from World War II to Hurricane Katrina*, 5.

99 "We've had enough ..." Ibid.

99 "You will have to look ..." Ibid.

99 "... a bit shocking ..." Michelle Krupa, "Good Cause Celeb," *Times-Picayune*, July 15, 2006.

99 "... a real opportunity ..." Reuters, "Brad Pitt Hopes to Build 'Green' in New Orleans," July 14, 2006.

100 a competition *Architecture Week*, June 2, 2006.

100 "... this is it" Krupa, "Celeb"; Stacey Plaisance, "Pitt, Jolie to Watch Hurricane-Wrecked Neighborhood Rebuild," Associated Press, August 31, 2006.

101 first black high school Valentine Pierce, "Clarification: McDonogh 35 Predates the 1930s," *Louisiana Weekly*, June 20, 2008.

101 privately run charters Waldman; Todd Ziebarth, "Top Ten Charter School Communities by Market Share," National Alliance for Public Charter Schools, www.publiccharters.org/files/publications/file_MarketShare2007.pdf.

102 nearly 60 percent Ziebarth.

104 In 1962 Katy Reckdahl, "The McDonough 3 Help Unveil Historical Marker at Their 1960 school," *Times-Picayune*, November 14, 2010.

109 the continuing worry Kari Lydersen, "Fight Continues over New Orleans's Lower Ninth Ward," *New Standard*, February 21, 2006.

110 16,000 acres Weeks, 211.

110 filled in swamps Jeff Williams, "Louisiana Coastal Wetlands: A Resource at Risk," U.S. Geological Survey, 1995, http://marine.usgs.gov/marine/fact-sheets/Wetlands/index.

110 **fastest-disappearing** Brian Merchant, "New Orleans Wetlands Now the Fastest-Disappearing Landmass on Earth," Treehugger.com, September 18, 2009.

110 **it calls for** "Holy Cross, Planning District 8, Rebuilding Plan," http://www .nolaplans.com/plans/Lambert%20Final/District_8_Final_Holy%20Cross.pdf.

111 **250,000** Bill Quigley, "Trying to Make It Home . . ."

111 **dropped to seventeenth** See *Bienville's Dilemma*, especially 229–33.

111 **one observer** Vigdor.

111 **the 1880's** *Bienville's Dilemma*, 41.

111 **pre-flood growth** Kelly Frailing and Dee Wood Harper, "Crime and Hurricanes in New Orleans," in Brunsma; see also Lewis, 114, 155–156.

111 **80 percent** Jeannine Aversa, "Job Market Has Weak Showing," Associated Press, December 4, 2010.

111 **first nation in the world** Victor R. Fuchs, "The First Service Economy," *National Affairs*, Winter 1966.

112 **Charity Hospital** Quigley, "Trying to Make It Home . . ."

112 **200 trauma patients** Richard A. Webster, "Trauma Caseload Tests New Orleans–area hospitals," *New Orleans City Business*, November 25, 2005.

112 **sixty-seven-acre** "City Limits Investigates," Special Edition, City Futures, Inc., August 29, 2008.

112 **lowest ranking** Liu et al., *Resilience and Opportunity: Lessons from the U.S. Gulf Coast After Katrina and Rita*, 46–47.

112 **upscale treatments** Roberta Brandes Gratz, "Why Was New Orleans' Charity Hospital Allowed to Die?" *Nation*, April 7, 2011; Carla K. Johnson, "Hospitals Caring for Poor on Brink of Closing," Associated Press, May 10, 2011.

112 **"Changing demographics . . ."** "City Limits Investigates"; Fritz Esker, "New Orleans Gets a Formal Level 1 Trauma Care Facility," *New Orleans City Business*, February 27, 2006.

Time Is Not the Same

123 **120,000** Kate Moran, "FEMA Trailers Called Health Hazards," *Times-Picayune*, May 29, 2007.

123 **respiratory problems** Union of Concerned Scientists, "FEMA Exposes Gulf Coast Residents to Formaldehyde," December 19, 2007, www.ucsusa .org/scientific_integrity/abuses_of_science/fema-exposes-gulf-coast.html.

123 **a spokesman** Mike Brunker, "Are FEMA Trailers Toxic Tin Cans?" MSNBC.com, July 25, 2006.

123 deadline has been extended Sean Alfano, "FEMA Trailers Will Stay in New Orleans," CBS News, September 23, 2006.

125 Reaching Road Home See Finger, 78.

125 thirteen checks Deon Roberts, "Louisiana's Road Home Program Proving to be Uphill Climb," *New Orleans City Business*, October 9, 2006.

128 40,000 miles of road Duany et al., *Suburban Nation: The Rise of Sprawl and the Decline of the American Dream*, 9.

128 ". . . a great subsidy . . ." Rabinowitz, 122–33.

128 suburbs Lewis, 80.

128 "logical growth corridor" New Orleans Land Use Plan, "Planning Districts Nine, Ten, and Eleven: New Orleans East," April 1999; Feireiss, 77.

128 construct a suburb Lewis, 80–81.

129 also had black leaders . . . halved. Wilson, 33.

129 number of refineries Colten, 127.

129 crude oil prices Matthew Brown, "Katrina May Mean MR-GO Has to Go," *Times-Picayune*, October 24, 2005.

129 hit particularly hard Kent B. Germany, "The Politics of Poverty and History: Racial Inequality and the Long Prelude to Katrina," *Journal of American History* 94, 3 (December 2007): 743–51.

129 75 percent black New Orleans Land Use Plan, April 1999.

129 fewer poor "Little Woods Neighborhood," Greater New Orleans Community Data Center, www.gnocdc.org/orleans/9/49/employment.html.

132 fifty-five and older Jeffrey A. Goren and Anne E. Polivka, "Going Home After Hurricane Katrina: Determinants of Return Migrants and Changes in Affected Areas," U.S. Bureau of Labor Statistics, Working Paper 428, September 2009.

133 "widespread ecological . . ." Brown.

133 a resolution "Report by Independent Levee Investigation team," July 31, 2006, www.ce.berkeley.edu/projects/neworleans/report/CH_12.pdf.

134 eighteen feet above Richard Campanella, "Geographical History and Future of New Orleans," http://cbr.tulane.edu/PDFs/Geo_NOLA.pdf.

134 company website www.bollingershipyards.com.

134 "probably the best . . ." Kimberley Solet, "Local Shipbuilding Magnate Talks Levees with President Bush," *Houma Today*, December 13, 2005.

134 "widespread sympathy . . . cease to exist" Brown.

134 in the process U.S. Army Corps of Engineers, "History of MR-GO," www.mrgo.gov/MRGO_History.aspx.

135 **a monolithic project** Mahoney and Flint, *This Land: The Battle over Sprawl and the Future of America*, 34.

135 **10,500** Arend, *Showdown in Desire*, 4–6.

135 **Dirty D** http://www.absoluteastronomy.com/topics/Desire_Projects #encyclopedia.

I Want to Keep Fighting Till . . .

138 **. . . already resigned** Mathieu Deflem and Suzanne Sutphin, "Policing Katrina: Managing Law Enforcement in New Orleans," *Policing* 3, 1 (2009): 41–49.

139 **debris-removal contracts** "FACTBOX—Top Private Contractors in Iraq/ Afghanistan," Reuters, November 20, 2007.

142 **a guerrilla movement** "Turncoat," *This American Life*, NPR, May 22, 2009.

142 **treason** Diana Welch, "The Informant," *Austin Chronicle*, January 23, 2009, http://www.austinchronicle.com/gyrobase/Issue/story?oid=oid%3A 729400.

143 **"authoritarian"** scott crow, "Anarchy and the Common Ground Collective," news.infoshop.org/article.php?story=20060313145800704.

143 **2,800 students** C. C. Campbell-Rock, "Grassroots Group Launches Development Project," *San Francisco Bay View*, May 31, 2006.

143 **". . . messed up in the head."** Welch.

144 **its own data** "One Year Later—Common Ground's Accomplishments," in *A Katrina Reader*, August 29, 2006, www.cwsworkshop.org/katrina reader.

147 **AmeriCorps** AmeriCorps, a federally funded community service program, grew out of the VISTA program of the mid-sixties.

148 **white Catholic majority** Rohrer and Edmonson, eds., *The Eighth Generation Grows Up: Culture and Personalities of New Orleans Negroes*, 32.

148 **declining** "New Orleans to Close Seven Parishes, Delay Openings of 23 Others," *Catholic Connection* 15, 8 (March 2006).

148 **situation worse** Bruce Nolan, "N.O. Church Closures Follow National Pattern," *Times-Picayune*, April 26, 2008.

148 **30 percent drop** Catholic Connection.

148 **budget deficit** Peter Finney Jr., "Archdiocese Realigns Deaneries to Reflect Plan," *Clarion Herald*, April 11, 2009.

148 post-Katrina realignment Randy J. Sparks, "An Anchor to the People: Hurricane Katrina, Religious Life, and Recovery in New Orleans," *Journal of Southern Religion*, http://jsr.fsu.edu/Katrina/Sparks.pdf.

148 determined, in part, Susan Hines-Brigger, "After Katrina: New Beginnings," *St. Anthony Messenger*, August 2006.

148 "... and confirmations." Peter Finney Jr., "Citing Sacrilege, New Orleans Archbishop Closes Historic Black Church," Catholic News Service, March 28, 2006.

148 "... new life ..." Finney, "Archdiocese Realigns."

148 pews for slaves Website of St. Augustine Catholic Church of New Orleans, "Summary of Church History," http://www.staugustinecatholicchurch -neworleans.org/hist-sum.htm.

148 "... and land grabbing." "St. Augustine Take Over," video at http://www.youtube.com/watch?v=QE4tJAIECNk.

148 one reverend Sparks.

151 outside priest Sparks.

152 "... the foreseeable future" Finney, "Citing Sacrilege."

152 "We have been able ..." "Historic African-American New Orleans Church Reopened After Weeks of Protest and Rectory Sit-in," *Democracy Now*, April 10, 2006, http://www.democracynow.org/2006/4/10/historic_afri can_american_new_orleans_church.

155 with the understanding Deon Roberts, "Failed Algiers Apartment Complex Sale Disputed," *New Orleans City Business*, December 11, 2006; "Hundreds Face Eviction in New Orleans," *Democracy Now*, November 27, 2006.

Nothing (Nothing) Has Been Decided (Has Been Decided)

157 average weekly wages Katrina Index, January 2007, www.gnocdc.org.

158 the number of permits Ibid.

158 new peaks Floyd Norris, "Studying Housing Through Distorted Indexes," *New York Times*, May 28, 2011.

158 "... move briskly" Deon Roberts, "University of New Orleans Real Estate Report Offers Mixed News," *New Orleans City Business*, June 7, 2006; Kathy Chu, "New Orleans Home Sellers Struggle," *USA Today*, July 27, 2007.

159 almost 60 percent Greater New Orleans Community Data Center, "Holy Cross Neighborhood: Housing and Housing Costs," www.gnocdc.org /Orleans/8/20/housing. html.

159 foreclosures in Louisiana "New Orleans Foreclosures," *New Orleans City Business*, July 13, 2007, www2.safeguardproperties.com/content/view/1616/106.

159 Greenola See Global Green website, www.globalgreen.org/press/55.

161 only 4,000 "The Katrina Index," Summary of Findings: January 2007, Brookings Institute Metropolitan Policy Program, www.gnocdc.org; "Mending the Urban Fabric: Blight in New Orleans." Part 1: Structure and Strategy, Bureau of Governmental Research, February 2008.

161 Houston—still home to Longman and Murphy.

163 The city's medical system Leslie Eaton, "New Orleans Recovery Is Slowed by Closed Hospitals," *New York Times*, July 24, 2007.

163 . . . electrical permits Gordon Russell and Richard Russell, "Patchy Progress Plays Out in N.O.," *Times-Picayune*, December 31, 2006.

164 ninety-two issued checks Deon Roberts, "Louisiana's Road Home Program to Be Uphill Climb," *Times-Picayune*, October 9, 2006.

164 more than thirteen years Becky Bohrer, "New Orleans Residents Losing Faith," Associated Press, February 12, 2007.

164 ICF's response David Hammer, "Recovery Grants Forecast Retracted," *Times-Picayune*, January 11, 2007.

164 $68,000 Leslie Eaton, "Slow Home Grants Stall Progress in New Orleans," *New York Times*, November 11, 2006.

164 the lower figure Finger, 61.

164 $50,000 less Ibid., 59.

165 "sustainable restoration" Holy Cross, Planning District 8 Rebuilding Plan, www.nolanrp.com/Data/Neighborhood//District_8_Final_Holy%20Cross.pdf.

165 ". . . a ripple effect . . ." "Sustainable Restoration: Holy Cross Historic District and Lower Ninth Ward," June 2006, http://davidrmacaulay.typepad.com/SustainableRestorationPlan.pdf.

166 117 checks "Four Years After the Storm: The Road Home's Impact on Greater New Orleans," congressional testimony of Alison Plyer, Greater New Orleans Community Data Center, August 20, 2008.

168 ". . . six people in the world . . ." David Hammer, "Recovery Czar Throws Down the Gauntlet Before LRA," *Times- Picayune*, February 13, 2007.

168 ". . . no idea where to start" Frank Donze, "N.O. Recovery Chief Chosen," *Times-Picayune*, December 5, 2006.

169 ". . . I quit" Hammer, February 13, 2007.

169 "Everybody should be allowed . . ." Donze.

169 TCA "TCA Appoints Thelma Harris French Its President and CEO," *Louisiana Weekly Newspaper*, December 28, 2009, http://www.louisianaweekly .com/news.php?viewStory=2188.

170 Citizens Council Fairclough, 260.

171 scheduled for demolition Bill Quigley, "Why Is HUD Using Tens of Millions in Katrina Money to Bulldoze 4,534 Public Housing Apartments in New Orleans When It Costs Less to Repair and Open Them Up? A Tale of Two Sisters," *CounterPunch*, December 29, 2006, http://www.counterpunch .org/quigley12292006.html.

171 Reverend Avery Alexander See New Orleans Merchant Boycotts & Sit-ins (1960–1963), Veterans of the Civil Rights Movement—Timeline, www.crm vet.org/tim/timhis60.htm.

172 Elmer Candy Mark Meister, "Robert Nelsen—Elmer Candy," *Tlanian*, Fall 2004, www2.tulane.edu/article_news_details.cfm?ArticleID=5530.

Still So Much Work

184 HUD's budget fell Wilson, 33; Habitat for Humanity, "National Housing Statistics," http://www.habitatnyc.org/pdf/Toolkit/NationalHousingStatistics .pdf.

184 HOPE VI Habitat for Humanity, "National Housing Statistics"; Katy Reckdahl, "Critics Question Whether New New Orleans Public Housing Will Meet Needs," *Times-Picayune*, December 8, 2008.

186 the archdiocese has made it clear "Forecast for New Orleans: Partly Sunny," Franciscan friars, *Province Newsletter* 2, 1 (2007).

188 "... crack down ..." "Thousands March Against New Orleans Crime," Associated Press, January 11, 2007.

188 RAINING BULLETS Liu et al., 64.

188 highest incarceration rate Ibid, 66.

191 Malik was twenty-two See Arend, especially 16–17.

191 Panthers were feeding Brice White, interviewer, "The 30th Anniversary of the Desire Shoot-Out: An Interview with Malik Rahim," WTUL (91.5 FM), March 13, 2000, http://minorjive.typepad.com/hungryblues/2005/09 /malik_rahim_on_b.html.

192 "a right to defend yourself ..." White.

192 Nationwide Moore, 70.

192 J. Edgar Hoover Arend, 70.

192 two undercover cops Arend, 77.

192 "... .357 revolvers ..." White.

192 "... would just pop" Arend, 55, 67, 70.

192 only prison chapter See Pamela Hamilton interview with Malik Rahim, Southern Oral History Program Collection, May 23, 2006, http://docsouth .unc.edu/sohp/playback.html?base_file=U-0252.

192 Angola Three Arend, 147; Michelle Garcia, "For a Former Panther, Solidarity After the Storm," *Washington Post*, December 4, 2005.

192 "... no longer proud of" Adam Fleming, "A Conversation with Malik Rahim," *Pittsburgh City Paper*, November 13, 2008.

192 armed robbery Horne, 220.

192 housing in San Francisco Leslie Goldberg, "Ex-Cons Take Over S.F. Tenant Group," *San Francisco Examiner*, February 21, 1995; Garcia.

192 Prejean crow, 61.

192 so-called African American Garcia.

193 shot a black man "Case Five: Henry Glover," Pro Publica, www.pro publica.org/nola/case/topic/case-five.

193 Danziger Bridge "Case Six; Danziger Bridge," Pro Publica, www.pro publica.org/nola/case/topic/case-six.

193 fundamental mistrust Arend, 217.

193 rely on this network See Karen DeSalvo, "Delivering High Quality, Accesible Health Care: The Rise of Community Centers," in Liu et al.

193 The idea for this one "Nursing the Lower Ninth," Help Holy Cross, August 31, 2007, www.helpholycross.org/2007/08/nursing-the-low.html.

194 a third of the hospital beds Gary Scheets, "Without Charity Hospital, the Poor and Uninsured Struggle to Find Health Care," NOLA.com, August 23, 2007; Daniel M. Rothschild, "Nursing the Ninth Ward," *Wall Street Journal*, August 11, 2007.

194 a third of the city's residents Rothschild.

If You're Gonna Leave Anybody Behind

199 two-thirds what it was "The New Orleans Index," November 13, 2007, Metropolitan Policy Program at the Brookings Institute, www.gnocdc.org /KI/KatrinaIndex.pdf.

201 less than 40 percent Adam Nossiter, "Patchwork City," *New York Times*, July 2, 2007.

202 seventeen "recovery zones" Keith I. Marszalek, "City Announces First 17 Target Recovery Zones," NOLA.com, March 29, 2007.

202 a "cat-fight" Michelle Krupa and Gordon Russell, "N.O. Post-K Blueprint Revealed," *Times-Picayune*, March 29, 2007.

202 ". . . don't trust the system . . ." Krupa and Russell.

202 ". . . right to return" Adam Nossiter, "Steering New Orleans's Recovery with a Clinical Eye," *New York Times*, April 9, 2007.

202 "cranes in the sky" Arian Wiltse, "Sustaining the Lower Nine," *Gambit Weekly*, June 26, 2007.

202 Lots Next Door Michelle Krupa, "Recovery Czar Says His Job Will Only Take One Year," *Times-Picayune*, April 5, 2007.

202 haven't bounced back Deon Roberts, "University of New Orleans Real Estate Report Offers Mixed News," *New Orleans City Business*, June 7, 2006.

203 estimated 7,000 David Hammer, "NORA Hears About Road Home Recovery," *Times-Picayune*, November 28, 2007.

203 in clusters Hammer, November 28, 2007.

203 first time in decades Ivan J. Miestchovich, "New Orleans Economy & Real Estate Market Redevelopment & Rebuilding," Institute for Economic Development & Real Estate Research, University of New Orleans.

203 60 percent white Michelle Krupa, "Minority Populations Still Growing in New Orleans Area, but Not as Fast," *Times-Picayune*, June 13, 2010.

203 fewer poor people Sarah Carr, "Higher LEAP Scores Add Fuel to Debate over Charter Schools," *Times-Picayune*, May 30, 2009.

206 "Some people . . ." Kathy Chu, "New Orleans Home Sellers Struggle," *USA Today*, July 27, 2007.

206 lowest rates of return Greater New Orleans Community Data Center, "Pontchartrain Park Neighborhood: People and Household Characteristics," www.gnocdc.org/orleans/6/31/people.html.

206 white-collar jobs "Sellers in New Orleans Home Market Desperate to Sell," *Real Estate Press*, July 25, 2007, www.realestatepress.org/latest/sellers -in-new-orleans-home-market-desperate-to-sell.html.

207 cost of homeowner's insurance Chu.

207 10 million Zandi, 168.

207 sixteen-year high Chu; Zandi.

207 3.5 million Zandi, 168.

208 500 checks Jeffrey Buchanan and Chris Krom, "Where Did the Katrina Money Go?" Institute for Southern Studies, September 5, 2007.

208 60 percent "Road Home Program Leaves Many Homeowners Waiting," Rand Gulf State Policy Institute, www.rand.org.

208 have had to wait Rick Eden and Patricia Boren, "Timely Assistance:

Evaluating the Speed of Road Home Grantmaking," Rand Gulf States Policy Institute, 2008.

208 Governor Blanco Liu et al., 86.

208 increased the payment Finger, 67.

208 fined ICF Finger, 67.

208 Senate oversight Finger, 62.

209 70 percent Ibid.

209 pace of returnees The New Orleans Index, Brookings Institution, November 13, 2007, www.gnocdc.org/KI/KatrinaIndex.pdf.

209 overall crime rate "New Orleans Has Highest Crime Rate: Report," Reuters, November 24, 2008.

210 about 200 homeless Katy Reckdahl, "Last 'Residents' Moved from Homeless Encampment at Claiborne Avenue and Canal Street," *Times-Picayune*, July 17, 2008.

210 $80 million Frank Donze and Katy Reckdahl, "Demolition Scheduled to Begin Next Week," *Times-Picayune*, December 4, 2007.

211 nearly doubled John Moreno Gonzales, "Homeless on the Rise in New Orleans," Associated Press, August 19, 2007.

211 Nobody knows Ibid.

211 600 fewer "Homeless Camp Outside New Orleans City Hall," Associated Press, November 16, 2007.

211 almost three times "New Orleans' Homeless Rate Swells to 1 in 25," Rick Jervis, *USA Today*, March 17, 2008.

212 demolish the Big Four Lewis Wallace, "First Came Katrina, Then Came HUD," *In These Times*, January 16, 2008.

213 not out-of-towners Katy Reckdahl, "Last 'Residents' Moved."

The Lucky Ones Still Standing

215 less than a third Alison Plyer, "Neighborhood Recovery Rates," Greater New Orleans Community Data Center, July 1, 2010, www.gnocdc.org/Recov eryByNeighborhood/index.html.

215 ". . . blank canvas" Sarah DeBacher, "Holy Cross School Update," October 23, 2007, www.helpholycross.org/2007/10/holy-cross-scho.html#tp.

216 George Washington Carver Bob Warren, "Recovery School District Opens Today," *Times-Picayune*, September 3, 2007.

216 "terrible" Kristen L. Buras, "It's All About the Dollars: Charter Schools, Educational Policy, and the Racial Market in New Orleans," in Watkins, 182.

217 second fall of operation Katrina Index, November 2007, and the New Orleans Index, Metropolitan Policy Program at Brookings Institution, August 2008, http://gnocdc.s3.amazonaws.com/NOLAIndex/NewOrleansIndexAug08.pdf.

217 2,000 students in need Weill, 119.

218 the deadline Sean Alfano, "FEMA Trailers Will Stay in New Orleans," Associated Press, September 23, 2006; "FEMA Phasing Out Louisiana Trailer Parks," Associated Press, November 29, 2007.

218 15,000 families "FEMA Phasing Out Louisiana Trailer Parks," Associated Press, November 29, 2007; Katrina Index, November 2007.

218 "predict the consequences" Union of Concerned Scientists, "FEMA Exposes Gulf Coast Residents to Formaldehyde," December 19, 2007.

221 $45,000 per National Trust for Historic Preservation, "Holy Cross Neighborhood Update," www.preservationnation.org/issues/gulf-coast-recovery/holy-cross-neighborhood.html; see also Kevin Mercadel, "Holy Cross Becomes HOMES AGAIN!" National Trust for Historic Preservation, www.preservationnation.org/issues/gulf-coast-recovery/home-again-program/holy-cross-home-again.html.

224 a couple thousand people Wiltse, June 26, 2007.

224 always resisted Steve Ritea, "The Dream Team," *Times-Picayune*, August 1, 2006.

224 "... the demise of education" "New Orleans: Coming Home to the Lower Ninth," *Education Week*, video interview, February 21, 2008, http://www.youtube.com/watch?v=mn9LofovY6A.

224 Paul Vallas Adamo.

224 1,100 teachers Warren; Paul Tough, "A Teachable Moment," *New York Times Magazine*, August 17, 2008.

224 only city Adamo.

224 "We have an opportunity . . ." Tough.

225 "No one tells me . . ." Weill, 120.

225 waiving national guidelines Dr. Raynard Saunders, "New Orleans Charter Schools: What Is the Problem?" Research on Reforms, www.researchonreforms.org.

225 "talented and gifted" Bill Quigley, "A Special Report on Katrina and Education," CounterPunch, http://www.counterpunch.org/quigley08062007.html.

225 "schools of last resort" Tough.

225 a third its former student population Adam Nossiter, "A Tamer of Schools Has Plan in New Orleans," *New York Times*, September 24, 2007.

225 fewer than half Ibid.

225 ". . . reopen" Ibid.

226 the only one in Louisiana Ritea.

226 twenty years' experience Ibid.

226 among the lowest Brentin Mock, "The Problem with New Orleans's Charter Schools," *Newsweek*, October 6, 2010.

226 President Bush "Bush Visits Gulf Coast on Katrina Anniversary," Associated Press, August 29, 2007.

227 "make it out" Alicia Dennis and Susan Schindehette, "Kendell Goes Back to School," *People*, August 27, 2007.

228 "beacon of hope" Christine Bordelon, "Catholic Church Reopens in New Orleans' Katrina-Damaged 9th Ward," Catholic News Service, March 24, 2009.

231 400 pink shapes Make It Right Lower 9th/Katrina Timeline, "The Pink Project," www.makeitrightnola.org/index.php/work_progress/timeline_pink _project.

232 a three-bedroom house Wayne Curtis, "Houses of the Future," *Atlantic*, November 2009, www.makeitrightnola.org/downloads/financial/2008_final _report.pdf.

232 more of a showcase Curtis.

232 "the hardest hit spot . . ." Feireiss, 471.

232 millions more Curtis.

We Fall Down, But We Get Up

239 around 310,000 Amy Liu and Allison Plyer, "State of Policy and Progress: Executive Summary," Brookings Institute, April 2008, www.brookings .edu/~/media/Files/rc/reports/2007/08neworleansindex/200804_katrinaES .pdf; Bret Schulte, "A Quiet Progress in New Orleans," *U.S. News and World Report*, June 11, 2008.

239 back by 40 percent Mike Longman and Jarret Murphy, "Shifting Winds: New Orleans Three Years Later," *City Limits* Special Edition, August 29, 2008.

239 ". . . is past." Schulte.

239 center of density Allison Plyer and Elaine Ortiz, "Who Lives in New Orleans and the Metro Area Now?" Greater New Orleans Community Data Center, October 2, 2009.

239 living in poverty Ibid.

239 monthly rents Alison Plyer, Elaine Ortiz, and Kathy Pettit, "Post-Katrina Housing Affordability," Greater New Orleans Community Data Center, October 13, 2009.

239 basic infrastructure Liu and Plyer, "State of Policy."

239 $6 billion Ibid.

240 "unhinged" Zandi, 213.

240 $5 billion Zandi, 176.

240 National unemployment "The New Orleans Index: Three Years Later," Brookings Institution, August 2008.

240 banking crisis Cassidy, 316, 320.

240 a recession Michael M. Grynbaum, "Recession Declared in U.S. as Stocks Tumble Worldwide," *New York Times*, December 1, 2008.

240 some two-thirds "The New Orleans Index: Three Years Later."

240 $6.5 billion Schulte.

242 ". . . in normal operations" David Hammer, "Blakely May Leave Post in January," *Times-Picayune*, October 23, 2008.

243 third anniversary Michelle Krupa, "Bush Touts Federal Money, Residents' Efforts to Revive New Orleans," *Times-Picayune*, August 20, 2008.

243 ". . . the entrepreneurial spirit" "President Bush's Speech on Gulf Coast Recovery," transcript on PBS NewsHour, August 20, 2008, http://www.pbs.org/newshour/bb/government_programs/july-dec08/bushnolaspeech_08-20.html.

243 less than half Douglas Ahers, Allison Plyer, and Frederic Weil, "Where Is the Money?" slide presentation, Greater New Orleans Community Data Center, January 2008.

244 . . . murder capital Brendan McCarthy, "Despite Drop in Crime, New Orleans' Murder Rate Continues to Lead Nation," *Times-Picayune*, June 1, 2009.

244 Some 2 million Ewen MacAskill and David Smith, "New Orleans Battens Down for Gustav with Curfew and Mass Evacuation," *Guardian*, September 1, 2008; Andrea Shaw, "New Orleans Sets New Curfew," *Times-Picayune*, September 5, 2008.

244 "It's smooth . . ." Becky Bohrer, "Gustav Gives Nagin a Second Chance to Get It Right," Associated Press, August 31, 2008.

245 "You be good . . ." Dane Schiller, "Levees Topped, but Holding," *Houston Chronicle*, September 1, 2008.

245 "blanket" the city Schiller.

246 deadline for its removal "New Orleans Issues Deadlines for Vacating FEMA Trailers," Associated Press, June 5, 2008.

248 a half dozen Feireiss, 87; see also makeitright.org.

248 "This to me . . ." Feireiss, 85.

248 ". . . in a catastrophe" Longman and Murphy.

249 Lower Ninth Ward Health Clinic "Nursing the Lower Ninth," *Help Holy Cross* Newsletter, August 31, 2007, www.helpholycross.org/2007/08/nursing _the_low.html.

252 Republican National Convention Welch.

252 "traditional nonprofit" crow, 163.

253 a tenth Bill Quigley, "Katrina Pain Index—New Orleans Three Years Later," CommonDreams.org, August 24, 2008.

253 4,000 and 7,000 David Hammer, "8,800 Road Home Properties to Return to Private Hands," *Times-Picayune*, October 18, 2008; "NORA Plans What to Do With 7,000 Road Home Properties," *City Business*, November 13, 2007, www.bnaconservancy.org/news/roundup/archives/811.

253 72,000 Quigley, "Katrina Pain."

253 leads the nation Allison Plyer and Elaine Ortiz, "Benchmark for Blight," Greater New Orleans Community Data Center, October 27, 2010.

253 concept of private property See Staughton Lynd, *Intellectual Origins of American Radicalism*.

254 largest number of vacant buildings "The New Orleans Index: Three Years Later."

255 "More Perfect Union" "Obama Race Speech: Read the Full Text," *Huffington Post*, March 18, 2008, www.huffingtonpost.com/2008/03/18/obama-race -speech-read-th_n_92077.html.

256 only 40 percent Lois E. Elie, "Pontchartrain Park's Trailblazing Spirit Is Being Rekindled," *Times-Picayune*, May 23, 2009.

256 one in every nine Ibid.

256 Wendell Pierce Ibid.

256 unanimously for demolition Adam Nossiter and Leslie Eaton, "New Orleans Council Votes for Demolition of Housing," *New York Times*, December 21, 2007.

256 by a third Coleman Warner, "Housing Officials Claim Surplus," *Times-Picayune*, December 18, 2007.

259 the stock market "Stock Market Crash of 2008," Money-zine.com, 2008, www.money-zine.com/Investing/Stocks/Stock-Market-Crash-of-2008.

259 TARP Cassidy, 329.

259 camps under I-10 Katy Reckdahl, "Social Workers Clear Camp for Homeless," *Times-Picayune*, July 18, 2008.

259 8,000 jobs Liu and Plyer, "The State of New Orleans Three Years After Katrina."

The Future Is What We Got in Front of Us

261 Green Party candidate Green Party Watch, "Malik Rahim Finishes with 3%; Democrat Loses," www.greenpartywatch.org/2008/12/07/malik-rahim -finishes-with-3-democrat-loses.

262 an open letter www.indymedia.org/pt/2008/12/918526.shtml.

262 November 2007 David Winkler-Schmidt, "Brandon Darby—FBI Informant & Common Ground Co-founder," *Gambit*, January 26, 2009.

262 ". . . faults of our own" Welch.

262 ". . . do something about it" Colin Moynihan, "Activist Unmasks Himself as Federal Informant in G.O.P. Convention Case," *New York Times*, January 5, 2009.

262 plead guilty James Walsh, "RNC Suspect Admits to Having Explosives," *St. Paul Star Tribune*, March 17, 2009.

262 agent provocateur Lisa Fithian, "Sexism, Egos, and Lies," *Rag Blog*, March 22, 2010, http://theragblog.blogspot.com:80/2010/03/lisa-fithian-fbi -informant-brandon.html.

262 "2006 or earlier" Austin Informant Working Group, "Statement on Brandon Darby, the 'Unnamed' Informant/Provocateur in the 'Texas 2,'" December 31, 2008, http://houston.indymedia.org/news/2008/12/66041.php.

263 "helping people" Welch.

263 early days after Katrina See A. C. Thompson, "Post-Katrina White Vigilantes Shot African-Americans with Impunity," ProPublica.org, December 19, 2008.

264 Suncere Facebook update, Suncere Shakur, June 7, 2011.

264 ". . . oppression or exploitation" Arend, 199.

265 10,000 jobs Paul Purpura, "Blueprint in Hand, Federal City Moves Forward in Algiers," *Times-Picayune*, October 18, 2010.

265 former congressman Tim Morris, "William Jefferson Verdict: Guilty on 11 of 16 Counts," *Times-Picayune*, August 5, 2009.

266 ". . . largest school construction . . ." Stephen Maloney, "Orleans Parish Public School Rebuild," *New Orleans City Business*, special supplement, "Top Construction Projects 2009."

266 "a model of . . ." Katy Reckdahl, "Algiers' Christopher Park Blight Has No Easy Answers," *Times-Picayune*, June 6, 2011.

266 "foothold . . ." Katy Reckdahl, "HANO Approves Sale of Demolition of Most Scattered Units," *Times-Picayune*, November 19, 2008.

268 "We're just scratching . . ." Mike Celizic, "Pitt on Mayoral Run: 'I Don't Have a Chance,' " Today Entertainment, MSNBC, August 13, 2009.

268 MR-GO was officially closed U.S. Army Corps of Engineers, New Orleans District, "MRGO Navigation Channel Closure," www.mrgo.gov/MRGO _Closure.aspx.

269 city has proposed Ramon Antonio Vargas, "Restoration of Bayou Near Lower 9th Ward Aims to Fix MR-GO Damage," *Times-Picayune*, August 15, 2009.

269 over $8 billion John McCusker, "ICF's Oversight of Road Home Program Comes to an End," *Times-Picayune*, June 10, 2009.

269 still waiting Bill Quigley and Davida Finger, "Katrina Pain Index," *CounterPunch*, CounterPunch.org, August 18, 2009.

269 filed suit Katy Reckdahl, "Road Home Settlements Will Benefit Nearly 1,500 Homeowners," *Times-Picayune*, July 6, 2011.

270 banning all apartment buildings Mary Elise DeCoursey, "St. Bernard Parish on Hook for Legal Fees in Rental Ordiance Fight," *Times-Picayune*, July 3, 2008.

270 "racially discriminatory" Chris Kirkham, "St. Bernard Officials Want Review of Rental Supply," *Times-Picayune*, June 10, 2009.

271 nearly 60 percent Gordon Russell, "It's Time for New Orleans to Admit It's a Shrinking City, Some Say," *Times-Picayune*, November 22, 2008.

271 aggressive Bruce Eggler, "While St. Bernard Razes, N.O. Holds Back, Creating Contrasting Landscapes," *Times-Picayune*, August 29, 2009.

272 presidential election "United States Presidential Election in Louisiana 2008," Wikipedia, http://en.wikipedia.org/wiki/United_States_presidential _election_in_Louisiana,_2008.

272 stimulus package See www.recovery.org.

272 2 million jobs www.recovery.org; Council of Economic Advisors, "The Economic Impact of the American Recovery and Reinvestment Act of 2009," Second Quarterly Report, Executive Office of the President, January 13, 2010.

272 ". . . clawing our way back" Peter S. Goodman and Jack Healy, "In Unemployed Reports, Signs of a Jobless Recovery," *New York Times*, September 4, 2009.

272 foreclosure rate James Thorner, "National Foreclosure Rate Highest in 3 Decades," September 5, 2008, www.tampabay.com/blogs/unrealestate/con

tent/national-foreclosure-rate-highest-3-decades; "US Foreclosure Rates Down but Still Almost 20% Higher than Year Ago, Report Shows," Property Wire, December 17, 2009, www.propertywire.com/news/north-america/fore closure-rates-down-again-200912173761.html.

272 Unemployment Goodman and Healy.

272 service sector Dustin Ensinger, "Service Economy Taking over U.S.," quoting U.S. Labor Department's 2009 Employment and Wages report, Economy in Crisis, July 14, 2010, http://economyincrisis.org/content/service -economy-taking-over-us.

273 twelve hundred blighted Alison Plyer, Elaine Ortiz, and Kathryn L. S. Pettit, "Optimizing Blight Strategies," Greater New Orleans Community Data Center, Annual Report, November 2010 [henceforth Plyer, Ortiz, and Pettit].

273 highest percentage of blight Ibid.

273 bulldozing whole neighborhoods Tom Leonard, "US Cities May Have to Be Bull-dozed to Survive," *Telegraph*, June 12, 2009.

273 losing jobs again Plyer, Ortiz, and Pettit.

274 Average rent in New Orleans Ibid.

275 Lot Next Door "The 'Lot Next Door' Program," Neighborhoods Partnership Network, www.npnnola.com/issues/view/16/the-lot-next-door-pro gram.

275 125 homeowners National Trust for Historic Preservation, "Holy Cross Neighborhood Update," www.preservationnation.org/issues/gulf-coast-recov ery/holy-cross-neighborhood.html.

276 "smart decline" Katy Reckdahl, "Critics Question Whether New New Orleans Public Housing Will Be Needed," *Times-Picayune*, December 8, 2008; Katy Reckdahl, "Three Years Later, 6,500 Subsidized New Orleans Apartments Fester," *Times-Picayune*, October 10, 2008.

276 waiting list Katy Reckdahl, "Iberville Residents Say HANO Skimping on Basic Maintenance, Recreation and Social Services," *Times-Picayune*, March 23, 2009.

277 pleaded guilty Louisiana violations, July 2008, www.lslbc.louisiana.gov /pdf/violations/violations-July08-residential.pdf.

280 selling twice as fast Plyer, Ortiz, and Pettit.

280 below $45,000 Ibid.

281 obituary of a priest "Father Bart Pax, St. Mary of the Angels Pastor Dies," *Clarion Herald*, August 8, 2009.

281 ninety-three percent . . . Michelle Krupa, "Minority Populations Still Growing in New Orleans Area, but Not as Fast," *Times-Picayune*, June 13, 2010.

281 The past fall's elections Michelle Krupa, "Katrina Changed Racial Landscape of Orleans Politics," *Times-Picayune*, October 18, 2008.

281 force of law Bruce Eggler, "Master Plan Given Force of Law," *Times-Picayune*, November 5, 2008.

281 "paranoia" Michelle Krupa, "Easter New Orleans Residents Still Fear the Area May Not Be Fully Redeveloped," *Times-Picayune*, November 14, 2008.

282 Reinventing the Crescent "New Orleans Riverfront Development May Be Key to City's Revival," Associated Press, May 3, 2006; Nicolai Ouroussoff, "Reinventing America's Cities: The Time Is Now," *New York Times*, March 29, 2009.

282 new urban demographic William H. Frey, "The New Urban Demographics: Race, Space and Boomer Aging," Brookings Institution, December 16, 2008.

282 often evacuating to Brookings Institution, "The Suburbanization of Poverty: Trends in Metropolitan American, 2000–2008," January 2010; Glen Ford, "No Black Plan for American Cities," *Black Agenda Report*, May 8, 2007, www.blackagendareport.com/node/10210.

282 trend continues Conor Dougherty, "The End of White Flight," *Wall Street Journal*, July 19, 2008.

282 bought the nearby mall David Hammer, "NORA Passes on Walmart, Sticks with Strip-Mall Plan for Gentilly Woods Site," *Times-Picayune*, December 17, 2009.

Epilogue

285 Mitch Landrieu Michelle Krupa and Frank Donze, "Mitch Landrieu Claims New Orleans Mayor's Office in a Landslide," *Times-Picayune*, February 6, 2010.

285 below pre-flood numbers Allison Plyer, "Hurricane Katrina Recovery," press release, Greater New Orleans Community Data Center, August 26, 2010.

285 "dramatically" whiter Michelle Krupa, "Racial Divides Amongst New Orleans Neighborhoods Expands," *Times-Picayune*, June 8, 2011.

285 real estate Rebecca Mowbray, "Orleans Parish Home Values Grew 9 Percent in 2010," *Times-Picayune*, February 20, 2011.

285 home values Rebecca Mowbray, "Home Prices Fell Throughout the New Orleans Area," *Times-Picayune*, August 21, 2011.

285 *Deepwater Horizin* Jon Bowermaster, "Measuring the Extent of Oil

Spillage," www.gadling.com/2010/11/29/bowermasters-adventures-measuring
-the-extent-of-oil-spillage.

286 almost 40 percent Plyer, "Hurricane Katrina Recovery"; Bruce Nolan, "Hurricane Katrina Altered Demographic Picture in New Orleans Area," *Times-Picayune*, August 25, 2010.

286 can't afford to pay Benjamin Alexander-Bloch, "St. Bernard Parish Discrimination Allegations on Trial," *Times Picayune*, August 17, 2011.

286 Obama declares "Transcript of President Barack Obama's Katrina Anniversary Speech at Xavier University," *Times-Picayune*, August 29, 2010.

286 about the size Allison Plyer, "Population Loss and Vacant Housing in New Orleans Neighborhoods," Greater New Orleans Community Data Center, April 15, 2011.

286 Holy Cross School Frank Donze, "Holy Cross School Makes Plans for Abandoned Lower Ninth Ward Campus," *Times-Picayune*, April 1, 2011.

287 St. Bernard at a medical center Benjamin Alexander-Bloch, "St. Bernard Hospital District Accepts Bid to Build Medical Offices," *Times Picayune*, August 16, 2011.

287 urgent-care center Bill Barrow, "24-Hour Urgent Care Center Sees Brisk Traffic in Eastern New Orleans," *Times Picayune*, August 9, 2011.

287 Evictions and demolition Wayne Curtis, "The Cost of Progress?" *Preservation*, May-June 2011.

288 raped "NOPD Asks for Public's Help in Finding Attacker," WDSU, October 26, 2010, www.wdsu.com/news/25520982/detail.html#ixzz1T85KNacP.

289 like Detroit Michelle Krupa, "FEMA to Restart Program for Demolishing Katrina-Damaged Buildings in New Orleans," *Times-Picayune,* March 30, 2011.

290 new high school Andrew Vanacore, "New Orleans School Construction Blueprint Revised," *Times Picayune*, June 30, 2011.

290 only 60 percent Plyer, "Hurricane Katrina Recovery."

290 fewer kids Allison Plyer and Elaine Ortiz, "Shifts in Population and Loss of Children Across the New Orleans Metro Area," Greater New Orleans Community Data Center, April 15, 2011.

290 ". . . a disaster" Nick Anderson, "Education Secretary Calls Hurricane Katrina Good for New Orleans Schools," *Washington Post*, January 30, 2010.

290 sixty-one charter schools Liu et al., 32, 39.

290 heck of a job Cindy Chang, "New Orleans Parents Complain That Charter Schools Are Leaving Most Vulnerable Students Behind," *Times-Picayune*, March 29, 2010.

290 **"systemic failure . . ."** Southern Poverty Law Center, "Children with Disabilities Face Discrimination in New Orleans Schools," July 28, 2010, www .splcenter.org/get-informed/news/splc-complaint-children-with-disabilities -face-discrimination-in-new-orleans-school.

290 **McDonogh 35 High School** Andrew Vanacore, "John McDonogh High School Supporters Get Disappointing News," *Times-Picayune*, June 24, 2011.

291 **HMGP** The Hazard Mitigation Grant Program administrated by FEMA.

291 **Danziger Bridge** Jordan Flaherty, "Danziger Bridge Police Trial Reveals NOPD Corruption . . . Again," Theloop21.com, July 11, 2011.

291 **"rumor to fact"** Trymaine Lee, "Rumor to Fact in Tales of Post-Katrina Violence," *New York Times*, August 26, 2010.

292 **". . . people like yourselves . . ."** See video "Malik Rahim at Occupy Eugene," added October 15, 2011, at www.youtube.com/watch?v-B4XsO5g bh8A.

292 **a different sort of** Welch; "Turncoat," *This American Life*, Chicago Public Media and Ira Glass, originally aired May 22, 2009, www.thisamericanlife .org/radio-archives/episode/381/turncoat.

292 **national PBS** Kelly Duane de la Vega and Katie Galloway, "Better This World," Loteria Films, 2011.

292 **a lot of speaking** Conversation with the author.

292 **". . . old pickup truck"** See "Sankofa Children's Free Breakfast Program," uploaded by AshevilleNow, YouTube, March 10, 2010, http://www.youtube .com/watch?v=ZwmgBXisXOg.

292 **more than 9,000** Katy Reckdahl, "Buildings Left Blighted by Hurricane Katrina House Thousands, Group Estimates," *Times-Picayune*, August 25, 2010.

292 **a quarter of the city** Allison Plyer and Elaine Ortiz, "Who Lives in New Orleans and the Metro Area Now?" Greater New Orleans Community Data Center, May 27, 2011.

292 **in the Big Four** Katy Reckdahl, "New C. J. Peete Complex Is Solid, Shiny—but Not as Social Some Residents Say," *Times-Picayune*, August 21, 2011.

293 **almost 45 percent** Alison Plyer, "Population Loss and Vacant Housing in New Orleans Neighborhoods," Greater New Orleans Community Data Center, Table 1, April 15, 2011.

293 **"interface with government . . ."** and **"Completely free market"** *The Rachel Maddow Show*, MSNBC, September 1, 2011.

293 **supermarket** Frank Donze, "Holy Cross Neighborhood Association Reviews Supermarket Proposal," *Times Picayune*, August 11, 2011.

293 Nationwide during 2010 Fred Magdoff, "The Jobs Disaster in the United States," *Monthly Review* 63, 2 (June 2011).

293 below the official poverty line Magdoff; Sabrina Tavernise, "Soaring Poverty Casts Spotlight on 'Lost Decade,'" *New York Times*, September 14, 2011.

293 decreasing African American Haya El Nasser, "Black Populations Fall in Major Cities," *USA Today*, March 22, 2011.

293 "The Whitening . . ." Glen Ford, "The Whitening of Chocolate City," *Black Agenda Report*, January 4, 2011.

293 "Public housing is . . ." Cara Buckley, "Agencies Lack Money to Mend Public Housing," *New York Times*, October 25, 2010.

293 almost 20 percent Carl Bialik, "Housing Statistics Hit Rough Waters," *Wall Street Journal*, January 8, 2011.

Selected Bibliography

Arend, Orissa. *Showdown in Desire*. Fayetteville: University of Arkansas Press, 2009.

Baker, Liva. *The Second Battle of New Orleans: The Hundred-Year Struggle to Integrate the Schools*. New York: Harper Collins, 1996.

Barry, John. *Rising Tide, The Great Mississippi Flood of 1927 and How It Changed America*. New York: Simon and Schuster, 1997.

Bergal, Jenny, et al., *City Adrift: New Orleans Before and After Katrina*. Baton Rouge: Louisiana State University Press, 2007.

Boger, John Charles, and Gary Orfield, eds. *School Resegregation: Must the South Turn Back?* Chapel Hill: University of North Carolina Press, 2005.

Bridges, Tyler. *The Rise of David Duke*. Jackson: University Press of Mississippi, 1994.

Bring New Orleans Back Commission. "Action Plan for New Orleans: The New American City." Urban Planning Committee, January 11, 2006.

Brothers, Thomas. *Louis Armstrong's New Orleans*. New York: W. W. Norton, 2006.

Brunsma, David L., David Overfelt, and J. Steven Pico, eds. *The Sociology of Katrina: Perspectives on a Modern Catastrophe*. Lanham, MD: Rowman and Littlefield, 2007.

Cable, Geroge Washington. *The Grandissimes*. New York: Hill and Wang, 1967.

———. *Old Creole Days*. New York: Heritage Press, 1943.

Campanella, Richard. *Bienville's Dilemma: A Historical Geography of New Orleans*. Center for Louisiana Studies, University of Louisiana at Lafayette, 2008.

Campanella, Richard, and Marina Campanella. *New Orleans Then and Now*. Gretna, LA: Pelican, 1999.

Cassidy, John. *How Markets Fail: The Logic of Economic Calamities.* New York: Farrar, Straus and Giroux, 2009.

Colten, Craig E. *An Unnatural Metropolis: Wrestling New Orleans from Nature.* Baton Rouge: Louisiana State University Press, 2005.

Cooper, Christopher, and Robert Block. *Disaster: Hurricane Katrina and the Failure of Homeland Security.* New York: Times Books/Henry Holt and Company, 2006.

crow, scott. *Black Flags and Windmills: Hope, Anarchy, and the Common Ground Collective.* Oakland, CA: PM Press, 2011.

Duany, Andres, Elizabeth Plater-Zyberk, and Jeff Speck. *Suburban Nation: The Rise of Sprawl and the Decline of the American Dream.* New York: North Point Press, 2000.

Earth Search, Inc. *Archaeological Survey and Testing in the Holy Cross Historic District, New Orleans, Louisiana.* 2 vols. For the U.S. Army Corps of Engineers, February 1992.

Fairclough, Adam. *Race and Democracy: The Civil Rights Struggle in Louisiana, 1915–1972.* Athens: University of Georgia Press, 1999.

Feireiss, Kristen, ed. *Architecture in Times of Need: Make It Right Rebuilding New Orleans' Lower Ninth Ward.* Munich: Prestel, 2009.

Flint, Anthony. *This Land: The Battle over Sprawl and the Future of America.* Baltimore: John Hopkins University Press, 2006.

Gunewardena, Nandini, and Mark Schuller, eds., *Capitalizing on Catastrophe: Neoliberal Strategies in Disaster Reconstruction (Globalization and the Environment).* Lanham, MD: AltaMira Press, 2008.

Hearn, Lafcadio. *Inventing New Orleans.* Ed. S. Frederick Starr. Jackson: University Press of Mississippi, 2001.

Horne, Jed. *Breach of Faith: Hurricane Katrina and the Near Death of a Great American City.* New York: Random House, 2006.

Johnson, Walter. *Soul by Soul: Life Inside the Antebellum Slave Market.* Cambridge, MA: Harvard University Press, 1999.

Lynd, Staughton. *Intellectual Origins of American Radicalism.* New York: Vintage Books, 1968.

Marable, Manning, ed. *Seeking Higher Ground: The Hurricane Katrina Crisis, Race, and Public Policy Reader.* New York: Palgrave Macmillan, 2007.

Medley, Keith Weldon. *We As Freeman: Plessy v. Ferguson.* Gretna, LA: Pelican Publishing, 2003.

Métraux, Alfred. *Voodoo in Haiti.* New York: Alfred Schocken Books, 1972.

Moore, Leonard N. *Black Rage in New Orleans: Police Brutality and African*

American Activism from World War II to Hurricane Katrina. Baton Rouge: Louisiana State University Press, 2010.

Needham, Maurice d'Arlan. *Negro Orleanian: Status and Stake in a City's Economy and Housing.* New Orleans: Tulane Publications, 1962.

Rabinowitz, Alan. *Urban Economies and Land Use in America: The Transformation of Cities in the Twentieth Century.* Armonk, NY: M. E. Sharpe, 2004.

Rohrer, John H., and Munro J. Edmonson, eds. *The Eighth Generation Grows Up: Culture and Personalities of New Orleans Negroes.* New York: Harper Torchbooks, 1960.

Ryan, James. *Five Miles Away, A World Apart: One City, Two Schools, and the Story of Educational Opportunity in Modern America.* Oxford: Oxford University Press, 2010.

Steinberg, Phil, and Rob Shields, eds. *What Is a City? Rethinking the Urban After Hurricane Katrina.* Athens: University of Georgia Press, 2008.

Sublette, Ned. *The World That Made New Orleans: From Spanish Silver to Congo Square.* Chicago: Lawrence Hill Books, 2008.

———. *The Year Before the Flood: A Story of New Orleans.* Chicago: Lawrence Hill Books, 2009.

Vlach, John Michael. *By the Work of Their Hands: Studies in Afro-American Folklife.* Charlottesville: University Press of Virginia, 1991.

Watkins, William H., ed. *The Assault in Public Education: Confronting the Politics of Corporate School Reform.* New York: Teachers College Press, 2012.

Wells, Ken. *The Good Pirates of the Forgotten Bayou: Fighting to Save a Way of Life in the Wake of Hurricane Katrina.* New Haven: Yale University Press, 2008.

Willinger, Beth, ed. *Katrina and the Women of New Orleans.* New Orleans: Newcomb College Center for Research in Women, Tulane University, December 2008.

Wilson, David. *Cities and Race: America's New Black Ghetto.* London: Routledge, 2007.

Woods, Clyde. *Development Arrested: The Blues and Plantation Power in the Mississippi Delta.* London: Verso, 1998.

Zandi, Mark. *Financial Shock: A 360° Look at the Subprime Mortgage Implosion and How to Avoid the Next Financial Crisis.* Upper Saddle River, NJ: Financial Times Press, 2009.

Index

A Note on the Author

Daniel Wolff is the author of *How Lincoln Learned to Read*, a *Chicago Tribune* Editor's Choice pick; *4th of July, Asbury Park*, a *New York Times Book Review* Editor's Choice pick; *You Send Me: The Life and Times of Sam Cooke*, a national bestseller; and two volumes of poetry, among other books. His journalism has appeared in publications ranging from *Vogue* to *Wooden Boat* to *Education Weekly*. Grammy-nominated, Wolff is also the coproducer, with Jonathan Demme, of *Right to Return*, an ongoing documentary film project about post-Katrina New Orleans. He lives in Nyack, New York.